Human Development in India

Challenges and Policies

Human Development in India

Challenges and Policies

Edited by

Himanshu Sekhar Rout
S. Bhyrava Murthy

P. G. Department of Economics
Dr. SRK Government Arts College
(Pondicherry University)
Yanam, India

in association with

New Century Publications
New Delhi, India

NEW CENTURY PUBLICATIONS
4800/24, Bharat Ram Road,
Ansari Road, Daryaganj,
New Delhi – 110 002 (India)

Tel.: 011-2324 7798, 4358 7398, 6539 6605
Fax: 011-4101 7798
E-mail: indiatax@vsnl.com • info@newcenturypublications.com
www.newcenturypublications.com

Editorial office:
LG–7, Aakarshan Bhawan,
4754-57/23, Ansari Road, Daryaganj,
New Delhi – 110 002

Tel.: 011-4356 0919

First Published: **July 2010**

ISBN: **978-81-7708-239-5**

Disclaimer: The findings, interpretations and conclusions expressed here are those of the author(s) and do not necessarily reflect either the views of the institutions they represent, or the views of the editors.

Published by New Century Publications and printed at Salasar Imaging Systems, New Delhi.

Designs: Patch Creative Unit, New Delhi.

PRINTED IN INDIA

Contents

About the Book

Human development demands that all social groups have equal access to the services provided by the State and equal opportunity for upward economic and social mobility. It is also necessary to ensure that there is no discrimination against any section of the society. The Constitution of India contains various provisions for the development of marginalized groups. Their individual and collective growth, however, cannot be ensured without improving their surroundings and providing basic necessities of life.

The major challenges of human development in India are (a) measurement and aggregation of human development, (b) manifestation of poverty in all dimensions of human life, (c) drop out and stagnation in primary education, (d) more demand for higher education than the available facilities, (e) decontextualization of present system of education (f) persistent regional disparities and social inequalities (g) unregulated human activities and unsustainable use of environmental resources and (h) gross under valuation of women's economic contribution.

The book, consisting of 24 scholarly articles, provides valuable material on various dimensions of human development in India. It also makes practicable recommendations in this context.

About the Editors

Dr. Himanshu Sekhar Rout and Dr. S. Bhyrava Murthy are with the Post-graduate Department of Economics, Dr. SRK Government Arts College (Pondicherry University), Yanam, India.

Preface

The objective of all development efforts is to raise the standard of living of the people as a whole. Development with human face is the new catchword of Five Year Plans in India.

There are many challenges to inclusive human development in India. However, the following challenges are identified for detailed examination in this book.

1. The problem of measurement and aggregation of human development—a debatable topic since the publication of Human Development Report by UNDP.
2. Conceptualizing poverty as a mere income deprivation is not enough. Poverty is manifested in all dimensions of human life. Even with decent income if a person is unable to access education or health services because of social taboos, he will be considered poor—not in terms of income but in terms of status. Human development is not possible without economic freedom which is a big challenge in India.
3. In the field of education, though primary enrolment ratio is over 85 percent, the 55th round of NSS data (1999-2000) indicated that around 53 percent of children dropped out of school before completing grade VIII. Further, the demand for higher education is likely to exceed the supply because of the changes in the age structure of Indian population.
4. The persistent regional disparities, increasing polarization, pervasive economic and social inequalities are the major hindrances in the process of human development in India. Both intra-State and inter-State disparities in development still continue. These factors increase the intensity of challenges in human development.
5. Persistent unregulated human activities have accelerated unsustainable use of environmental resources. This is adversely affecting human development. Therefore, judicious use of natural resources and modern environmental governance are challenges for human

development strategies.

6. The development of both men and women constitute human development. Human development, if not engendered, is endangered. Removing gender inequality has nothing to do with national income. However, unequal gender relations in legal, social, political and economic powers can contribute to lowering of human development index.

More importantly, following are some of the suggestions made in this book for human development in India.

1. There is an urgent need of real political willpower, irrespective of different party ideologies, to improve human development.
2. Poverty is area-specific. Hence, policies should be area-specific and target-oriented. General policy will not produce desirable results.
3. Make people aware about their rights and responsibilities at all levels—from grassroots to national. That will enable them to claim their entitlements, seek accountability for redressal of grievances.
4. There is a need for fundamental change in the structure and pattern of Indian education to make it contextualized. There should be a holistic blend of theory and practical knowledge in education.
5. The health planners and administrators may be involved in the planning process of the government to reduce poverty and adopt policies for more equitable distribution of income.
6. The specific problems of backward regions should be looked into to ensure sustainable development with social cohesion.

Acknowledgments

We express our deep sense of gratitude to all our resource persons and paper contributors who made this volume see the light of the day. Our sincere thanks are due to University

Grants Commission (UGC), New Delhi; National Bank for Agriculture and Rural Development (NABARD), Mumbai; and Regency Ceramics Limited (RCL), Yanam for their sponsorships.

We would also like to extend our sincere thanks to Mr. Sandeep Sury of New Century Publications, New Delhi for accepting our proposal to publish this volume and extending his co-operation in every respect.

It is hoped that the volume will provide valuable inputs to the academicians, researchers, policy makers, government functionaries, and all others who are interested in human face of development in India.

Yanam

Himanshu Sekhar Rout
S. Bhyrava Murthy

Contributors and Their Affiliations

Atulya Bhoi	Assistant Professor, Department of Commerce, Dr. SRK Government Arts College, Yanam.
B. Suresh Babu	Doctoral Scholar, Department of Economics, University of Hyderabad, Hyderabad.
B. Thrinadha Rao	Research Scholar, Department of Tourism Studies, Pondicherry University, Puducherry.
Barun Kumar Thakur	Research Associate, Madras School of Economics, Chennai.
Bidyadhar Majhi	Assistant Professor of Economics, Indian Institute of Foreign Trade, New Delhi.
Dipali Bosumatari	Doctoral Scholar, Department of Economics, University of Hyderabad, Hyderabad.
Dukhabandhu Sahoo	Assistant Professor of Economics, Department of Paper Technology, IIT Roorkee.
K. Joseph Raj	Assistant Professor of Economics, S. T. Hindu College, Nagercoil, Tamil Nadu.
L . Ganesan	Assistant Professor of Economics, S. T. Hindu College, Nagercoil, Tamil Nadu.
M. Indira	Professor, Department of Economics and Cooperation, and Director, Centre for Women's Studies, University of Mysore, Mysore.
Mitrajit Chatterjee	Research Scholar, Department of Geography, University of Burdwan, Burdwan.
Narayan Chandra Nayak	Associate Professor of Economics, Department of Humanities and Social Sciences, IIT, Kharagpur.
Nirmal Chandra Sahu	Professor, Department of Economics, Berhampur University, Berhampur, Orissa.

P. Nayak	Director, Textiles Committee, Ministry of Textiles, Government of India, Mumbai.
Phanindra Goyari	Assistant Professor, Department of Economics, University of Hyderabad, Hyderabad.
Rajni Kapoor	Lecturer in Economics, Asia-Pacific Institute of Management Studies, New Delhi.
Ranjeeta	Research Scholar, CSRD, School of Social Sciences, Jawaharlal Nehru University, New Delhi.
Robin Singhal	Research Scholar, Centre for Economic Studies and Planning (CESP), Jawaharlal Nehru University (JNU), New Delhi.
Ruchira Bhattacharya	Research Scholar, CSRD, School of Social Sciences, Jawaharlal Nehru University, New Delhi.
Sangram Kumar Rout	Research Scholar, Department of Politics and International Studies, Pondicherry University, Puducherry.
Sujay Ghosh	Reader in Political Science, Uluberia College, Howrah, West Bengal.
Swarna Sadavsivam Vepa	Visiting Professor, Madras School of Economics, Chennai.
T. Subba Lakshmi	M. Phil. Scholar, Department of Economics, Pondicherry University, Puducherry.
Umesh Chandra Pati	Reader in Economics, Nayagarh Autonomous College, Nayagarh, Orissa.
V. G. Siddaraju	Associate Director (ICSSR-RP), Centre for Women's Studies, University of Mysore, Mysore.
Y. Venkata Rao	Reader, Department of Tourism Studies, Pondicherry University, Puducherry.
Yoginder Singh	Assistant Professor, Department of Commerce, Dr. SRK Government Arts College, Yanam.

1

Trends in Human Development Among SAARC Countries

M. Indira[1] and V. G. Siddaraju[2]

I. Introduction

The concept of human development was first operationalized by UNDP Report in 1990. It conceptualizes development as a process of enlarging people's choices indicated by improved health, education and income status. Human development creates human capabilities that lead to productivity enhancement and acceleration in economic growth. The concept of human development is much broader than economic development. According to this all efforts of development should be directed towards the people and their well-being who are considered to be the main objective of economic growth. The concept of human development encompasses the welfare of not only the present generation, but also the future generation as well (HDR 1995).

Amartya Sen has defined Development in terms of expansion in capabilities and freedom, freedom from hunger, being free to participate in the political process, being adequately sheltered, having access to health and education etc. Capabilities refer to what a person can do or can be. In this frame work human development has two sides i.e., the formation of human capabilities, such as - improved health, knowledge and skills and the use of theirs acquired capabilities for productive purposes, for leisure or for being active in cultural, social and political affairs.

Economic development of a country was traditionally judged in terms of Gross Domestic Product (GDP). The greater the volume of GDP per capita, higher the state of development and prosperity. But, the GDP measure of development completely ignores the welfare of

[1] Professor of Economics, DOS in Economics and Cooperation, University of Mysore, Mysore – 570006, India

[2] Associate Director (ICSSR – RP), Centre for Women's Studies, University of Mysore, Mysore – 570006, India

the people. It is not necessarily true that high GDP generates well-being to the people. It is not the volume of GDP per se, but its distribution that matters much for the well-being to the people. It is for these reasons that economists like Nobel laureate Amartya Sen and Mahbub Ul Haq have considered GDP as an inadequate measure of development and instead advocated the concept of human development.

Based on the contributions of these economists, Human Development Index (HDI) was developed and first Human Development Report was published by UNDP in 1990. It clearly stressed the primary message of the human centered approach to development.

According to the HDR, Human Development Index (HDI) measures the average achievement in three basic dimensions of human development:

1. A long and healthy life, as measured by life expectancy at birth.
2. Knowledge, as measured by the adult literacy rate (with two-thirds weight) and the combined primary, secondary and tertiary gross enrolment ratio (with one-third weight).
3. A decent standard of living, as measured by GDP per capita (PPP US$).

Sustainable Human Development

With the introduction of the concept of human development there is a paradigm shift in the development thinking. However, sustainability of the human development became important in the process. Human Development Report of 1994 focuses on the sustainable human development

According to the UNDP Administrator, Mr. James Gustave Speth, "sustainable human development is development that not only generates economic growth but distributes its benefits equitably; that regenerates the environment rather than destroying it; that empowers people rather than marginalizing them. It gives priority to the poor, enlarging their choices and opportunities and providing for their participation in decisions affecting them. It is development that is pro-poor, pro-nature, pro-jobs, pro-women and pro-children".

According to Sukehiro Hasegawa (2001) Sustainable Human Development requires 7 freedoms:

1. Freedom from **discrimination** (by gender, race, ethnicity, national origin or religion).
2. Freedom from **want** (to enjoy a decent standard of living and well being).
3. Freedom to **develop** and **realize** one's human potential.
4. Freedom from **fear** (of threats to personal security, torture, arbitrary arrest and other violent acts).
5. Freedom from **injustice** and violations of the rule of law.
6. Freedom of **thought, opinion and to participate** in decision making and form associations.
7. Freedom for decent **work** without exploitation.

II. Objectives and Methodology

In this context an attempt is made in the present paper to analyze the trends in human development among SAARC countries. Sustainable human development has been conceptualized in terms of trends in Human Development and freedom from discrimination. Trends and variation in human development reflect on sustainability in access to health, education and decent standard of living which are basic minimum requirements affecting the capabilities of human beings. The second indicator of sustainable human development is freedom from discrimination based on gender discrimination in terms of human development. Trends and variation in Gender Development Index (GDI) across SAARC countries has been analyzed over a period of ten years from 1998.

South Asian Association for Regional Cooperation (SAARC) came into existence in 1985 with the objective of raising the standard of living in South Asia through greater economic cooperation. The member countries are Bangladesh, Bhutan, India, Maldives, Nepal, Pakistan and Sri Lanka.

In the global scenario, South Asia remained backward in terms of both economic and social development. The region represents nearly 23 per cent of the world population, but shares only 2.5 per cent of the world's gross national income (US$1,339 Billion in 2007). The region ranks low in human development and gender development indicators. The average per capita income of this region is US $ 880; which is only 11 per cent of the world's average of US $7,995. Though the region is rich in resources, it is confronted with low literacy levels, higher poverty and low quality of living.

III. Income and Poverty among SAARC Countries

SAARC countries are placed under the middle income group. The following table explains the relative position of different countries in SAARC in terms of economic progress and the incidence of poverty.

In terms of per capita income Maldives stands out among the Asian countries. The per capita GDP in Maldives is estimated to be \$2345. Nepal has the lowest per capita GDP. It is interesting to observe that though the per capita GDP is lowest in Nepal, 24 per cent of the population are earning below \$1 per day. But in the case of Bangladesh, though per capita GDP is 406, 36 per cent are earning below one dollar per day. Sri Lanka has the least percentage of population with an earning of below one dollar per day. In terms of human poverty rank, Maldives and Sri Lanka are ranked better compared to the other SAARC countries. Among the SAARC countries Bangladesh and Bhutan are ranking very low in human poverty. While the value of human poverty is as high as 44.2 per cent in Bangladesh, it is 39 per cent in the case of Bhutan. Bangladesh has highest percentage of population with earning of bellow 1 \$ per day. Human poverty measured in terms of health, knowledge and a decent standard of living (HPI -1) was least in Maldives and Sri Lanka among the SAARC countries. The data presented in table 1 also clearly shows the inadequacy of GDP as an indicator of human development.

Table 1: Income and Poverty among SAARC Countries

Countries	GDP per capita income (PPP US \$)	% of Population under-nourished	Population with below 1 \$ per day (per cent)	Human Poverty Rank (2004)	HPI Value
Bangladesh	406	24.7	36.0	85	44.2
Bhutan	751	10.8	-	71	39.0
India	640	28.5	34.7	55	31.3
Maldives	2345	29.2	-	36	16.9
Nepal	252	15.3	24.1	68	38.1
Pakistan	632	34.5	17.0	65	36.3
Sri Lanka	1033	15.2	5.6	38	17.7

Source: UNDP Reports

Maldives, which has attained highest per capita GDP among the SAARC countries ($2345) also, has the highest percentage of population under nourished. Twenty nine percent of population in Maldives is estimated to be under nourished.

IV. Education and Health Status Among the SAARC Countries

Health and education are the basic minimum requirements for the human development when development is conceptualized as improving the choices of the people. Access to good education and health facilities influences the capabilities of the people to exercises the choices. The following table explains the status of education among the SAARC countries.

Table 2: Education Status in SAARC Countries

Sl. No	Countries	Percentage of Children enrolled	Adult Literacy	Expenditure on education as per cent of GDP
1	Bangladesh	56.0	41.1	1.5
2	Bhutan	-	47.0	-
3	India	61.0	61.0	3.7
4	Maldives	65.8	96.3	7.0
5	Nepal	58.1	48.6	2.0
6	Pakistan	40.0	49.9	2.6
7	Sri Lanka	62.7	90.7	3.2

Source: UNDP Reports

Adult literacy rate indicates the access to knowledge. Adult literacy rate among the SAARC countries is low compared to the developed countries. Within SAARC countries also greater variation could be observed. While 96 per cent of the adults are literate in Maldives, only 41 per cent of the adults are literates in Bangladesh. Among the SAARC countries, Maldives and Sri Lanka attained grater literacy status compared to their neighbouring countries. India is in the middle range with 61 per cent of male literacy rate. Percentage of children enrolled at primary and secondary levels show that there is not much variation among the SAARC countries except in Pakistan where the rate of enrollment is as low as 40 per cent during 2004. In all the SAARC countries only 60 per cent of the children are enrolled. Expenditure on education as a percentage to GDP indicates the amount of resources allocated for the promotion of education. As on 2004, the expenditure on education is only 1.5 per cent of GDP in Bangladesh which is the lowest among the SAARC countries. Maldives which has attained the 96 per cent adult literacy is spending highest amount on education (7 per cent of GDP). India is spending around 3.7 per cent of GDP on education.

Access to clean drinking water and improved sanitation is a per-requisite for human development. Deprivation of these services results in chronic diseases leading to loss of human resources. While expenditure on health services indicates the efforts to provide health services, Infant Mortality Rate (IMR), percentage of population with access to improved sanitation and water reflect the health status of the people. The following table gives a picture of health status in SAARC countries.

Table 3: Health Status in SAARC Countries

Sl. No	Countries	Public expenditure on Health (per cent GDP)	Per capita Health expenditure (PPP US$) 2003	Population with access to water
1	Bangladesh	1.1	68	74
2	Bhutan	2.6	59	62
3	India	1.2	82	86
4	Maldives	5.5	364	83
5	Nepal	1.5	64	90
6	Pakistan	0.7	48	91
7	Sri Lanka	1.6	121	79

contd...

Sl. No	Countries	Access to improved sanitation	Infant Mortality Rate (2004)
1	Bangladesh	39	56
2	Bhutan	70	67
3	India	33	62

4	Maldives	59	35
5	Nepal	35	59
6	Pakistan	59	80
7	Sri Lanka	91	12

Source: UNDP Reports.

It can be observed that per capita health expenditure is lowest in Pakistan ($48). Among the SAARC countries, Maldives is spending $ 364 per capita on health issues. Sri Lanka is another country with reasonable health expenditure. India spends $82 per capita. Correspondingly Infant Mortality Rate is highest in Pakistan. One important observation is that in the case of Maldives, though per capita health expenditure is high, IMR is 35 per 1000 live births. Bhutan and India are the other two countries with high IMR. Higher IMR in Maldives can be partially explained with the access to sanitation facilities. In the case of Maldives only 59 per cent have access to improved sanitation facilities. But in the case of Pakistan, though 59 per cent have access to improved sanitation, IMR is highest at 80 per cent. India is one of the countries with poor access to sanitation. As on 2004, 33 per cent of the Indians have access to improved sanitation. Sri Lanka is the only country which attained 91 per cent access to improved sanitation. Public expenditure on health indicates the commitment of the government in improving the health status. During 2003-04, Maldives government has spent 5.5 per cent of the GDP on health sector. In case of the India, 1.2 per cent of the GDP was allocated for health. Bhutan is another country with 2.6 per cent of the GDP spent on health care.

V. Trends and Variation in Human Development

Trends and variation in human development among the SAARC countries over a period of 10 years has been analyzed to understand the sustainability of human development. From the data it can be observed that during 2007, among the member countries, Maldives ranks first with the HDI value of 0.771 followed by Sri Lanka (0.759). In the case of Maldives the value increased from 0.725 to 0.771 during the 10 years period. Bangladesh ranks least among SAARC countries. Based on the trends in the value of HDI it is observed that Sri Lanka and Maldives have attained higher values of human development consistently. These countries have shown least variation in the value of HDI over the past 10 years. While the variation in the HDI value was 1.52 per cent in Sri Lanka, it is 1.93 per cent in the case of Maldives. The average value is around 0.74 in both the countries. But in the case of India, the variation is 3.13 per cent. The progress of human development is not stable in the case of Bhutan. The variation is around 9.30 per cent. The other possible reason for larger CV is due to low human development index value in the later part of 1990's. It has picked up in later part of 2000. The value of HDI increased from 0.483 in 1998 to 0.619 in 2007 in Bhutan. Nepal did not show much improved. Though Bhutan and Nepal were equally placed during 1998, Bhutan improved to 0.619 by 2007. But Nepal could reach only 0.553 by 2007. Same is the case with Bangladesh. But these countries have lower CV, as their human development index is consistently low.

VI. Trends and Variation in Gender Development Index (GDI)

Gender related development index measure the gap between men and women in attaining human development. Higher the value, lower the gender gap. In terms of GDI also Sri Lanka and Maldives rank higher among the neighbors. Both countries have attained a GDI value of 0.756 and 0.767 respectively during 2007. These countries have attained higher human development in 1998 itself compared to the other countries. For example, the HDI of Maldives and Sri Lanka was 0.72 when it was 0.54 in India during 1998. It was as lower 0.44 in Bangladesh. HDI has improved to 0.594 in Indian context by 2007. But in the case of Bangladesh it remained at 0.536 by 2007. Bhutan is another country with a relatively better HDI among the SAARC countries.

VII. Quality of Life and Human Development

It is interesting to observe the relationship between the quality of life and human development. While human development rank shows the status of human development in a particular country in terms of access to health, education and income, quality of life index shows the quality of life in a particular country in terms of access to other services and living conditions. It is calculated by taking into consideration the community life, political stability and security, job security, political freedom and gender equality. Logically a country with a large number of literates and healthy people with sufficient income to lead their life should also be the country where the quality of life is high.

Table 4: Trends and Variation in Human Development Index

Country	Sri Lanka	Maldives	India	Pakistan
1998	0.733	0.725	0.563	0.522
1999	0.735	0.739	0.571	0.498
2000	0.729	0.73	0.579	..
2001	0.73	0.751	0.590	0.499
2002	0.74	0.752	0.595	0.497
2003	0.751	0.745	0.602	0.527
2004	0.755	0.739	0.611	0.539
2005	0.743	0.741	0.619	0.551
2006	0.755	0.765	0.604	0.568
2007	0.759	0.771	0.612	0.572
Average	0.74	0.750	0.590	0.530
CV	1.52	1.930	3.140	5.530

contd...

Country	Bhutan	Nepal	Bangladesh
1998	0.483	0.474	0.461
1999	0.477	0.480	0.470
2000	..	0.488	0.497
2001	0.511	0.499	0.502
2002	0.536	0.504	0.509
2003	0.536	0.526	0.520
2004	0.538	0.527	0.530
2005	0.579	0.534	0.547
2006	0.608	0.547	0.535
2007	0.619	0.553	0.543
Average	0.54	0.510	0.510
CV	9.30	5.460	5.760

Source: Human Development Reports (*various years*).

An attempt is made to understand the relationship between the quality of life and human development among the SAARC countries. As it is observed, Maldives and Sri Lanka are ranking one and two among the SAARC countries in terms of HDI ranking during 2007. But, Maldives is not the country with highest quality of life index. The aggregate score of quality of life index is highest in Bhutan and Sri Lanka. Maldives, which is ranking highest in human development, is having the score of 55 in quality of life index and where as Bhutan with lower human development index has attained the score of 58 in quality of life index. Similarly, Bangladesh, which is ranking lowest among SAARC countries in human development, has also reached the quality of life index of 53.

VIII. Conclusions

SAARC came into existence with the objective of improving human development among the South Asian countries by developing close network among the member countries. However, still SAARC countries are lagging behind in human development. But among the SAARC countries Maldives and Sri Lanka are performing well compared to other members. These two countries could attain above 90 per cent adult literacy rate where as Bangladesh, Nepal and Bhutan are staggering at around 45 per cent. This partly explains the difference in GDP per capita based on purchasing power of parity.

Table 5: Trends and Variation in Gender Development Index

Country	Sri Lanka	Maldives	India	Pakistan
1998	0.727	0.72	0.545	0.489
1999	0.732	0.735	0.553	0.466
2000	0.737	0.739	0.56	0.468
2001	0.726	-	0.574	0.469
2002	0.738	-	0.572	0.471
2003	0.747	-	0.586	0.508
2004	0.749	-	0.591	0.513
2005	0.735	0.744	0.6	-
2007	0.756	0.767	0.594	0.532
Average	0.74	0.74	0.58	0.49
CV	1.38	2.30	3.36	5.17

contd...

Country	Bhutan	Nepal	Bangladesh
1998	-	0.449	0.441
1999	-	0.461	0.459
2000	-	0.47	0.468
2001	-	0.479	0.495
2002	-	0.484	0.499
2003	-	0.511	0.514
2004	-	0.513	0.524
2005	0.525	0.52	0.539
2007	0.605	0.545	0.536
Average	0.14	0.49	0.50
CV	40.05	6.39	7.01

Source: Human Development Reports (*various years*).

Table 6: Human Development and Quality of Life

Sl. No	Countries	Quality of Life Index Rank, 2007	HDI Rank 2007
1	Bangladesh	144	146
2	Bhutan	108	132
3	India	108	134
4	Maldives	130	95
5	Nepal	137	144
6	Pakistan	175	141
7	Sri Lanka	108	102

Source: International Living,
http://www1.internationalliving.com/qofl2009

Bangladesh has the least per capita GDP among the SAARC countries. Human Poverty (HPI-I) valued in terms of health, knowledge and decent standard of living is highest in Bangladesh and Bhutan. However one important observation which needs further research is that Maldives with highest per capita GDP has more percentage of people under-nourished (29.2 per cent) than in Bangladesh (24.7 per cent) which has lowest per capita GDP. This probably reflects on the distribution of income. When the distribution is skewed, the under-nourished people are more in Maldives. India ranks in the middle among the SAARC countries in all the human development indicators. Human development and quality of life are closely associated, though quality of life in a country also requires more favorable geographic, political and social environment. The analysis shows that countries ranking high in human development are not the countries with best quality of life. Maldives is ranking number one among SAARC countries in human development. But in terms of quality of living Bhutan which is ranking 3 in human development is ranking one in quality of life. This clearly shows that apart from providing access to health and education and creating income earning opportunities, it is also important for the government to ensure safety provide political stability and freedom, healthy community life in order to provide quality of life to the people.

References

Sukehiro, Hasegawa (2001): Development Cooperation, paper presented at the UNU Global Seminar "Global Issues and the United Nations" held on 20 November 2001.

International Living, http://www1.internationalliving.com/qofl2009.

UNDP, Human Development Reports, Various Issues.

2

Human Development: A Citizenship Approach

Sujay Ghosh[1]

I. Rationale

Human development (HD) aims to enable people 'develop their full potential and lead productive, creative lives in accord with their needs and interests.' The key to this aim lies in broadening the range of basic human capabilities: leading healthy life, having access to knowledge and necessary resources and participation in the life of the community (HDR Website). Conceptually, citizenship emanates from the word 'citizen.' In ancient and mediaeval Europe, residents of the city were considered as citizens. Democracy considers citizen to be the 'person who can hold her or his head high and participate fully and with dignity in the life of her or his society' (King and Waldron 1988: 443).

Such a changed concept of the citizen has enriched citizenship into a framework to analyse diverse social issues. Citizenship might also be envisaged to analyse HD, which has attracted significant academic interest in recent times. Towards this endeavour, we shall first briefly trace the genesis of the key concepts: HD and citizenship. Next, we shall identify some of the issues which form their common agenda: citizenship articulates their demands and ultimately those agendas promise to achieve human development.

II. Objective: Conceptualising HD and Citizenship

In order to conceptualise HD, we first need to understand development: the way its' meaning has evolved over time. Again, we need to understand the relationship between the state, society and individual for conceptualising citizenship.

HD: Developing the Human Beings

In a dictionary sense, development implies the improvement of current state of affairs. This definition is however, too inadequate to

[1] Associate Professor of Political Science, Uluberia College, Howarh, West Bengal

address socio-economic issues satisfactorily. Academically, the discipline – 'Development Studies' has emerged after Second World War, particularly in consonance with the emergence of Third World as a significant subject in international politics and power games. A significant number of journals on development studies are in circulation at present and almost all major international publishers regularly publish books on this subject. However, development has been predominantly understood in terms of economic growth, probably because achievements in these fields are visible, glaring, spectacular and relatively quick. Growth indicates an increase in the amount of economic goods (commodities and services) that are produced in a society…and a concomitant increase in the inhabitants' ability to acquire economic goods (Dale 2000: 17).

Still, in the long run, the social audit occurs to evaluate whether growth can lead to comprehensively beneficial human consequences. It favours the impulse to comprehend development, which denotes *improvements in the quality of life of people, extending much beyond direct gains from increased production of commodities and services* (Dale 2000: 17; emphasis added).

The difference between these two concepts mark a shift: the social, political and cultural – in sum, the human dimensions of development have now become important, both at policy-making and academic levels. In terms of policy, particularly in developing countries following market economy during the Cold War, democracy was seen as antithetical to development. However, since the late 1980s, democracy appeared to be a strategically better option for governance.

As Fisher points out, these governments were increasingly challenged by the population-poverty-environment crisis; power created from below and growing demands of human rights has been constantly challenging these governments. Accordingly, they came to realise 'their capacity to repress is unequal to the capacity to govern' (Fisher 1998: 26). In addition, non-democratic regimes by and large, save a few ones in South-East Asia, have not proven spectacular success in economic growth.

At academic level, the dimensions of development has broadened manifold. For instance, DEPENDS approach sets forth a number of criteria for 'just development' or 'good governance': development of infrastructure, economic growth, poverty alleviation, equity, natural resource base protection, democracy and social justice

(Clark 1991: 26-30). It implies that alongside economic, the social and political aspects are also integral to the notions of development. Politics is concerned with the distribution of power in society and its attendant dimensions. Such distribution inevitably involves the relationship between state, society and individuals.

The 'Right to Development' should be understood in this context. It unifies civil and political rights with economic, social and cultural rights. It is an 'inalienable' right derived from the concept of human dignity, focussing primarily on individual's participation at all levels of decision-making, equal opportunity of the access to resources and fair distribution of the benefits of development (Sengupta 2000). The discourse of development acquires a normative dimension with HD, as it is concerned with developing human beings in a given social context. According to Gasper and Truong (2005:374), development ethics 'supports a politics of social change that accepts human dignity as a priority.' From both of these accounts, we find human dignity is a basic pre-requisite of developmental thinking. In fact, HD is a step ahead of social development – the latter is rather a public policy-centric concept, focussing on certain issues such as health, education, poverty eradication, access to safe drinking water and so on. Conceptually, HD is broader as it is open to accommodate many other issues such as participation; specific in the sense that it's original focus lies on developing the human beings.

Mukherjee Reed (2008) identifies three approaches to analyse HD: capability approach, human face approach and her own 'social power' approach. We shall turn to capability and social power approach later, as they address HD more definitely and comprehensively. The 'Human Face' approach argues that people would treat fellow human beings with dignity if the vision of a 'fully equal human society' is realised (Bagchi 2000: 4417). This approach however, is too broad and normative. In effect, the approach is too uncompromising to visualise the possibility of HD in a foreseeable future. In addition, Khalakdina (2008) studies HD in terms of psychological and cognitive development of the individual. This approach is too narrow for our purpose: it does not sufficiently address HD in social terms.

Amartya Sen is the pioneer of capability approach: he identifies the expansion of freedom both as a primary end and principal means of development. In this view, participation in politics, dissent constitutes development because it allows one something 'she has reason to value.' If deprived, then development suffers. Freedom can also act as a means – play 'instrumental' role in promoting development in five ways: political freedom; economic facilities; social opportunities such as access to education, healthcare and so on; transparency guarantees for upholding the relations of trust; and 'protective security' providing safety nets to prevent affected people from being reduced to extreme poverty. 'These instrumental freedoms contribute to the general capability of a person to live more freely' (Sen 2000: 36-40). Capability approach thus provides the vision and content of HD.

Another approach understands HD in terms of 'reconfiguration of the matrices of social power' (Mukherjee Reed 2008: 23). This is social power approach, having three components: the basic *social structures* which condition goals and outcomes; structural differences and inequalities; and the nature of 'agency' for reconfiguring social power through collective attempts (*Ibid*). Corollary to the capability approach, which envisages ends, the social power approach points out possible pathways to realise those ends.

HD tries to move much beyond the 'economism' of development approach (Gasper and Truong 2005: 375-76). In addition, HD broadens the vision and thinking in development: it presents a holistic viewpoint cutting across the diversity of people and academic disciplines. It attempts to locate the place of 'self': neither totally detached from, nor absolutely predetermined by society.

Understanding Citizenship

Citizenship has the potential to provide the essential keys to understand and analyse HD. It would be clear after we understand citizenship in contemporary times which, we have seen, has roots in the word 'citizen.' Broadly, there are two conceptions of citizenship: (i) *state citizenship* – where the emergence of the modern state has been accompanied by the elaboration of formal legal status of an individual; (ii) *democratic citizenship* – which refers to shared membership of a political community (Stewart 1995: 63). Democracy envisages the individual not as a 'subject', but a 'citizen' (Chandoke 2003: 2957-58). Rights become a crucial factor in this transformation. They express a 'claim' to civilised life, which entails 'a claim to be admitted to a share in the social heritage, which in turn means a claim to be accepted as full members of society...as citizens (Marshall 1977: 76).

Freeden argues that individuals need rights from society, because the latter is responsible for their well-being, otherwise they will be dehumanised and incapable of full development. Secondly, human action and development often face constraints due to 'social malorganization, error or incompetence', which people have the right to avoid or receive compensations. Finally, society benefits from the ability and contribution of its members; rights enable them to develop these faculties (Freeden 1998:71).

However, citizenship did not usher into modern society automatically. Its dimensions enlarged after many reversals and setbacks. It is a historical than a 'universal' category, having different characteristics from one country to another (Beteille 1999: 2588-89). With the example of Britain, Marshall (1977) argues, citizenship has evolved through three stages: civil rights, political rights ands social rights. Recent works however argue that the factors that prompted the growth of national citizenship: war, work and family have undergone drastic change themselves. Rights have assumed new character under changed social circumstances – they are now much more global and universal in nature, such as human rights, ecological rights and cultural rights. They guarantee the 'ontological security' against the onslaught of global capitalism (Turner 2001).

However, in the context of countries like India, where the state is primarily responsible in promoting development and eradicating poverty, it is too early to conclude that the quest for global citizenship should occur at the expense of national context. The global context is certainly not irrelevant, particularly in the age of globalisation: not only of economy and culture, but also of social movements and human rights. However, there is only a vague deductive reasoning that if the world prospers, we shall also prosper. Yet no clear assurance is available that an overwhelming zeal for 'global citizenship' would not neglect the national context. At this point, the role of the state is crucial. Currie (2001: 84) opines that that the 'political community' comprising of both government and civil authority has the 'antecedent responsibility' to ensure 'security and well-being' of their subjects. Again, with the entry of state, the impulse for 'global' is somehow restricted.

As we have seen, rights are the defining feature of the modern conception of citizenship – national or global. Yet, rights in effect represent only one side of the relationship between the state, society and individuals. Bellamy invokes the duty-based concept of citizenship. He proceeds from the rights-based arguments which envisage human rights as the defining and delimiting the political sphere for protecting individual liberties from governmental interference. However, a moral framework of politics requires citizens to participate in collective decision-making and treat the views of fellow citizens seriously. Consent must be open to refusal or renegotiation in order to avoid the problems of coercion or false consensus. Rights require identification and compossibility for avoiding self-contradiction. Duties on the other hand, can be successfully identified through the rejection of those actions violating the principle of heterogeneous public sphere where everybody participates on roughly equal terms. In addition, as a framework of action, duties chart out what is ought to be done. With collective arrangements in mind, we may consider the feasible methods for exercising rights. Moreover, institutional rights emerge from political deliberation if the duty to participation is undertaken. It strengthens democratic bodies like smaller local organisations and legislatures, thus counters concentration and centralisation of decision-making power (Bellamy 1993: 63-69).

Marshall (1977: 129) argued that duties are generally 'vague.' However, the argument was originally made in 1950. In the light of later-day experiences, broadly two types of duties can be associated with modern citizenship: to exercise own rights and respect others' rights. Rights are hard-won achievements of democratic citizenship. If not exercised, they lose their meaning, relevance and significance. Again, if others' rights are not respected, the dominant and powerful groups and individuals in a given social context may apportion the larger share of benefits and entitlements at the expense of many others.

Duties thus have the potential to operationalise rights. Accordingly, citizenship today means a set of practices (juridical, economic and cultural) which define a person as a competent member of society, and which as a consequence shape the flow of resources to persons and social groups (Turner 1993:2).

Turner elaborates the definition himself: a 'general theory of citizenship' should address the content, type and forms of social rights and obligations, various social forces producing such practices and social arrangements to distribute the accruing benefits among various segments of society (Ibid 2-3).

The 'capability approach' sums up HD's vision and social power approach outlines the probable means to achieve them in most realistic ways. Many factors like rampant corruption, asymmetrical power relations stand in the way of realising HD in a meaningful way. Citizenship however, represents both the vision and means. It concurs with HD towards achieving the essentials of civilised human existence. On the other hand, it simultaneously emphasises upon the existence of rights and duties, which includes a person as a competent member of society. This status works as a means to enable claim the benefits of human development. This paper believes that the inductive method of citizenship is better suitable for achieving HD: to emphasise the national context where deprivations can be located and analysed.

III. Methodology and Data: Human Development through Citizenship: A Civility Framework

In this section, we identify a few issues adjacent and peripheral to the concept of citizenship, which at the same time can be envisaged to secure HD. The category is representative, and by no means an exhaustive one. These issues primarily figured in the discourse of citizenship, but now form the essence of HD. Healthy physical and social environment, education and social inclusion are germane to citizenship. Hence, they are adjacent concepts. Democratic governance is somewhat a peripheral concept: it is more about a strategy as it intends to ensure citizens a congenial socio-political environment to realise HD.

The above-mentioned issues link HD with citizenship under the framework of civility. Civility can be perceived in a number of ways: 'broadly…as those ideas, values and practices, both at individual and collective levels' for securing a civilised human existence (Ghosh 2008: 547). Nearer to citizenship, Marshall (1977: 76) perceives civility on account of goods consumed or services enjoyed towards a qualitative assessment of life in terms of the essential elements of civilization or culture.

In his opinion, citizenship entails a claim to civilised life. Beteille (2005: 278) adds another dimension:

Civility ensures the free and frank exchange of opinions among persons with divergent political attachments and indeed, with *divergent conceptions of a good society* (emphasis added).

These definitions encompass an individual's relationship with state and society. Civility is necessary for the flourishing of human lives. As an anti-thesis to dehumanisation, civility aims for collective social existence where people can have access to material and non-material resources to lead life in accordance with their values and priorities.

Physical and Social Environment

Citizenship articulates the impulse to this fundamental claim in a meaningful way. There might be various parameters of good life and good society, but two overarching conditions encompass them all: healthy physical environment and secure social environment. Healthy physical environment protects one – to a considerable extent, from illness. Consequently, the individual can afford to invest time, physical and mental energy and resources for purposes which he or she has reasons to value.

A secure social environment is marked by reason and non-domination: it enables one to exercise his or her own preferences in a way which he or she considers to be enriching for life. At the same time, such claims would also require to respect others' preferences. It presupposes the existence of appropriate consciousness, which in turn strengthens the spirit of citizenship. Violence is inimical to the requirements of secure social environment. Much of violence may occur at psychological levels: various sorts of humiliation such as sarcasms, non-recognition, baseless or motivated condemnation and like, threats, blackmailing are most visible ones in daily social life. However, those acts cannot be substantiated with empirical data. Hence we shall examine the occurrences of violent crimes in India. Figures in the Table 1 below suggest that the states such as Kerala, Himachal Pradesh, Tamil Nadu and Punjab, who score higher in 'Social Development Indicators' both at rural and urban levels also have lesser degree of violent crimes.

Table 1: Occurrence of Crimes in India[2]

State	Occurrences of Crime in 2006 against...			Social Development Ranking (2005)	
	Body	Property	Public Order	Rural Areas	Urban Areas
A. P.	66,214	32,674	3,928	09	11
Assam	11,790	11,606	3,172	08	13
Bihar	25,031	18,593	9,044	20	20
Chhatisgarh	11,138	9,392	1,167	16	15
Gujarat	17,812	25,277	1,855	10	06
Haryana	8,637	15,257	1,298	12	10
H. P.	2,099	1,602	681	02	01
J and K	2,768	3,410	1,400	03	03
Jharkhand	7,511	8,961	2,828	19	16
Karnataka	23,764	22,666	6,451	06	12
Kerala	20,275	10,621	6,800	01	02
M. P.	45,157	34,735	3,123	17	18
Maharashtra	46,037	65,910	8,641	11	07
Orissa	11,822	11,186	1,906	14	17
Punjab	10,494	6,490	71	05	04
Rajasthan	32,482	23,739	2,318	15	14
Tamil Nadu	28,747	17,500	2,298	04	05
Uttar Pradesh	32,985	27,352	4.073	18	19
Uttaranchal	2,119	2,356	528	07	09
West Bengal	13,191	14,999	2,496	13	08

Sources: National Crime Records Bureau (2007: 220-22); Council for Social Development (2008: 308-11).

The study understands social development in terms of demography, access to healthcare, basic amenities, education, economic deprivation and social deprivation – HD also shares these same concerns. Although the data are not of exactly the same year, they are not too distant either. Two fundamental requirements that

[2] Jammu and Kashmir (J and K) certainly presents an exceptional case, but the prolonged political disturbance there does not offer much scope for a credible generalisation under our framework.

assure the attainment of necessary physical and social environments are *education* and *social inclusion*.

Education

Education contributes to the growth of consciousness for citizens to develop appropriate values and dispositions necessary for democracies to flourish. In fact, democratic citizenship needs education for various reasons. First, it enables pupils understand about themselves and their social roles; they are empowered to participate as informed and responsible members in a society (Halliday 1999: 44). Secondly, education for citizenship requires an understanding of politics. The political world is an inalienable part of an individual's social existence. Moreover, it involves many normative questions relevant to an individual's life: justice, rights and other values. Understanding politics might enable citizens reflect critically on these issues (Wringe 1984: 90-93). Citizens learn to confront the controversial issues – not as 'unfortunate by-product', but as a core and vital element of democracy. Discussing controversial issues would enrich democratic thinking (Hess 2004: 257), because pupils would have the opportunities of learning viewpoints other than their own. Even if they do not agree, they would at least be familiar with reasons of the other side. Such process of learning also involves developing qualities such as mutual tolerance and respect. This leads towards the third necessity: citizens learn to organise pluralism and differences – they must learn both 'to rule and *being ruled*' (Gunsteren 1996: 84-90; emphasis added). This is an important lesson for HD: 'being ruled', an individual learns necessary social obligations where he or she has little expertise; yet, in their own areas of competence, learns the necessity to take responsibility. It increases their capacities: they acquire skills necessary for collective social existence arising from participation. Education is necessary at this point because, otherwise citizens may enter the political arena with no skills and tools, they will waste their time and energy, and eventually give up, become frustrated and alienated and cease participating (de-Shalit 2004: 804).

It is true that there are many problems with participation: most prominently, it does not indicate how empowerment might occur; again, excessive obsession with the 'local' tends to ignore the wider context of injustice and oppression (Hickey and Mohan 2005: 241-42). Yet, where participation at local level empowers truly and substantially, decision-making power is distributed somewhat more evenly.

Diversity is an essential feature of modern societies. The attempt to avoid diversity and heterogeneity motivates the attitude of segregation in learning. However, it is disadvantageous: the learning process remains incomplete; citizens cannot broaden their 'social network' beyond ascribed identities, nor can they learn about 'others' (Anderson 2007: 600-04). In India, the state neglects education for poor children, resulting into massive illiteracy and dropout rates. On the other hand, such segregation – a 'divisive school system' has promoted the growth of expensive private schools to cater the children from privileged social backgrounds. Such exclusivity contradicts the diversity existing in their immediate environments which therefore cannot act as a resource for learning. Hence, without much significant contribution to original fields of civilisation such as science, sports or arts, these schools produce huge number of bureaucrats or technocrats (Kumar 2004: 43-47), who rather than innovation and originality, are accustomed to carry out tasks set by others. This is detrimental for HD, because progress in human civilisation cannot occur unless citizens are psychologically equipped to deal with new problems or find creative solutions to the existing problems and necessities. Carrying out the routine business at best ensures the existing stability and works well in a society which does neither experience, nor require massive social changes.

Education for citizenship disapproves such segregation. It rather hopes to reduce the number of disaffected, sometimes violent and disruptive students and include them into 'learning society' (Halliday 1999: 44). 'Learning society' is related to citizenship in many ways: it approximates to the notion of a good society, 'where educational opportunities are available to all.' Again, the 'good citizen' is also a learner; finally, it prepares the citizen to meet the uncertainties and risks of today's globalized and knowledge-based society (Brooks and Holford 2009: 89).

Education is the primary and most organised source of knowledge: this way it does address the prime concern of HD. Nussbaum advocates three values for securing a 'decent minimally just society', which would also promote HD among students: 'self-criticism', whereby learners reflect on their own traditions and question the power holders keen to exploit that tradition; respecting diversity; and developing the ability for 'narrative imagination' –

understanding other's stories, sufferings, wishes and desires (Nussbaum 2008: 377-84). Such an education creates a vision for social inclusion: children who are 'privileged' (such as in Indian context) to have access to education get opportunities to know and feel about their underprivileged fellow citizens. Such knowledge and feelings may prevent many of them from being self-centred to the point of being inhuman.[3] Moreover, they may also lead to concerted efforts among some of them to change the lot: attack the factors that deprive many from realising HD.

Social Inclusion

A society cannot prosper if some of its citizens are deprived from access to common human heritage: hence the necessity of social inclusion. Social inclusion emanates from the concept of social exclusion, which is a 'rupture of social bonds' (Haan 2008:7). It conceives a deliberate and systematic denial of the status as members of society for some people or groups and accordingly legitimises their deprivation and attendant entitlements from common social goods and resources.

Social exclusion justifies social inequality on the basis of history and culture, which is morally indefensible in terms of civilisation and culture (Bader 1995: 212-15). These are the ideological and ideational foundations of exclusion, which segregates the advantaged from the disadvantaged on the basis of gender, caste, class, religion and various other social origins. In South Asia for instance, religion generates two types of exclusions: from the domain of religious equality and liberty; and denying the non-religious sphere of liberty and equality (Bhargava 2007: 69). This forms the application part of social exclusion.

In addition, various social practices, such as encouraging 'unruly practices' – not implementing anti-discrimination laws; 'social closure' – deliberately excluding a group on the basis of social origin and mobilising institutional bias to allow beneficiaries 'defend and promote vested interests' (Kabeer 2008) lead towards consolidating the forces of social exclusion. Again, social exclusion is manifested in poverty, preventing a person to 'appear in public without shame.' Moreover, exclusion from social relations may also lead to other deprivations, such as one may not receive credit. In these senses,

[3] If we analyse the instances of misbehaviour or misconduct that harms many others, we may find in most cases, blind human selfishness the primary reason.

social exclusion ends up into capability deprivation in a pervasive way (Sen 2004: 5).

Yet, social exclusion enables us identify the deficiencies of citizenship; therefore, social inclusion 'may be viewed as a strategy, even an instrument for the fuller realization of citizenship' (Jayal 2009: 366). Inclusion is an agenda for democratic citizenship: it leads to social justice. Fraser proposes a two-pronged approach to realise social justice through parity of participation: *redistribution of resources* to transform the economic structures in society that generate injustice, marginalisation and deprivation; and *recognition* of cultural, ethnic and social minorities as full members of society (Fraser 2008).

Social exclusion might occur both on economic as well as socio-cultural grounds, separately or simultaneously: a poor person who cannot access reasonable entitlements such as healthcare facilities suffer economic exclusion. If an economically well-off person in India with *dalit* background is denied access to public forums such as temples, then social exclusion occurs on socio-cultural ground. Again, a poor person from traditionally depressed class suffers exclusion both on economic and socio-cultural grounds. Establishment of social justice enables the recipients, particularly the historically excluded and deprived groups of people, to access the opportunities for self-development.

Citizenship attempts to respond to various social divisions and ensure justice through inclusion. In the process, it confronts the values and practices that justify discrimination at ideational, ideological and application levels, thus promises access to HD for the hitherto excluded group of people. It makes a strong normative plea, as well as a framework for action to obtain social inclusion. It enables them to claim the status of membership into society and attendant benefits necessary for a comprehensive HD. Accordingly, social inclusion results into the empowerment of people hitherto excluded from the access to society's common heritage. Empowerment is the human ability to use one sort of capability, or one type of freedom, to boost other types of capacity or freedom (de-Shalit 2004:804).

Citizenship conceives about social inclusion, which empowers a wide section of the population to envision a life worthy to lead; at least the political impediments are removed to a considerable extent.

In this sense, social inclusion acts as a bridge between citizenship and HD.

Democratic Governance

Governance essentially denotes 'efficient administration'; we have seen above that democracy is a strategically sound method of governance under contemporary circumstances. Democracy, by its own logic, incessantly spreads to various aspects of social life: new areas of injustice, asymmetries of power relations are continuously unearthed. For instance, women's unequal access to social positions both at family and workplace led to the emergence of Feminism at ideological, conceptual and policy-making levels.

Democratic governance, we shall argue, works as an insurance for HD. We shall take recourse to a hypothetical Research Proposal to substantiate this claim.

Does participation by people matter? Case of drinking water project in Village 'A'.

First we have to identify the universe: the demographic profile and geographical features of Village A; what percentage of the population in the village had access to drinking water previously; and whether people from underprivileged backgrounds had such access in past. Next we shall examine the nature of participation: whether people from all sections of society in Village A participate in the project; whether they educate themselves on the necessity of the project and the constructive roles they might play; whether they have access to relevant information and the means to elicit accountability from the elites who implement the project. Finally, we shall compare past with present: find out if there are noticeable positive changes in the access to drinking water and if it had led to positive changes in the life-styles of various segments of the population in the village.

Participation and accountability are the key requirements of democratic governance. Participation is also the defining feature of modern citizenship and accountability involves ensuring adherence to proper conduct in a given context, such as implementation of water project in village A. The above research proposal thus indicates that while participating, citizens exercise both their rights and responsibilities to realise a common good: in this context, a fundamental human necessity.

IV. Results

Citizenship articulates the vision; HD represents the application part of the same social concerns. While studying the relationship between the occurrences of violence and social development rankings, we find they are inversely related: more violence, less social development. Violence is locked into the vicious circle with other factors that lead to capability deprivation. Lack of healthcare facilities, basic amenities and access to education coupled with widespread socio-economic deprivation stultifies the normal course of mobilisation through human efforts and faculties. Yet, the alluring vision of socio-economic mobilisation and the gaps in the possibility of realising them sometimes make people desperate to compromise with the norms of civility. Violence is one outcome of such circumstances, which again has the potential to be a governing norm of human behaviour. Social exclusion deepens because might determine rights and weaker people are left with little realistic means to seek justice. Accordingly, other requirements of human development, such as participation, which depends on healthy inter-personal relationships, suffer: it prevents people to claim collectively the requirements of HD. This way it also impairs the potential of democratic governance.

V. Conclusion

The quest for a civilised human existence, for people to lead a happy, prosperous and productive life is ingrained in human psyche since time immemorial. Various instances of creative works such as religious texts, literary and cultural pursuits as well as many conscious social endeavours (such as fight against slavery) by various social agents (political, social, religious or other voluntary activists) testify to this fact. This natural human impulse, together with an academic treatment of development, forms the roots of HD.

Yet, the process to realise HD is not a smooth one: it has encountered many difficulties and impediments from various social forces from time to time. In this context, citizenship can be perceived as a meaningful approach to understand HD because it clearly demarcates the place of citizens in society and polity. As an ensemble of rights and duties, individuals are made aware of their role in shaping their destiny, to achieve the life they have reason to value. As citizenship rights emerge from the 'humdrum politics of everyday life in democratic societies' (Isin and Turner 2007: 16), citizens acquire spaces to interrogate power structures that stand in the way of realising their capabilities.

Citizenship has various agendas relevant for HD. The attainment of civility in social relations is an incentive towards HD. It provides the emotional resource, by legitimising claims for material and non-material entitlements necessary for free interaction among citizens. Education for citizenship carries the process forward, because citizens learn both about their rights and obligations as members of society. Social inclusion promises to realise HD for greater number of people, in the sense it designates the status to everybody as a member of society in a meaningful way, when it throws light in the areas deficient of citizenship.

References

Anderson, Elizabeth (2007): Fair Opportunity in Education: A Democratic Equality Perspective, *Ethics*, 117(4): 595-622.

Bagchi, Amiya K. (2000): Freedom and Development and End of Alienation, *Economic and Political Weekly,* 35(50): 4408-20.

Bader, Veit (1995): Citizenship and Exclusion: Radical Democracy, Community and Justice. Or, what is wrong with Communitarianism?, *Political Theory*, 23(2): 211-46.

Bellamy, Richard (1993): Citizenship and Rights, In Richard Bellamy (ed.) *Theories and Concepts of Politics*, Manchester University Press, Manchester, pp. 43-76.

Beteille, Andre (1999): Citizenship, State and Civil Society, *Economic and Political Weekly,* 34(36): 2588-91.

Beteille, Andre (2005): Civil Society and the Good Society, In N. Jayaram (ed.) *On Civil Society: Issues and Perspectives*, Sage Publications, New Delhi, pp. 273-93.

Bhargava, Rajeev (2007): Inclusion and Exclusion in South Asia: The Role of Religion in India, Pakistan and Bangladesh, *Indian Journal of Human Development*, 1(1): 67-98.

Brooks, Rachel M. and John A. K. Holford (2009): Citizenship, Learning and Education: Themes and Issues, *Citizenship Studies*, 13(2): 85-103.

Chandoke, Neera (2003): Governance and the Pluralisation of the State: Implications for Democratic Citizenship, *Economic and Political Weekly,* 38(36): 2597-68.

Clark, John (1991): *Democratizing Development: The Role of Voluntary Organizations*, Earthscan, London.

Council for Social Development (2008): *India: Social Development Report – Development and Displacement*, Oxford University Press, New Delhi.

Currie, Bob (2001): Political Authority, Public Deliberation and the Politics of Poverty Reduction, In Niraja Gopal Jayal and Sudha Pai (eds.) *Democratic Governance in India: Challenges of Poverty, Development and Identity*, Sage Publications, New Delhi, pp. 66-108.

de-Shalit, Avner (2004): Political Philosophy and Empowering Citizens, *Political Studies*, 52(4): 802-18.

Dale, Reider (2000): *Organisations and Development: Strategies, Structures and Processes*, Sage Publications, New Delhi.

Fraser, Nancy (2008): *Social Justice in the Age of Identity Politics*, Critical Quest, New Delhi.

Fisher, Julie (1998): *Nongovernments: NGOs and the Political Development of the Third World*, Kumarian, Connecticut.

Freeden, Michael (1998): *Rights*, Worldview, Delhi.

Gasper, Des and Thanh-Dan Truong (2005): Deepening Development Ethics: From Economism to Human Development to Human Security, *European Journal of Development Research*, 17(3): 372-84.

Ghosh, Sujay (2008): Civility through Character Education: A Voluntary Effort, *Indian Journal of Political Science,* 69(3): 547-64.

Haan, Arjan de (2008): Social Exclusion: Towards a Holistic Understanding of Deprivation, In Arjaan de Haan and Naila Kabeer, *Social Exclusion: Two Essays*,Critical Quest, New Delhi, pp. 3-18.

Halliday, John (1999): Political Liberalism and Citizenship Education: Towards Curriculum Reform, *British Journal of Educational Studies,* 47(1): 43-55.

HDR Website: <http://hdr.undp.org/en/humandev> accessed on dated 2 August 2008.

Hickey, Sam and Giles Mohan (2005): Relocating Participation within a Radical Politics of Development, *Development and Change*, 36(2): 237-62.

Isin, Engin F. and Bryan S. Turner (2007): Investigating Citizenship: Towards an Agenda for Citizenship Studies, *Citizenship Studies*, 11(1): 5-17.

Jayal, Niraja Gopal (2009): The Challenge of Human Development: Inclusion or Democratic Citizenship?, *Journal of Human Development and Capabilities*, 10(3): 359-74.

Kabeer, Naila (2008): Social Exclusion, Poverty and Discrimination: Towards an Analytical Framework, In Arjaan de Haan and Naila Kabeer, *Social Exclusion: Two Essays*, Critical Quest, New Delhi, pp. 19-40.

Khalakdina, Margaret (2008): *Human Development in the Indian Context: A Socio-Cultural Focus*, Sage Publications, New Delhi.

King, Desmond S. and Jeremy Waldron (1988): Citizenship, Social Citizenship and the Defence of Welfare Provision, *British Journal of Political Science*, 18(4): 415-43.

Kumar, Krishna (2004): *What is Worth Teaching?* Orient Longman, New Delhi.

Marshall, T.H. (1977): Citizenship and Social Class, In S.M. Lipset (ed.) *Class, Citizenship and Social Development*, University of Chicago Press, Chicago, pp. 71-134.

Mukherjee Reed, Ananya (2008): *Human Development and Social Power: Perspectives from South Asia*, Routledge, London.

National Crime Records Bureau (2007): *Crime in India, Part –II*, Ministry of Home Affairs, New Delhi.

Nussbaum, Martha C. (2008): Education for Profit, Education for Freedom, *Journal of Educational Planning and Administration*, 22(4): 369-88.

Sen, Amartya (2000): *Development as Freedom,* Oxford University, Press, New Delhi.

Sen, Amartya (2004): *Social Exclusion: Concept, Application and Scrutiny*, Critical Quest, New Delhi.

Sengupta, Arjun (2000): Realizing the Right to Development, *Development and Change*, 31(3): 553-78.

Stewart, Angus (1995): Two Conceptions of Citizenship, *British Journal of Sociology,* 46(1): 63-78.

Turner, Bryan S. (1993): Contemporary Problems in the Theory of Citizenship, In Bryan S. Turner (ed.) *Citizenship and Social Theory*, Sage Publications, London, pp. 1-18.

Turner, Bryan S. (2001): The Erosion of Citizenship, *British Journal of Sociology,* 52(2): 189-209.

Wringe, Collin (1984): *Democracy, Schooling and Political Education*, George Allen and Unwin, London.

3

Robust Relation among Human Development and Economic Freedom: An Empirical Study on South Asian Perspective

Rajni Kapoor[1]

I. Rationale

The United Nations advocated the concept of Human Development as the goal of all member countries. Without economic freedom the opportunities to develop human capabilities couldn't be increased. Economic theory indicates that economic freedom affects incentives, productive efforts and the effectiveness of resource use. From the time of Adam Smith, freedom had been used to choose supply resources, competition in business, trade and secure property rights for economic progress. Without exchange and entrepreneurial activity coordinated through markets, modern living standards would be impossible. The realization of human development is depended on the presence of sound money, rule of law, and security of property rights, among other factors.

The qualitative model proposed for understanding the relationship between human capital and economic development confirms the importance of institutions (HDR 2003). An approach to the quantification of economic freedom has lately been undertaken by researchers from the Heritage Foundation and, as a result, the Index of Economic Freedom was edited and first published in 1995. As a measure of the level of economic freedom of a particular country Economic Freedom Index is also defined as a measure of globalization or as an institutional measure of sustainable development (Kowalczewski 2000; Pionek 2002).

II. Literature Review

There is general acceptance regarding the relation between human development and economic freedom. Human development is

[1] Assistant Professor of Economics, Asia Pacific Institute of Management Studies, New Delhi

defined as the process of enlarging people's choices (UNDP; 1990). Choices include political freedom, guaranteed human rights, ingredients of self-reliance and self-esteem (Mahbub Ul Haq, 1995). These quotes define that economic freedom is very much related with human development. Moreover, from Adam Smith's, "Wealth of Nations" (1776) to Sen. (1999) "Development as Freedom", the economic theory presumes direct and positive relation between the two. Adam Smith emphasized the working of "invisible hand" or "natural law" in the economy, he advised the countries to let the citizens free and they all can do the best for themselves. Thus Adam Smith was in the favor of absolute freedom for development of the nations. Similarly, Sen in his popular book Development as Freedom states *"Freedoms," "are not only the primary ends of development, they are also among its principal means."* Development should be seen as a process of expanding freedoms. In the word of Sen, "*the solution of the problem of population growth (like the solution of so many other social and economic problems) can lie in expanding the freedom of the people whose interest are most directly affected by over frequent child-bearing and child-rearing. The solution of the population problem calls for more freedom, not less*." It seems Sen doesn't want government interference in economic activities. China's population growth is the good example of the violation of Sen.'s views regarding population growth. In China, population growth is controlled by the government itself. Similarly, in Japan, government's main objective is the Improvement and Enrichment of Higher Education. Hence in these cases, freedom is not required. This study is an attempt to test and examine whether the components of economic freedom index are robustly related with human development or not.

In the previous literature of economic development, various empirical studies describe significant relationship between human capital development and economic freedom. Strong correlations have been found between economic freedom and GDP per capita, economic growth, employment, human development, life expectancy, literacy and abatement of poverty (Grubel 1998). The evolution of the concept of economic freedom and its close relationship has already been found in the work of Sen. (Prendergast 2005). Sen insisted importance of positive freedom and the expansion of capabilities that people have to lead the kind of lives they value (Sen. 1999). Various indicators of economic freedom have been used and proved that increase in economic freedom robustly related to economic growth (Sturm; Haan; 1999). Human capital and institutions are the soft factors of economic growth. In his study, Juri had taken an example of 119 countries and proved relationship between human development and economic freedom. (J. S. 2000). New Human Development Index introduced; named, Ethics augmented human development index (E-HDI) as a new indicator of socio-economic change and development. The E-HDI incorporates freedom, faith, environmental concerns and the institution of family in the HDI (H. A. Dar 2004). Secure private property rights is found to be a most significant positive causal variable as is sound money, whereas moderate amounts of labor regulation and big government are not found to be bad for the economy (Altman 2008).

III. Objectives

This study attempts to test statistically significant relation among human development and economic freedom. The paper would like to analyze the impact of the components of economic freedom on human development. In other words, it is an attempt to test and examine whether the components of economic freedom index are robustly related with human development or not. It helps in identifying the most significant component of economic freedom index that affects human development the most and the result would be able to guide the countries to develop that significant component of economic freedom to develop human being.

IV. Data and Methodology

For the analysis, Five South Asian countries have been taken; these are India, Sri Lanka, Pakistan, Bangladesh and Nepal. Time-series data has been constructed for 10 years trend from 1980 to 2005. Human development and economic freedom have been evaluated with the help of human development index (HDI) and economic freedom index (EFI) respectively. The measurement of economic freedom used in this paper is based on the index developed by (Gwartney; Lawson; Block 1996), which was subsequently updated by (Gwartney; Lawson 1997) and Data Base 2009 published by the Economic Freedom Network (EFN).

Human Development Index is a summary measure of human development. It was evolved by UNDP in 1991, taking into account three basic dimensions of human development, namely, the right to live a long and healthy life as measured by life expectancy at birth, education, as measured by the adult literacy rate and a decent standard of living, as measured by GDP per capita (PPP US$). Life expectancy is chosen as an index of longevity, adult literacy and gross enrolment ratio (years of schooling) combined to construct the education index. Per capital Gross Domestic Product (PPP US$) adjusted as an index of decent life. Therefore, a methodology is developed to construct a composite index. It is expressed in terms of a numerical value between 0 and 1.

Economic freedom index seeks to measure the consistency of the institutions and policies of various countries with voluntary exchange and the other dimensions of economic freedom. The Freedom House in New York, Heritage Foundation in Washington, D.C., and the Fraser Institute of Vancouver, all three of them developed indices to measure economic freedom. The centre for Civil Society is a co-publisher of the Fraser Institute's Economic Freedom of the World. The Fraser Index of Economic Freedom takes into account seven different areas while in Heritage Foundation, there are 10 components of economic freedom. This section discusses how the concept of economic freedom can be quantified. This quantification serves several purposes. First, if economic freedom can be measured, it is then possible to test directly the strength of the relationship between economic freedom and economic growth. Second, a quantification of economic freedom also makes it possible to compare its contribution with that of other factors contributing to economic growth.

Data for each of the component of economic freedom index compiled for more than 100 countries and statistical procedures used to assign each country a component rating ranging between zero and ten. A higher component rating—a rating toward the ten end of the scale—is indicative of institutions and/or policies more consistent with economic freedom, and vice-versa. The Economic Frcedom index is subdivided into five major areas:

(1) Size of the government: It indicates the extent to which countries rely on the political process to allocate resources, goods and services. When government spending increases relative to spending by individuals, households, and businesses, then Government decision-making is substituted for personal choice and economic freedom is reduced. For example; when government consumption is a larger share of the total then political choice is

substituted for personal choice. Similarly, when governments tax some people in order to provide transfers to others, they reduce the freedom of individuals to keep what they earn.

(2) Private property rights: Protection of persons and their rightfully acquired property is a central element of economic freedom and a civil society. Security of property rights, protected by the rule of law, provides the foundation for economic freedom. For example, freedom to exchange is meaningless if individuals do not have secure rights to property. Countries with major deficiencies in this area are unlikely to prosper human development.

(3) Sound money: Sound money or Hard or strong currency refers to a globally traded currency that can serve as a reliable and stable store of value. Factors contributing to a currency's *hard* status can include political stability, low inflation, and consistent monetary and fiscal policies, backing by reserves of precious metals, and long-term stable or upward-trending valuation against other currencies on a trade-weighted basis. As of 2008, hard currencies could be argued to include the United States dollar, Euro, Swiss franc, British pound sterling, Norwegian krone, Swedish krona, Canadian dollar, Japanese yen, and Australian dollar. Therefore, it is concluded that Money oils the wheels of exchange.

> "*High rates of monetary growth invariably lead to inflation. Similarly, when the rate of inflation increases, it also tends to become more volatile. High and volatile rates of inflation distort relative prices, alter the fundamental terms of long-term contracts, and make it virtually impossible for individuals and businesses to plan sensibly for the future. Sound money is essential to protect property rights and, thus, economic freedom. Inflation erodes the value of property held in monetary instruments. When governments use money creation to finance their expenditures, in effect, they are expropriating the property and violating the economic freedom of their citizens.*"[2]

(4) Free international trade: It includes freedom of exchange across national boundaries. It is a key ingredient of economic

[2] Economic Freedom of the World; 2008 Annual Report xxi page no. 6; Executive summary.

freedom and designed to measure a wide variety of restraints that affect international exchange: tariffs, quotas, hidden administrative restraints, and exchange rate and capital controls. In order to get a high rating in this area, a country must have low tariffs, a trade sector larger than expected, easy clearance and efficient administration of customs, a freely convertible currency, and few controls on the movement of capital.

(5) Business regulations. It is designed to identify the extent to which regulations and bureaucratic procedures control entry and reduce competition. In order to score high in this portion of the index, countries must allow markets to determine prices and refrain from regulatory activities that delay entry into business and increase the cost of producing products. For example, countries that use a private banking system to allocate credit to private parties and refrain from controlling interest rates receive higher ratings for this regulatory component.

Hypotheses: Corresponding to the objectives of the study, the hypotheses to be designed are as under:

h_1 : There is significant robust relationship among human development and economic freedom.

h_2 : There is significant impact of economic freedom's indicators on human development.

To measure the reliability of the coefficients of economic freedom has been tested with't-test' at 95 per cent significance level.

Models Specifications:

Model 1:

$$HDI_i = \varphi_0 + \gamma_0 EFI_i + u_{1i}$$

Model 2:

$$HDI_i = \theta_0 + \phi_0 PRR_i + \phi_1 FIT_i + \phi_2 SOG_i + \phi_3 SM_i + \phi_4 BSR_i + u_{21}$$

Model 1 is constructed for examining statistical significant relation between human development and economic freedom. Table 1 reveals the results by applying OLS to the regression model. Parameter of economic freedom is estimated based on time series data on South-Asian perspective. T-test has been used to check the statistical significance of the parameters. Human development Index value is the dependent variable and economic freedom is independent variable. φ_0 is constant coefficient and γ_0 is Economic freedom index parameter. U_i is random variable in the model. 'i' is used for five countries, it will be equal to 1, 2, 3, 4, and 5.

Model 2 has been used for examining significant relationship between HDI and various indicators of economic freedom. It is helpful in analyzing the indicator of economic freedom that has significant affect on human development. Only five indicators have been taken in this model. These are Private Property Rights (PRR), Free International Trade (FIT), Size of Government (SOG), Sound Money (SM) and Business Regulations (BSR).

V. Empirical Results

Regression result of examining relation among human development and economic freedom: The study ran the regression using SPSS 16.0 version among the human development index value and economic freedom index value for the five South-Asian countries. It can be shown with the Table 1

Table 1 revealed that in India, the computed value of γt (the computed value of t-test) is 6.910 which is greater than the table value of 't' (2.50 at 95 per cent significance level). Thus, the unit hypothesis (h_1) is accepted that there is statistical significant relation among human development and economic freedom. The R value is 0.909 it means there is high degree of positive correlation between the two. R^2 value indicates that 82.7 per cent variation in human development is regressed by the freedom of the economy. In Sri Lanka, the computed value of γt (the computed value of t-test) is 3.428 which are greater than the table value of 't' (2.50). Thus, the unit hypothesis (h_1) is accepted that there is statistical significant relation among human development and economic freedom. The R value is 0.771 it means there is high degree of positive correlation among HDI and EFI values. R^2 value is 0.595 which indicates that 59 per cent variation in human development is regressed because of economic freedom. In Sri Lanka, human development is comparative less affected by economic freedom. Economic freedom is able to explain approximately 59 per cent variation in human development and rest 40 per cent of the variation is not explained yet.

Table 1: Regression Results of Model 1

South-Asian Countries	φ	γ	φ t	γ t	R	R^2
India	.130 (.074)	0.074 (.011)	2.059	6.910*	0.909	0.827
Sri Lanka	.348 (.108)	.064 (.019)	3.235	3.428*	0.771	0.595
Bangladesh	.068 (.049)	.078 (.009)	1.386	8.289*	0.896	0.896
Pakistan	-.204 (.109)	.126 (..020)	- 1.876	6.318*	0.913	0.833
Nepal	.775 (.499)	-.057 (.091)	1.554	- .623**	0.215	0.046

*significant at 95 per cent level of significance
** Non-significant at 95 per cent level of significance

Both in Bangladesh and Pakistan, regression results show robust and positive relation among human development and economic freedom. The computed values of γ t (the computed value of t-test) for these countries are 8.289 and 6.318 respectively these are greater than the table value of 't' (2.50). The R values are 0.896 and 0.913 respectively it means there is high degree of positive correlation among HDI and EFI values. R^2 values are 0.896 and 0.833 that indicates that 89 per cent and 83 per cent variation in human development is regressed respectively in both the countries.

In Nepal, the study got the opposite results; computed 't' value (-.623) is less than the table value of 't' (2.50). The EFI Coefficient value is -.057, negative sign shows inverse relation among human development and economic freedom. It means higher the economic freedom, lower is the development of human resource. Moreover, in Nepal the correlation coefficient is very low i.e. .215. R^2 is .047 means only 4 per cent variation in human development is regressed by the economic freedom. Thus economic freedom does not have significantly effect on human development of Nepal.

The Impact of Economic Freedom's components on Human Development have been revealed with Table 2: This table examines which component of economic freedom has a separate affect on human development. This paper has taken five main components of economic freedom in model 2. In India, impact of sound money is significant at 95 per cent significance level and computed 't' value ϕ_3 i.e. 3.042867 is greater than the table value of 't' (2.50). Thus h_2 hypothesis is accepted and sound money has significant impact on human development.

The Spearman's correlation coefficient between human development and sound money is 0.94 which implies positive and high degree of correlation between the two. R^2 value states that 89 per cent variation in human development in India is regressed by the sound money. Hence these components have a valuable affect on human development. Business Regulations is significant at 90 per cent significance level, but has a negative and low correlation with human development (see Table 2) for correlation coefficient. R^2 is 0.19 which states that only 20 per cent variation in human development is explained by the business regulations.

Table 2: Regression Results of Model 2

India					
	ϕ's	$S.E.\phi$	ϕ_t	R	R^2
θ_0	-0.187	0.278	-0.67**		
SOG	0.001	0.015	0.052**	0.938	0.883
PRR	0.021	0.019	1.056**	0.628	0.394
SM	0.144	0.047	3.043*	0.947	0.895
FIT	-0.001	0.017	-0.04**	0.909	0.827
BR	-0.063	0.026	-2.43**	-0.442	0.194
Sri Lanka					
θ_0	0.517	0.055	9.388*		
SOG	0.022	0.005	4.458*	0.895	0.801
PRR	0.013	0.007	1.838**	0.390	0.152
SM	0.023	0.010	2.311**	0.733	0.537
FIT	-0.012	0.011	-1.04**	0.751	0.565
BR	-0.014	0.006	-2.24**	-0.479	0.23

Pakistan					
θ_0	-0.384	0.364	-1.06**		
SOG	0.035	0.010	3.302*	0.842	0.709
PRR	0.020	0.011	1.721**	0.160	0.025
SM	0.038	0.027	1.422**	-0.141	0.019
FIT	-0.002	0.030	-0.08**	0.675	0.455
BR	0.057	0.053	1.069**	0.565	0.319
Bangladesh					
θ_0	0.1706	0.081	2.106**		
SOG	0.008	0.013	0.631**	0.894	0.800
PRR	8.74E-05	0.011	0.007**	0.256	0.065
SM	0.018	0.018	1.032**	0.788	0.620
FIT	0.027	0.007	3.879*	0.943	0.889
BR	0.001	0.010	0.019**	-0.135	0.018
Nepal					
θ_0	1.220	7.626	0.160**		
SOG	-0.16	0.981	-0.16**	-0.51	0.262
PRR	-0.02	0.072	-0.22**	-0.418	0.175
SM	-0.02	0.324	-0.05**	0.4376	0.191
FIT	0.038	0.345	0.111**	0.229	0.052
BR	0.007	0.393	0.017**	0.676	0.457

* Significant at 95 per cent confidence θ_0 constants in model 2.
**non-significant at 95 per cent confidence
ϕ's parameters of EFI $S.E.\phi$ standard error of ϕ
R Correlation Coefficient R^2 Square of correlation coefficient

In Bangladesh, the coefficient of free international trade is statistical significant at 95 per cent level of significance. Spearman correlation coefficient (R = 0.94) shows high degree correlation between human development and free international trade. R^2 value shows 88 per cent variation in human development is regressed by the free international trade. In Nepal, it is proved in table 1 that there is no significant relationship between human development and economic freedom and no one indicator of economic freedom is found statistically significant in Nepal. The important cause of getting the different results of five countries is the covered area, size and growth of population, political stability, and liberalization policies.

Test for Multicollinearity: Model 2 is a multiple regression model. While analyzing the relation between human development and components of economic freedom, it is possible that there exist the problem of multicollinearity. In such a case, independent variables might be highly correlated to each other and it will violate the assumption of no-multicollinearity of the regression model. It is difficult to separate the affect of each component of economic freedom on human development. It is (delete also) difficult to estimate the values of parameters. (delete also) It is necessary to test multicollinearity of the independent variable. A t-test for the pattern of multicollinearity has been used in this study which aims at the detection of the variable that causes multicollinearity.

This test is developed by Frrar and Glauber. It is a set of three tests; Chi-Square test for the detection of the existence of multicollinearity in the model. The second test is F-test for locating which variables are multicollinear. The third test is t-test for determining which factor is responsible for the appearance of multicollinearity (delete variable). Table 3 reveals that statistical significance of partial correlation coefficients at 95 per cent significance level. If partial correlation coefficients are significant it means, null hypothesis is rejected and there exists multicollinearity among the indicators of economic freedom. In India, private property rights and sound money are significantly correlated to each other as in this case computed 't' value is greater than the table value of 't' (2.50) at 95 per cent significance level. Partial correlation coefficient value (-0.80) shows negative but high correlation between private property rights and sound money. In Sri Lanka, private property right and free international trade are significantly correlated to each other. The partial correlation coefficient value (0.78) shows high and positive correlation between the two.

In Pakistan, business regulations are significantly correlated with sound money and free international trade. The partial correlation coefficient value (-0.68) of sound money and business regulations shows negative and moderate degree correlation between the two. But the partial correlation coefficient value (0.80) of business regulations and free international trade shows positive and high degree correlation between them. In Bangladesh, size of the government is significantly correlated with sound money. In case of Nepal, all indicators of economic freedom are significantly correlated to each other; hence the study can't separate the affect of one indicator to another. That is why; Economic Freedom Index value in case of Nepal is not able to estimate the value of human development.

Table 3: Statistical Significance of Partial Correlation Coefficients

		India				
No.	Indicators	SOG	PRR	SM	*FIT*	*BR*
1.	SOG	--				
2.	PRR	$r_{SOG.PRR} = .57$ t =1.56	--			
3.	SM	$r_{SOG.SM} = .60$ t =1.68	$r_{PRR.SM} = -.80$ t = -2.98*	--		
4.	FIT	$r_{SOG.FIT} = .32$ t =0.79	$r_{PRR.FIT} = .51$ t =1.32	$r_{SM.FIT} = .49$ t =1.25	--	
5.	BR	$r_{SOG.BR} = -.59$ t = -1.65	$r_{PRR.BR} = .53$ t =1.40	$r_{SM.BR} = .44$ t =1.225	$r_{FIT.BR} = .4$ *t =1.25*	--
		Sri Lanka				
No.	Indicators	SOG	PRR	SM	FIT	BR
1.	SOG	--				
2.	PRR	$r_{SOG.PRR} = -.40$ t = -0.96	--			
3.	SM	$r_{SOG.SM} = .19$ t = 0.43	$r_{PRR.SM} = -.22$ t = -0.51	--		
4.	FIT	$r_{SOG.FIT} = .45$ t =1.25	$r_{PRR.FIT} = .78$ t = 2.76*	$r_{SM.FIT} = .54$ t =1.69	--	
5.	BR	$r_{SOG.BR} = -.10$ t = -0.22	$r_{PRR.BR} = .37$ t = 0.96	$r_{SM.BR} = .37$ t =0.96	$r_{FIT.BR} = -.$ t =1.34	--
		Pakistan				
No.	Indicators	SOG	PRR	SM	FIT	BR
1.	SOG	--				
2.	PRR	$r_{SOG.PRR} = .048$ t = -0.11	--			
3.	SM	$r_{SOG.SM} = -.30$ t = -0.74	$r_{PRR.SM} = -.29$ t = -0.7	--		

No.	Indicators	SOG	PRR	SM	FIT	BR
4.	FIT	$r_{SOG.FIT} = .34$ t = 0.85	$r_{PRR.FIT} = .32$ t = 0.80	$r_{SM.FIT} = .63$ t = 2.31	--	
5.	BR	$r_{SOG.BR} = .002$ t = .0044	$r_{PRR.BR} = -.49$ t = -1.25	$r_{SM.BR} = -.68$ t = -2.81*	$r_{FIT.BR} = .8$ t =2.98*	--
			Bangladesh			
No.	Indicators	SOG	PRR	SM	FIT	BR
1.	SOG	--				
2.	PRR	$r_{SOG.PRR} = .63$ t = 2.31	--			
3.	SM	$r_{SOG.SM} = .80$ t = 2.98*	$r_{PRR.SM} = -.47$ t = -1.34	--		
4.	FIT	$r_{SOG.FIT} = .66$ t = 1.97	$r_{PRR.FIT} = -.31$ t = -.72	$r_{SM.FIT} = -.27$ t = -0.62	--	
5.	BR	$r_{SOG.BR} = -.32$ t = -0.80	$r_{PRR.BR} = .44$ t = 1.225	$r_{SM.BR} = .24$ t = 0.55	$r_{FIT.BR} = .1$ t = 0.22	--
			Nepal			
No.	Indicators	SOG	PRR	SM	FIT	BR
1.	SOG	--				
2.	PRR	$r_{SOG.PRR} = -.89$ t = -4.42*	--			
3.	SM	$r_{SOG.SM} = -.82$ t = -3.22*	$r_{PRR.SM} = -.89$ t = 4.42*	--		
4.	FIT	$r_{SOG.FIT} = .89$ t = 4.42*	$r_{PRR.FIT} = .96$ t = 7.69*	$r_{SM.FIT} = .95$ t = 21.3*	--	
5.	BR	$r_{SOG.BR} = -.95$ t = -21.3*	$r_{PRR.BR} = -.92$ t = 5.15*	$r_{SM.BR} = -.81$ t =2.98*	$r_{FIT.BR} = .9$ t = 4.83*	--
significant at 95 per cent level of significance						

References

Altman, M. (2008): How much economic freedom is necessary for economic growth? Theory and Evidence, *Economics Bulletin*, 15(2): 1-20.

Carlsson, F. and Lundstrom, S. (2002): Economic freedom and growth: decomposing the effects, *Public Choice*, 112(3-4): 335-344.

Dhar, H. A. (2004): On making human development more humane, *International Journal of Social Economics*, 31 (11-12): 1071-1088.

Grubel, H. G. (1998): Economic freedom and human welfare: Some empirical findings, *Cato Journal*, 18(2): 287-304.

Gwartney, J., Lawson, R. (2003): *Economic Freedom of the World 2003, Annual Report*, Fraser Institute, Vancouver, B.C.

Gwartney, J., R. Lawson; W. Block (1996): *Economic Freedom in the World, 1975-1995*, Fraser Institute, Vancouver, B.C.

Haan, J. de and Sturm, Jan-Egbert (2000): On the relationship between economic freedom and economic growth, *European Journal of Political Economy*, 16(2): 215- 241.

Haq, Mahbub Ul, Jolly, R., Streeten, P. And Haq, Khadija (1995): *The UN and the Bretton Woods Institutions: New Challenges for the Twenty-First Century*, St. Martin's Press, New York.

Heckelman, J. C. (2007): Economic freedom and economic growth: A short-run causal investigation, *Journal of Applied Economics*, 3(1): 71-91.

Prendergast, R. (2005): The concept of freedom and its relation to economic development- a critical appreciation of the work of A. Sen, *Cambridge Journal of Economics*, 29(6): 1145-1170.

Romer, Paul M. (1990): Endogenous Technological Change, Journal of Political Economy, 98(5): S71-S102.

Romer, Paul M. (1994): The Origins of Endogenous Growth, *The Journal of Economic Perspectives*, 8(1): 3-22.

Sen, A. (1999): Development as Freedom, Oxford, Oxford University Press, New York.

Sepp, J. (2006): *Soft Factors of Economic Development: Human Capital and Institutions*, Paper presented at XIV Conference of the Economic Policy Research; Värska Tartu, Estonia, June 29-July 1 2006.

Smith, Adam (1976): The Wealth of Nations, Bantam Dell, New York.

UNDP (1990): Human Development Report 2003, Oxford University Press, New York.
UNDP (2003): Human Development Report 2003, Oxford University Press, New York.

4

Gender Equality: An Important Issue of Human Development

Umesh Chandra Pati[1]

I. Rationale

Human development is an important objective of development planning. Economic growth is to be accompanied by improvement in the quality of life of people, so that social face of India will be bright. Rightly, the 11th five year plan has given emphasis to inclusive growth which relates essentially to equality of opportunity to all for a productive and meaningful life with freedom and dignity. It includes Human Development and economic and social mobility for all sections of the society and in particular for the poor and disadvantaged groups. Human development necessarily encompasses the issue of Gender Equality. Gender gaps exist in equal rights, access, control of resources, economic opportunities as well as power and political representation. Women still posses less of a range of productive resources, including land, education and financial resources (World bank-2000). Gender inequality leads to higher levels of malnutrition, poverty ,illness and other deprivations with an adverse impact on the quality of life, productivity of farms and enterprises and governance ,all leading to a poor position in the Human Development Index and Gender Development Index.

The quality of life in India continues to be appalling with the country ranked poorly at 134 among 182 countries on the Human Development Index of the United Nations Development Program (UNDP) released in 2009.The ranking clearly shows that India has slipped in terms of ensuring a better quality of life for its citizens compared to 2007 and 2008. India ranked 128 during this period while the position the year before was 126.

---

[1] Associate Professor of Economics, Nayagarh Autonomous College, Nayagarh, Orissa

The HDI measures average achievements in a country, but it does not incorporate the degree of gender imbalance in these achievements. The gender-related development index (GDI), introduced in Human Development Report 1995, measures achievements in the same dimensions using the same indicators as the HDI but captures inequalities in achievement between women and men. It is simply the HDI adjusted downward for gender inequality. The greater the gender disparity in basic human development, the lower is a country's GDI relative to its HDI.

India's GDI value, 0.594 should be compared to its HDI value of 0.612. Its GDI value is 97.1 per cent of its HDI value. Out of the 155 countries with both HDI and GDI values, 138 countries have a better ratio than India's.

II. Objectives and Methodology

The objective of the study is to find out the significance of gender equality for achieving human development and promoting social wellbeing along with equitable and sustainable growth. It will critically examine certain key components of Human Development related to gender question and highlight the achievements till date with a suggestion to consolidate and accelerate the gains. The study will focus on the achievement of the state vis-a vis some important gender parameters of the country. It reflects the underlying features of Human Development in Orissa focusing on women who are exposed to all kinds of ill treatments by nature as well as institutions of state and are powerless to influence key decisions with expanding human choices.

Study is based on secondary data collected from various Government reports, studies and area research related to education and health.

III. The Backdrop of Orissa

Orissa endowed with abundant natural resources and renowned for its cultural heritage is making sustained progress on Human Development. The absolute value of human development index of Orissa has risen by 51.3 percent between 1981 and 2001. The Government of Orissa through its legislations, budgetary provisions, administrative measures and concerted actions with community based organizations is implementing a comprehensive development program for ensuring growth with social justice. But the black spots are still found in IMR, MMR, Literacy, provision of health care and others leading to a low position in development index. The inter district disparities and regional imbalances are evidenced in terms of net national product and access to educational, health and other HDI/GEM indicators. Tribal backwardness, area backwardness and backwardness due to severe natural calamities combine to perpetuate inter district disparities.

The HDI of Orissa is 0.579 which is much lower than the HDI of India and many other states. The pattern and extent of variation in respect of HDI, EI. HI and GDI in different districts with their ranks are analyzed in Table 1.

It is observed that Khurda tops the list followed by Jharsuguda in HDI and the tribal district of Malkangiri is at the lowest position. A look at education index reveals the same district having topmost position followed by Jagatsinghpur and the same Malkangiri at the lowest position. The mission of total literacy programme of Government has not made any progress in the tribal districts. With regard to the health index Mayurbhanj tops the list followed by Deogarh and another tribal district of Kandhamal is at the lowest position. This may be due to more number of missionaries working in these districts on the health front. Looking at the gender development index, the district of Jharsuguda tops the list followed by Sundargarh and the district of Malkangiri is at the lowest position. There is prevalence of more gender disparity in coastal districts than the tribal districts. Hence assessed from all fronts Malkangiri is the least developed district and the fruits of planning have not reached the people in that area. The trend reveals that the tribal dominated districts in southern and western Orissa have low position in development fronts. These districts are noted for economic/social backwardness, low mobilization for political causes, growing red militancy and widening chasm between classes and castes, the possible causes are lower access to opportunities. Table 2 reveals that the six tribal districts are at the lowest ebb of human development of less than 0.5.

Table 1: Human Development Index in Orissa, 2004

Sl. No	Districts	HDI	HDI Rank	EI	EI Rank	HI	HI Rank	GDI	GDI Rank
1	Angul	0.663	06	0.760	12	0.481	12	0.637	04
2	Bolangir	0.546	21	0.666	21	0.468	14	0.518	16
3	Balasore	0.559	18	0.770	10	0.442	10	0.519	14
4	Baragarh	0.565	17	0.727	16	0.449	17	0.528	13
5	Bhadrak	0.646	08	0.803	06	0.673	08	0.497	21
6	Boudh	0.536	23	0.688	20	0.423	20	0.509	19
7	Cuttack	0.695	03	0.813	05	0.686	07	0.618	07
8	Deogarh	0.669	05	0.698	19	0.776	02	0.647	03
9	Dhenkanal	0.591	12	0.773	09	0.468	15	0.531	12
10	Gajapati	0.431	28	0.561	26	0.173	28	0.401	27
11	Ganjam	0.551	20	0.718	17	0.404	21	0.518	15
12	Jagatsinghpur	0.557	19	0.833	02	0.288	25	0.491	22
13	Jajpur	0.540	22	0.786	07	0.333	24	0.386	28
14	Jharsuguda	0.722	02	0.773	08	0.635	09	0.687	01
15	Kalahandi	0.606	11	0.585	24	0.763	03	0.579	08
16	Kandhamal	0.389	29	0.645	23	0.006	30	0.372	29
17	Kendrapara	0.626	10	0.815	04	0.596	11	0.516	18
18	Keonjhar	0.530	24	0.704	18	0.340	22	0.504	20
19	Khurda	0.736	01	0.845	01	0.724	04	0.632	05
20	Koraput	0.431	27	0.535	27	0.218	27	0.415	26
21	Malkangiri	0.370	30	0.491	30	0.122	29	0.362	30
22	Mayurbhanj	0.639	09	0.647	22	0.782	01	0.621	06
23	Nabarangpur	0.436	26	0.516	29	0.340	23	0.422	25
24	Nayagarh	0.571	15	0.766	11	0.462	16	0.452	23
25	Nuapara	0.581	14	0.582	25	0.692	05	0.561	09
26	Puri	0.657	07	0.823	03	0.622	10	0.516	17
27	Rayagada	0.443	25	0.531	28	0.250	26	0.428	24
28	Sambalpur	0.589	13	0.742	13	0.436	19	0.560	10
29	Sonpur	0.566	16	0.731	15	0.474	13	0.543	11
30	Sundargarh	0.683	04	0.740	14	0.692	06	0.659	02
	ORISSA	0.579	-	0.723	-	0.468	-	0.546	-

Source: Compiled from the Human Development Report, Government of Orissa, 2004.

IV. Levels of Human Development

The HDI value for each district indicates how far that district has developed on HD front. The most desirable value of HDI is given as unity. The closer this value of a district is to one, the smaller the distance to be travelled by that district. UNDP has categorized human development into high HDI as above 0.8, medium as between 0.5 to 0.8, low as between 0.4 and 0.5, lowest as below 0.4. None of the districts in Orissa falls under the category of high HD category. Hence the present study has categorized high HD as above 0.6, medium between 0.5 and 0.6 and low as below 0.5.

Data in Table 2 reflecting the levels of human development in different districts of the State reveal how the coastal districts are more developed than the tribal districts.

Table 2: Levels of Human Development

Districts	Levels of HD
Khurda, Jharsuguda, Cuttack, Sundargarh, Deogarh, Angul, Puri, Bhadrak, Mayurbhanj, Kendrapara, kalahandi (11)	High (> 0.6)
Dhenkanal, Sambalpur, Nuapada, Nayagarh, Sonpur, Baragarh, Balesore, Jagatsinghpur, Ganjam, Bolangir, Boudh, Keonjhar (12)	Medium (> 0.5 and < 0.6)
Rayagada, Nabarangpur, Koraput, Gajapati,Kandhamal, Malkangiri	Low (< 0.5)

Source: Compiled from the Human Development Report, Government of Orissa, 2004.

Literacy

Literacy is an important indicator of the relative development of a society and has a strong impact on the individuals' earnings leading to higher income and a more equal distribution of such income. With the phenomenal expansion of the formal education system since independence there has been noticeable progress in overall literacy rate, but there is an undesirable continuance of gender disparity. Though overall literacy rates in Orissa has increased between 1951 and 2001 from 15.80 to 63.61 but there is existence of gender disparity. As per 2001 census Orissa still ranks a lowly 24th among the states/ union territories. There also exists a significant gender and regional disparities in the state. The comparative study of literacy in India and Orissa reveal the following.

Table 3 shows the literacy rates of India during the last five decades from 1951 to 2001 reflecting the efficiency of education policies of Government of India in bridging the gap of gender disparity. For the first time the country witnessed a faster growth in female literacy, that is 14.9 per cent points during 1991-2001 which is higher than the increase in male literacy of 11.7 per cent. The gender gap has declined from 1981 and remained more than 20 per cent. This denotes the Government's commitment towards women education and empowerment on the one hand and existence of gender disparity on the other. In 2001, 75 percent of males and just 54 percent of females were literate (Census of India 2001). Rural women are twice as likely to be illiterate. Gender bias intersects with social exclusion: reaching girls from scheduled castes and tribes is particularly challenging.

Table 3: Gender Gap in Literacy after Independence
(in percentage)

Census Year	Persons	Males	Females	Gender Gap
1951	18.33 (15.80)	27.16 (27.23)	08.86 (04.52)	18.30 (22.71)
1961	28.30 (21.66)	40.40 (34.68)	15.35 (08.65)	25.05 (26.03)
1971	34.45 (26.18)	45.96 (38.29)	21.97 (13.92)	23.98 (24.37)
1981	43.57 (33.62)	56.38 (46.39)	29.76 (20.60)	26.62 (25.79)
1991	52.21 (49.09)	64.13 (63.09)	39.29 (34.68)	24.84 (28.41)
2001	65.38 (63.61)	75.85 (75.95)	54.16 (50.97)	21.70 (24.98)

Note: Figures in parenthesis indicate data of Orissa
Source: Census of India, part III, 2001, Census of India-2001, Series-22, Orissa

The same picture is pertinent in case of Orissa and for all the years the gender gap is more than that of India except 1981. This leads to poor quality of health care, high IMR, high MMR, and malnutrition. All these directly affect economic growth by lowering the state's position in HDI and GDI. Finally that is reflected in the provision of employment opportunities and discriminatory practices against them in the labour market and other societal activity.

Women Empowerment

The employment situation in the state as shown in Table 4 reflects that very few women are employed in the organized sector.

The women employees in the public sector increased from 0.89 lakh during 2000 to 0.92 lakh during 2007, an increase of 3.37 per cent and women employees in the private sector remained almost the same. The percentage of women employees to total has increased from 12.4 per cent to 14.8 percent but is very low.

Table 4: Employment in the Organized Sector and Women
(in '000)

Year	Public Sector		Private Sector		Total Employ-ment	Women Employees	Per cent of women to total
	Total	Women	Total	Women			
2000	711	89	87	10	798	99	12.4
2001	717	92	89	10	806	102	12.7
2002	692	93	79	10	771	103	13.4
2003	680	96	87	10	767	106	13.8
2004	657	96	89	11	746	107	14.3
2005	655	100	90	11	745	111	14.9
2006	627	100	89	11	716	111	14.9
2007	598	92	90	10	688	102	14.8

Source: Directorate of Employment, Orissa, Bhubaneswar *(various years*).

The status of women when viewed in respect of higher education leadership and their role to play in decision making is also very disheartening as shown in Table 5. Of the eight positions the percentage of women in Academic Council is more being 15 percent and in all others it is less than that. This is a matter of great concern and needs rethinking when we are talking of Human Development.

Women in Elected bodies

The representation of women in elected bodies as shown in Table 6 is not satisfactory except the local bodies where the policy of reservation is in operation. There is no women representative from Orissa in Lok Sabha now. There were only two women MLAs in the first state legislative assembly which has increased to 14 in 2000. The number is 07 in the current assembly (2009). In terms of percentage it was always less than 10 percent.

Hence promoting women's rights and increasing their participation in public life may contribute to better governance and strong voice in the society. Institutional changes that establish gender equality in basic rights are important factors for gender equality in political participation and voice.

Table 5: Gender Distribution of Administrators in Higher Education in 2000

Sl No	Positions	Number		Percentage of women
		Men	Women	
1	Vice Chancellor	70	09	11
2	Pro Vice Chancellor	24	02	08
3	Registrar	77	06	07
4	Deputy Registrar	298	27	08
5	Assistant Registrar	504	67	12
6	Controller of Examinations	57	05	08
7	Finance Officer	66	03	04
8	Academic Council	4216	723	15

Source: Discussion Paper in the UGC sponsored workshop on *"Capacity Building of Women Managers in Higher Education"* held at Women's College, Kolkata from 14-12-09 to 18-12-09.

Health Facilities

Women are not only discriminated on the education front but also in terms of their access to health care facilities, reproductive rights, proper diagnosis of their diseases and nutritious food. There is gender bias in health care access and practices. Child bearing and poor reproductive health care lead to depletion of maternal health, thereby affecting women's survival.

Health is considered as fundamental to human right. Good health is both means and ends of development. The goal of Health for All is a distant dream for the large percentage of women in India. The sex ratio remains pitted against women. India continues to share the lowest rung in comparison to the world average sex ratio. Even countries like Nigeria, Tajikistan, Vietnam, Brazil and Indonesia fare better. No doubt India has created a large network of health care facilities during the last more than five decades, but women are yet to receive significant benefits.

Table 6: Women MLAs in Orissa

Sl No	Year	Total strength of MLAs	Women MLAs	Percentage of women MLAs
1	1937	60	02	3.3
2	1946	91	03	3.3
3	1952	140	03	2.1
4	1957	140	05	3.8
5	1961	140	05	3.8
6	1967	140	05	3.8
7	1971	140	01	0.7
8	1974	140	04	2.9
9	1977	147	07	4.8
10	1980	147	05	3.4
11	1985	147	08	5.4
12	1990	147	07	4.8
13	1995	147	08	5.4
14	2000	147	14	9.52
15	2004	147	11	7.48
16	2009	147	07	4.8

Source: Government. of Orissa, Statistical Information on General Elections to Orissa Legislative Assembly (*different years*).

A patriarchal social structure with a strong male preference predominates in many communities, resulting in gender disparities in all human development indicators (Filmer, King, and Prichett 1998; Siddhanta and Nandy 2003). Discrimination against girls begins before birth—abortion, infanticide, and neglect contribute to a skewed gender balance, with only 933 females for every 1,000 males (Census of India 2001). This adds up to 20 million missing females. In recent years the gender balance has become even more skewed in the economically advanced states and Union Territories, such as Punjab and New Delhi, where readily available ultrasound technology can identify the gender of the foetus (Census of India 2001). The balance is also more skewed among children in the highest-spending households (measured by monthly per capita expenditure). The top 5 percent of rural households have 804 female children for every 1,000 male children (891 in urban households), compared with 946 female children in the bottom 5 percent (903 in urban households) (Siddhanta, Nandy, and Agnihotri 2005).

There is no denying the fact that health standards in India have improved significantly over the years since independence. Better socio economic conditions along with concerted efforts in expanding health infrastructure have given us results we can feel proud of. Life expectancy has doubled from 32 in 1947 to 66 now. IMR has fallen to 55 (see Table 7). We have managed to eradicate small pox and polio. Leprosy cases have come down, Malaria is under control. We have made deeper inroads into rural areas with focused schemes like the NRHM and started health insurance for the poor. Yet these achievements notwithstanding we are nowhere near world standards in public health and we compare poorly even with many of the developing and similarly placed countries. Our IMR may have fallen sharply, but the figure of 55 is still alarming when Srilanka has a rate of 27, China -19 and Thailand only 06. Same is the case with MMR.

Table 7: Selected Health Indicators of Human Development

	Life Expectancy (2007)			IMR(2007)			BR (2007)	DR (2007)	Overall sex ratio (2001)	Sex Ratio 0-6 year age group (2001)
	M	F	Total	M	F	Total				
Orissa	59.5	59.6	59.6	70	72	71	21.5	9.2	972	950
India	62.0	64.9	63.4	55	56	55	23.1	7.4	933	

Source: Compiled and computed from Economic Survey, Government of Orissa, 2008-09 and Economic Survey, Government of India, 2008-09.

The key health indicators as shown in Table 8 and compared in three National Family Health Survey Reports reflect a very sorry picture. Though some improvements in the health care facilities have been there but it is less than the prescribed standard. The prevalence of more percentage of underweight children and more anemic pregnant women lead to high IMR and MMR. The women's role in decision making is also very less which is a matter of great concern and that increasingly excludes women from the development process.

There is a need for a different approach to the existing delivery system. In order to bring about an overall change in the health condition of women, the NGOs and village Panchayats can be involved. The PPP model can also be adopted to bring about improvement in the health condition of women in the country.

Table 8: Key Health Indicators for Orissa

Sl No	Indicators	NFHS-1 (1992-93)	NFHS-2 (1998-99)	NFHS-3 (2005-06)
1	Women age 20-24 married by age 18 (per cent)	45.5	37.6	37.2
2	Men age 25-29 married by age 21 (per cent)	NA	NA	22.2
3	Total fertility Rate	2.9	2.5	2.4
4	Women age 15-19 who were mothers or pregnant at the time of survey (per cent)	NA	NA	14.4
5	Family planning method used by women (per cent)	36.3	46.8	50.7
6	Child births assisted by medical personnel (per cent)	19.0	33.4	46.5
7	Children 12-23 months fully immunized (per cent)	36.1	43.7	51.8
8	Children under 3 years who are underweight (per cent)	50.0	50.3	39.5
9	Women whose body mass index is below normal (per cent)	NA	NA	40.5
10	Pregnant women age 15-49 who are anemic (per cent)	NA	60.5	68.1
11	Women who have heard of AIDS (per cent)	NA	39.0	62.1
12	Currently married women who usually participate in household decisions (per cent)	NA	NA	41.8

Source: Compiled from NFHS Reports for different years.

V. Conclusion and Suggestions

The initial years of planning process were based on the trickle down theory on the belief that the fruits of development and growth will spread out equally among all regions and all sections of the society. But this did not happen as a large segment of our population especially women have been left outside the growth process. Even among women those in rural areas are more disadvantaged as compared to those in urban areas. There is rural urban divide and the divide between different states and districts. The socio economic parameters of HDI including health and education are not in favour of women. It is in this background the UPA Government introduced for the first time a statement on gender budgeting in Union Budget 2005-06. The 11th plan has given emphasis on including the excluded. The 11th plan takes care of the special needs of women and made appropriate provision for that. Opportunities have to be enhanced for women so that they can generate income and can be self supportive. The patriarchal values need to change and public awareness that a nation cannot be healthy unless its women are healthy. Gender equality can bring efficiency in all economic sectors. This requires concerted efforts at all levels to make this endeavour a success.

There is necessity for a participatory method in preparation of village/block level plan instead of top down approach. A considerable investment by central and state government to correct the historical wrong of long standing is the need of the hour. Proper monitoring, review and implementation of the programs in association with local retired Government personnel, Panchayat members, social workers with due weightage to women and backward classes will fulfil the vision of human development.

Construing gender equality as an important issue of human development would entail both immediate measures to address various reasons as well as placing women's well being firmly on the development agenda. So gender equality is an important issue of human development not an isolated issue.

References

Ahluwalia, Montek, S. (2009): Growth, Distribution and Inclusiveness: Reflections on India's Experience, in Kausik Basu and Ravi Kanbur (Eds), *Arguments for a better world-*

Essays in honour of Amartya Sen, Vol.II : Society, Institutions and Development, Oxford University press, New Delhi.

Census of India (2001): *Final Population Totals: Orissa*, Director of Census Operations and Joint Registrar General, Orissa.

Express News Service (2009): *Gender Disparity Still Remains High*, 22nd December.

Government of Orissa (2004): Human Development Report, Bhubaneswar.

Government of Orissa, Finance Accounts for different years, Bhubaneswar.

Government of Orissa (2008): Economic Survey, Bhubaneswar.

Government of India (2008): Economic Survey, Ministry of Finance, New Delhi.

Kamdar, S. and Basak, A. (2005): Beyond the Human Development Index, Preliminary notes on Deprivation and Inequality, *Economic and Political Weekly*, 40(34): 3759-3765.

Shetty, S. L (2009), *Growing Inequality, A serious Challenge to the Indian Society and Polity, Dr V K R V Rao memorial lecture*, Bangalore, Institute for Economic and Social Change.

The Hindu (2006): *Confronting Gender Disparity*, March, 2 (Editorial).

UNDP, *Human Development Reports*, Various Issues.

5

Role of Geographical Indications for Economic Empowerment and Human Development: Evidences from a GI Registered Product

P. Nayak[1]

I. Introduction

Global competitiveness is a key determinant for trade and economic prosperity of a country in World Trade Organization (WTO) era. Trade Related Aspects of Intellectual Property Rights (TRIPS) as a part of agreements agreed upon under the framework of WTO are emerging as a key determinant for enhancing the rural economy, human development, increases international trade and leads to global competitiveness. TRIPS agreement stipulates protection of Intellectual Property through patents, designs, trademarks, copyrights, trade secrets and Geographical Indications (GI), etc. The protection creates a system for innovator to benefit from his inventions/ innovations/creations.

Geographical Indications (GI) is the newest addition to Intellectual Property Rights (IPRs) and defined as Indications, which identify a good as originating in the territory of a member country, or a region or locality in that territory, where a given quality, reputation or other characteristics of a good is essentially attributable to its geographical origin. In other words, some geographical regions acquire a reputation for origin of a product with some specific quality and uniqueness. It is the quality or reputation that distinguishes the product from others all over the world.

The GI is a unique form of Intellectual Property Rights (IPRs) provided to the community of producers who have acquired traditional knowledge from generations and produce products with unique characteristics. The GIs are further linked to their place of

---

[1] Director (Market Research), Textiles Committee, Ministry of Textiles, Government of India, Mumbai

origin. The main objectives of GI is (i) to provide legal protection to the product by safeguarding unauthorized usage of the product by other countries/manufacturers; (ii) promotion of economic prosperity of the producer of the goods/idea; (iii) assigning a form of "collective monopoly right" to the producer either within or outside the relevant geographical area; and (iv) empowering the registered proprietor to initiate legal action against unauthorized users.

Protection to traditional knowledge based industries, of late, has drawn considerable international attention. Traditional knowledge could be often described as different varieties of product available in the society as an outcome of tradition based intellectual activity. They are normally based on the knowledge systems, which are transmitted from generations and constantly evolving over time.

Protection to these traditional knowledge have never been an issue of debate in the TRIPS council rather liberal granting of patents to the new invention in the arena of traditional knowledge based generic resources to the developed countries particularly the EU and USA in a way pushed the developing countries to demand protection to their traditional knowledge based industries[2].

In this context, the possibilities of protecting the traditional knowledge based systems emerged. The new concept of GI as introduced in the TRIPS agreement recognizes quality reputation or other characteristics of the goods as conditions of protection. Since the quality, reputation and other characteristics are the result of continuous innovation in the traditional methods of production or use of specific formulae from generations, it was strongly pitched for protection through GI[3].

These traditional knowledge systems have also been instrumental in transforming the social and human development besides preserving the cultural heritage of the countries. It has also been suggested that since the GIs has always provided a sustained development of the socio economic conditions of the producers of the GIs; as has been witnessed in case of wines and spirits of Europe; the prospects of protecting the traditional knowledge holders in India holds a lots of hope.

---

[2] Ameena-Gurib-Fakim, Bridging the Gap between TRIPs and the CBD. Available at http://irfd.org/events/wfsids/virtual/papers/sids _guribfakim2.pdf

[3] Sergio Escudero, "Working paper on international Protection of Geographical Indications for Developing countries", July 2001, South Centre available at http//www.southcentre.org/publications/working papers/wp10.pdf

II. Objectives

In view of the above, this paper tries to examine and restate the role of the GI in economic empowerment and human development from some of the recent experiences of a GI registered product.

III. Socio-Economic Rationale

Historically, a range of professions (e.g. carpenters, stone carvers, tile manufacturers, potters, printers) and distinctive signs helped distinguish products and protect the goodwill of the consumers (Azmi et al., 1997). The role of goodwill protection was enhanced with the formation of guilds and their territorial control of trade in the middle ages. Inherent here is the economic rationale and legal principles between IGOs and trade marks, emerges from the economic theories to do with information and reputation (OECD, 2000)

India has been a store house of traditional knowledge. The stream of knowledge transcendent to almost all spheres of life; whether it is the system of Ayurved or Unani or unique handloom products, special plants and biodiversity and so on. The geo-climatic conditions and the cultural ethos have always influenced these products and their innovation. It requires no mention that the traditional knowledge in the handlooms of India is a timeless facet of the rich cultural heritage. Though the bold contours of these traditional art forms have displayed a strong blend of artisanal imagination linked to their faiths and natural surroundings, it has always provided enough space for appealing dynamism. In fact, the hand-woven is unparalleled in its flexibility and versatility, always permitted experimentation and encouraged innovation. The geographical reputation of these products was carefully built and painstakingly maintained by the producers or the developers by combining the best of nature and man; and continued as a generational legacy. Distinctively known by its name, created their brand value and commanded a premium price.

In spite of the above, the handlooms and handcrafted sector which is one of the treasures of the country in terms of the skill, knowledge and tradition has the weakness of economies of scale of production. The traditional textile products could establish themselves owing to royal patronage, cultural preferences etc. which over the period created a well established brand image for them. But the unorganized nature of production and lack of economies of scale has always attracted infringement from other segments besides the global players. The infringement deprives the producers to retain the existing market shares, and also over a period of time, the name associated with the product for its quality and reputation gets fast eroded. As a result, the premium price which the weaver/ artisan were deriving is siphoned away by the infringer. This has always been an impediment to the growth profile of the GI, retards the space of social growth and many times has fueled significant occupational mobility.

The Indian parliament passed the geographical indications at (registration and protection) Act 1999 in December 1999. The geographical indications (registrations and protections) rules also came into being in the year 2002. The act has come into force with effect from 15 September 2003. Under this act, the central government has established a 'geographical indication registry' with all India jurisdictions at Chennai, where the right holders can register their respective GIs. The GI act is to be administered by the controller general of patents, designs and trademarks who is the registrar of geographical indications. It is interesting to note that though Article 23 of TRIPS provides a higher level of protection to GIs relating to wines and spirits only, the corresponding provisions in the Indian act does not restrict themselves to wines and spirits alone. Rather it has been left in the discretion of the central government to decide which goods or classes of goods should be granted such a higher level of protection. This discretion has deliberately been maintained by Indian lawmakers with the aim of ensuring the absolute protection of article 23 or the GIs associated with products of India's export interest. Once a product registered under GI act, the applicant for a group of applicants can be registered proprietor of that product. In order to identify the goods, which can be registered under GI, the act stipulates that the persons dealing with three categories of goods are covered as producers of GI registration i.e. agricultural goods including production, processing, trading or dealing of such goods, natural gods including exploitation, trading or dealing of such goods, handicrafts or industrial goods including making, manufacturing, trading or dealing of such goods. The registration of GI products is predominantly a case of reorganization and governance of supply chains. These two themes reflect the dual requirement of GI protection: coherence in terms of distinguishing the characteristics between the products produced in different firms and authenticity that the production process is consistent with the given quality.

The product market protection though Geographical Indications (GI) has unleashed a new era of human development in terms their knowledge spheres in blending the traditional knowledge to the contemporary ones without losing its originality, securing a market meant for them only and ultimately benefiting from the effort to strengthen their life from the incremental income. The Geographical Indication Act, 1999 created new avenues to these unique products as it stipulates protection from infringement. As of today, more than 150 products have been protected under the GI Act. The producers who are economically backward can really harvest the premium price associated with the products and hence can increase their income, productivity, and maintain quality of their product which leads to development of human resources. The paper delves into a post GI effect study of a unique handloom product of Pochampally to delineate the ushering of the human development in a geographical area close to Hyderabad. The famous Pochampally tie and dye sari has won Intellectual Property Rights Protection, more than a year after it was applied. It is the first traditional Indian craft to receive this status of geographical branding. In the above context, we examine below the case of Pochampally Ikat in the post GI scenario.

IV. Pochampally Ikat

Pochampally a small village in the Nalgonda district of Andhra Pradesh is a major centre of handlooms and has received prominence for Ikat productions from silk and cotton fibers. Ikat is a traditional technique resulting in a streaky effect, created by tying and dying of the length of yarn before weaving. Wherever colour is not required in a particular portion of the yarn to provide a special effect in the weaving design, the yarn bundles are tied with rubber strips before the yarn in given a dye bath. Over the years, Pochampally is manufacturing tie and dye silk saris, mostly in geometric designs. There are other forms of Ikat in India particularly the ones practiced in Gujarat and Orissa.

Of late, Pochampally has entered into the diversification mode and now producing dress materials, home furnishings and wall hangings in both silk and cotton for catering to the growing demand of the consumers. Since most of the artisans are resource poor and depending on the money lenders and the master craftsmen for their requirement of credit, quick shift from a product design to other has always been a matter of great stress on their production schedule. Sometimes change in design/product costed the artisan more on account of increased use of the yarn and labour, making the initiative less attractive.

Besides the Pochampally, large number weavers are located in the surrounding areas in the districts of Nalgonda and Mehbubnagar. They wove fine cotton saris both plain and checked/striped, chitki saris, telia rumals[4], and tie-dye designed fabric. Tie and dye saris (both silk and cotton) of different counts are woven. The Pochampally designs started during the period of Nizam when Ikat technique was brought from Chirala, a place in Andhra Pradesh. Weavers, basically Hindus of the *Padmasali* community have been marketing their products in the name of Pochampally Handlooms for a long time. Presently, the "Pochampally Handloom Weavers Cooperative Society Ltd" a society registered under the society registration Act and the "Pochampally Handloom Tie and Dye Silk Manufactures Association" are two most important marketing organizations which regulate the marketing of the Pochampally products. During 1950s and 1960s, cotton saris were being produced in Pochampally and this cotton sari production received a short in the arm in 1956, when Kamladevi Chattopadhyaya, a strong proponent of the handlooms and crafts, visited the place during her chairmanship of the All India Handloom Board and persuaded the artisans to produce cotton saris by using the local Ikat technique. This persuasion and subsequent popularity of the product provided a new dimension to the Pochampally Ikat. By the mid 1960s, silk tie and dyed saris from Pochampally began to enter the market and by 1970s became popular especially at the upper end of the market. Within a decade, weaving in the entire region shifted to silk from cotton. Silk was preferred as wages were higher, the yarn was stronger and easier to weave; and silk yarn absorbs colour well providing the cloth a vibrancy in colour disposition. Around this time, many weavers migrated from Medak, Khammam, Mehbubnagar, Guntur and other places into the Pochampally-

[4] The "*Telia Rumal*" is piece of long cloth from Ikat design specially processed through oil which is mainly used like a turban (head gear) so as to protect the head from the scorching heat. The product became very popular and famous in the Middle East countries, particularly in the Muslim communities and a large amount of Telia Rumal exports were made to Burma, and Africa; and known as "Asian Telia Rumal".

Koyyalagudem belt. In Pochampally, weft tie-dyed is more popular today, though earlier double Ikat production was also done. Since the product was a very popular one and commanding a good market segment, in no time, Pochampally saris began to face the problem of infringement from power looms and mills. The demand for the authentic handloom silk saris fell and undercutting in terms of price competitions and wage squeezes has become very common. Currently mainly master weavers are servicing the market. Master weavers/traders control the business aspect by in turn linking up with traders from outside the state (i.e. the traders often get orders and then seek to get the production organized through several master weavers). The manufacturers have an association called "Pochampally Handloom Tie and Dye Manufacturers Association", which consists of more than 100 master weavers. They use the office space of the association more for lobbying with Government when there is stock pile up, or for controlling and deciding wage limits, or for devising ways of dealing with credit defaulters. Apart from these functions, there is no common procurement of raw materials or marketing. But the real threat of infringement kept the market squeezed and expansion of the market remained a distant dream. Obviously the producers were deprived of their market and the premium price they were earning earlier. On the enactment of the Geographical Indication Act and rules in India, the Textiles Committee in association with the government of Andhra Pradesh and Andhra Pradesh Technology Development Council (an initiative of Confederation of Indian Industries and the government of AP) started the process of registering the product under GI Act and it got registered during November 2004.

Immediately on registration of the product under the GI, a metamorphosis has happened. First, the product got national and international attention as the first textile product receiving protection under the GI in India and many national level bodies were encouraged to share the reputation by procuring and using these products to enhance their brand equity. The prominent among them are the Air India's procurement of saris for the air hostesses and interest of Tata group of industries to use the Pochampally Ikat for interior designing of their office spaces. There was a general demand increase of the product and the weavers looked for the changes in the preference pattern of the consumers.

Given this scenario, we attempted to map the trajectory of successful handloom enterprises and locate them in the context of the growth of the handloom industry of Pochampally. In the above background, we examined the efficacy of Geographical Indication to protect the Intellectual Property Rights of the handloom weaver with reference to Pochampally Ikat and the effect of the GI Act registration on various parameters like skill, increase in productivity, improvement in designs, supply chain management and earning of the artisans. The results that follow from here.

Nature of Production Activity[5]

About 800 looms are in the co-operative sector under the fold of "Pochampally Handloom Weavers Co-operative Society Limited" while the majority of the rest is working for the master weavers. Though production in the co-operative sector was predominant, only 15 to 20 percent of the looms in the sector are active today and most weavers are depending on job-work. Traders procure orders and organize production through a network of master weavers. There are over 100 master weavers are operating in Pochampally. These master weavers/manufacturers are having the association called "Pochampally Handloom Tie and Dye Manufacturers Association". General prevailing practice of the cluster is Society or the master weaver supply the silk yarns to the weavers and the weavers carry out de-gumming, mercerizing, dyeing, weaving preparatory and weaving at their units mostly placed in their homes. For each design, society or master weavers supply the raw materials for 8 saris (a standard used for convenience). To complete this, weaver will take minimum 30 to 45 days (depending on the design of the Saris the duration varies), for which entire family members will be on job. For 8 saris weaver gets on an average Rs. 1800/- to Rs. 2500/- as conversion charges. The rates vary from design to design.

Size Structure of Units

Since the handloom weavers are generally economically backward and the occupation has been largely family based, the number of looms is generally restricted for the enterprise on the basis of the size of the family. However in case of associations and

[5] The data used in the paper has been largely borrowed from a survey conducted by the Textiles Committee, a statutory organisation under the Ministry of Textiles and one of the Organisations initiated the registration of the Pochampally products under GI Act.

recently developed consortia they manage larger size of units as compared to household units. The field data has been organized for three time points, i.e., 2004, 2006 and 2008 for the purpose of comparison of the size structure between the pre and post Geographical Indication (GI) registration periods. Though there is a limitation to the analytical prospective of the size structure of looms for such a small period, the changes registered are very insignificant in terms of increase in size of loomage or even increase in the workforce for the units. It is an obvious fact that changes in the size structure will need investment, the entry of new artisanal force to the industry and the extent of influence of the market demand. Though the market for the product increased many fold, the incorporation of more looms and increase of the labour into the units remained largely sluggish on account of non-availability of the desired looms, which forms the main capital investment of the enterprise. So much so, the scanty knowledge of the entrepreneurs on the source of the looms is also another negative factor for rapid changes in the size structure.

Supply Chain and quality

The supply chains of the GI products are distinguished from other products on account of fundamental requirement for the product, irrespective of its origin in terms of manufacturing unit to exploit the distinguishable characteristics, quality or reputation that is essentially attributable to its geographical origin. Chappuis and Sans (2000) also hold the view that a range of firms in the geographical area that are legally and economically distinct units produce the very same product.

There are two important raw materials required for maintaining of the desired quality of the product: the yarn and dyes. As Pochampally specializes in silk saris and dress material, the silk yarn becomes an important issue in the supply chain for the final product. It is found that yarn is bought from Karnataka. Charka fine quality silk yarn is used for making tie and dye silk saris. In warp they are using 16-18 denier and in weft 24-26 denier. In most cases, the weaver receives poor quality of yarn as well as dyes from the local markets, since master weavers are also involved in the production process, they supply yarn which, many times, is better but use of sub standard yarn is also not ruled out. Further, even though, they are having few complaints like more percentage loss of silk yarn after de-gumming, poor quality of dyes, adulteration in dyes etc. poor financial position forces them to accept the substandard raw materials.

For maintaining the quality of Pochampally silks and cloth items, the government of Andhra Pradesh has taken a number of measures. In the case of weavers who are members of the society, quality control technicians are appointed in each of the branches to provide training to the weavers and also suggest new designs. In the processing side; the weavers use to dye their yarn trough tumble dyeing method which has seen a change and few weavers have adopted winch dying systems and the weavers have acquired new knowledge in this area.

Market in Post GI

Even when, textile items produced by Pochampally were in great demand both in domestic and in West Asian countries, market was only in hands of traders. Artisans/weavers were to only supply or sell to these traders. Because of this reason, when the traders went away after Nijam's rule, they were failed to survive, as they were not having any idea about their own market. But within short period it was able to withstand with the help of Co-operative movement and by HYCO, which was made special effort to market in the initial stages. Then thanks to 'Bhoodan' movement, where it attracted persons from various places. During this period, this new product attracted by many visitors and got advertised without the marketing efforts of Pochampally weavers. So, inflow of the traders to Pochampally, and newness in the product was made Pochampally in to demand oriented market. Mill and power-loom people who started copying these designs during the 1990s slowly captured this. During the period, Pochampally was not made sufficient efforts to withstand the competition by way of product/design diversification. Less exposure to market also further worsened the situation.

The weavers at Pochampally don't have any systematic market strategy as the marketing is largely carried out by the Master Weaver through their shops/show rooms at Pochampally. The domestic buyers and traders from different places of the country come to Pochampally and source products for their retail sales. Besides the marketing of the product is largely controlled by the Handloom Weavers Co-operative Society and the Pochampally Handloom Tie and Dye Silk Sarees Manufacturers Association, a body representing the weavers who are not the members of the Society. The Society gives materials for weaving to its members and the weavers get a 12 percent margin for the final product but are not allowed to sale their product in open market. The society sells 50 percent of the product through the Andhra Pradesh Cooperative Society and the rest is sold directly in the open market and through exhibitions. The government of Andhra Pradesh provides a rebate of 20 percent during festival seasons. Major market for Pochampally textiles lies in Gujarat, Maharashtra and West Bengal. Poor market access and strategy of weavers is the reasons for poor product diversification. They don't have proper market linkages to get information on fashion trends. Internal price competition amongst these artisans lowered their own margins.

The post GI period witnessed complete structural changes in the marketing of the product. The consortium formed for the purpose of the GI registration of the product becomes the main architect of shaping the production, design development, marketing, export and publicity of the Pochampally products. The first measure adopted by the consortium is to appoint reputed designers to support new designs and product diversification without compromising the essence of the GI which involves a diamond in the chowka and aggressively popularized the concept of GI as a legal measure for the genuine producers so as to contain the infringement action. Secondly, the consortium followed a systematic marketing strategy such as participation in national and international markets for getting orders and making spot sales. This led to large orders and compelled the artisans to pool their production to achieve economies of scale so as to help the consortium meet the deadlines of the orders. The weavers also become receptive to the training imparted by the consortium and skill levels in respect of finer Ikat technique, weaving and finishing. The occupational mobility and non adoption of family avocation by the younger Turks has been reduced in a significant extent. A common pool of yarn requirement led to sourcing quality yarn at reduced cost and that too become available any time the weaver required the yarn. To day, the Pochampally Ikat has found large international market for its product and the artisans are comfortable to deal with the overseas market with ease; further the consortium receives their international orders through their dedicated web portal. The most important happening is the establishment of the Handloom park one of its kind in India which has provided the economies of scale advantage besides the technological advantage. Experienced with the supply constraints, the consortium approached the Government of AP & Government of India for supporting the weaver's community in this initiative. The Governments proactively supported the consortium in the process of developing an integrated handloom park in the Kanumukkula Village, about 10 kms away from Pochampally. The park housed a large number of loom sheds and provided common facilities for processing and display of the key product among other necessary services.

Family income in post GI

Increase in productivity, price and sales turnover is the effects of the Pochampally Ikat, the moment it received publicity and discovered newer markets. The publicity not only started in the web as soon as it received GI but also in newspapers, magazines and also in exhibitions. The Pochampally Ikat being the first textile product to be registered under GI in India, it has received enormous attention from the research and practicing community as well. In fact, the Pochampally has been converted into an experimental lab for many institutions and organizations. The information suggest National Institute of Rural Development (NIRD), National Institute of Small Industries Extension and Training (NISIET), some of the institutions under Indian Institute of Handloom Technology (IIHT) and many foreign institutions visited Pochampally to understand the resultant changes in the production, marketing and lifestyles of the weaving community of Pochampally after GI. The big brand customers like the Air India started procuring the Pochampally Ikat products. The product design and quality has been defined by the Air India itself and the test parameters are ascertained by the Textiles Committee. The increase in productivity indirectly provided higher earnings to the weavers and hence a better leaving standards to the weaving households.

The most important finding of the study is the clear evidence of the increase in disposable income of the artisans in the cluster in the post GI period. The increase in the income seems to be quite promising due to the fact that when almost all clusters in the country are increasingly experiencing declining incomes during the past years, Pochampally provided better income to the manufacturers. The upward trend of income may be due to the increase in the demand pattern for the product after the IPR protection and the product diversification, the weavers have been adopting due to wide scale intervention by government and international agencies in post registration period.

It was observed from the field that the silk weavers are earning around Rs 3200 in 2008, Rs 2800 per month in 2006 as compared to Rs 2200 in 2004 (Table 1). The earnings have been increased by around 36 percent in 2008 as compared to 2004 indicating a sustained growth of the levels of earning of the weavers from 2004. The growth of the wage earning has been steady and indicating a monotonously increasing trend. Though increase in the wage earning is not an exact indicator of the net earnings of the each weaver in the household as most of the members put their effort in the entire exercise and part timers' wage calculation becomes a Herculean task. But undoubtedly the trend of earning has been significantly upward. Similarly, the income of cotton weavers has increased by 54 percent during the period. This is being attributed to the production of diversified products like home furnishings, ladies dress materials etc. and increase in demand for the products both in domestic and export market.

Table 1: Income of the Weavers

Income in INR	Year		
	2004	2006	2008
Silk Weaver	2200	2800	3200
Cotton Weaver	1200	1850	2000

Source: Calculated from primary data by the author

V. Conclusion

The protection of the Pochampally Ikat through Geographical Indications has provided enough space and opportunities for growth and empowerment of the Ikat handloom weavers. This has not only increased the levels of awareness on the protection of their rights, the weavers have been able to convert the protection rights to their advantage ushering a new era in socio-economic development in general and human development in particular. However, it is evident that the producers of the GI do not have cultural mindset conducive for a legal protection of the GIs at the community level. This has taken the toll of the real market away from the right holders and results in widespread use of GIs by members outside the community and as a consequence leads to economic loss of the actual producers of the GIs. Further, the post GI initiatives taken by the right holders of Pochampally have demonstrated that it is a case of successful GI in India and corroborate to many such experiences of the west particularly the Europe.

References

Arasaratanam, S (1990): Weavers, Merchants and Company: The Handloom Industry in South Eastern India, 1750 – 1790, In S. Subramanyam (ed), Merchants, Markets and the State in Early Modern India, Oxford University Press, Delhi.

Azmi, Ida Maidieha, Spyros Maniatis and Bankole Sodipo, (1997): Distinctive signs and early markets: Europe, Africa and Islam, In Alison Firth, (Ed.,) The pre history and development of intellectual property systems; London, Sweet and Maxwell.

Blaug, M (1986): Entrepreneurship Before and After Schumpeter, In Economic History and the History of Economics, New York University Press, New York, pp 219 – 30.

Boddewyn, J. J. (2003): Understanding and Advancing the Concept of Non-Market, *Business and Society*, 42(3): 297 – 327.

Brennig, J. J. (1990): Textile Producers and Production in Late 17th Century Coromandel, In S. Subramanyam (Ed), Merchants, Markets and the State in Early Modern India, Oxford University Press, Delhi.

Chappuis, J M and P Sans (2000): Actors coordination: governance structures and institutions in supply chains of protected designation of origin, In B Sylvander, D Borjolle, F Arfini,eds, The Socio Economics of Origin Labelled Products in Agri-food Supply Chains: Spatial, institutional and coordination aspects, ACTES et Communications.

Correa, J. (2001): Traditional knowledge and intellectual property: issues and options surrounding the protection of traditional knowledge, Quaker United Nations Office Discussion Paper 18.

Fowler, B.J. (2004): Preventing counterfeit craft designs, In Finger, J.M. and Schuler, P. (Eds), Poor People's Knowledge: Promoting Intellectual Property in Developing Countries, The World Bank, Washington DC, pp. 113 – 131.

Gopalkrishnan, N S et al (2007): Exploring the Relationship between Geographical Indications and Traditional Knowledge, ICTSD programme on sustainable development.

Harnetty, P (1991): De-industrialization Visited: the Handloom Weavers of the Central Provinces of India, c1800-1947, *Modern Asian Studies*, 25(3): 445-510.

Mukund, K and B Syamasundari (2001): *Traditional Industry in the New Market Economy: The Cotton Handlooms of Andhra Pradesh*, Sage Publications, New- Delhi.

OECD (2000): Appellations of Origin and geographical indications in OECD member countries: economic and legal implications, Working party on Agricultural Policies and Markets of the committee for Agriculture, joint working party of the committee for Agriculture and the trade committee.

Rangnekar, Dwijen (2003): The socio economics of Geographical Indications: A review of Empirical evidence of Europe, Centre for the Study of Globalization and Regionalization, Warwick University, Coventry.

Rangnekar, Dwijen (2004): Demanding Stronger Protection for Geographical Indications: The Relationship between Local Knowledge, Information and Reputation, INTECH Discussion Paper.

Roy, T (1998): Economic Reforms and Textile Industry in India, *Economic and Political Weekly*, 33(32): 2173-2182.

——(1999): Traditional Industry in the Economy of Colonial India, Cambridge University Press, Cambridge.

6

Public Expenditure and Human Development in India

Ranjeeta[1]

I. Introduction

Human development has recently been advanced as the ultimate objective of human activity in place of economic growth. Human development has been defined as enlarging people's choices in a way which enables them to lead longer, healthier and fuller lives. Empirical findings show that countries at similar levels of per capita income can have significantly different human development indicators depending on how that income was used. According to Kuznets inverted U shaped curve, as the economy develops the in equality increases in the initial stage. The inequality promotes poverty which creates obstacles in the path of human development. It is well known that economic growth is a necessary but not a sufficient condition for the eradication of poverty. The policy makers should, therefore, not only need to understand the factors that affect growth of a particular economy, but also the factors that help redistribute the effects of growth more effectively. Traditionally, tax and expenditures on public goods have been used as the most important forms of redistribution instruments. In recent years, however, public expenditures on education and health have been used as prominent mechanisms for effecting redistribution.

Since the role of a government is to enhance social welfare, therefore public spending is a considered as a powerful instrument for achieving this goal. Public expenditures can overcome market failures that exacerbate poverty, such as the inability of the poor to borrow for education, their lack of information about preventive health care, or the externalities that exacerbate public health hazards

[1] Research Scholar, Centre for the Study of Regional Development, Jawaharlal Nehru University, New Delhi

to which the poor are most exposed. The importance of public expenditure in the process of human development is well recognized.

This paper examines the trends and pattern of public expenditure on human development in India and compares it with the public expenditure of other countries. The paper is divided into seven sections. In the next section we have looked at the earlier literatures on the role of public expenditure in promoting the Human development. In section 3 we analyses, in a more formal way, the overall pattern of public expenditure on Human Development in general and health and education in particular. The section 4 we illustrate the position of India compared vis-à-vis other countries in terms of public expenditure on health and education. In section we further examine in detail the composition of public expenditure in sectors that are important for human development. In section 5, we have looked at the quality of public expenditure. In section 7, we conclude.

II. Literature Review

Traditionally public expenditure represents a form of government intervention designed to promote allocative efficiency through correction of market failures, redistribute resources equitably and promote economic growth and stability (Musgrave, 1959). The redistributive powers of the state, through public expenditure, emanates from the normative arguments in favour of greater equality (Marshall, 1950; Rawls, 1971).

To analyze how public spending on human development can be designed and monitored, UNDP's Human Development Report 1991 uses four ratios. These are:

- Public expenditure ratio (PER), defined as the total budgetary expenditures as a proportion of GDP,
- Social Allocation Ratio (SAR), defined as the share of budgetary expenditure on the social sector in total budgetary expenditure,
- Social Priority Ratio (SPR), defined as the proportion of social sector expenditure that is spent on human priority areas, and
- Human expenditure ratio (HER), which is a product of the first three ratios and measures the budgetary expenditures in human priority areas as a proportion of GDP.

In addition to these ratios, studies have also used trends in per capita expenditure on social and human priority sectors to measure public spending for human development. It is important to examine trends in per capita expenditure along with the UNDP ratios as the UNDP ratios measure the human development expenditure in relation to income and do not indicate the absolute level of expenditure on human development in a Country. So, in this analysis apart from the ratios proposed by UNDP, per capita expenditure on Social and Human priority and the change in its composition over the period has also been analyzed.

Several important policy conclusions emerge from the UNDP's analysis of public expenditure on human development[2].

a. The human expenditure ratio may need to be around 5 per cent if a country wishes to do well in human development.
b. This can be achieved in different ways both efficient and inefficient. A preferred option is to keep the public expenditure ratio moderate (around 25 per cent), allocate much of this to the social sectors (more than 40 per cent) and focus on the social priority areas (giving them more than 50 per cent). An inefficient option is to withdraw a large proportion of national income into the public sector to depress private investment and initiative and to restrict the economic growth and resource expansion that can ultimately finance human development. In several cases, total public expenditure can be cut back (that might encourage more private investment) and yet the government can spend more public money on human concerns.
c. Budgetary interventions need not be extensive if GNP growth is rapid and equitable or if the private sector and non-governmental organizations are extremely active in social pending. Even when the funding is public, the implementation can still be private. Many governments find that the private sector and NGOs can provide social services more efficiently, and are increasingly channeling public funds through them.
d. High government spending with low social priorities is the worst case. If 25 per cent or more of national income is channeled through the government budget, and yet less than

[2] UNDP(1991): Human Development Report, 1991, Oxford University Press, New York

> 1 per cent of GNP goes into human priority concerns, this is the worst of all possible worlds. The public sector is huge yet the majority of the population does not benefit from public social expenditure.

The human expenditure ratio should increasingly become one of the principal guides to public spending policy. When resource is tight, greater attention must be paid to allocation priorities and efficiency in spending. It is wrong, however, to confuse a plea for greater efficiency with indifference to the mobilization of additional resources. The best argument for mobilizing more resources is spending existing resources well.

III. Overall Pattern of Public Expenditure on Human Development

In this section, trends in both the UNDP ratios and the per capita expenditures have been analyzed. The first step towards such an analysis is to define what constitutes social sector and the human priority areas. In this paper, social sector is defined to comprise expenditure on broad budgetary heads called Social Services and Rural Development. Social Services include following subheads: (i) Education, Sports, Art and culture; (ii) Medical and Public Health; (iii) Family Welfare; (iv) Water Supply and Sanitation; (v) Housing; (vi) Urban Development; (vii) Welfare of Scheduled Castes, Scheduled Tribes and Other Backward Castes; (viii) Labour and Labour Welfare; (viii) Social Security and Welfare; (ix) Nutrition; (x) Relief on Account of Natural Calamities; (x) Other Social Services. Within the social sector, social priority areas are defined to comprise education, art and culture, health and family welfare, nutrition, water supply and sanitation and rural development. These are sectors that are particularly important for human development.

Human Expenditure Ratio has remained approximately constant during the period under consideration. Social Priority ratio has declined from 84.44 per cent in 2001-02 to 73.33 in 2008-09.

Public Expenditure Ratio (PER)

A high public expenditure ratio is neither a virtue nor a necessity. Public policy and public spending must facilitate, encourage and complement private spending to ensure that human development needs are met. If a government is to allow for sufficient spending on priority areas, a public expenditure ratio of 20-25 per cent is probably desirable.

If we look at the period 1986-87 to 2008-09, average public expenditure ratio (PER) has been around 29 per cent. The minimum was 25.83 around 1996-97 and maximum was 31.62 around 1986-87. The overall public expenditure in India as a share of GDP, as reflected in PER estimates presented in Table 1, declined from about 31.62 per cent in 1986-87 to about 26 per cent in 1996-97. This was mainly due to the tightening fiscal policy of the government after the reform period. There was an increase in PER between 1996-97 and 2003-04 due to the implementation off pay revision by the government, it increased from 25.83 per cent to 30.05 per cent. If we look at the public expenditure, it has increased at an increasing rate during this period (figure 1), but, PER has not increased at a very high rate mainly due to high growth rate of GDP.

Figure 1: Public Expenditure Ratio

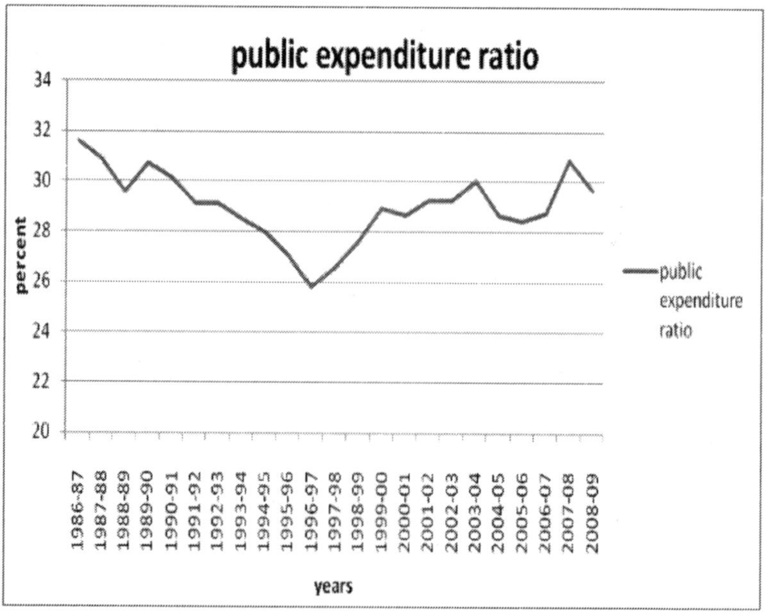

Table 1: Indicators of Expenditure on Human Development in India

(in percent)

Year	PER	SAR	SPR	HER
1988-89	29.57	24.41	81.67	5.89
1989-90	30.71	24.29	82.66	6.16
1990-91	30.12	23.28	83.12	5.83
1991-92	29.11	23.20	81.47	5.50
1992-93	29.12	22.45	83.23	5.44
1993-94	28.51	23.15	83.77	5.53
1994-95	27.98	23.61	83.59	5.52
1995-96	27.06	24.09	82.96	5.41
1996-97	25.83	24.78	80.90	5.18
1997-98	26.60	24.55	81.13	5.30
1998-99	27.60	24.91	81.88	5.63
1999-00	28.94	24.49	82.67	5.86
2000-01	28.68	23.32	82.09	5.49
2001-02	29.25	22.06	84.44	5.45
2002-03	29.26	22.77	82.08	5.47
2003-04	30.05	22.02	80.62	5.34
2004-05	28.65	22.87	79.51	5.21
2005-06	28.44	24.21	79.82	5.50
2006-07	28.75	24.84	78.67	5.62
2007-08	30.85	25.07	75.53	5.84
2008-09(BE)	29.66	27.17	73.77	5.95

Notes: PER= Public Expenditure/GDP

SAR= Expenditure in the social sector/public expenditure; SPR= Expenditure in Human Priority Areas/Expenditure in the Social sector; HER= Expenditure in Human Priority Areas/GDP.

Expenditure under different heads has been estimated as the sum of revenue expenditure and capital expenditure of both centre and country.

Social Allocation Ratio (SAR)

"Social spending" includes that on education, health, rural development, welfare, social security, water, sanitation, housing and amenities. According to UNDP's Human Development Report 1991, high social spender devotes over 40 per cent of public expenditure to the social sector, and the low spender, 20 per cent or less.

A high social allocation ratio does not guarantee a good human development performance, but it does make an important contribution. Some developing countries have high social allocation ratio and social priority ratio and have all attained high levels of human development. Almost all start from large public expenditure ratios-one-third or more of GNP. But many of countries could find ways to reduce the size of the public sectors and yet maintain, or even increase, their human development spending.

In terms of allocation to social services, the SAR in India has always remained lower than the 40 per cent norm suggested by the UNDP. Average Social Allocation Ratio (SAR) in India during the period 1986-87 and 2008-09 has been about 23.73 per cent with a minimum value of 20.01 per cent in 1986-87 and maximum value of 27.17 per cent in 2008-09 (see Figure 2). Social Allocation Ratio has increased from 22.06 to 27.17 per cent in the period 2001-02 to 2008-09.

Figure 2: Social Allocation Ratio

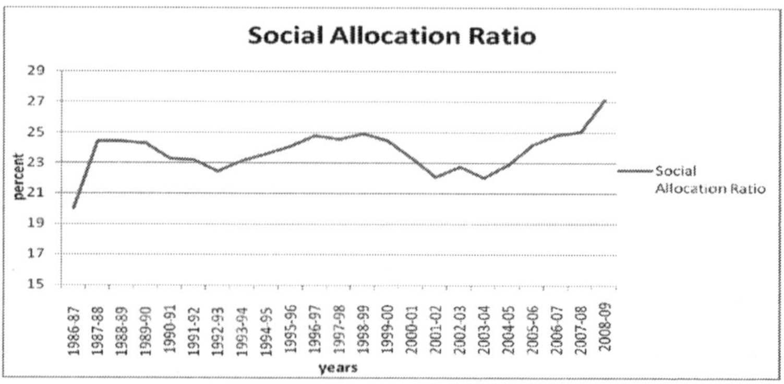

Financing human development usually involves switching resources from other areas of government expenditure. But restructuring budgets can be difficult. Each government has existing commitment to fulfill and operates under political constraints. Still, it is easy to exaggerate these constraints and encourage passive attitudes toward highly undesirable spending pattern.

Human development and economic growth need to be promoted together. Expenditure on economic item -including infrastructure such as roads and telecommunications is very important for overall development. So, increasing social expenditure should not mean diverting resource from the economic sector. There may be some potential for savings in this sector, but widespread economic cut-back could undermine the potential for growth. But there are a number of other expenditure items where savings no doubt can be made. Defence is one of the largest components in this category-and a prime candidate for cutbacks.

It is seen that in many poor countries, military spending is two to three times higher than spending on education and health. Beyond defence spending the other area that have a great potential for releasing funds for more productive uses are external debt, internal debt, internal policing, and public enterprise losses.

Social Priority Ratio (SPR)

The social priority ratio is the percentage of social expenditure directed at the priority areas. What is considered to be a priority will naturally change from one country to another, and change over time as human development proceeds. Countries that have already achieved high standards of literacy may well regard higher education as their next priority area. Where basic standards of health have been achieved, health ministry will want to increase attention to more sophisticated kinds of curative care.

It is seen that many developing countries have very low standards of public health, education and water. For them, the priority must be basic education, primary health care and the extension of basic water systems to poor areas of both cities and rural areas.

Average Social Priority Ratio in India has been around 81 per cent during the period 1986-87 and 2008-09. Minimum value of Social Priority Ratio during this period was 73.77 per cent in 2008-09 and maximum was 84.44 per cent in 2001-02. Social Priority ratio has declined from 84.44 per cent in 2001-02 to 73.33 in 2008-09 (see Figure 3). In this study, social priority areas are defined to comprise education, art and culture, health and family welfare, nutrition, water supply and sanitation and rural development. This analysis shows that although the social sector spending is low in India but whatever is spent in the name of social sector, its major share goes to the priority sector.

Figure 3: Social Priority Ratio

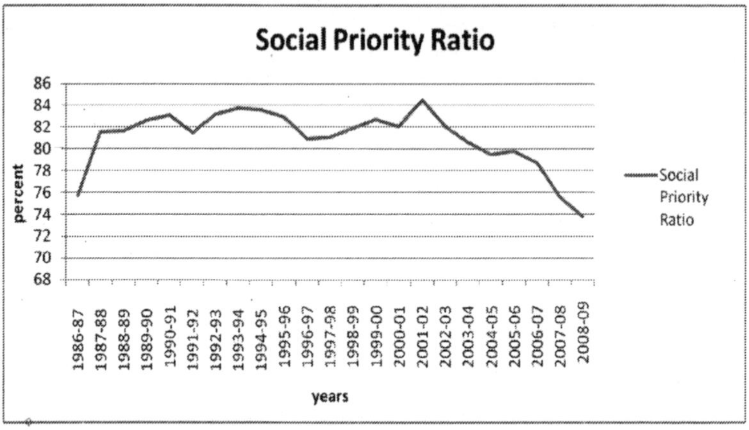

Human Expenditure Ratio (HER)

The percentage of national income devoted to human priority concerns is called Human Expenditure Ratio (HER). The Human Expenditure Ratio is the product of the first three ratios. It is a powerful operational tool that allows policy-makers who want to restructure their budgets to see existing imbalances and the available options.

According to UNDP if a country wishes to do well in human development the Human Expenditure Ratio may need to be around 5 per cent. This also indicates a good political commitment from the government to Human priority or Social priority concern. In India Human Expenditure Ratio has been around 5.56 per cent on an average during the period 1986-87 and 2008-09 (see Figure 4).

Figure 4: Human Expenditure Ratio

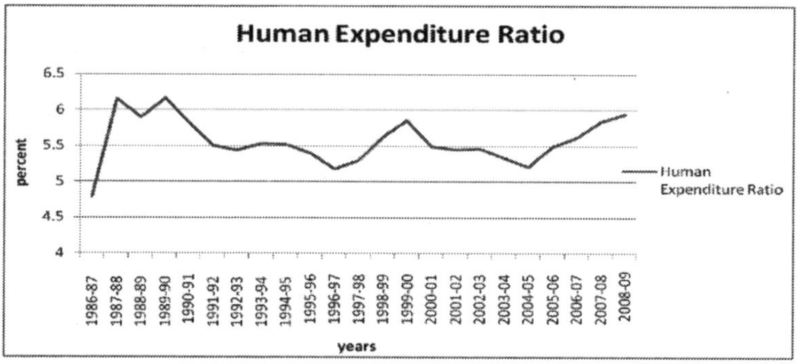

However, HER by itself cannot reveal the true picture of human development, unless human development spending per person in absolute terms is taken into account. Therefore the per capita Public Expenditure, per capita Social Sector expenditure and per capita Social Priority expenditure are presented in Table 2.

Figure 5 shows the trends in real per capita public expenditure on social sector and social priority areas in India between 1986-87 and 2008-09. The figure shows that there was a significant increase in per capita public expenditure over this period. The per capita public expenditure increased from Rs. 3487 in 1986-87 to Rs. 8584 in 2008-09. The expenditure on per capita social sector expenditure increased from Rs. 528.21 per capita in 1986-87 to Rs. 2332.39 per capita in 2008-09. Per capita social priority expenditure increased from Rs.528.21 to Rs.1720.61 in the period 1986-87 to 2008-09. Since the rate of growth of per capita expenditure is far greater than the rate of growth of par capita social sector and social priority sector. Therefore from this analysis a very interesting fact comes out. This increase in per capita expenditure over this period is mainly on the non developmental expenditure heads which primarily consists of defence expenditure, interest payments, wages and salaries etc. The increase in per capita social sector expenditure and social priority expenditure is very moderate. However, there is a very less gap in, per capita Social Sector expenditure and per capita Social Priority expenditure. This again shows that whatever is spent in the name of social sector, its major share goes to the priority sector.

Table 2: Per Capita Real Expenditure on Human Development in India

(*in Rupees*)

Year	Per Capita Public Expenditure	Per Capita Social Sector Expenditure	Per Capita Social Priority Expenditure
1986-87	3486.57	697.83	528.21
1987-88	3454.99	843.49	688.16
1988-89	3561.64	869.49	710.11
1989-90	3844.66	933.77	771.84
1990-91	3890.36	905.74	752.84
1991-92	3736.98	867.00	706.36
1992-93	3867.79	868.21	722.62
1993-94	3911.55	905.65	758.68
1994-95	4003.23	945.04	789.94
1995-96	4073.02	981.25	814.03
1996-97	4118.20	1020.43	825.58
1997-98	4341.84	1065.79	864.69
1998-99	4711.91	1173.85	961.19
1999-00	5165.39	1264.82	1045.64
2000-01	5247.40	1223.49	1004.30
2001-02	5548.01	1223.94	1033.51
2002-03	5675.24	1292.10	1060.56
2003-04	6231.14	1372.17	1106.25
2004-05	6284.64	1437.51	1142.93
2005-06	6728.06	1629.09	1300.28
2006-07	7357.06	1827.71	1437.84
2007-08	8483.88	2126.93	1606.40
2008-09	8583.87	2332.39	1720.61

Note: Expenditure under different heads has been estimated as the sum of revenue expenditure and capital expenditure.

(Base year: 1999-00)

Source: Based on data from Indian Public Finance Statistics, various issues.

Figure 5: Trends in Per Capita Real Expenditure on Human Development in India (Rupees)

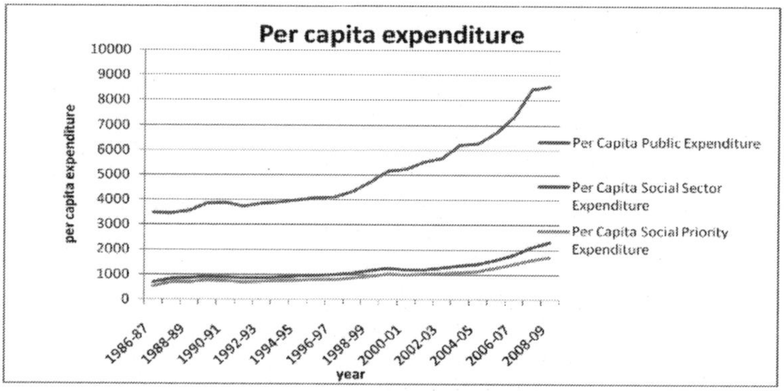

Public Expenditure on Education and Health

From around the mid 1990s, a number of studies have investigated the effectiveness of public spending in education and health on social development outcomes, such as enrolment rates, infant mortality, life expectancy, and other outcome indicators. The effectiveness of government spending goes down if allocations are skewed towards higher education and curative (tertiary) rather than preventive (primary) healthcare[3].

Public intervention in the area of education, particularly elementary education, is universally accepted. From the lens of education as a fundamental right, such intervention directly follows from the basic features of the paradigm. The role of education in economic development has been recognized for quite some time in mainstream economic literature. Education has both intrinsic and instrumental value: it is desirable not only for the individual but also for the society as a whole[4].

It is well known that health expenditure in India is dominated by private spending. To a large extent this is a reflection of the inadequate public spending. This is particularly unfortunate because of the large positive externalities associated with health spending, which make health spending a clear merit good. The greater reliance

[3] Mukherjee Anit K, (2007),Public expenditure on education: A Review of selected issues and evidence.: NIPFP, WP HD51

[4] Sen, Amartya (1999). *Development as Freedom*. Oxford: Oxford university press

on private delivery of health infrastructure and health services therefore means that overall these will be socially underprovided by private agents, and also denies adequate access to the poor. This in turn has adverse outcomes not only for the affected population but for society as a whole[5].

Per capita expenditure on health and education both show on an increasing trend (see Figure 6). The average per capita expenditure on education is Rs.548 and the average per capita expenditure on health is Rs.126. The per capita expenditure on education is increasing at a greater rate than those on health. Therefore the gap in the per capita expenditures in education and health is widening.

Figure 6: Per Capita Expenditure on Health and Education

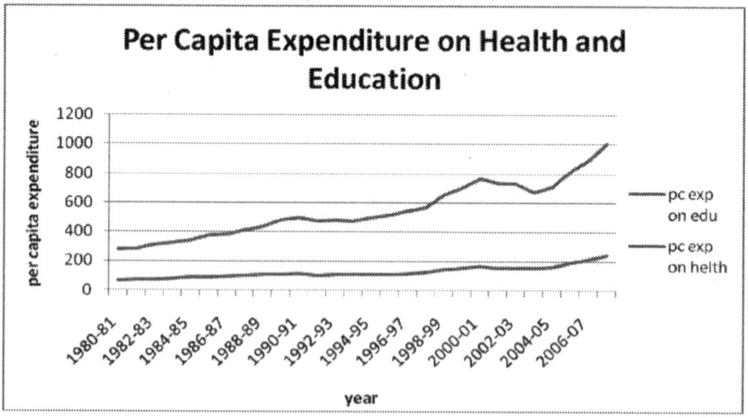

IV. International Comparison

Health expenditure is highly unequal across the globe. As is to be expected, the developed countries spend the most on health per person. OECD countries accounted for less than 20 per cent of the world's population in the year 2000 but were responsible for almost 90 per cent of the world's health spending. Therefore 80 per cent of world's population spent only 10 per cent of the total expenditure on health[6]. The expenditure on education also tells the similar story.

---

[5] Government Health Expenditure in India: A Benchmark Study, (2006) Economic Research Foundation New Delhi

[6] World Health Report, 2003

For this section of the paper we have selected 77 countries, out of which there are 26 very high Human Developed, 18 high Human Developed, 26 medium Human Developed and 7 medium Human Developed countries. The main data source is the data bases of World Health Organization (WHO) and US data base, the time period of analysis is 2006-07.

Health Expenditure

There is much higher ratio of public health spending to private spending in the developed countries. By contrast, in middle developed and low developed countries, either private expenditure dominates or there is very little difference between the shares of private and public expenditure, although in general both tend to be low. It is notable that India has the third lowest ratio of public to private health expenditure among all the 77 countries taken for this study, including the poorest countries. This is inherently regressive and puts a disproportionate burden for health care on poor households.

Education Expenditure

Looking at the Education expenditure as a percent of GDP, all the developed countries have high education expenditure, the only exception is Japan. In middle developed countries the average expenditure on education comes out to be 4.2 per cent. India is a low spending country (3.2 per cent) among this group. The average Education expenditure as a percent of GDP in very high Human Developed country is 5.3 per cent, it is 5.1 per cent for high Human Developed countries and 3.8 per cent for low Human Developed countries.

Public Expenditure and Different Development Outcomes[7]

In Table 3, the correlation between public expenditure on education and various education outcomes and public expenditure on health and different health outcomes has been calculated. Assuming that the pattern of public expenditure has remained same, it is seen that the correlation between public expenditure on health and life expectancy at birth is 0.72. This shows life expectancy is positively related with public expenditure on health. Further if we look at the

[7] Data can be provided by the author on request.

correlation between public expenditure on health and Infant Mortality Rate it is highly negatively correlated with value -0.67. Correlation between public expenditure on health and Human Development Index comes to be 0.78, which shows a high very association. Correlation between public expenditure on education and adult literacy rate comes out to be 0.45 which is not very high, but it is positive. Further if we look at the correlation between public expenditure on education and combined Gross enrolment ratio it is positively correlated with value 0.58. Finally the table shows that the correlation between public expenditure on education and Human Development Index is 0.61. Which shows Human Development Index is positively related with public expenditure on education.

Table 3: Correlation between Public Expenditure on Health and Education and the Development Outcomes

	Life Expectancy at birth (2007)	IMR (2007)	HDI (2007)
Pub Exp on Health as per cent of GDP (2007)	0.72	- 0.67	0.78
	Adult Literacy Rate (2007)	Combined GER (2007)	HDI (2007)
Pub Exp on Edn. as per cent of GDP (2007)	0.45	0.58	0.61

Source: Calculated by the author on the basis of WHO and UN database

V. Composition of Social Sector Spending in India

In this section of the paper, the composition of social sector spending has been analyzed. The comparison of the composition of the social sector spending in India has been done at two time period 1986-87 and 2006-07. The data has been taken from National Public Finance Statistics (various rounds). In this analysis the broad heads of social sector expenditure are expenditure on Education, Art and culture, expenditure on Medicine, Public Health, Sanitation and

Water supply, expenditure on Family Welfare, expenditure on Rural Development, expenditure on Housing, expenditure on Urban Development, expenditure on Broadcasting, expenditure on labour and Employment, expenditure on relief on account of natural calamities, expenditure on Social Security and other social expenditure.

Chart 1 and 2 show the composition of social sector spending in India. There is a fall in the share of expenditure of almost all the heads of social sector except Rural development, Urban Development and Social Security. The expenditure on Education, Art and culture was 52.5 per cent in 1986-87, it fall by 7.5 per cent point in 2006-07. The expenditure on Medicine, Public Health, Sanitation and Water supply was 23.9 per cent in 1986-87, it fall by 6.3 per cent point to become 17.3 per cent in 2006-07. The largest gainer in this redistribution was expenditure on Rural development. It was just 0.1 per cent in 1986-87 and grew by 16 per cent point to become 16.1 per cent in 2006-07.

Chart 1: Composition of Social Sector Spending in India (1986-87)

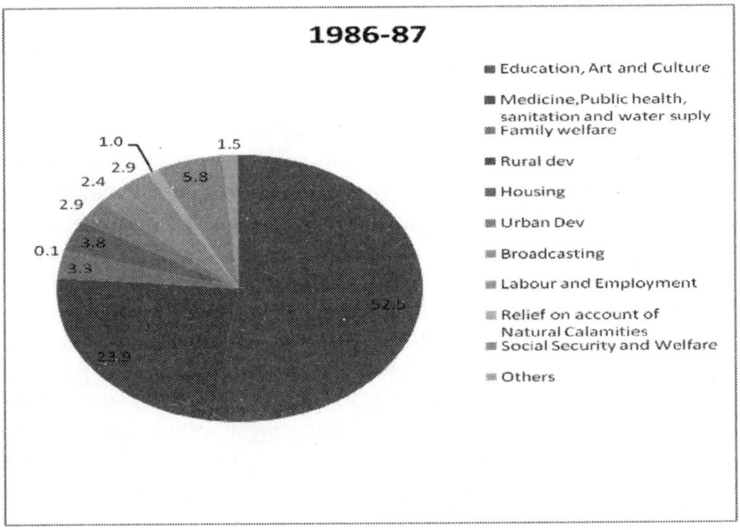

Chart 2: Composition of Social Sector Spending in India (2006-07)

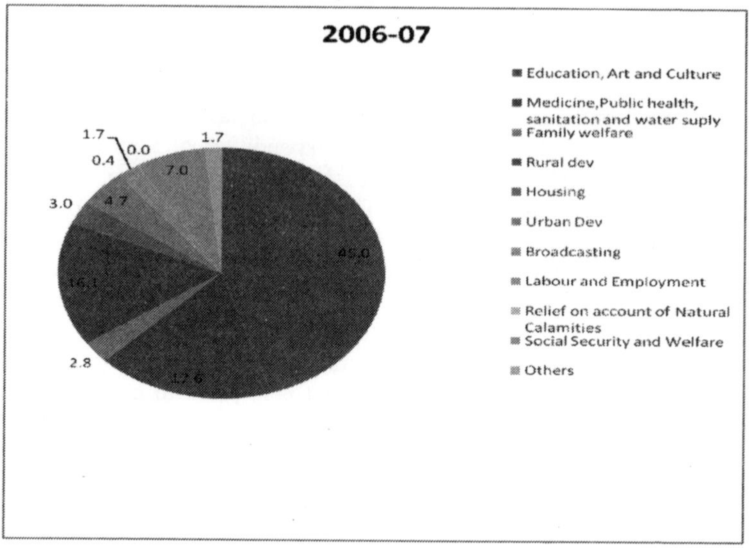

Composition of Education Expenditure

The significant contribution of education and health on economic growth and development calls for a significant role of the government in the provision and delivery of these social services. The nature and scope of the interventions vary, depending on the stage of development and the characteristics of the society. Therefore it is argued that in the initial stage of development the expenditure or the public intervention particularly in the area elementary education is universally accepted.

Chart 3 and 4 show the composition of education expenditure in India Over this period of twenty years the expenditure on elementary education in India increased by 8.3 per cent point. Therefore elementary education accounted for a share of 54.2 per cent of the total expenditure on education in the year 2006-07. On all the other heads there in a minor decrease ranging from 0.7 per cent point to 2 per cent point is been observed.

Chart 3: Composition of Education Expenditure in India (1986-87)

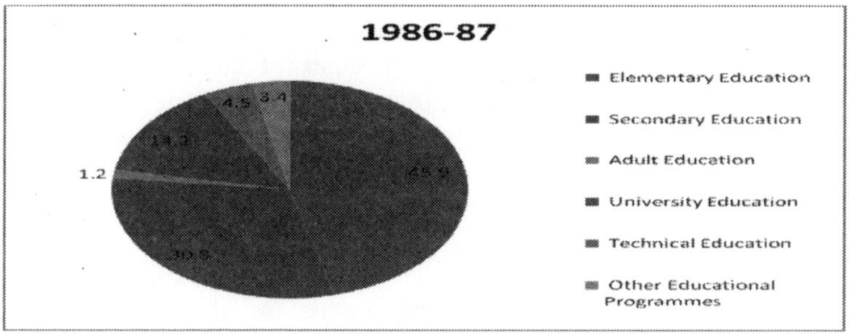

Chart 4: Composition of Education Expenditure in India (2006-07)

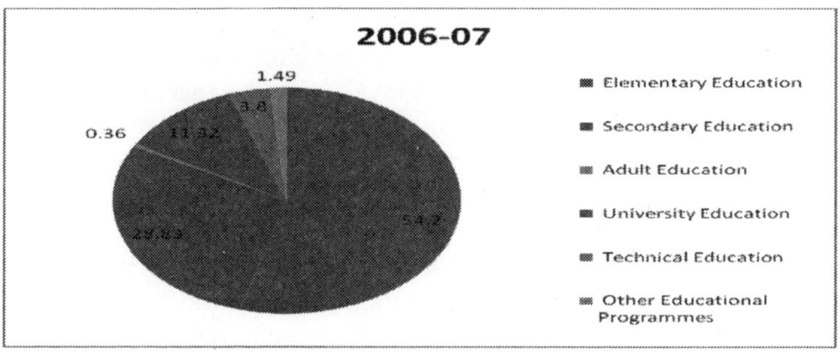

VI. Quality of Social Sector Expenditure

Just the higher allocations for the social sectors are not enough for the improvement in the Human Development. The allocated amounts need to be spent properly. Since the Social sector schemes are community-oriented and the sector-related problems faced at the ground level are best known to the local community itself. It is therefore imperative that the schemes meant to address such problems are designed and implemented in consultation with the local community. Local community is capable of managing its own affairs. It has the ability to innovate and solve its own problems, provided it is allowed to do so. It has been seen that Community participation has reduced the scope for corruption, and resulted into better outcomes of village school and health centres, wherever it has been encouraged. So if there is in a transparent community discussion and debate on the design of the scheme and its implementation, its relevance increases and the scope for corruption and political patronage reduces. There is greater efficiency in the use of funds under the scheme. The schemes of social development should be such that it provides an opportunity to the local community and the intended beneficiaries to come up with ingenious and innovative solutions that would not cross the minds of the bureaucrats in the centre or the state.

VII. Conclusion

In this paper, we examined trends in the social sector expenditure in India for 1986-87 to 2008-09. In this analysis we included social services as well as rural development expenditure. UNDP in its Human Development Report 1991 used the above four ratio to analyze how public expenditure can be designed and monitored. These four ratios provide a kind of tool for observing and formulating public expenditure policies for human development. The other way of looking at the above ratio is that how public expenditure can affect the human development. The above analysis shows that PER is well above the desirable level of 20-25 per cent. India is a medium social spender; it devotes about 27.17 per cent in comparison to high spender who spends 40 per cent of public expenditure to the social sector, and the low spender, 20 per cent or less. The desirable level of Human Expenditure Ratio in order to do well in human development is around 5 per cent. India has the HER of around 5.56 per cent. It is concluded from this study that the social sector spending is low in India but whatever is spent in the name of social sector, its major share goes to the priority sector.

The government expenditure on education in India is more satisfactory than that of health. So, the government needs to concentrate more on health sector. Over the time the share of expenditure on rural development has remarkably increased. This shows the inclination of government policies towards the rural sector.

It is also concluded that although the per capita expenditure in India has followed an increasing trend but this increase in per capita expenditure is mainly on the non developmental expenditure heads which mainly consists of defence expenditure, interest payments, wages and salaries etc. The increase in per capita social sector expenditure and social priority expenditure is very moderate.

Just the higher allocations for the social sectors are not enough for the improvement in the Human Development. The allocated amounts need to be spent properly. Therefore the government should be very careful in this regard and in policy formulation.

References

Choudhary Meeta, (2007): *Public Expenditure on Human Development in Tripura*, Background paper, Tripura Human Development Report.

Mahendra Dev, S and Jos Mooij (2002): Social Sector Expenditures in the 1990s: Analysis of Central and State Budgets, *Economic and Political Weekly*, 37(9): 853-866.

Mukherjee Anit K, (2007): '*Public expenditure on education*: A Review of selected issues and evidence', WP HD51, National Institute of Public Finance and Policy, New Delhi.

Mundle, S and M G Rao (1997): *Public Expenditure in India: Trends and Issues*, In S Mundle (ed), Public Finance: Policy Issues for India, Oxford University Press, Delhi.

Marshall, T.H. (1950): *Citizenship and Social Class and Other Essays*, Cambridge University Press.

Musgrave, R. (1959): *The Theory of Public Finance*, Mc Graw-Hill, New York.

Prabhu, S (1997): *Social Sector Expenditures in India: Trends and Implications*, Background paper for UNDP.

Rawls, J. (1971): *A Theory of Justice*, Harvard University Press.

Sen, Amartya (1999): *Development as Freedom*, Oxford University Press, Oxford.

UNDP (1991): *Human Development Report 1991*, Oxford University Press, New York.

UNDP (2004): *Orissa Human Development Report*, Oxford University Press.

7

Dimensions of Poverty and its Regional Variation

Ruchira Bhattacharya[1]

I. Rationale

Poverty is the greatest impediment in the way of successful implementation of any human development policy. Therefore, it is a problem that demands serious attention and proper monitoring. The basic problem however lies in the contemporary conceptualization and measurement of poverty itself.

Conventional method of measuring poverty by defining a poverty line on the basis of a single factor of consumer index and making head count ratios has been criticized by scholars as it does not count the aspect of distribution (Planning Commission, 1993). The conceptual and methodological problems regarding the determination of the minimum consumer expenditure to define poverty line has been pointed out by Kundu (Kundu, 1993). The consumer price expenditure has been worked out only for 1960-61 and 1973-74 and updated using CSO's consumer price index which is not available for the whole country. CSO estimate is taken to be larger than that of NSS. Adjusting all the NSS estimates upwards by a uniform percentage of total private consumption as estimated from NAS to the total estimated from NSS, therefore, gave a lower value of poverty. But NSS estimate on food and fuel consumption which indeed is the main source of expenditure for any poor household is higher than CSO. Therefore, there was an underestimation. Kundu (1993) also pointed out that the poverty estimates for India when state level estimates are aggregated are higher than those computed by using one poverty line for whole country. Thus head count ratio has been termed "notorious" by Andre Beteille (Beteille, 2003). A very important departure from contemporary poverty measures and

[1] Research Scholar, Centre for the Study of Regional Development, School of Social Sciences, Jawaharlal Nehru University, New Delhi-110067, India

an attempt to capture multi-dimension of development was the introduction of Human Development Index by UNDP in the publication of the 1991 report. But this measure also faced criticisms from several authors on the ground that it did not catch the totality of deprivation by using indicators that only partly show human welfare (Sansui, 2008).

The greatest challenge is that there are several dimensions that poverty can manifest it in. The conceptualization of poverty as multidimensional dates back to the 70's and 80's with the Capability approach of Sen (Sansui, 2008). But most recent studies in this line have attempted to calculate poverty as a function of multiple dimensions of social life adding these dimensions into one single index (Partridge and Rickman, 2008).

But a single household can show different performances in different dimensions of poverty (Geranda, 2008). Bourguignon and Chakraborty (2003) and Geranda (2008) make poverty line in separate dimension and count heads under those lines. The definition of threshold in social indicators is relative in concept. For education primary level has been taken as a threshold (Bourguignon and Chakravarty, 2003; Geranda, 2008)· But in Indian context primary education would not provide any gainful employment thus cannot be taken as a minimum required level. Moreover, poverty is a household phenomenon affecting individual's life and choices. Thus making an ideal threshold line and calculating deviations from it or creating a single index of development does not really show the ground scenario. Monitoring poverty has to be done on the basis of indicators that show the real level of living of individuals. These are essentially the socio-economic indicators that are outcomes of level of living. The performance of a region may vary in different dimensions of development which shows how much access the people of that region have to the basic necessities of life. Thus poverty should truly be redefined in terms of the outcomes a region shows in socio-economic dimensions which reflect the development of its people. Income and expenditure might affect development to a great extent but there are other factors that determine individual's access to social necessities. There are intra-household differentials of income and expenditure that can be captured from inequalities in the social outcomes. This paper analyses the performances of Indian states in different dimensions of development separately to compare whether development in one dimension coincides with other. This would show whether single dimensional policy making would be of any effect.

II. Objectives

The objectives of the paper are to:

a) measure the level of development of the major states in the dimensions of health, social-infrastructural, gender and economy on the basis of outcome indicators and compare the performance of states in different dimensions of development. These are the four main dimensions in which development policies are made;
b) compare development in different dimensions at a district level for the states which show a dismal level of development among different dimensions; and
c) observe whether the states showing good performance in all the dimensions show similar performance at a district level.

III. Data and Methodology

Percentage using any contraceptive, receiving antenatal care, attended by a doctor, getting vaccinated, percentage of deliveries in health facility, Female school attendance and media exposure of females in reproductive age has been obtained from NFHS III, 2005-06. These reflect access to health and social amenities which is assumed to reflect the level of socio-economic development of the states because women being the victims of social deprivation would receive schooling and exposure where some social development has taken place.

Percentage of higher educated (Higher Secondary and Graduates and above), child sex ratio, percentage of urban population has been computed from C-Series, Census 2001. Higher education shows social development as a low level of education can hardly bring any gainful employment. Proportion of workers in manufacturing in urban areas and percentage of main workers has been computed from B-Series, Census 2001. These indicators reflect economic security and gainful employment of an individual.

Gender parity in primary enrolment from Flash Statistics, 2006, DISE, National University of Educational Planning and Administration and MHRD, Gov of India; Proportion of girls in primary enrolment, and Gross Enrolment Ratio from DISE, 2005-06, MHRD, Gov. of India etc. are proxy for overall gender equality as these ensure equitable distribution of resources among the two gender group thus reducing poverty and deprivation. Child sex ratio is an important proxy of gender parity as its value is free from the influence of migration factor. Thus a lower value shows a son preference of society and implicit in it is the negligence of female children.

Data for households with electricity, drinking water, and toilet, National Health Profile, 2006, Ministry of Health and Family Welfare; for monthly per capita consumer expenditure in urban and rural areas, NSSO 61st round Consumer Expenditure Survey; Wage earnings in urban and rural areas and state wise secondary sector workers, NSSO Employment-Unemployment survey 2004-05 and State wise Per Capita Income, 2005-06 from CSO at 1999-2000 prices have been used.

Ratio of secondary sector to urbanization has been taken as a measure of informalisation of urban economy which is one of the root causes of poverty. Per capita income and consumer expenditure levels are directly related to individual welfare and should be high in economically developed states. Proportion of manufacturing workers in urban areas is a proxy for tertiarisation of urban economy which emphasizes an informalisation as well.

Using Principal Component Analysis (Weights in Table 1) the indicators have been grouped into four separate composite indices (Table 5). Delivery at a health facility, percentage using any contraceptive, percentage receiving antenatal care, percentage attended by a doctor, and percentage getting vaccinated have been combined to form the Index of Health Development. These indicators show the individual's access to health care facilities which is positive for a state's development.

Higher education i.e. percentage of Higher secondary and graduates, proportion of urban population, households with electricity, drinking water, and toilet have been combined to form Index of Social and Infrastructural Development. The index shows individual's access to housing and proper education.

Index of Gender Empowerment has been prepared combining Gender parity in primary enrolment, child sex ratio, school attendance of females and media exposure of females in reproductive age.

Table 1: Weights: State Level Indicators

Health Indicators[1]		Social Indicators[2]	
Delivery_HFacility	.959	HEDU	.922
Contraceptive_use	.818	UPOP	.889
Antenatal_Care	.920	HH_Electr	.899
Attended_Doctor	.946	HH_Drinking Water	.479
All_Vaccination	.858	HH_Toilet	.596

contd...

Gender Parity Indicators[3]		Economic Indicators[4]	
GPI_Enr	.899	SECW_U	-.300
ChildSR	.800	MPCE_R	.886
SchAt_F	.462	MPCE_U	.920
MediaExp_F	.238	Wage_r	.405
		Wage_u	-.376
		PCI	.933

Sources:

1. Computed by the author from NFHS III, 2005-06 using PCA.
2. Computed by the author from C-Series B-Series, National Health Profile 2004-05 using PCA.
3. Computed by the author from Census 2001, DISE, 2005-06 using PCA.
4. Computed by the author from NFHS III, 2005-06, Census 2001, NSSO 61st Round EUS and CES, CSO using PCA.

Table 2: Weights: District Level Indicators

	Gender emp. Index	
States\indicators	per cent_Girls_Primary	Child_SR
Maharashtra	0.89	0.89
Guiarat	0.865	0.865
Harvana	0.795	0.795
Puniab	0.783	0.783
Kerala	0.825	-0.825

contd...

Social development index			Economic welfare index	
LQ_Urban	Pr_Enr	HSGRAD	WFP_Mn	per cent_MAN_U
0.958	0.489	0.945	0.649	0.649
0.922	-0.891	0.857	0.82	0.82
0.911	-0.466	0.887	-0.778	0.778
0.855	-0.791	0.871	0.857	0.857
0.651	-0.795	0.89	0.834	0.834

Source: Computed from DISE, 2004-05, B Series and C Series, Census 2001 using PCA.

Index of Economic Development has been made combining proportion of secondary sector workers in urban areas, Monthly per capita consumer expenditure in urban and rural areas, wage earnings in urban and rural areas and per capita income.

Due to data constraints at district level three indices have been made (Weights in Table 2 in above page). Using PCA proportion of girls in primary enrolment and child sex ratio has been combined into Index of Gender Empowerment. Location quotient of urbanization, percentage primary enrolment, and percentage higher educated has been combined into Index of Social Development, and Work Force Participation of main workers and Percentage of manufacturing workers in urban population has been combined in to Index of Economic Welfare (Table 6).

States and Districts have been ranked on the basis of four indices and Rank Correlation Matrices have been used to compare performances of states in different dimensions.

States and districts have been divided into quartiles on the basis of performance in different dimensions and state names in the quartiles according to ranks in different dimensions have been tabulated. It is the ranks of the states in certain dimension that determine its level of development that dimension.

Composite mapping has been created to compare the performances clearly.

IV. Results

Rank Correlation between four indices shows that the indices of Health, Social Infrastructural and Economic development are positively correlated but with Index of Gender empowerment none of the correlations are significant (Table 3). The rank correlation value of Health and social-infrastructural development is 0.755, and between Economic development and Health is 0.728 both significant at 1 per cent level. Between Economy and Social Infrastructural development *rho* value is 0.838 significant at 1 per cent level. But rest of the correlations with gender empowerment is statistically insignificant. This shows that the states performing well in economic, infrastructural, social or health dimensions are not showing any good performance when distributive aspect is considered. Gender development level is much lower for the economically or infrastructural developed states. A composite index joining all aspects of development would overshadow this aspect.

Table 3: India - Correlation

	Health	Socio Infrastructure	Gender	Economy
Health	1	.755**	0.328	.728**
Socio Infrastructure	.755**	1	-0.12	.838**
Gender	0.328	-0.12	1	-0.11
Economy	.728**	.838**	-0.11	1

** Correlation is significant at the 0.01 level (2-tailed).
Source: Computed from Table 5 and 6.

To observe closely how the states perform in different dimensions all the states have been arranged in descending order of the dimensions and then divided into four quartiles (Table 7). If some state is not falling in the top quartile or at least top two quartiles of all the dimensions that state shows dismal levels of development among different dimensions.

It is observed that Kerala is the only state that remains in top quartile for all four dimensions (Map 1). Tamil Nadu, Andhra Pradesh and Karnataka fluctuate between first and second quartile. Tamil Nadu is in first quartile for the health and social infrastructural development but for gender and economic development indices it is in second quartile. It ranks 9th in gender empowerment which is the last rank in second quartile. Andhra Pradesh is in second quartile in Social and Infrastructural development and economic welfare indices whereas Karnataka in Gender development and economic welfare indices.

The problem states are Maharashtra, Punjab, Haryana and Gujarat. These states are developed when health, social, infrastructural or economic welfare dimensions are considered but in gender dimensions they are poor. Maharashtra comes in third quartile with a rank 11; Haryana, Gujarat, and Punjab come in fourth quartile with Bihar. Punjab is last ranking state in gender empowerment index. The contradiction is shocking as these are the states which lie with Kerala when economic welfare is considered. It reaffirms the fact that the distribution of development is a neglected dimension of development. Thus although in other dimensions the states of Punjab, Haryana, Gujarat and Maharashtra are developed in gender dimension they are poor.

Table 4: Correlation Matrix of the Five States

	Maharashtra			Gujarat		
	Gender	Social	Economy	Gender	Social	Economy
Gender	1	-.01	-0.436	1	-.39*	0.115
Social	-0.01	1	-0.098	-.39*	1	0.175
Economy	-0.43	-.09	1	0.115	0.175	1

contd....

Punjab			Haryana			Kerala		
Gender	Social	Economy	Gender	Social	Economy	Gender	Social	Economy
1	0.235	-0.231	1	-.31	0.29	1	0.235	-0.231
0.235	1	-0.424	-0.31	1	-0.074	0.235	1	-0.424
-0.23	-0.42	1	0.293	-.07	1	-0.23	-0.42	1

* Correlation significant at 0.05 levels (2-tailed).
Source: Computed from Table 5 and 6.

West Bengal, Assam and Madhya Pradesh perform well in gender dimension but in other three dimensions West Bengal is in the second quartile and Assam and MP fluctuate between third and fourth quartile. Although economically underdeveloped, MP shows a higher rank in gender empowerment index. But from the highest ranking state (Kerala) it is lot lower and for a less developed state distribution hardly has significance. If economic and other development are not accompanied by gender development, that becomes a problem.

The composite map (Map 1) has been prepared showing performances in all four dimensions. The darkest shade means that the district is in the top quartile, and light shade means it is in the lower quartile. The economic dimension has been shown with bars where height of the bar shows in which quartile it is in.

Table 5: State-Level Composite Indices of Different Dimensions

State	Health	Socio-Infra	Gender	Economy
Andhra Pradesh	0.80	0.39	1.08	-0.26
Assam	-0.61	-0.97	1.00	-0.31
Bihar	-1.32	-1.50	-1.32	-1.27
Chhattisgarh	-0.62	-0.85	0.57	-0.65
Gujarat	0.38	1.01	-1.42	0.43
Haryana	0.02	0.70	-1.25	2.04
Jharkhand	-1.16	-1.34	-0.36	-0.39
Karnataka	0.78	0.70	0.76	-0.25
Kerala	2.17	0.83	1.30	1.64
Madhya Pradesh	-0.72	-0.29	0.83	-1.16
Maharashtra	0.73	1.48	-0.16	0.66
Orissa	-0.15	-1.22	0.39	-1.11
Punjab	0.32	1.36	-1.96	1.62
Rajasthan	-0.98	-0.74	-0.54	-0.27
Tamil Nadu	1.40	0.98	0.14	0.13
Uttar Pradesh	-1.36	-0.55	0.07	-0.90
West Bengal	0.32	0.02	0.86	0.05

Source: Computed from CSO, NFHS III, DISE, 2004-05, B Series and C Series, Census 2001, National Health Profile 2004-05 using PCA

The performance in health index shows a south to north decrease but in gender dimensions even southern states do not show parity with economic or health dimensions. Negative correlation of gender and economic dimensions is alarming and it questions the very concept of poverty as mere low consumer expenditure.

If consumer expenditure or per capita income were only reflectors of developments then the states with a good performance in these would not have shown opposite performance in gender development which is a proxy of social distributive justice.

Map 1: Composite Map Levels of Development in Different Dimensions of India

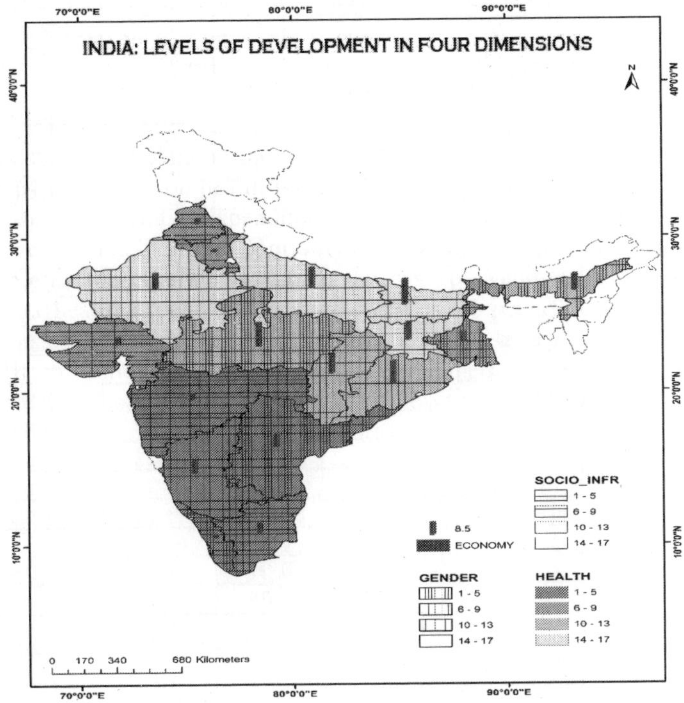

Source: Created by the author using data from Table 5 and 6

Table 6: District-Level Composite Indices of Different Dimensions

State	District	Gender	Social	Economy
Punjab	Gurdaspur	0.61	-0.08	-1.32
	Amritsar	0.33	1.04	-0.78
	Kapurthala	-1.39	0.32	-0.22
	Jalandhar	-0.05	1.71	-0.58
	Hoshiarpur	0.50	-0.52	-0.41
	Nawanshahr*	-0.33	-0.99	3.18
	Rupnagar 07	0.29	1.38	0.43
	Fatehgarh Sahib*	-1.94	-0.02	0.69

	Ludhiana	0.61	1.80	0.59
	Moga*	0.12	-1.09	0.58
	Firozpur	1.87	-0.75	-0.90
	Muktsar*	1.69	-0.99	-0.24
	Faridkot	0.51	-0.60	-0.60
	Bathinda	-0.98	-0.64	-0.31
	Mansa	-0.73	-1.20	-0.10
	Sangrur	-0.20	-0.12	0.36
	Patiala	-0.93	0.75	-0.37
Haryana	Panchkula	-1.01	2.06	-0.98
	Ambala	-1.35	1.05	0.15
	Yamunanagar	-0.79	0.69	0.73
	Kurukshetra	-1.75	0.05	-0.85
	Kaithal	-1.17	-1.13	0.09
	Karnal	-0.39	-0.10	0.30
	Panipat	-0.20	0.75	1.16
	Sonipat	-0.31	0.11	0.18
	Jind	0.34	-0.97	-0.85
	Fatehabad*	0.05	-1.23	-0.66
	Sirsa	-0.46	-0.92	-1.63
	Hisar	0.68	-0.11	-1.43
	Bhiwani	1.79	-0.94	-0.38
	Rohtak	0.02	0.49	-1.05
	Jhajjar*	0.08	-0.13	0.78
	Mahendragarh	1.30	-1.16	1.44
	Rewari	0.33	-0.84	1.72
	Gurgaon	1.54	0.41	1.24
	Faridabad	1.29	1.92	0.07
Gujarat	Raigarh	0.74	-0.27	-1.83
	Kachchh	0.23	-0.34	-1.07
	Banas Kantha	0.17	-1.27	0.25
	Patan*	-1.18	-0.33	-0.35
Gujarat	Mahesana	-1.51	-0.01	0.87
	Sabar Kantha	0.03	-0.48	-0.47
	Gandhinagar	-1.62	0.66	0.03
	Ahmadabad	-0.39	2.50	-1.14
	Surendranagar	-0.71	-0.60	0.13
	Rajkot	-0.86	1.17	0.04
	Jamnagar	-0.53	0.69	-0.59
	Porbandar*	-0.86	0.20	-1.15
	Junagadh	-0.18	-0.22	-0.92
	Amreli	0.44	-0.29	0.81
	Anand*	-1.73	-0.05	-0.20

	Kheda	-0.41	-0.41	-0.17
	Panch Mahals	1.06	-0.76	-0.97
	Dohad*	1.54	-1.30	-1.44
	Vadodara	0.00	1.52	-0.46
	Vadodara	0.00	1.52	-0.58
	Narmada*	1.62	-0.70	0.30
	Bharuch	0.15	-0.10	0.33
	Surat	0.74	1.60	2.46
	The Dangs	1.88	-2.18	-0.48
	Navsari*	0.57	0.55	1.81
	Valsad	0.88	0.15	1.90
	Nandurbar*	1.01	-0.71	0.02
	Dhule	-0.38	-0.08	-0.19
	Jalgaon	-1.23	-0.18	0.34
	Buldana	-0.35	-0.54	1.48
	Akola	0.70	0.27	0.64
	Washim*	0.15	-0.50	1.14
Maharashtra	Amravati	0.70	0.25	0.49
	Wardha	0.94	0.19	0.16
	Nagpur	1.16	1.47	-0.32
	Bhandara	1.21	-0.34	-1.65
	Gondiya*	1.37	-0.66	-3.09
	Gadchiroli	1.84	-1.01	-0.57
	Chandrapur	0.69	-0.05	-0.14
	Yavatmal	0.31	-0.47	0.91
	Nanded	0.01	-0.37	0.00
	Hingoli*	1.50	-0.93	1.52
	Parbhani	-0.01	-0.45	0.85
	Jalna	-0.77	-0.94	0.64
	Aurangabad	-0.75	0.13	0.22
	Nashik	0.08	0.18	0.53
	Thane	0.41	1.62	-0.47
	Mumbai (Suburban)*	-1.51	2.20	-0.03
	Mumbai	-0.42	3.91	0.58
	Pune	-0.34	1.21	0.32
Maharashtra	Ahmadnagar	-1.03	-0.36	0.50
	Bid	-0.56	-0.48	0.82
	Latur	-0.92	-0.19	0.12
	Osmanabad	-1.11	-0.61	0.45
	Solapur	-0.41	-0.30	0.24
	Satara	-0.95	-0.42	-0.33
	Ratnagiri	1.13	-0.92	-1.16
	Sindhudurg	0.68	-0.67	-2.38

	Kolhapur	-2.18	0.11	0.09
	Sangli	-1.72	-0.12	0.10
Kerala	Kasaragod	-0.27	-0.84	0.48
	Kannur	-0.70	0.69	-0.86
	Wayanad	-0.56	-1.75	1.34
	Kozhikode	0.03	-0.17	-1.57
	Malappuram	-0.36	-1.46	-1.27
	Palakkad	-0.68	-0.94	0.88
	Thrissur	1.45	0.13	0.25
	Ernakulam	1.68	1.55	-0.19
	Idukki	-1.49	-0.52	1.99
	Kottayam	-0.62	0.63	0.18
	Alappuzha	1.72	0.42	0.00
	Pathanamthitta	-0.90	0.92	-0.56
	Kollam	0.39	0.08	0.53
	Thiruvananthapuram	0.31	1.26	-0.87

Source: Computed by the author from DISE, 2004-05, B Series and C Series, Census 2001 using PCA.

Intra State Comparison of Levels of Development

The states which show a difference in the level of development among different dimensions are Maharashtra, Gujarat, Punjab, and Haryana. The only state showing good performance in all the dimensions was Kerala. Therefore for these five states analysis has been repeated at a district level.

Maharashtra

The rank correlations within the state showed that in none of the dimensions the state ranks are positively and significantly correlated (Table 4). This means that the districts showing high economic development are not developed in social or gender dimensions. Similarly districts which perform well in social dimension are not the good performers in gender dimensions. Thus although the state shows good performance in economic, health, social dimensions as a whole within the states the development in different dimensions do not accompany each other. Thus the distribution of development is very low in the districts of Maharashtra.

The district names have been tabulated in three dimensions according to their ranks and then divided into quartiles (Table 8). It can be seen that the only districts that perform comparatively well in all three dimensions are Wardha and Nashik although their ranks fluctuate from 8 and 10 in Gender to 8 and 9 in social and 13 and 18 in economic welfare respectively.

Table 7: Quartiles of Performances in Different Dimensions of States

Rank	Health	Socio_Infra	Gender	Economy
1	Kerala	Maharashtra	Kerala	Haryana
2	Tamil Nadu	Punjab	Andhra Pradesh	Kerala
3	Andhra Pradesh	Gujarat	Assam	Punjab
4	Karnataka	Tamil Nadu	West Bengal	Maharashtra
5	Maharashtra	Kerala	Madhya Pradesh	Gujarat
6	Gujarat	Haryana	Karnataka	Tamil Nadu
7	Punjab	Karnataka	Chhattisgarh	West Bengal
8	West Bengal	Andhra Pradesh	Orissa	Karnataka
9	Haryana	West Bengal	Tamil Nadu	Andhra Pradesh
10	Orissa	Madhya Pradesh	Uttar Pradesh	Rajasthan
11	Assam	Uttar Pradesh	Maharashtra	Assam
12	Chhattisgarh	Rajasthan	Jharkhand	Jharkhand
13	Madhya Pradesh	Chhattisgarh	Rajasthan	Chhattisgarh
14	Rajasthan	Assam	Haryana	Uttar Pradesh
15	Jharkhand	Orissa	Bihar	Orissa
16	Bihar	Jharkhand	Gujarat	Madhya Pradesh
17	Uttar Pradesh	Bihar	Punjab	Bihar

Source: Computed from Table 5 and 6.

Districts of Buldhana, Ahmednagar, Kolhapur, Bid, Jalna, and Osmanabad etc are in top quartile in economic welfare index but in gender and social development indices they are in third or fourth quartile.

Curiously the urbanized districts of Mumbai, Pune and Mumbai suburbs show lowest rank in economic welfare. This is because the indicators taken are not usual macro-economic indicators of income or overall employment. This shows that the proportions of manufacturing and main workers in these districts are actually low which means that the casual workers constitute bulk of employed in the district which increases insecurity of income and resultant poverty. However social dimensions are developed in the districts due mainly to urbanization (urbanization got highest weightage in PCA). The distribution of this development is quite low as in Gender dimension the districts come in the last two quartiles.

Table 8: Quartiles of Performances in Different Dimensions of Maharashtra

Ranks	Gender	Social	Economy
1	Gadchiroli	Mumbai	Hingoli
2	Hingoli	Mumbai (Suburban)	Buldana
3	Gondiya	Thane	Ahmadnagar
4	Bhandara	Nagpur	Kolhapur
5	Nagpur	Pune	Washim
6	Ratnagiri	Akola	Bid
7	Nandurbar	Amravati	Yavatmal
8	Wardha	Wardha	Jalna
9	Raigarh	Nashik	Osmanabad
10	Akola	Aurangabad	Satara
11	Amravati	Kolhapur	Solapur
12	Chandrapur	Chandrapur	Sangli
13	Sindhudurg	Dhule	Nashik
14	Thane	Sangli	Parbhani
15	Yavatmal	Jalgaon	Gadchiroli
16	Washim	Latur	Nandurbar
17	Nashik	Raigarh	Jalgaon
18	Nanded	Solapur	Wardha
19	Parbhani	Bhandara	Aurangabad
20	Pune	Ahmadnagar	Akola
21	Buldana	Nanded	Latur
22	Dhule	Satara	Ratnagiri
23	Solapur	Parbhani	Pune
24	Mumbai	Yavatmal	Nanded
25	Bid	Bid	Amravati
26	Aurangabad	Washim	Gondiya
27	Jalna	Buldana	Dhule
28	Latur	Osmanabad	Bhandara
29	Satara	Gondiya	Chandrapur
30	Ahmadnagar	Sindhudurg	Mumbai (Suburban)
31	Osmanabad	Nandurbar	Raigarh
32	Jalgaon	Ratnagiri	Thane

33	Mumbai (Suburban)	Hingoli	Sindhudurg
34	Sangli	Jalna	Nagpur
35	Kolhapur	Gadchiroli	Mumbai

Source: Computed from Table 5 and 6.

Some of the districts e.g. Akola, Gondiya, Bhandara, Raigarh et cetera fall in the first quartile for Gender dimensions but these are hardly important as at a low level of economic development distribution does not mean much and these districts fall in the third or fourth quartile for economic welfare indicators or social indicators.

Map 2 shows that central Maharashtra performs badly in all dimensions while the border districts and more precisely urbanized districts have a dismal ranking in the three dimensions of development. High urbanization has not brought gender development along with it and the economy is mainly of casual nature which means economic insecurity.

Gujarat

The correlation matrix (Table 4) prepared for districts of Gujarat showed that the dimensions of economic welfare and social and gender development are not significantly correlated. This only shows that the economic development within the state is not bringing any social development. Distribution of fruits of development among the gender group is not there.

The dismal levels of development in different dimensions is clear when correlations between social and gender development is observed. The correlation is negative and statistically significant, rho value being -0.39 significant at 5 per cent level. The districts which are developed in social indicators are poor in gender empowerment indicators. Therefore, the social development of the districts of Gujarat is only for half the population. The development of females is not a part of the social development of the districts.

The districts which are in top two quartiles in all three dimensions are Valsad, Surat, and Navsari (Map 3). Mehsana, Kheda, and Patan rank very low in gender dimension, but in economic dimension they are in top two quartiles. Similarly The Dangs, Panch Mahal show low ranks in social dimensions.

The districts of Ahmadabad, Porbandar, Rajkot, Vadodara etc rank high in social development index as the urbanization level is high but their workforce is mainly casual. So in the economic welfare index these districts rank lowest. In the gender development index these districts rank very low (Table 9). Thus the social development is neither distributed nor is accompanied by economic welfare of population.

Map 2: Composite Map Levels of Development in Different Dimensions of Maharashtra

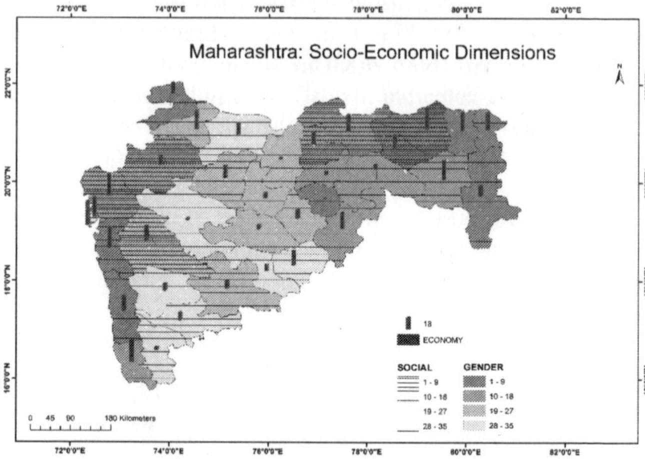

Source: Created by the author using data from Table 5 and 6.

Map 3: Composite Map Levels of Development in Different Dimensions of Gujarat

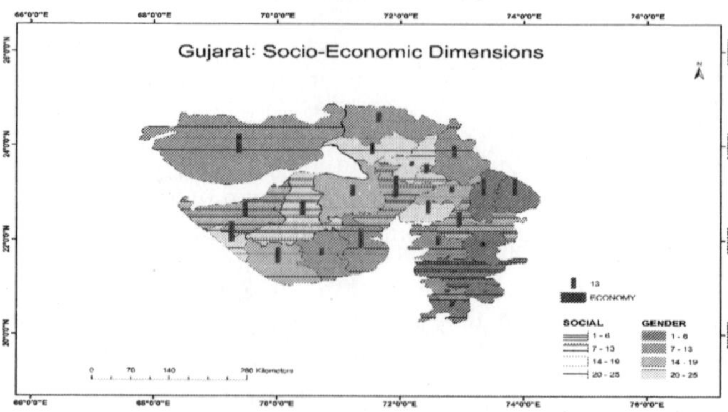

Source: Created by the author using data from Table 5 and 6.

Table 9: Quartiles of Performances in Different Dimensions of Gujarat

Rank	Gender	Social	Economy
1	The Dangs	Ahmadabad	The Dangs
2	Narmada *	Surat	Surat
3	Dohad *	Vadodara	Navsari *
4	Panch Mahals	Rajkot	Mahesana
5	Valsad	Jamnagar	Narmada *
6	Surat	Gandhinagar	Valsad
7	Bharuch	Navsari *	Kheda
8	Navsari *	Porbandar *	Amreli
9	Amreli	Valsad	Bharuch
10	Kachchh	Bharuch	Gandhinagar
11	Banas Kantha	Mahesana	Banas Kantha
12	Bhavnagar	Anand *	Patan *
13	Sabar Kantha	Bhavnagar	Surendranagar
14	Vadodara	Junagadh	Sabar Kantha
15	Junagadh	Amreli	Anand *
16	Ahmadabad	Patan *	Rajkot
17	Kheda	Kachchh	Vadodara
18	Jamnagar	Kheda	Junagadh
19	Surendranagar	Sabar Kantha	Jamnagar
20	Porbandar *	Surendranagar	Panch Mahals
21	Rajkot	Narmada *	Dohad *
22	Patan *	Panch Mahals	Kachchh
23	Mahesana	Banas Kantha	Bhavnagar
24	Gandhinagar	Dohad *	Porbandar *
25	Anand *	The Dangs	Ahmadabad

Source: Computed from Table 5 and 6.

Punjab

The rank correlations among the three dimensions are not positive or statistically significant (Table 4). Within Punjab also the districts show dismal performance in different dimensions of development.

Map 4: Composite Map Levels of Development in Different Dimensions of Punjab

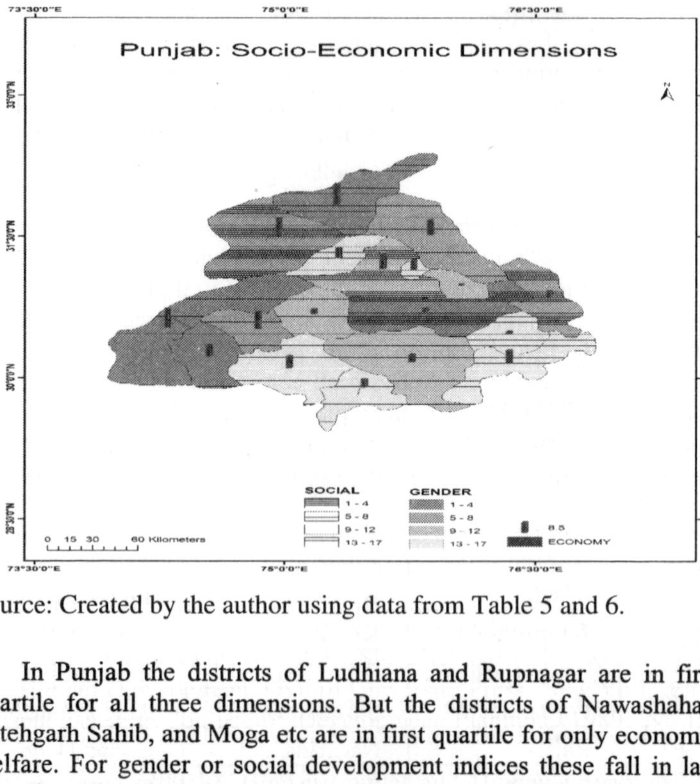

Source: Created by the author using data from Table 5 and 6.

In Punjab the districts of Ludhiana and Rupnagar are in first quartile for all three dimensions. But the districts of Nawashahar, Fatehgarh Sahib, and Moga etc are in first quartile for only economic welfare. For gender or social development indices these fall in last quartiles. Therefore the economic development of these districts has not been accompanied by gender development.

Amritsar, Gurdaspur etc show very low ranks in economic welfare index, which shows that the proportion of unemployed, casual workers and marginal workers is high. Their rank in social dimension goes up as the urbanization is high and in gender dimension also they fall in top two quartiles (Table 10).

Table 10: Quartiles of Performances in Different Dimensions of Punjab

Ranks	Gender	Social	Economy
1	Firozpur	Ludhiana	Nawanshahr
2	Muktsar	Jalandhar	Fatehgarh Sahib
3	Ludhiana	Rupnagar	Ludhiana
4	Gurdaspur	Amritsar	Moga
5	Faridkot	Patiala	Rupnagar
6	Hoshiarpur	Kapurthala	Sangrur
7	Amritsar	Fatehgarh Sahib	Mansa
8	Rupnagar	Gurdaspur	Kapurthala
9	Moga	Sangrur	Muktsar
10	Jalandhar	Hoshiarpur	Bathinda
11	Sangrur	Faridkot	Patiala
12	Nawanshahr	Bathinda	Hoshiarpur
13	Mansa	Firozpur	Jalandhar
14	Patiala	Muktsar	Faridkot
15	Bathinda	Nawanshahr	Amritsar
16	Kapurthala	Moga	Firozpur
17	Fatehgarh Sahib	Mansa	Gurdaspur

Source: Computed from Table 5 and 6

Map 4 shows that the performances of the eastern districts near Haryana are some of the worst in Gender dimensions. In western part there is more parity in the levels of development in all dimensions. The performances of Amritsar and Gurdaspur in economic dimensions however are bad because of the aforesaid factors. The dismal performance in different dimensions is clear from the map.

Haryana

Within Haryana also the correlations between different dimensions of development are insignificant (Table 4).

Both Table 11 and Map 5 show that except for the district of Faridabad, all other districts ranking in different dimensions. Panchkula, Ambala, Panipat, and Yamunanagar fall in first two quartiles for the economic welfare and social development index but in gender development they rank lowest. The districts which rank high in gender development are at a very low level of social development e.g. Bhiwani. Therefore distribution in these districts hardly means anything. Gurgaon shows a low rank in economic welfare which proves the casual nature of its workforce (Table 11).

Map 5: Composite Map Levels of Development in Different Dimensions of Haryana

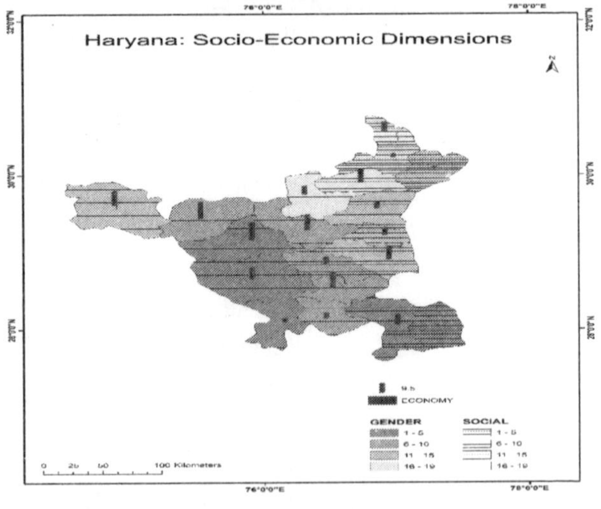

Source: Created by the author using data from Table 5 and 6.

Kerala

Kerala was the only state in state level analysis showing similar performance in all the dimensions but when a district level analysis is done it showed no significant correlations among the different dimensions of development (Table 4). Therefore, it is clear that the within state performance of the districts in the three dimensions of development is not getting reflected in the overall state analysis. Although Kerala is counted as a socially developed district absence of significant correlation between social and gender development points out the dismal levels of development.

The districts of Idukki, Wayanad, Palakkad, Kottayam, Kasaragod, and Pathanamthitta fall in top quartiles for economic welfare but in social and gender development indices their ranks are one of the lowest. The performance in the gender dimension is particularly low in the northern and inland districts.

Table 11: Quartiles of Performances in Different Dimensions of Haryana

Ranks	Gender	Social	Economy
1	Bhiwani	Panchkula *	Faridabad
2	Gurgaon	Faridabad	Yamunanagar
3	Mahendragarh	Ambala	Ambala
4	Faridabad	Panipat	Mahendragarh
5	Hisar	Yamunanagar	Rewari
6	Jind	Rohtak	Karnal
7	Rewari	Gurgaon	Panipat
8	Jhajjar *	Sonipat	Rohtak
9	Fatehabad *	Kurukshetra	Kaithal
10	Rohtak	Karnal	Panchkula *
11	Panipat	Hisar	Gurgaon
12	Sonipat	Jhajjar *	Bhiwani
13	Karnal	Rewari	Sonipat
14	Sirsa	Sirsa	Kurukshetra
15	Yamunanagar	Bhiwani	Sirsa
16	Panchkula *	Jind	Jind
17	Kaithal	Kaithal	Jhajjar *
18	Ambala	Mahendragarh	Fatehabad *
19	Kurukshetra	Fatehabad *	Hisar

Source: Computed from Table 5 and 6.

Thrissur, Ernakulam, Alappuzha, and Thiruvananthapuram show low ranks in economic welfare even with high social and gender development which means that although urbanization and associated development of education has taken place the nature of urban workforce is largely non manufacturer and casual (Table 12). The southern and coastal districts perform well in gender and social dimensions while the northern and inland districts perform poorly. Opposite is true for economic welfare index (Map 6).

Table 12: Quartiles of Performances in Different Dimensions of Kerala

Ranks	Gender	Social	Economy
1	Alappuzha	Ernakulam	Idukki
2	Ernakulam	Thiruvananthapuram	Wayanad
3	Thrissur	Pathanamthitta	Palakkad
4	Kollam	Kannur	Kottayam
5	Thiruvananthapuram	Kottayam	Kasaragod
6	Kozhikode	Alappuzha	Pathanamthitta
7	Kasaragod	Thrissur	Kollam
8	Malappuram	Kollam	Thrissur
9	Wayanad	Kozhikode	Ernakulam
10	Kottayam	Idukki	Alappuzha
11	Palakkad	Kasaragod	Thiruvananthapuram
12	Kannur	Palakkad	Malappuram
13	Pathanamthitta	Malappuram	Kannur
14	Idukki	Wayanad	Kozhikode

Source: Computed from Table 5 and 6

The key points that emerge out of the analysis are:

a) Overall the states which are stronger in economic dimension show very bad performance when distributive aspect e.g. gender development is considered. Most striking are highly developed states of Punjab, Haryana, and Maharashtra etc.
b) The district level study shows that even within the states the economically developed districts are very low ranking in social development and gender empowerment.
c) This only leads to conclusion that good performance in one dimension of development does not necessarily guarantee similar performance in all other dimensions.

Map 6: Composite Map Levels of Development in Different Dimensions of Kerala

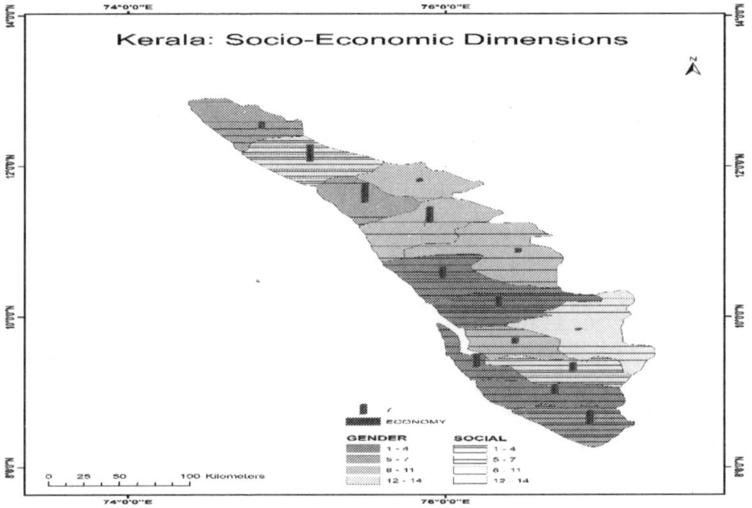

Source: Created by the author using data from Table 5 and 6

d) Kerala, the only state that showed comparably similar performance in all the dimensions in state level analysis showed that the districts with high rank in social development index have low rank in economic welfare index and high rank in economic development index have low rank in gender development index. Thus at a micro-level study the intra regional variation of Kerala's performances in different dimensions became clear which were overshadowed in a macro analysis.

e) The opposite performance of districts in social and economic welfare indices may be due to the fact that the urbanization which is an important part of social development in India is mostly by Non- Manufacturing Workforce – mainly casual and informal types. The performance of states in social dimension alone thus does not reflect the real welfare of population. Casual nature of work adds to economic insecurity and poverty.

If the poverty alleviation policies merely focus on the income generation programs the welfare of population will be hardly addressed. The development levels of Indian states and districts vary in social, infrastructural, health, gender or economic dimensions. If levels of development in social or gender dimension other than income are low it will be impeding any successful implementation of simple poverty alleviation or income guarantee programs. Programs have to target the distributional aspect of any income generation, housing or health schemes directly otherwise the real purpose of providing long healthy and productive life to all population will not be served.

Different regions of India suffer from different kind of under development. A single policy for all regions will not be enough. Thus districts that show low gender development even with high economic and social development should be target for special gender empowerment program. Similarly urban districts with large proportion of casual labourers should be target of programs that ensure a healthy living for informal workers.

The multiple dimensions of human development cannot be recognized with single indices. Policy targets have to be decided based on separate indices in each dimension. The state which performs badly in all dimensions has a different policy requirement than the state which performs well in some dimensions and performs badly in other. Human development has to be analyzed for as small regional unit as possible because at a micro analysis the performance of a region may be totally different from that in a macro analysis. The multi-dimensional aspect of poverty has to be acknowledged while policy building. Otherwise disparity between development levels in different dimensions will remain.

References

Beteille, A. (2003): Poverty and Inequality, *Economic and Political Weekly,* 38(42): 4455-4463.

Francois, B. and and Chakravarty, S. R. (2003): The Measurement of Multidimensional Poverty, *Journal of Economic Inequality*, 1(1): 25–49.

Kundu, A. (1993): *In The Name of Urban Poor: Access to Basic Amenities*, Sage Publications, New Delhi.

Notten, G. (2008): Multidimensional Poverty in the Republic of Congo: Being Poor Simultaneously in Many Ways, *BWPI Working Paper 65*, accessed on the 8th September, 2009 at www.bwpi.manchester.ac.uk/resources/Working-Papers/bwpi-wp-6508.pdf

Partridge, M. D. and Rickman, D. S. (2008): Does a Rising Tide Lift All Metropolitan Boats? Assessing Poverty Dynamics by Metropolitan Size and County Type, *Growth and Change*, 39(2): 283–312.

Planning Commission (1993): Report of the Expert Group on Estimation of Proportion and Number of Poor, Perspective Planning Division, Government of India, New Delhi, accessed on the 10th July, 2009 at www.planningcommission.gov.in/reports/publications/pub93_nopoors.pdf

Sansui, Y. A. (2008): Application of human development index to measurement of deprivations among urban households in Minna, Nigeria. *Habitat International*, 32(3): 384–398.

8

Human Development, other Side of the Coin of National Rural Employment Guarantee Scheme (NREGS)

B. Suresh Babu[1]

I. Introduction

Human development as a concept is broad and comprehensive. But it is guided by a simple idea – people always come first. It concerns all activities- from production processes, to institutional changes, to policy dialogues. It is the development that focused on people and their well–being. Human development is much more about the rise or fall of national incomes. It is about creating an environment in which people can develop their full potential and lead productive, creative lives in according to their need and interests.

Definition

Human Development apart from income, relates to the general well being and economic capabilities of the people (HDR, 2007). Human development is defined by the expansion of capabilities, because fundamentals to enlarging human choices is building human capabilities-the range of things that people can do or be in life. Unlike income, capabilities are ends, and they are reflected not in inputs, but in human outcomes in the quality of people's lives. Deprivation is reflected in a lack of basic capabilities, when people are unable to reach a certain level of their choices. Leading a life free of avoidable morbidity is one such capability, being informed and educated another, and being well nourished a third. Ideally, in measuring deprivation incapability's, indicators should be used that directly reflect capability short-falls. Deprivation incapability is the result of lack of opportunity – signifying that society has not provided people with access to the means to develop or maintain

[1] Research Scholar, Department of Economics, University of Hyderabad, Hyderabad, Andhra Pradesh, India

their essential capabilities. If indicators of the full range of essential capabilities were available, there would be little need to use an indirect monetary indicator such as income or expenditure to monitor deprivation.

II. Human Development in India and Global Context

Since 1990, UNDP (United Nations Development Program) has been constructing HDI and the details are published in its annual report Capita Income, GDP and PQL, HDI is a better measure of level of human development and hence level of development of country. It represents average value of a variables viz. Expectancy of Life at Birth, Literacy and Education Standards, and Per Capita Income. In considering incomes, if a country's per capita income is above certain level, the income is discounted because contribution of very high levels of Real Per Capita GDP in Purchasing Power Parity (PPP, It is based on the relative purchasing power of two currencies in the case of all the produced goods and services are internationally traded). As per 2001 HDR, India's per Capita Income in PPP was US$2248 but at market exchange rate US$440(and in Rs.16500). In the 2001 HDR, for 162 nations HDI values are given. At the top (1st rank) of human development stands Norway, followed by Australia and Canada (the rank of US 6th and UK 7th) and at the bottom Sierra Leona (162nd Rank). India's Rank is 115th, with HDI value of around 0.57. India graduated to Medium HD from Low HD in 1999. (High Human Development is defined as HDI value exceeding 0.8. Medium means HDI value 0.5+ to 0.8 and Low means HDI value less than 0.5). The HDI value of India is 0.571 and among the 162 countries, the rank of India is 115.

World Human Development Report-2007 released on 27th November, 2007 in New Delhi. United Nations Organization affiliated UNDP 2007 has taken into consideration of 177 countries it has developed and released a report on human development. The fresh reports witnessed that Britain, American, some other European countries and western countries are listed in the world human development index (HDI) the countries human development levels are declined. Indian declined to second rank in the index. Major concepts of human being's life span period in years, education, living standards, per capita income which all included in the human development index. The development will be accounted on the per capita income and life period of the human being. In the index most of the countries levels are declined. In the year 2000 as the HDI Ranking, most of the countries have lost their best ranks declined into a deeper depth. In the year 2000 index listed to 177 countries.

In the year 2007 Human Development Index, India ranked 128. Last year India has ranked 126.now it declined two points. Sub continent Sri Lanka rank declined. This country has declined from rank 84 to 99. Indian country neighbour Pakistan declined single digit resting on 136 ranks. Other side, in and around India some other countries developed its ranks in the human development index. Bangladesh climbed its rank level from 146 to 140. Nepal rank picked up from 144 to 142. Bhutan rank picked up from 142 to 133. Last six years shown results of the human development index, Norway slipped to second country. First rank gained by Iceland. Second, third, fourth, fifth ranks gained by Australia, Canada, Ireland.

III. Background and Comparative Status in Andhra Pradesh

Andhra Pradesh is one of the major states in India and ranks fifth in terms of population. The population of the states was about 75.7 million in 2001 (Census 2001). The projected population would be around 83 million in March 2007 accounting for 7.4 percent of country's population. In terms of population the state is bigger than many countries in the world. Its geographical spread of 274.4 lakh hectares accounting for 8.37 percent of the total area of the country makes it the fourth largest state in the country. The state capital Hyderabad has become an A1 city in 2007 with 54 lakh population. There are 23 districts and 1,127 mandals in the state. Andhra Pradesh has three regions which are distinct in terms of socio-economic characteristics owing to historical reasons and region specific resource base. Of the 23 districts, nine are in Costal Andhra; ten are in Telangana and four in Rayalaseema.

Viewed against the resource base and economic activities, the relative performance of Andhra Pradesh among Indian states in terms of the growth of SDP and per capital income began in the state from the late 1970s, while the 1980s was the golden era of high economic growth in the state. The growth rate of GSDP in A.P was lower than all-India in the 1990s but there was a turnaround in GSDP growth during 2003-07. However, per capital GSDP in A.P has been lower than in all-India throughout, through it has been catching up in recent years with the all-India average. In fact, the per capita GSDP in

2005-06 (in 1999-2000 prices) in A.P (Rs. 21277) was slightly higher than in all- India (Rs.20734).

Andhra Pradesh has done reasonably well in terms of fiscal performance. Till the mid-1980s A.P. used to have a surplus budget and these surpluses were used for productive capita expenditure on irrigation and power generation. The surplus budgets disappeared after the mid-1980s with the introduction of populist welfare policy initiatives such as distribution of rice at the rate of Rs.2/kg through the Public Distribution System (PDS) and prohibition, through alcohol was one of the major sources of excise duty contributing to state revenues. Fiscal reforms undertaken since 1995-96 have led to an improvement in some indicators of fiscal management. At the same time the state also faced fiscal problems similar to other states of India in the second half of the 1990s. Debt/GSDP ratio for A.P increased from 1995-96 to 2000-01. However, despite rising indebtedness, the outstanding public debt for A.P at 25.6 percent of GSDP in 2000-01 was lower than for all the major states, the all-states average being 30.7 per cent. The ratio of debt-GSDP ratio in 2005-06 was eight (in ascending order) among 29 states. In other words, 21 states in India have higher debt-GDP ratio than Andhra Pradesh. There seems to have been an improvement in revenue generation and decline in revenue deficit in recent years so that the fiscal performance of the state does not seem bad in a comparative perspective.

The state was at a relative disadvantages in terms of manufacturing activity in the non-household sector unlike some states which were ahead of the rest in terms of industrial development even at the time of independence. For instance, A.P. does not have a strong background and tradition of industrial development, like the neighbouring state of Tamil Nadu in terms of entrepreneurship, technical skills and infrastructure. Industry is predominantly a central subject in the Indian Constitution. As a result, the relatively underdeveloped states rarely had a separate industrial policy, at least in their early stages of development. In A.P., the first-ever industrial policy statement was announced only in the early 1990s.

The performance of the social sector in A.P. has not been satisfactory as compared to many states in India, particularly the other southern states like Kerala and Tamilnadu. The state has, however, done well in terms of income poverty. Official estimates show that poverty was only around 15 percent in the year 2004–05. This level of poverty is one of the lowest in the country. The state has also done remarkably well in reducing population growth. Further, as noted above, the women's self-help group movement with seven lakh groups is also a success in the state. On the other hand, the human development index is very low and the state rank tenth among 15 states. In spite of better economic growth, the state is lagging behind in social development. The performance of the state in education had been very good in the 1990s. Despite this the literacy level in state is one of the lowest in the country. Similarly, it ranks eleventh among 17 states in infant mortality. The low poverty ratios and the high incidence of child labour/educational deprivation of children indicate a paradoxical situation specific to the state. It as the highest incidence of child labour among the Indian states whereas it has the lowest level of the poverty and poverty levels have also declined sharply in the past decade. The infrastructure index shows that the state is lacking in infrastructure and in fact has the lowest status (CMIE, 2000).

Inter-regional disparities are very high in the state. Districts like Mahabubnagar and Adilabad in Telangana, Vizianagaram and Srikakulam in North Costal Andhra and Anantapur in Rayalaseema are among the poorest districts in the state. In general, south Telangana districts, some districts of Rayalaseema and North Costal Andhra are poorer than south Costal Andhra and North Telangana.

Historically, in terms of economic and social development, Andhra Pradesh was behind Travancore and Mysore state, but was ahead of Madhya Pradesh and other poorer sates. The same situation continues to some extent even today fifty years after the formation of the state. In terms of economic growth and per capita income it is now closer to all-India. In short, the state has to concentrate more on 'inclusive growth' or equitable development.

IV. About National Rural Employment Guarantee Scheme (NREGS)

NREGA (recently 'Mahatma Gandhi' was prefixed to the scheme on the account of birthday of Father of Nation from 2nd October, 2009) launched on February 2, 2006 by our Prime Minister Dr. Manmohan Singh in a district name called Ananthapur of Andhra Pradesh and this February it has witnessed the third anniversary. Initially 200 most backward districts were identified to begin with, has been expanded to 330 districts in the second phase beginning from 1st April 2007. The remaining 266 districts have been notified on September 28, 2007 where the scheme came into effect from April 1, 2008. As against the employment demanded by 2.61 crore rural households, 2.57 households have been provided wage employment during 2007-08. A budget allocation of Rs. 12,000 crore was made for 2007-08 and Rs. 10.501.02 Crore has been released till 30-01-2008. Recent budget allocation under NREGS increased by 144 per cent to Rs.39,100 crore in Budget Estimate in 2009-10 over Budget Estimate of 2008-09 to increase productivity of assets and resources under NREGA, convergence with other schemes relating to agriculture, forests, water resources, land resources, rural roads initiated. In the first stage 115 pilot districts selected for convergence (Union Budget 2009-10).

Objectives of the Act

The objective of the Act is to enhance livelihood security in rural areas by providing at least 100 days of guaranteed wage employment in a financial year to every household whose adult members volunteer to do unskilled manual work.

Goals

a) Strong social safety net for the vulnerable groups by providing a fall-back employment source, when other employment alternatives are scarce or inadequate;
b) Growth engine for sustainable development of an agricultural economy. Through the process of providing employment on works that address causes of chronic poverty such as drought, deforestation and soil erosion, the Act seeks to strengthen the natural resource base of rural livelihood and create durable assets in rural areas. Effectively implemented, NREGA has the potential to transform the geography of poverty;
c) Empowerment of rural poor through the processes of a rights-based Law;
d) New ways of doing business, as a model of governance reform anchored on the principles of transparency and grass root democracy.

V. Previous Strategies of Employment for Human Development

Prior employment strategies associated with public works programs have identified a number of shortcomings like improper maintenance of records, leakage and rent seeking by the implementing authorities (Kumar, Misra and Panda, 2004). The main lacuna in the wage employment programs has been the inadequacies of planning suitable projects and the consequent inability to build productive assets through employment. Still, this is considered necessary to supplement the results of overall growth in poverty reduction but the need to make them more effective by better integration with the overall development process is well recognized (Papola, 2004). Here an attempt is made to show the previous employment strategies taken by the government to transform the rural face.

Since the end of the third plan in post independent India providing social security through wage employment for rural poor is a common phenomenon. The Rural Manpower Program (RMP) (1960-61) was launched as a pilot project for providing 100 days employment to at least 2.5 million people against the backdrop of seasonal unemployment and under employment in rural areas. There after this program had taken different names in different time period which has been captured below in an outline form:

The 1970s: the Fourth and Fifth plans: During the fourth five years plan period Crash Scheme for Rural Employment (CRSE) was introduced to provide wage employment for 1000 persons in 350 districts of the country followed by Pilot Intensive Rural Employment Program (PIREP) [1972], Small Farmers Development Agency (SFDA), Marginal Farmers and Agricultural Labour Scheme (MFAL) to benefit the poorest of the poor. In 1977 these experiments were translated into a full-fledged wage-employment program in the form of Food for Work Program (FWP).

The Sixth Five Year Plan (1980–85): National Rural Employment Program (NREP) was launched to provide wage employment for the rural people 'with no assets' or 'with grossly inadequate assets'and during 1980-81 to 1984-85, Rural Landless Employment Guarantee Program (RLEGP) was introduced for assuring **100 days** of employment to at least one member of each landless household in the rural areas.

The Seventh Five Year Plan (1985-86 to 1990-91): During the seventh five years plan RLEGP and NREP were merged together in the name of Jawahar Rozgar Yojana (JRY). It is to note that while RLEGP was a completely central sponsored program, JRY has been designed to have 20 percent contribution from the state governments.

The Eighth five year plan (1992-1997): During the eight five years plan Employment Assurance Scheme (EAS) was launched in 1778 economically backward blocks. It became universal since April 1, 1997 to cover all 5448 blocks of the country. The primary objective of the program was to generate employment along with the secondary objective of creation of economic infrastructure and community assets in the rural areas for sustained employment and development.

The Ninth five year plan (1997 – 2002): JRY was revamped as Jawahar Gram Samriddhi Yojana (JGSY) and Swarnajayanthi Grameen Rozgar Yojana (SGRY) to create economic infrastructure and community assets for sustained employment and local development.

The Tenth five year plan (2002–2007): National Food for Work Program (NFFWP) was started in 2004 to address the hunger and also providing daily labour with payment in the form of kind mostly. In February 2006, National Rural Guarantee Employment Program (NREGP) was initiated by the Union government to solve the employment delicacy.

VI. Andhra Pradesh – An Overview

Andhra Pradesh state is the fifth largest economy in the country. The state of Andhra Pradesh has a population of 7.6 cores of which 73 per cent live in rural areas. The scheduled castes constitute 16.19 per cent and scheduled tribes 6.59 per cent of the total population. 76 per cent of the workforce consists of cultivators and agriculture labourers in the state. Andhra Pradesh Government has been implementing development projects under various schemes to address food security, rural poverty, unemployment, health and education with support from the Government of India, bilateral and multilateral donor agencies.

In its endeavour to provide employment opportunities to rural poor, the Government of Andhra Pradesh has embarked on new approach to development with the advent of National Rural Employment Guarantee Act that provides 100 days of employment to poor, a state obligation. For the purpose the state Government has formulated Andhra Pradesh Rural Employment Guarantee Scheme (APREGS) under NREGA.

The Andhra Pradesh Rural Employment Guarantee Scheme (APREGS) under NREGA came into force on 2nd February2006, on the same day on which NREGA was notified by the Government of India. In 2006-07, the Scheme was operational in 13 districts of AP, i.e., Adilabad, Ananthapur, Chittoor, Karimnagar, Khammam, Kadapa, Medak, Mehaboobnagar, Nizamabad, Nalgonda, Ranga Reddy, Vizianagaram and Warangal and 6 districts in 2007-08, 3 districts in 2007-08 were incorporated (Ministry of Rural Development, Government of India). The Government of Andhra Pradesh (GoAP), realizing the potential of NREGA to alter the poverty profile of Andhra Pradesh - has accorded highest priority to the implementation of APREGS. APREGS has pioneered many **"firsts"** in the country in implementing the NREGA. Andhra is India's no.1 NREGA implementer.

VII. APREGS and Human Development

Every objective of the NREGS (APREGS in Andhra Pradesh) is intended i.e. to enhance livelihood security in the rural huts in the other way seeks to human development. The rural mass public works programs (PWPs) are programmatic efforts to generate non-farm employment so as to sustain incomes and consumption, especially during conditions of distress such as those caused by drought, natural disasters, market failure in distribution of food items and so on (Sen, 1981; Dreze 1990).

This paper elaborates that each and every objective is correlated directly and indirectly intended to uplift or to reach the unreached millions of the favor seeking people from the government and this is explained in the following lines.

Demand and Supply of the Employment

Demand for employment under NREGA implies a job card that makes an individual eligible for a manual employment. This is followed by an application for employment to be provided by the program officials with in a period of 15 days. Employment supply, on the other hand, is described by the provision for employment provided to the applicant by the Gram Sabha/Gram Panchayat.

To help the focus on the Demand and Supply I have amalgamated in Table 1 where the data presents us with an edifying picture of employment under the scheme. First the demand i.e. job cards demanded in the initial years was overwhelming and response to that the supply part in the form of employment in person days is high in terms of average in 2008-09 year.

Table 1: Demand and Supply of the Employment: (at state level)

Person days are in lakhs

Year	Job cards demanded	Employment provided (in Person days)	Average Person days created
2006– 07	50,29,402	21,73,319	29.78
2007– 08	46,51,225	25,11,676	90.90
2008– 09	16,47,857	10,19,635	103.50
2009– 10*	4,87,536	7,64,502	98.21

* Up to December 2009.

Source: Andhra Pradesh Rural Employment Guarantee Scheme (APREGS), website: www.apregs.gov.in

100 days wage employment

Main objective of the Act is to provide 100 days of guaranteed wage employment in a financial year to every household whose adult members volunteer to do unskilled manual work. Results in providing 100 days of work varies due to the phase method of the scheme which clearly depicts that there is an increase of HHs who have participated and employed for 100 days. There is a notable rise in the percentage of HHs who has reached the objectivity from 3.1 per cent in 2006-07 to 14.8 per cent in 2009-10 (See Table 2 and Figure 1). This replicates that NREGA has enabled HHs to have wage employment and having three meals a day.

Table 2: 100 days Employment to HH: (at state level)

Year	Total No. of HH working	No. of HHs completed 100 days	Per cent HHs completed 100 days
2006–07	2174730	67242	3.1 (13 districts)
2007- 08	4684995	410517	8.8 (19 districts)
2008–09	5703613	481004	8.4 (22 districts)
2009–10*	5616646	830692	14.8 (22 districts)

* Up to December 2009.

Source: Andhra Pradesh Rural Employment Guarantee Scheme (APREGS), website: www.apregs.gov.in

Figure 1: 100 Days Employment to HH: (at state level)

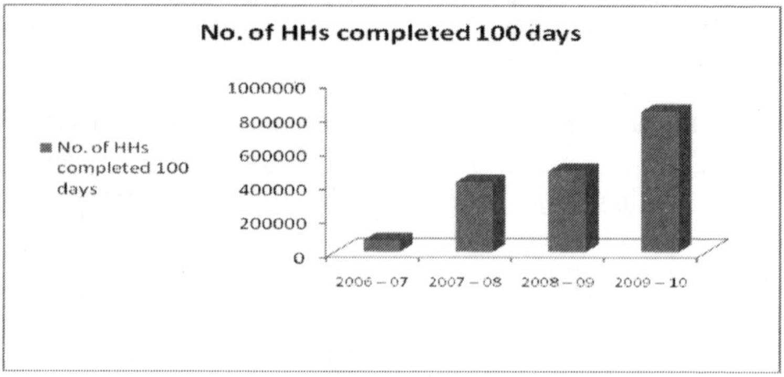

Generate productive assets and protecting the environment

Efforts under APREGS are focused on innovations that regenerate rural assets and promote the building of viable, self sustaining rural communities. As per Schedule I of the Act, the focus of the Rural Employment Guarantee Scheme (REGS) shall be on the following works: water conservation and water harvesting; drought proofing, including afforestation and tree plantation; irrigation canals, including micro and minor irrigation works; provision of irrigation facility to land owned by households belonging to the SC/ST, or to land of the beneficiaries of land reforms, or to land of the beneficiaries under the Indira Awas Yojana; renovation of traditional water bodies, including de-silting of tanks; land development; flood-control and protection works, including drainage in waterlogged areas; rural connectivity to provide all-weather access. The construction of roads may include culverts where necessary, and within the village area may be taken up along with drains; any other work that may be notified by the Central Government in consultation with the State Government.

In view of the guidelines, works undertaken by the government has increased during the period 2006-07 to 2009-10 (See Table 3and Figure 2) though the strategy of completion is slight varies with the selection of works but it gives an outlook that it is generating productive assets and protecting the environment. Completion of works has also accelerated over the period.

Table 3: Total Works under the Scheme (at state level)

Year	Total No .of works taken up	No. of works completed	per cent Works completed	Expenditure (Rs. in Lakhs)
2006– 07	276489	104938	38.0 (13 dists.)	58726.25
2007 – 08	543140	119122	21.9 (19 dists.)	200982.26
2008 – 09	1038444	181781	17.5 (22 dists.)	250990.4
2009– 10*	1602540	417559	26.1 (22 dists.)	217944.04

* Up to December 2009.
Source: Andhra Pradesh Rural Employment Guarantee Scheme (APREGS), website: www.apregs.gov.in

Figure 2: Total Works under the Scheme (at state level)

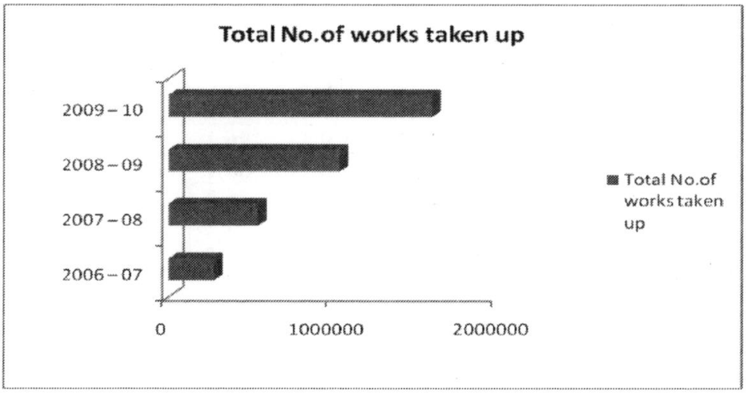

Empowering rural women

There are several provisions of the Act which are of special interest to women workers. First, the Act mandates that at least one-third of the workers should be women. This combined with the fact that the Act places no restriction on how each household's quota of 100 days is shared within the household, means that there is ample scope for women's participation in NREGA works. Second, the wage earned is equal for both men and women. Besides this, the NREGA also provides for childcare facilities at the worksite when more than five children under six years of age are present at the worksite. This is an important provision but in large parts of the country, there are no childcare arrangements (e g, functional anganwadis) for working women (Reetika Khera, Nandini Nayak, 2009). Region-wise analysis of employment sharing by the women and other groups brings out an healthy line among the females which depicts of about 58 per cent have involved in the employment with *right* sharing increased with the margin of 4 per cent i.e. from 54.7 per cent in 2006-07 to 58 per cent in 2008-09 (See Table 4). Andhra Pradesh speaks about there is an active participation of women in employment, social audits, gatherings etc. In 2006-07, women participation is quite good in Telangana region and notable change can be seen in the Coastal area. Except in Telangana, the share of women is accumulative over the years of initiation.

Table 4: Region-wise Employment Sharing by Women and other Groups

Year	Region	SC	ST	Others	Total	Women
2006-07	Telangana	16.8	10.0	27.8	54.7	29.2
	Coastal	1.1	0.7	4.2	5.9	2.4
	Rayalaseema	11.4	1.9	26.1	39.4	23.1
	AP	**29.3**	**11.6**	**58.1**	**100.0**	**54.7**
2007-08	Telangana	14.3	8.7	25.8	48.7	29.1
	Coastal	5.3	2.9	13.2	21.5	11.0
	Rayalaseema	8.0	1.2	20.5	29.8	17.7
	AP	**27.6**	**12.8**	**59.6**	**100.0**	**57.8**
2008-09	Telangana	11.9	8.3	24.5	44.6	27.1
	Coastal	7.1	3.7	18.8	29.6	16.4
	Rayalaseema	7.0	1.0	17.7	25.8	14.5
	AP	**26.0**	**13.0**	**61.0**	**100.0**	**58.0**

* Up to December 2009.

Source: Andhra Pradesh Rural Employment Guarantee Scheme (APREGS), website: www.apregs.gov.in

Fostering social equity

Regular employment is a recent good change observed by the rural community in Andhra Pradesh. In the very first year i.e. 2006-07 of APREGS deploying, it is noted that cumulative number of households which completed 100 days of employment are 37,311 households. Among the social groups it is identified that except in Scheduled Caste there is an increase trend of employment generated in person days in Scheduled Tribe and others section of rural society. In 2006-07, 29.27 per cent is the employment generated in the Scheduled Caste and its is slight declined to 25.38 per cent and among in Scheduled Caste it is noted that from 12.67 per cent in 2006-07 is increased to 13.06 per cent, whereas in other sections there is notable increase in the employment generated from 2006-07 i.e. 58.07 to 61.56 per cent in 2009-10 (See Table 5and Figure 3).

Table 5: Employment Generated in Person days among Social Groups (at state level)

Employment Generated in Person days among Social Group in Andhra Pradesh (within three financial year)						
Year	(per cent of employment generated up to December, 2009)					
	Schedule Caste		Schedule Tribes		Others	
	Employment generated in Person days	per cent of employment generated	Employment generated in Person days	per cent	Employment generated in Person days	per cent
2006- 07	19172967	29.27	8297053	12.67	38037977	58.07
2007– 08	54953679	27.61	25658104	12.89	118398844	59.49
2008- 09	58884216	26.06	29293460	12.97	137746006	60.97
2009– 10*	54061128	25.38	27814178	13.06	131133883	61.56

*Up to December 2009.

Source: Andhra Pradesh Rural Employment Guarantee Scheme (APREGS), website: www.apregs.gov.in

Figure 3: Employment generated in Person days among Social groups (at state level)

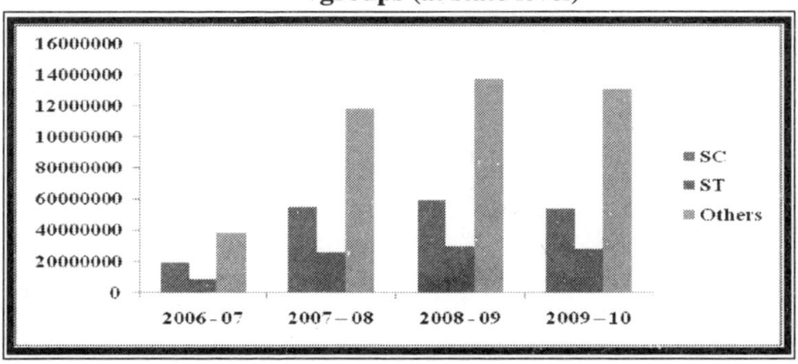

VIII. Conclusion

As a conclusive note, Human Development is the other side of the coin of National Rural Employment Guarantee Scheme (NREGS) in transforming rural society in diluting the bias of gender discrimination, reducing poverty, creation of community rural assets and infrastructure, improved incomes in labour intensive works in rural community even though it has coupled with the complications, critiques from the all sections of the society from the ground level of implementation of the scheme. Many in India argue that the NREGA is one of the most important pieces of socio-economic legislation passed in recent times to change the face of the rural structure. Indeed, it is doing the right and it has the potential not only to strengthen social security and transformations in rural India, but also to strengthen community mobilization, ensure better responsiveness of local governments to community needs and priorities, and most of all enhance governance outcomes. Realizing the potential of NREGA, Andhra Pradesh is in work to alter the poverty profile of Andhra Pradesh - has accorded highest priority to the implementation of APREGS. A reformed and expanded NREGA program holds out the prospect of not only transforming livelihoods of the poorest people of our country but also heralding a revolution in rural governance in India.

Case Study

Victory over Discrimination

Name : Vallepu Sattemma
Name of the Village : Aaleru
Mandal : Aaleru
District : Nalgonda
Job Card number : 232830505005010143

Sattemma in hope of a better future

141

Sattemma is a daily labourer and belongs Vaddera community, a dalit community which had been facing suppression over centuries. She had been facing discrimination in the villages on two-fronts – firstly because she is women and secondly she is a dalit. As a young girl she used to go for labour work to the nearby construction sites and used give all her earnings to the family. After her marriage with Narsimha sufferings continued because he is ordinary labourer and had to work daily to ensure that there was enough to eat in the family. She had two daughters and they lived in a thatched kutcha house. For her elder daughter's marriage they raised some loans from landlords. Because of her condition, she and her husband joined in the service of rich landlords to repay the loans. There she faced lot of insults, humiliations and discrimination. After they came to know about Rural Employment Scheme, they stopped working under landlords and enrolled under the scheme. They worked for 143 days and earned Rs.30,000/-. All the labourers worked in harmony and there was no discrimination at the work. The best fall out of the scheme was the upper caste people understood and they were provided irrigation facilities to their lands. Dalit community is treated equal with the upper castes. This is a positive change within the social system in the village.

References

Dreze, J. (2007): NREGA: Dismantling the Contractor Raj, *The Hindu,* 20th November.

Dreze, Jean, Reetika Khera, and Siddhartha (2008): Corruption in NREGA: Myths and Reality, *The Hindu*, January 22.

Ganesh Kumar, A., Mishra, S. and Panda, M. (2004): Employment Guarantee for Rural India, *Economic and Political weekly*, 39(1): 5359-5361.

GoI (2008): Annual Reports, Ministry of Rural Development, Government of India, India.

Human Development Report (2007): Human Development Report, 2007, prepared by Andhra Pradesh by *Centre for Economic and Social Studies*, Begumpet, Hyderabad.

Hirway, I. (2004): Providing Employment Guarantee in India: Some Critical Issues, *Economic and Political weekly*, 39(48): 5117-5124.

Khera, R., Nayak, N. (2009): Women Workers and Perceptions of the National Rural Employment Guarantee Act, *Economic and Political Weekly*, 44(43): 49 – 57.

—— (2007): 100 Days, 100 Hopes, Transforming Lives: EGS in Andhra Pradesh, SPIU, Department of Rural Development, Government of Andhra Pradesh, Hyderabad.

Mathur, L. (2007): Employment Guarantee; Progress so far, *Economic and Political Weekly*, 42(52): 17-20.

Shah, M. (2007): Employment Guarantee, Civil Society and Indian Democracy, *Economic and Political Weekly*, 42(45-46): 43 – 51.

Government of Andhra Pradesh (2007): Annual Reports 2006-07, Ministry of Rural Development, Hyderabad.

——(2008): Annual Reports 2007-08, Ministry of Rural Development, Hyderabad.

——(2009): Annual Reports 2008-09, Ministry of Rural Development, Hyderabad.

Mick, M. and Putzel J. (1999): *Politics of poverty*, background paper for the World Development Report 2000/1.

Papola, T.S (2004): The Question of Unemployment, In B. Jalan (Ed) *The Indian Economy, Problem and Prospects*, Penguin Books.

9

Role of National Rural Employment Guarantee Act in Human Development

Atulya Bhoi[1] and Yoginder Singh[2]

I. Introduction

People are the real wealth of the country. Every country should create a conducive environment in which people can develop, use their full potential, and lead a productive and creative life depending on their needs and interest .The founder of human development report Mahabul Ul Haqu (1999) has pointed out that the objectives of human development is to create an enabling environment for people to enjoy long, healthy and creative lives .Human Development requires a situation where people can freely identify and select their choice (Antony and Laxmaiah, 2008). According to Shah (2004) the most basic capability of human development are to lead long and healthy life, to be knowledgeable, to have access to resources needed for a decent standard of living and to be able to participate in the life of the community. Basically the human development includes (a) long healthy life (b) education (c) decent standard of living (d) increase in per capital monthly consumption expenditure and (e) participation in community life.

In order to fulfill the basic requirement of human development, a person must have minimum resources/ income. Without minimum financial resources it is impossible to think about human development. No doubt human development is more than the poverty eradication. But poverty eradication and economic empowerment form the foundation for human development. Siva Kumar (1991) has concluded in his work that human development must promise to eliminate the worst forms of human deprivation.

---

[1] Assistant Professor, P. G. Department of Commerce, Dr. SRK Government Arts College, Yanam

[2] Assistant Professor, P. G. Department of Commerce, Dr. SRK Government Arts College, Yanam

Krishna and et al (2003) have concluded in their work that economic growth is important but not the panacea for human development. They argue that the present nature of growth is jobless and it does not provide social and economic security to the majority of the people in fact it generates more and more insecurity and inequality in the society. Smith and Middleton (2007) have rightly pointed out in their research that the loss of employment is the most significant cause to poverty in UK. The eighth five year plan of India (1992-97) has clearly identified that human development should be the ultimate goal of a states. Accordingly it aims at creating jobs, eradicating illiteracy, universalisation to elementary education, providing safe drinking water and primary health care facilities. Similarly the eleventh plan (2007- 2012) has also emphasized on inclusive economic growth, empowerment and quality life of the people.

II. Material and Methods

The objective of the study is to study the role of National Rural Employment Guarantee Acts (NREGA) in human development. For the present study the secondary data have been used. A brief review has been made regarding human development, poverty eradication, importance of wages, different poverty eradication programs and NREGA. An attempt has been made to study the performance of NREGA in human developments in the last four years. The performance has been assessed by taking total expenditure, total employment generation, social inclusion, number of work undertaken etc.

III. Human Development and Poverty

In India human development is a synonymous to poverty eradication. While resuming the charge of 1st Prime Ministership of free India in 1947, Nehru stressed on the ending of poverty, ignorance, diseases and inequality of opportunities. Gandhiji always emphasized on taking care of poor. According to Gandhiji true independence means the poorest among poor would be free from human suffering. Every five year plan has strongly emphasized on human development and has promised to eliminate the worst form of human deprivation.

Now the biggest question arises regarding our achievement in the last 60 year of independence. India has the fourth highest number of dollar- billionaires in the world; behind only the United States, Germany and Russia. India has 1, 00,000 dollar –millionaires but 800 million in the country existed on less than Rs.20 per day. Our position is 134th out 186 countries in human development (Sainath, 2007).

Box 1: Facts about Human Development in India

- 134th rank out 186 countries in Human development index
- 27.5per cent are poor and are below poverty line
- 66th among 88 countries in global hunger index
- 50 per cent of the world's hungry people live in India
- 350 million i.e. 35 per cent of the total Indian population are considered as food insecure
- 47 per cent children suffer from malnutrition and under weight (below 5years age)
- 800 million people exist on less than Rs.20 per day
- 80 per cent of total poor are SC, ST and OBC
- 18 million rural people do not have a shelter over their head
- Rs.356 is the monthly per capita consumption expenditure for rural area and Rs.539 for urban area in 2004-05
- 100000 $ millionaire are in India
- It is the fourth highest in dollar billionaires in the world
- Gender development index is 116 out of 157 countries (2006)

Source: Compiled from Economic Survey of India 2008-09, 11th Five Year Plan, Sainath (2007)

The detail facts about India have been reflected in Box-1. By looking at these figures we can know where we are after 60 year of planned development. About half of the poor are chronic poor (poor person/house who have been poor for a long duration). The incidences of chronic poverty are higher among rural casual labourers household (24 per cent), 45 per cent of rural agricultural labourers are chronic poor. (Radha Krishna et al, 2006). In this juncture reduction of poverty is the utmost need for human development. Without eradication of poverty in India defining human development is a very complex issue. In reality, poverty is the major social problem that India is facing.

Increasing purchasing power of poor and vulnerable group is a prerequisite for poverty reduction and social cohesion. For inclusive growth it is an integral part of the planning process. Increasing purchasing power is a form of economic empowerment of vulnerable groups. Government of India has been implementing series of development programs for the eradication of poverty since the inception of the planning era. Accordingly many rural wage employment programs have been implemented. Radha Krishna (2008) has rightly pointed out that the provision of gainful employment for all the labour force is essential for reducing poverty and achieving inclusive growth as wage income is the main source of income for the poor. Creation of employment increases the purchasing power of the people and this leads to increase consumption and employment which is known as multiplier effect of employment. Creation of assets through employment enhances capital formation and also helps to enhance the GDP (Chatterjee, 2009).

In order to eradicate the extreme poverty through employment generation, many wage employment programs have been implemented in different names during the last sixty year of planning. In the year 1980 National Rural Employment Program (NREP) was launched to use unemployment and under employed workers to build community assets. Accordingly Rs.980cr. had been allocated to this program in 6th plan. Again in the year 1983 Rural Landless Employment Guarantee Scheme (RLEGS) was launched to provide 100 days of guaranteed employment to one member of each rural landless household. Accordingly 500 cores were allocated in 6th plan. In the year 1989, *Jawahar Rozgar Yojana* (JRY) was launched by combining NREP and RLEGS. Again in the year 1993, Employment Assurance Scheme (EAS) was launched to provide employment during the lean agricultural season. In April 2002, both JRY and EAS were merged and named as *Sampoorna Grameen Rozgar Yojana* (SGRY). Again in order to generate employment in rural area in late 2004, National food for work program was launched in 150 backward districts of India.

Although various rural wage employment generation schemes have been implemented in India since the inception of planning era under different attractive names on the whole, there has been a decreasing trend of achievement in terms of man-day employment generated (Dogra, 2005). These programs usually failed to achieve the target due to ineffective targeting, leakages, poor quality of asset creation (Aiyar and Salimah, 2006), corruption and inefficiency (Sinhna, 2005).

In order to overcome all the deficiency of all rural wage employment generation programs, a new program in the name of National Rural Employment Guarantee Act has been launched on 2nd February of 2006. Eradication of poverty and hunger, decline in per capita output in Indian agriculture in the last decade, failure of series of rural wage employment program in India since 1960, increasing jobless growth, failure to operationalise the concept the right to work are the base of NREGA (Rout, 2007).

IV. Analysis of NREGA

NREGA was launched on 2nd February 2006 from Anantpur district of Andhra Pradesh. Initially it was confined to 200 districts only of 27 states. It is one of the most flagship schemes of the United Progressive Alliance Government. Now it has been expanded to 614 districts across of the country in the year 2008-09. It is one of the main planks of rapid poverty reduction program in the Eleventh five year plan. An allocation of Rs. 1,00,000 crores has been made in the eleventh plan to NREGA. Now NREGA is renamed as Mahatma Gandhi National rural employment guarantee scheme.

NREGA is the first nation wide scheme that guarantees employment legally to the rural population of India. It guarantees 100 days unskilled jobs per household which are below poverty line in a financial year. It eradicates the extreme poverty through productive asset creation in rural area. These 100 days guaranteed wage employment can be judiciously and rationally utilized by the landless and rural poor during lean and distress season. It will reduce the distress migration for the sake of minimum wages to eke out the livelihood for survival rather than better wages. It is expected to enhance people's livelihood on a sustained basis by developing economic and social activities in rural areas.

The Act provides a legal guarantee of 100 days of wage employment in a financial year. All the works are unskilled manual works. The work will be provided within fifteen days of demand .If it is not provided within fifteen days then unemployment allowance will be paid .Normally the work should be within five kilometers .If it is above five kilometers than transport allowance will be paid. The wages is Rs.100 per days. The payment will be given within fifteen days of work. The basic worksite facilities will be provided in the worksite. There will be no interference of contractor .Every dispute will be settled in the *panchayat* level.

NREGA is a workforce program. It is not supply driven but it is demand driven. It provides a legal right for 100days employment .Typically it provides work to unskilled worker in short term employment on public work. Normally the work is provided during lean season .The assets which are created under NREGA having multiplier effect of income. It provides livelihood and economic security in rural area. It helps in bringing more rural poor to the social safety net. The Act is based on participatory approach. Full transparency is maintained in each and every level. There is no discrimination is made in registration in terms of caste, creed and gender. It stops distress rural migration for the sake of minimum wages.

NREGA works are intended to create permanent assets in rural areas for future needs. These assets have a multiplier effects in the rural economy. Normally the plan of works under NREGA are water conservation and water harvesting ,land development, flood protection, rural connectivity, minor irrigation work, renovation of traditional water bodies, drought proofing activities(including plantation and afforestation),works approved by ministry of rural development. Table 1 contains detail work undertaken and completed under the scheme NREGA during 2009-10.

The details of total expenditure and wages distributed under NREGA are given in Table 2. As it is evident from Table 2 that the total outlay in NREGA is 167824.14 cores out which Rs.41061.27 cores has been spent on wage distribution till August 2009. The Table 3 contains the details of employment generation under NREGA. It has been observed that 522.15 cores persons day have been created up to August 2009. 12.27croes households have been benefited under the scheme so for. The average day per household is 42.6 days in a year. Similarly the NREGA has a great role in social inclusion in the rural employment process as far as the participation of SC, ST and women are concerned. The participation of these vulnerable groups is highly encouraging it is clearly observed from Table 4.

Table 1: Performance of NREGA during the Year 2009-10

Works under NREGA	No. work undertaken	No. of works completed
Rural Connectivity	335873	44177
Flood control& Protection works	46980	9830
Water Conservation & Water Harvesting	442125	57958
Drought Proofing	143945	9991
Micro Irrigation Works	112677	15638
Provision of Irrigation facilities to land owned by farmer	394223	72053
Renovation of Traditional Water Bodies	209049	24953
Land Development Works	258345	31658
Work approved by Ministry of Rural Development	17478	1270

Sources: (1) http://nrega.nic/states/nregampr.asp, (2) Kar (2009)

Table 2: Total Outlays of Wages Distributed under NREGA

Year	Amount Spent on Wages (Rs. Core)	Distributed Under NREGA
2006-07	5842.37	8823.35
2007-08	10738.47	15856.89
2008-09	18165.57	134582.29
2009-2010	6314.86	8561.65
Total	41061.27	167824.18

Source: www.nrega.nic.in

Table 3: Employment Generation under NREGA

Year	Person day in Core	No of Household Provided Employment in Core	Average day Per household
2006-07	90.5	2.1	43.1
2007-08	143.59	3.39	42.4
2008-09	214.56	4.5	47.7
2009-10	73.5	2.28	32.2
Total up to August 2009.	522.15	12.27	42.6

Source: www.nrega.nic.in

Table 4: Participation of SC, ST and Women

(in percentage)

Year	SC	ST	Women
2006-07	25	36	41
2007-08	27	29	43
2008-09	29.3	25.4	47.9
2009-10 (Up to August 2009)	28.9	24	25

Source: www.nrega.nic.in

V. Conclusions and Policy Implications

NREGA has the potentiality to increase the purchasing power of rural poor, stop the distress migration for the sake of minimum wages, develop long-term assets in rural areas which having multiplier effects, increase the wage in rural areas, provide employment during lean season, boost the message of economic women empowerment, increase the quality of life of the rural poor, transform the face of rural India, thus, make the foundation for human development in rural areas.

NREGA makes a paradigm shift from all earlier and existing wage employment programs because it is an act and not a scheme. It provides a legal right to rural poor for 100 day employment in a financial year. The scheme has a great impact on the employment of rural poor. Consequently it increases the wages income of the vulnerable class of rural India. It is a step towards the economic and social empowerment of rural poor. The act is a very bold and a revolutionary step to eradicate the chronic poverty in rural India. In rural India NREGA is not a supply driven act but it is demand driven. In order to achieve 100 days target in a year per poor family lot of awareness is required among the rural poor. From the aforementioned discussion it can be concluded that the NGERA has played a significant role in transforming the face of human development in rural India.

References

Aiyar, Yamini and Salimah Samaji (2006): Improving the effectiveness of National Rural Employment Guarantee Act, *Economic and Political Weekly*, 41(4): 320-326.

Antony G. M. and Laxmaiah, A. (2008): Human development, poverty, health and nutrition situation in India, *Indian Journal Medical Research*, 128(2): 198-205.

Chatterjee, S. (2009): Rural employment program fuelling development of Indian Economy, *Kurukeshtra*, 57(12): 26-33.

Dogra, Bharat (2005): Rural Employment Scheme: Rhetoric of Reality, *Economic and Political Weekly*, 40(18): 1809-1810

Government of India (2008): Economic Survey 2008-09, Ministry of Finance, New Delhi.

Haq, Mahbub Ul (1999): Reflection on Human Development, Oxford University press Delhi.

Kar, S. (2009): NREGA to change the face of Rural India, Kurukshetra, 57(12): 50-53.

Krishna A., Kapila M., Porwal M., Singh V. (2003): Failing into Poverty in a High Growth State: Escaping Poverty and becoming Poor in Gujarat Village, *Economic and Political Weekly*, 38(49): 5171.

Radhakrishana R., Rao H., Ravi C and Reddy S. (2006): Estimation and determination of chronic poverty in India: an alternative approach, *Working Paper No. wp-2006-07*, Indira Gandhi Institute of Development and Research, Mumbai.

Rout, H. S. (2007): National Rural Employment Guarantee Act – Issues and Challenges, in K. K. Bagchi (Ed.), *Employment and Poverty Alleviation Programs in India*, Abhijeet Publication, New Delhi.

Sainath P. (2007): Farmer Suicides the Symptom, *The Hindu*, Vishakhapatnam Edition, 7th September.

Shah, G. (2004): Growth, poverty and human development in India, www.sasnet.iu.se/EASASpaper/PHDShah.Pdf , accessed on 12th March 2010.

Sinha, Ajit (2005): Minimum Income Entitlement, *Economic and Political Weekly*, 40(27): 2896-2898.

Siva Kumar A. K. (1991): Poverty in human development in India: Getting priorities right, http://hdr.undp.org/docs/publication/ocational-paper/oc30 html, accessed on 3rd December 2009.

Smith Noel and Middleton (2007): Poverty research in the UK, http://www.jrf.org.uk/publication/poverty/-dynamics-reserch accessed on 24th December 2009.

10

Role of Governance towards Growth and Human Development

Sangram Kumar Rout[1]

I. Introduction

The ultimate objective of all human endeavours is the attainment of happiness and welfare. It is rightly acknowledged that the true parameter of development is removal of poverty, unemployment and inequality. The success of development efforts is expressed in terms of our capacity 'to wipe out tears from the eyes of the poor' or 'to bring smile on the face of the common man' or to achieve economic development with 'human face'. The issues of growth, governance and human development in the economic sphere are most widely discussed and yet largely remained as unresolved question of government policy. This issue has a substantial degree of historical specificity. It has gained additional significance in to-day's context of economic growth and neo-liberal advocacy.

Economic growth primarily concerns the economic well being and material development of a nation. Attaining and sustaining a high level of human development for all people is the prime concern of nation. Adam Smith, J.S. Mill, Kant and others considered human beings as the real end of all activities. Albert Hirschman opines that growth is only a means not the end. According to him the end is human development. The ultimate objective of growth process is the attainment of happiness and welfare. The true parameters of development are removal of poverty, unemployment and inequality. But the most modern governments put excessive accent on growth and miss the people for whom such growth is meant. They take full care of the means and miss the ends.

II. Growth -- Value Neutral

Growth and Development are two different things. While rapid economic growth is necessary for a steady improvement in the

[1] Resaerch Scholar, Department of Politics & International Studies, Pondicherry University, Puducherry

quality of life, growth by itself, does not automatically lead to better life for the majority. Economic growth alone has not improved the standard of living of all sections of the people. The gains of the growth will not automatically percolate to the lowest layer of society. Growth is value-neutral. It does not carry any in-built mechanism to translate itself in to human development. It ensures neither the equal opportunity for all to participate in the growth process nor the equitable disposal of the fruits of growth among the people. For example, the per capita income of India is higher than that of Bangladesh. But the infant mortality rate in Bangladesh is 51 per 1000 and for India it is 67 per 1000 according to the latest Human Development Report. Similarly 90 percent of the population in Bangladesh has access to improve sanitation compared with 28 percent in India.

III. Governance and Good governance: An overview

The concept of 'governance' is not new. It is as old as human civilization. Simply put "governance" means: the process of decision making and the process by which decisions are implemented (or not implemented). Governance can be used in several contexts such as corporate governance, international governance, national governance and local governance.

The World Bank defines governance as "the exercise of political authority and the use of institutional resources manage to society's problems and affairs. An alternative definition suggests that governance is the use of institutions, structures of authority and even collaboration to allocate resources and coordinate or control activity in society or the economy.

According to UNDP's Regional Project on local governance for Latin America "Governance has been defined as the rules of political system to solve conflicts between actors and adopt decision (legality). It has also been used to describe the 'proper functioning of the institutions and their acceptance by the public (legitimacy). And it has been used to invoke the efficacy of government and the achievement of consensus by democratic means (Participation).

The World Bank for the first time, raised the issue of governance in the context of Sub-Saharan Africa where it stated – "Underlying the litany of Africa's development problem is a crisis of governance. By governance, it is meant the exercise of political power to manage a nation's affairs." This definition of World Bank on governance is not only neutral between forms of government, i.e. democracy or authoritarian but even between 'good' or 'bad' governance since both would in their own ways qualify as the exercise of political power to manage a nation's affairs. Therefore, in view of these deficiencies, the Bank further elaborated its definition on governance. This has been done in the World Development Report of 1992 Governance and Development, where governance is defined as "the manner in which power is exercised in the management of a country's economic and social resources for the development.

Good Governance looks at decision making and the process by which decisions are implemented in a manner essentially free of abuse and corruption and with due regards for the rule of law. It defines an ideal which is difficult to achieve in its totality. However, to ensure sustainable human development, actions must be taken to work towards this ideal. Major donors and international financial institutions, like the IMF or World Bank, is increasingly basing their aid and loans on the condition that reform ensuring good governance is undertaken.

Characteristics of Good Governance

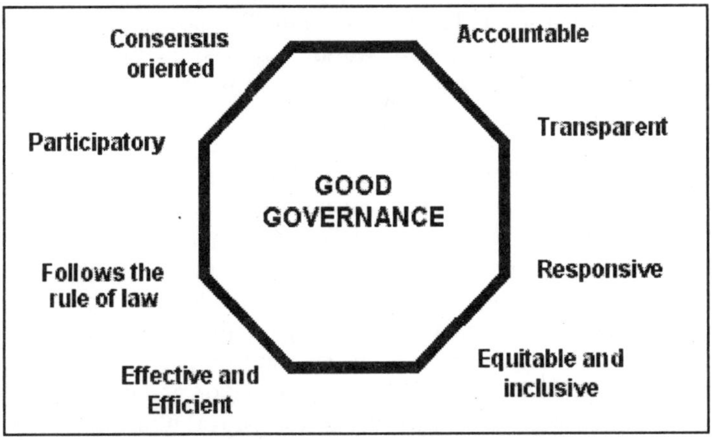

From the above discussion, these characteristics assure that

- Corruption is minimized,
- The views of minorities are taken into account, and
- That the voices of the most vulnerable in society are heard in decision-making.

Though on paper and theoretically, India had a grandiose framework of ideas, the real state of life and governmental dispensing of the future vision and lofty missions that we had during the initial years after independence were lost by the way side. The government became paradoxically, a prisoner of its magnificent obsession and lost initiative, drive and direction. There was genuine leadership vacuum, with none to lead the people from the front. There were plenty of leaders, no doubt, but they were out there to pursue their own selfish ends, and promote and consolidate clannish interests. "People" was the first thing they talked of and the last thing they bothered about. It was a sordid state of deception and deceit, extraordinary example of hypocrisy and dishonesty and classic case of blatant betrayal of the people who, shattered in hope and battered by battles of life, suffered in silence and bled. In fact, administration deteriorated making "good governance" a mirage. The reasons of deterioration are clear in a visible spectrum.

IV. Focus on Governance: Immediate Context

As it has been already stated, the World Bank identified governance as an issue in the development debate. There are several reasons accounted for it. The first is the inefficiency in state owned enterprises. In most of the third world countries, the public sector undertakings were incurring heavy losses on the state due to their ineffective functioning.

Secondly, fiscal crises made countries unable to repay their debt burden. Thirdly, corruption is acutely paralyzing the economy and has become an obstacle for development. Fourthly, mismanagement of funds borrowed from the World Bank and other institutions. In these countries, corruption is acute and as a result, resources are being misutilized. Fifthly, there were movements for democracies, as the authoritarian administrators in many of these countries were ruthless in the implementation of the reform packages without looking into their adverse effects on its population and economy. In order to make the government's 'clean' for the real utilization of the World Bank's funded money and effective implementation of reform programs, the World Bank started talking about good governance.

V. Good Governance in Indian Context

In the Indian context, the idea of good governance can be traced back to the Third Century B.C. when Kautilya in his treatise 'Arthasastra' proposed rules for the king-that the king's happiness should lie in the happiness of his subjects, which means that the king has to work for the well-being of the common people. Later, the Mughal rule brought drastic changes in the governmental systems by combining Arabic administrative concepts (like governorship [Amir] as head of the military and police and treasurer [Amil] as the head of the revenue, finance etc.) with certain classical Indian Practices (Hindu Revenue System). Even during the British period, there were many acts like Act of 1857, 1891,1909,1919,1935 etc., where in administrative procedures kept on changing for the better.

After independence, in 1949, N. Gopalaswamy Ayyenger suggested to create an organizational and method division in the Central Government set up. A. D. Gorwala, in his report (1951) stressed for clean, efficient and impartial administration. Similarly, P. H. Appleby, in his reports of 1953 and 1956, dealt with reforming the Indian Administrative System and he recommended the setting up of an O and M Organization in the Union Government and an institute of Public Administration. In 1964, K. Santhanama's report dealt with corruption. L.K. Jha's 'The Economic Administrative Reforms Commission' (1983) felt the need for accountability, so that importance can be given to performance than mere adherence to rules and procedure. In 1993, the 73rd and 74th Amendments to the Constitution brought Three- Tier representative Governance at the district level and below so that people's involvement in governance will increase.

Today, the Government of India is using the measure of Good Governance in order to tackle the problems of poor governance like lack of sensitivity, transparency and accountability in many facets of working of state machinery, which was eroded to such an extent that common people have lost faith in the credibility of Governmental institutions. In order to regain the confidence of the people, good governance is the only instrument working like ray of hope for Government of India.

Administration in many respects should be self managed and closer to the people and at door steps. There is, however, need to use democratic institutions in the service of the people and reduce the role of bureaucracy. These bodies could be less formal and more accommodating in taking care of the many day to day problems of the people. Really, democracy is now regarded as the universal chapter of good governance of global sustainability. Then the most pertinent question is ***which type of democracy is needed for good***

governance? Gandhi advocated true democracy in which power flows upward from the people. He also advocated a need based non exploitative economic system accountable to local communication. Gandhian ideology is based on the 4000 years democratic ethos and experience in India in which local entities control local resources and decision making. And the State provides only infrastructure and plays a role of facilitator and coordinator. As result, because of social control State cannot exploit. Rejection of Gandhi by society has led to all around social, environmental, economic and political degradation in India. It has also deprived the World of the path of realizing sustainable global society.

VI. Good Governance in India: Problems and Prospects

True good governance in India is a Herculean task. But it is possible. The nation needs to chant the mantra 'the only constant in life is change'. Most of our "bad aspects" need to be reformed by the system. The changes should be on five fronts: political reforms, judicial reforms, administrative reforms, socio-institutional reforms and human reforms.

The first three involves system and sub-systems. The fourth involves the entire gamut of plural society and diversified institutions. And the fifth deals with man, his mind, his character and psyche, the world of the morals and values. Even if the first four battles are own-which is extremely difficult, finally, the war can not be won, unless, the individual is able to score a decisive victory in the fifth. Admittedly, it is the most intricate, more time consuming, completely substantive and fully comprehensive. India committed the original sin by not attempting internal decolonization while designing a democratic super structure of the independent republic. It was a blunder of the highest magnitude – the Westminster model is unworkable in India and it is not performing well.

A new constituent assembly should be constituted, elected on the basis of adult franchise, which should write a new constitution providing for presidential model of government at union and state levels- a government fully federal and considerably decentralized, with a responsive and involved bureaucracy which also needs total overhauling. Regarding judicial reforms, reforms should be started from the top. Appointment of judges should be meticulously handled. Speedy justice is to be given to the masses at low cost which is a hall mark of good governance. Judgment should not be lengthy. Necessary arrangement must be made in the police culture to promote human rights. Coming to the administrative reform, which is the single most important instrumentality for good governance, it may be noted that the Indian Administrative system suffers from four major deficiencies: ideology-idiom incompatibility with consequential goal derailment; structural gigantism bordering on hydra headed monstrosity, procedural jungle leading to functional blind alley, and massive population explosion.

To bring reforms in governance or to make it good or effective, political reforms must take place. When there is a talk about good governance in the context of India, the need for political reform occupies the most prominent place. In this connection, the single greatest problem plaguing Indian polity for more than a decade has been the instability of governments not only at the centre but at the state level as well. If well organized, ideologically-oriented, fairly stable system of two major political parties have not evolved at the national level for obvious reasons associated with the proliferation of political parties. Multi-party pluralist democracy has become inevitable in view of the craving for political space by caste and ethnicity oriented factions. They cannot cease to exist. The resulting coalition experiment has altered the political fabric of Indian society to the extent that even dominant political parties like the Congress and the B.J.P cannot dream of occupying the seat of power on their own individual strengths.

Political reforms cannot be completed without electoral reforms. So that good candidates are elected. In this election, the election commission should be authorized to disqualify a person found guilty of corrupt practices and criminal track record. Criminalization of politics and politicization of both religions and criminals have gone so deep and entrenched into the functioning of Indian democracy that it would be a Herculean task for people of proven integrity and honesty to enter the electoral processes and claim power. Under the circumstances the Gresham Law, the bad driving the good from circulation, inevitably, operates in the political arena and the entire governance mechanism has gone into shambles leading to impoverishment of poor and the weak.

VII. Linking Growth and Human Development

Human development is a fundamental prerequisite to economic development with serial justice. In poor developing countries the presentation and protection of human lives is of vital importance. Healthy, educated, trained, motivated and dedicated manpower will not only accelerate development process but will also make it equitable and just. Healthy and educated manpower will surely help in providing the millions of people relief from poverty, unemployment and suffering. Aspiring for a higher rate growth, the government should not neglect people's immediate interests. Industry and agriculture are two economic sectors that have a direct and vital bearing on the people's standard of living. Neglecting them brings about unfavourable results and causes serious imbalances in the economy.

The government should not only develop modernization but also improve people's lives. Only by doing so, the state can lay a solid foundation for modernization as well as human development. The purpose of modernization for achieving a higher rate of growth is to serve people's long term interests. Moreover, to safeguard people's well-being and fruits of growth, the government must rely on the people. If the government ignores their immediate interests and instead asks them to tighten their belts to an unreasonable extent, their living standard will decline. This, in turn, will make it hard for them to display full enthusiasm and initiative production. The result will be an insufficient accumulation of funds, which will bring the growth process to a halt.

The investment on human development can not be viewed as counter- productive, poor, the fatalistic, the malnourished and the uneducated can hardly be enthused in achieving higher growth rates. Human development is a sine quo none for any development program and it is an invisible development. Investment ultimately results in general improvement in the quality of human life. Economic growth is incomplete and lop-sided, if human development does not take place simultaneously. The investment in human resources, which was earlier considered unproductive, fruitless and wasteful, is now being treated as highly productive. It ensures labour productivity which in turn ensures a high rate of growth. It augments the process of economic growth positive and self sustaining in the long run. Government activities should focus on human dimension in stead of income-centered economic growth.

VIII. Governance: Key to Growth and Human Development

Why is governance so important? In a market driven economy with competing players and minimal state intervention, governance plays a vital role for growth and social justice. Standing between the two is an administrative machine corroded by apathy and corruption. To be clearer, the governance subsidies fail to reach the poor, its schools fail to teach them and its rural clinics fail to treat them. If we look at UNDP, European Commission and World Bank, clearly and precisely describe the concept.

UNDP describe that "governance is the system of values, policies and institutions by which a society manages its economic, political and social affairs through interactions within and among the state, civil society and private sector ... It is the rules, institutions and practices that set limits and provide incentives for individuals, organization and firms". European commission describes "governance as that which concerns the state's ability to serve the citizens. It refers to the rules processes and behaviours by which interests are articulated, resources are managed and power is exercised in the society. The ways in which public functions are carried out, public resources are managed and public regulatory powers are exercised is the major issue to be addressed in the context". World Bank describes "governance as the traditions and institutions by which authority in a country is exercised for the common good. This includes (i) the process by which those in authority are selected, monitored and replaced (ii) the capacity of the government to effectively manage its resources and implement sound policies and (iii) the respect of citizens and the state for the institutions that govern economic and social interactions among them". For the measurement of growth and social justice, six components of governance are identified to facilitate it, viz:

Voice and Accountability: It measures the extent to which a country's citizens are able to participate in selecting their government as well as freedom of expression, freedom of association and a free media.

Political Stability and absence of violence: It measures perception of the likelihood that the government will be destabilized or over thrown by unconstitutional or violent means including domestic violence and terrorism.

Government Effectiveness: It measures the quality of public service, the quality of the civil service and the degree of its independence from political pressures, the quality of policy formulation and implementation and the credibility of the government commitment to such policies.

Regulatory Quality: It measures the ability of the government to formulate and implement sound policies and regulations that permit and promote private sector development.

Rule of law: It measures the extent which agents have confidence in and abide by the rules of society and in particular the quality of contract enforcement, the policies and the courts as well as the likelihood of crime and violence.

Control of Corruption: It measures the extent to which public power is exercised for private gain, including both petty and grand forms of corruption, as well as "capture" of the state by the elite and private interests.

While everybody is proud of India's democracy, it is observed that Indian democracy is based on corruption. Why is it so? Because, every political party needs funds and every political party collects money in cash which is mostly black money. This means that black money which is the oxygen for corruption is the life blood of financing the political process of the country. Political corruption leads to a vicious cycle of business corruption, bureaucratic corruption and criminalization of politics. Hence our 'system' itself is based on corruption. When it comes to government policies too anyone can find that many a time they encourage corrupt behaviour or reward corrupt behaviour. Can the system be changed? Is there a way out? There is, if the people are able to change the character of them. It is worth recalling at this stage to think about national character, which is the key stone on which rests the fate and future of a nation's public affairs.

Ganndhiji it had been often stated wished to spiritualize politics. He firmly held the view that the citizens can keep politics and morality a part. Indeed, he wanted politics to be rebuilt, based on a true and reliable foundation viz, individual honesty. There is a correlation between national progress and how the moral calibre of individual decides the fate of the nation. The nation can progress only if there is *good governance*. There can be no good governance unless moral values are inculcated in the people.

IX. Conclusion

The fate of a nation depends on its people. India has more natural resources than Taiwan, Japan or Singapore. But, those countries are richer and economically more advanced. Why is it so? It is because ultimately the wealth of a nation depends upon its people and their performance. It is the quality of the people and their skills that will help the country make progress. If the character based on values like integrity, helpfulness, love and corrupt are not there, nations which may progress economically temporarily may ultimately stand to lose. The nation if it has to progress, has to have good people. In this age of globalization, everyone including the World Bank recognizes that there is need for observing values. Honesty is the best policy- is a truth that is being rediscovered in the 21st century.

References

Collingwood, Vivian (2003): *Good Governance and the World Bank, Sub Saharan Africa: From crisis to Sustainable Growth*, Oxford University Press, Oxford.

Doig, Alan and McIvor, Stephanie (1999): Corruption and its Control in the Developmental Context: An Analysis and Selective Review of the Literatures, *Third World Quarterly*, 20(3): 657-676

Hirschman, A. O. (1958): *The Strategies for Economic Development*, New Haven, Yale University press, USA.

Leftwich, Adrain (2000): *Origin and Emergence of the Concept of Governance*, Oxford University Press, Oxford.

Nauro, Paolo (1995): Corruption and Growth, *The Quarterly Journal of Economics*, 110(3): 681-712.

Pagden, Antony (1998): The genesis of governance and enlightenment conceptions of the cosmopolitan order, *International Social Science Journal*, 50(155): 7-15.

Ramakanta Rao, M. G. (2008): *Good Governance: Modern and Regional Perspectives*, Kanishka Publishers, New Delhi.

Rao, Bhanoji (2008): Governance is Key to Growth and Social Justice, *The Hindu Business Line,* April 29.

Vittal, N (2003): *Corruption in India: The Road Block to National Prosperity*, Academic Foundation, New Delhi.

World Bank (1997): World Development Report 1997: The States in a Changing World, Oxford University Press, New York.

11

Dynamics of Health Status and Health care in Assam

Dukhabandhu Sahoo[1]

I. Introduction

The larger human development paradigm stresses on human beings as *ends* in themselves and not so much as *means* of development[2]. Further, the ends can be in multiple domains. It is in this context that Mahbub ul Haq, the founder of *Human Development Reports*[3], considers one-dimensionality as the most serious drawback of the income-based measures. This led to the birth of the Human Development Index (HDI) (Haq 2003). The calculation of HDI involves three dimensions – health, education and the ability to achieve a decent standard of living. Health, h, is measured by life expectancy at birth; education, e, is measured in terms of weighted average of adult literacy rate and enrolment ratio[4]; and standard of living, y, is measured through logarithm of income[5]. All the three dimensions are normalized such that $0 \leq h,e,y \leq 1$[6]. The composite HDI for each country is calculated by linear averaging (LA) of the above three dimensions. Acknowledging the importance of HDI, all most all the countries and even the provinces of a country have prepared the Human Development Report (HDR) with an aim to supplement

[1] Assistant Professor of Economics, School of Humanities, Social Sciences and Management, IIT Bhubaneswar, Orissa

[2] For discussions on this see Haq (2003) and Sen (2003a, 2003b and 1999) among others.

[3] The human development report is being published annually since 1990 and serves as a cornerstone in terms of philosophy as well as an approach of the United Nations Development Programme.

[4] Adult literacy rate is given 2/3rd weight and enrolment ratio is given 1/3rd weight.

[5] Logarithm of income represents diminishing returns to an increase in income.

[6] The normalization used: Index=(actual-minimum)/(maximum-minimum).

their policy decisions'. In lieu of this, the state of Assam also came up with its first HDR that highlighted the various dimensions of human well-being in the state at a district level. Without going into the rationale of choosing the particular three indices or the way these three individual indices are measured, scaled, weighed and normalized this paper tries to unearth the dynamics of the Health status and Health care facilities in Assam as reported in her first HDR, 2003. The rest of the paper is organized as follows. The following section highlights the importance of health care services and facilities in India and Assam. The third section examines key health indicators such as life expectancy at birth (LEB), infant mortality rates (IMR), birth and death rates, and the morbidity pattern. It also looks at issues of maternal and child health. An analysis is made of the medical infrastructure, its accessibility and utilization in the same section. It also includes the issues of sanitation and water supply, two areas that are closely related to health. Based on the analysis, the last section analyses the data at the district level and concludes the study with some policy suggestions.

II. Importance of Health Care Services and Facilities in India and in Assam

The priority agenda of the Government of Assam is the provision of 'health for all'. It is a commitment and an objective that encompasses an array of actions and policies. Health is an indicator of well-being that has immediate implications for the quality of life as well as for productive capacities and capabilities. To build a healthy society is to lay the foundations of a prosperous and dynamic society, and a contented and strong people. The Government of Assam is deeply conscious of its responsibility to the people of the State. The Constitution of India is uncompromising on the issue of health and the people. It states in that 'the enjoyment of the highest achievable standard of health is one of the fundamental rights of every human being, without distinction of race, religion, political, economic or social condition'. In a declaration adopted by the world community in 1978, and reflected in the Alma Ata declaration of the World Health Organization (WHO), health is classified as a human right. The 'health' of a person or of a group of people is a comprehensive concept that incorporates many dimensions, not just the absence of illness. In fact, the Charter of the World Health Organization (WHO) explicitly defines 'health' as 'a state of complete physical, mental and social well-being and not merely the absence of disease and infirmity'. This is a definition that recognizes the many dimensions of health and well- being, and one that requires action on many different fronts.

The National Health Policy of 1983 and the approach of the Government of Assam reflect a multi-faceted approach to health care. Such an approach was initially advocated by the Alma Ata declaration, and is notable for its principal focus on primary health care. Assam has been moving towards the attainment of the goal of 'health for all'. The State Government has emphasized not only the adequate provision of primary health care, but other pivotal concerns as well. These include education and awareness of heath issues, dissemination of information on prevention, hygiene and healthy practices, food security and nutrition, safe drinking water and good sanitation, maternal and child health and family welfare. Also taken up for State and schematic support are immunization against major infectious diseases, prevention and control of locally endemic diseases; treatment of common ailments and the provision of essential drugs. These are critical objectives and significant activities. To measure the progress and observe the impact of the 'health for all' strategy is, however, not an easy task. In some cases for instance, on the long term goals of major reductions in morbidity and mortality, we need to look at data over a long period of time – perhaps even three or four decades - to evaluate the success of a particular approach. In other cases, especially where private and informal health care systems are involved, data may not be easily forthcoming. Information available from routine reporting is not adequate to give a comprehensive picture of the disease profile of the State and its people. A combination of routine reporting, disease prevalence studies and some hospital-based data can help to assess the level of morbidity and mortality in respect of particular diseases. The State has established fairly efficient disease specific surveillance systems for some major diseases such as polio and leprosy. There is more work to be done in terms of strengthening of data and its availability, from the State health care network, and from other sources. Beyond data collection and organization, capabilities need to be built for analysis and its conversion to inputs for the planning framework. It is however possible to form an assessment of health status from key indicators such as infant mortality, crude birth rate, crude death rate, life expectancy and nutritional status. The accessibility to health services tells us about the status of the health service delivery system. The quality of services being provided has a bearing on the utilization of services, especially if alternatives are available.

All over the world, development, the rise in incomes and the application of science and technology have led to people living longer and healthier lives. However, it is pertinent to at this juncture to have a look at the overall human development indicators of Assam vis-a-vis India and the same across different districts of Assam. As is observed from the Table 1 there are differences in HDI values across regions; suggesting differences in the development across the states. However, the dispersion of HDI (as measured by CV) across states is declining over the study period (Figure 1). This may be due to the fact that there is a sharp reduction in inequality across states in education index, as is evident from Figure 2. Since, education is one of the components in HDI; reducing inequality in this section can reduce the overall HDI inequality, provided inequalities in other dimensions of HDI does not get worse off. It may be noted that some of the states, having attained poor HDI score in 1980-81, have performed better over a period of 20 years. Table 1 brings to the fore that states like Assam, Bihar, Orissa, Uttar Pradesh and West Bengal have recorded fairly higher scores in 2000-01 over the initial period 1980-81. However, since the already developed states have maintained higher HDI score all through, the ranking of the state have not changed much, except for Tamil Nadu, whose rank jumped to 3 by 2001 from 7 in 1981. The appreciable improvement in the HDI rank of Tamil Nadu can be attributed to its good performance in all the three dimensions of HDI over the years. This trend is in sharp contrast to the observed rise in inequalities till late eighties as highlighted by some research studies (Das, Barua and Ghosh, 1993).

The state wise variation in Health index is given in Table 2. It is evident from Table 2 that Orissa and Madhya Pradesh are consistently low performers in regard of health index, whereas Kerala and Maharashtra have continuously registered good performance. Among the poor states, Assam which had a score of 0.40 in 1991-92 recorded a lower figure of 0.11 in 2005-06, implying poor performance of the state over the period of time. Among the highest per-capita income states, Haryana has almost aped Assam in this respect. This was the state which occupied fifth position in 1991-02 but was replaced by Punjab in 2001-02. This is a strange phenomenon as the advanced states generally fare better in the health index. Looking into the value of coefficient of variation, it is evident that the disparity in health index has increased over the years.

Figure 1: CV of HDI Across Indian States

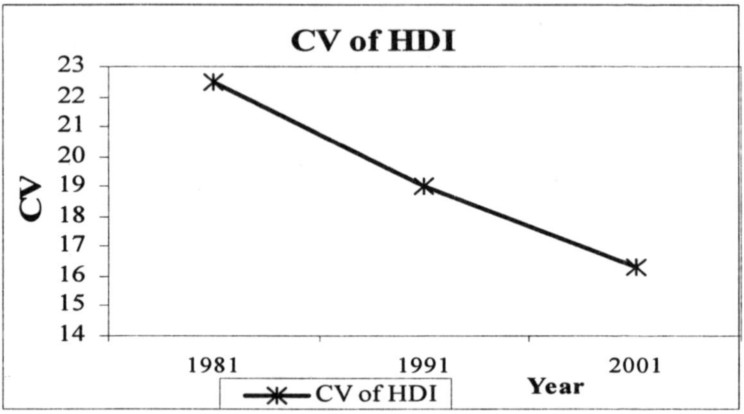

Figure 2: CV of Education Index across Indian States

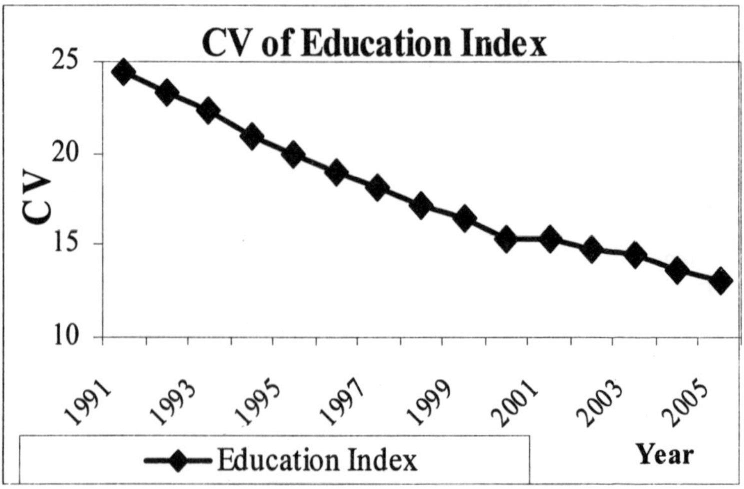

Table 1: HDI Score and Rank of the States According to their Respective HDI from 1981 to 2001

Year \ States		Andhra Pradesh	Assam	Bihar	Gujarat	Haryana	Karnataka	Kerala	Madhya Pradesh	Maharashtra	Orissa	Punjab	Rajasthan	Tamil Nadu	Uttar Pradesh	West Bengal
Score	1981	0.3	0.27	0.24	0.36	0.36	0.35	0.50	0.25	0.36	0.27	0.41	0.26	0.34	0.26	0.31
	1991	0.38	0.35	0.31	0.43	0.44	0.41	0.59	0.33	0.45	0.35	0.48	0.35	0.47	0.31	0.4
	2001	0.42	0.39	0.37	0.48	0.51	0.48	0.64	0.39	0.52	0.4	0.54	0.42	0.53	0.39	0.47
Rank	1981	9	10	15	4	5	6	1	14	3	11	2	12	7	13	8
	1991	9	10	15	6	5	7	1	13	4	12	2	11	3	14	8
	2001	10	14	15	6	5	7	1	12	4	11	2	9	3	13	8

Source: National Human Development Report, Planning Commission, Government of India.

Table 2: State-wise Health Index (HI) in Descending Order

1991-92		2001-02		2005-06	
States	HI	States	HI	States	HI
Kerala	1.00	Kerala	1.00	Kerala	1.00
Punjab	0.66	Maharashta	0.58	Maharashtra	0.64
Tamil Nadu	0.62	Tamil Nadu	0.53	Tamil Nadu	0.62
Maharashtra	0.59	West Bengal	0.50	West Bengal	0.61
Haryana	0.52	Punjab	0.49	Punjab	0.51
Gujarat	0.51	Karnataka	0.41	Karnataka	0.41
Bihar	0.51	Gujarat	0.39	Gujarat	0.34
West Bengal	0.49	Bihar	0.36	Bihar	0.32
Andhra Pradesh	0.47	Uttar Pradesh	0.32	Andhra Pradesh	0.30
Karnataka	0.44	Haryana	0.31	Uttar Pradesh	0.29 .
Rajasthan	0.42	Andhra Pradesh	0.31	Haryana	0.25
Assam	0.40	Assam	0.21	Rajasthan	0.11
Uttar Pradesh	0.25	Rajasthan	0.14	Assam	0.11
Madhya Pradesh	0.06	Madhya Pradesh	0.12	Madhya Pradesh	0.09
CV	51.75		62.65		71.13

Source: Authors' Compilation from indiastat database.

The various dimensions of HDI with regards to Assam are presented in Table 3 and Table 4. Data shows that the most developed district in Assam is Jorhat while Dhurbi (a district of the Char area of Assam) is languishing at the bottom. Various measures of dispersions like Coefficient of Variation, Standard Deviation of Logarithm and Sen's Index (SI)[7] shows that there is a wide variation in all most all the components of HDI across the states of Assam.

---

[7] There are various ways of defining the Gini coefficient, and a bit of manipulation (done by Prof. Amartya Sen and commonly known as Sen's Index) as it is-reveals that it is exactly one-half of the relative mean difference, which is defined as the arithmetic average of the absolute values of difference between all pairs of incomes.

$$S = (1/2n^2\mu) \sum_{i=1}^{n} \sum_{j=1}^{n} |y_i - y_j| = 1-(1/n^2 \mu) \sum_{i=1}^{n} \sum_{j=1}^{n} \mathrm{Min}(y_i, y_j)$$

$$S = 1+(1/n)-(2/n^2\mu)[y_1+2y_2+ \dots\dots +ny_n] \quad \dots\dots\dots(2.23)$$

$$\text{for } y_1 \langle\, y_2 \langle \dots\dots \langle\, y_n.$$

The variations is highest with respect to the income index (the value of Sen's Index is 0.40) implying that there is huge disparities with respect to income. However, the disparity is less with respect to the overall HDI (the value of Sen's Index is 0.15, much less than the Sen's Index for income index). This may be due to the fact that the disparities with respect to education and health are less. As could be evidenced from Table 3, Sen's Index with respect to percentage of Literacy and Combined Enrolment Ratio (CER) is merely 0.06 and 0.07 respectively. The variation in education index is 0.08. However, there are little higher variations in the health index and its components. The table shows that the Sen's Index for Infant Mortality Rate (IMR) and IMR index is 0.13 and 0.25 respectively, indicating a comparative higher disparity in the health sector across the districts of Assam.

The gender dimension of HDI is presented in Table 4. A perusal of Table 4 reveals the fact that there are widespread gender disparities across the districts of Assam. The data also reveal that, the gender disparity is higher in the plains than the hill areas (The NC Hill is the best performer with respect to Gender Development Index, the GDI). This could be because of the fact that the hills are generally inhabited by the tribes who do not have much of the gender biasness. On the other hand, the economically developed plains which are mostly populated by the upper cast generals have miserable performance in GDI. This is an indication of the fact that in these areas probably the social structure and system encourages preferential treatment towards the male and females as a social group get the residual treatment. As a result, there may be a tendency towards female foeticides and negligence towards the education and health care of the female siblings of the family. This is a major cause of concern not only in Assam but also in the whole country as there has been a steady decline in the sex ratio in all most all parts of the country baring some few exceptions. This calls for urgent social and administrative reforms nationwide.

III. Key Health Indicators of Assam

Health indicators in Assam reveal inequity-between districts, and between income and other groupings. There is a rural–urban divide, and a gender gap. This can be observed as follows:

Table 3: Various Dimensions of HDI with Regards to Assam

Districts	Literacy	CER (1991)	EI	IMR
Jorhat	77.9	60.7	0.72	47
Kamrup	74.7	60.8	0.7	77
Golaghat	70.4	54.3	0.65	61
Morigaon	59.5	46.4	0.55	88
Karbi Anglong	58.8	42.8	0.54	76
Dibrugarh	71.2	53.7	0.65	51
Sibsagar	75.3	59.9	0.7	75
Cachar	68.4	53.3	0.63	97
Barpeta	57.4	43.5	0.53	101
Tinsukia	63.3	44.7	0.57	73
Hailakandi	59.8	49.1	0.56	99
NC Hills	68.6	57.7	0.65	108
Sonitpur	60.3	45	0.55	77
Nagaon	62.3	50.4	0.58	97
Kokrajhar	52.6	37.2	0.47	78
Nalbari	68.1	56.2	0.64	96
Lakhimpur	69.6	58	0.66	112
Goalpara	58.6	43.7	0.54	106
Karimganj	67.2	51.5	0.62	111
Dhemaji	66	54.6	0.62	114
Bongaigaon	60.3	46.6	0.56	122
Darrang	55.9	42.3	0.51	111
Dhubri	49.9	36.5	0.45	128
ASSAM	**64.3**	**49.8**	**0.6**	**92**
CV*	11.24	14.31	11.99	23.54
SDoL*	0.17	0.22	0.18	0.40
SI*	0.06	0.08	0.07	0.13

contd...

IMR index	Income	Income Index	HDI Index	HDI Rank
0.66	11222	0.56	0.65	1
0.45	11424	0.57	0.57	2
0.56	8021	0.41	0.54	3
0.37	11152	0.56	0.49	4
0.46	9588	0.49	0.49	4
0.64	4713	0.16	0.48	6
0.46	5602	0.24	0.47	7
0.31	5897	0.27	0.4	8
0.28	7616	0.39	0.4	9
0.48	3966	0.08	0.38	10
0.29	5507	0.23	0.36	11
0.23	5234	0.21	0.36	11
0.45	3869	0.07	0.36	13
0.31	4893	0.18	0.36	14
0.44	4544	0.15	0.35	15
0.31	3911	0.08	0.34	16
0.2	4636	0.15	0.34	17
0.24	4548	0.15	0.31	18
0.21	3931	0.08	0.3	19
0.19	3511	0.03	0.28	20
0.13	4150	0.1	0.26	21
0.21	3755	0.06	0.26	22
0.09	4144	0.1	0.21	23
0.34	**6158**	**0.29**	**0.41**	
44.42	42.95	74.95	27.38	
0.79	0.55	1.31	0.40	
0.25	0.22	0.40	0.15	

Source: Assam Human Development Report, 2003.
* *Author's Calculations*

Table 4: Gender Dimension of HDI and the GDI of Assam

	Literacy		CER	
	Male	Female	Male	Female
N.C. Hills	64.7	49.47	60.95	54.16
Morigaon	53.95	42.51	48.85	43.8
Jorhat	72.55	63.62	64.62	56.75
Kamrup	70.66	58.11	64.03	57.46
Dibrugarh	68.59	53.25	58.47	48.8
Hailakandi	56.06	41.76	54.55	43.37
Golaghat	66.83	52.82	58.22	50.31
Lakhimpur	65.51	50.52	60.83	52.83
Sibsagar	71.22	58.61	63.49	56.29
Barpeta	54	39.23	47.36	39.39
Kokrajhar	50.7	34.86	42.02	32.31
Goalpara	53.1	41.55	47.58	39.65
Dhemaji	62.85	46.72	60.2	48.95
Cachar	64.88	50.64	56.91	49.68
Sonitpur	57.2	43.98	49.9	40.04
Bongaigaon	56.86	41.97	50.82	42.23
Nalbari	66.31	49.99	60.94	51.33
Darrang	53.3	38.64	46.19	38.32
Tinsukia	61.24	44.83	49.66	39.84
Dhubri	45.37	33.82	41.33	31.27
Nagaon	56.53	45.41	52.82	47.93
Karimganj	61.5	49.65	55.4	47.36
ASSAM	**71.93**	**56.03**	**53.81**	**45.61**
CV*	11.64	15.56	12.46	15.67
SDoL*	0.18	0.23	0.20	0.25
SI*	0.15	0.17	0.15	0.17

IMR		EEI		GDI	GDI Rank
Male	Female	Male	Female		
109	100	35,248	14715	0.877	1
106	97	31,898	8240	0.759	2
47	48	20,208	7336	0.701	3
80	78	20,462	5347	0.642	4
56	45	13,805	6511	0.642	4
101	97	17,504	4908	0.609	6
66	56	13,538	5443	0.608	7
138	104	6,173	4366	0.491	8
81	68	7,478	3411	0.468	9
97	104	13,595	2629	0.448	10
56	75	5,779	2959	0.418	11
109	103	9,475	2473	0.413	12
113	117	4,690	3148	0.41	13
99	85	10,387	2379	0.409	14
75	77	5,936	2621	0.397	15
93	124	7,218	2255	0.376	16
102	70	6,540	2103	0.357	17
118	86	6,204	1840	0.317	18
82	63	3,964	1896	0.3	19
123	132	7,667	1269	0.206	21
104	89	4,617	916	0.068	22
105	97	3,935	818	0.012	23
96	**87**	**6,744**	**5530**	**0.537**	
22.80	25.57	71.42	75.68	44.48	
0.41	0.42	0.96	1.07	0.83	
0.21	0.22	0.42	0.43	0.31	

Source: Assam Human Development Report, 2003.
* *Author's Calculations*
Note: Data on Karbi Anglong was not available.

Life Expectancy at Birth

Life Expectancy at Birth (LEB) is defined as the number of

years a person may be expected to live when he is born, given the prevailing mortality rates in the population to which he belongs. In India, life expectancy has more than doubled in the last fifty years. From just around thirty years at Independence, it is now over 60 years. The data for Assam shows trends similar to the rest of the country; it does, however, point to the fact that life expectancy in Assam is below that of the country as a whole, and is one of the lowest amongst major Indian States. In the 1970s men at birth could expect to live longer than women. This has since been reversed; women can now expect to live longer than men. This is a trend that began to take place initially in urban areas, but is now true of rural areas as well. The LEB in Assam is lower than the average LEB for the country as a whole. Amongst the major States of India, LEB in Assam was the second lowest. The only major State with a lower LEB than Assam was Madhya Pradesh. In the period 1992-96, LEB was 56.2 years for Assam and 60.7 years for the country. The encouraging aspect in the case of Assam is the positive change in the LEB for women. For the first time, in the period 1991-95, women in Assam had a higher LEB than men (it was 56.1 for women and 55.7 for men, Figure 3). In 1992-96, LEB for women was 56.6 years while for men it was 56.1 years. There is still a very significant gap between the LEB for rural and for urban areas. In the period 1992-96, the LEB in urban areas was 64.6 years. In rural areas it was almost ten years less, at 55.6 years (Figure 4).

Infant Mortality Rate (IMR)

The infant mortality rate is defined as the probability of a child dying before he attains the age of one year, and is calculated per 1000 live births. Through the 1990s there was a secular decline in the Infant Mortality Rate in Assam[4] from 81 per 1000 live births (1991) to 76 per 1000 live births by the end of the decade (1999). This is a positive development. There is however cause for concern. There is a growing divergence between the IMR status of Assam, and that of the rest of the country and a substantial rural-urban gap within Assam as well (Figure 5). Across districts there are major differences; the data shows that while some districts have IMR rates lower than the national average and are therefore performing very well, there are others with high IMR rates.

Figure 3: Gender Gap in LEB for Assam

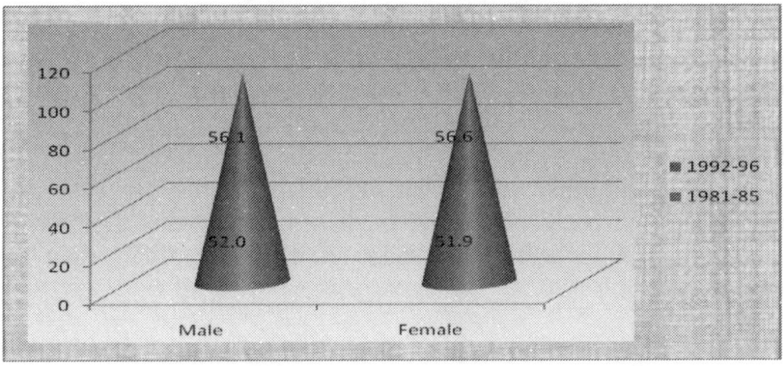

Figure 4: Rural-Urban Gap in LEB for Assam

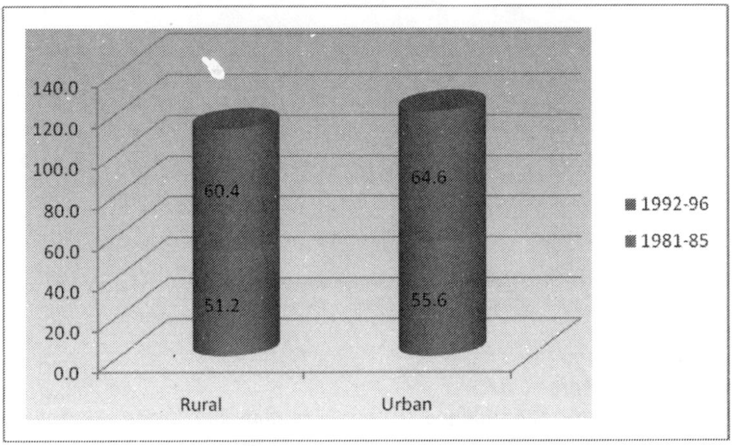

The IMR for the country as a whole was 80 per 1000 live births, a figure that declined to 70 per 1000 live births by 1999. At the beginning of the decade Assam was only one point away from the national average figure. At decade's end, the difference between the IMR for the State and that of the country was as much as six points. There has been little change in the IMR at all in the period 1996-99. This may be attributable to high peri- natal mortality and stillbirths, (both of which remained unchanged) which contribute significantly to IMR.

The rural-urban gap is extremely high. Urban IMRs were less than half the rural IMRs, in the entire period. The IMR for urban Assam is substantially lower than the all India average (36 per 1,000 as against 44 per 1000 for India), while in rural Assam the IMR is higher than that for rural India (79 per 1000 against 75 per 1,000 for India) in 1999. There were extensive variations in the IMR across districts in Assam. At the extremes were the districts of Dhubri (128 per 1000 live births) and Jorhat (47 infant deaths per 1000 live births) – a difference of over 272 per cent. Three districts, Jorhat, Dibrugarh and Golaghat had substantially lower IMRs than the others.

Figure 5: Trend in IMR for Assam and India

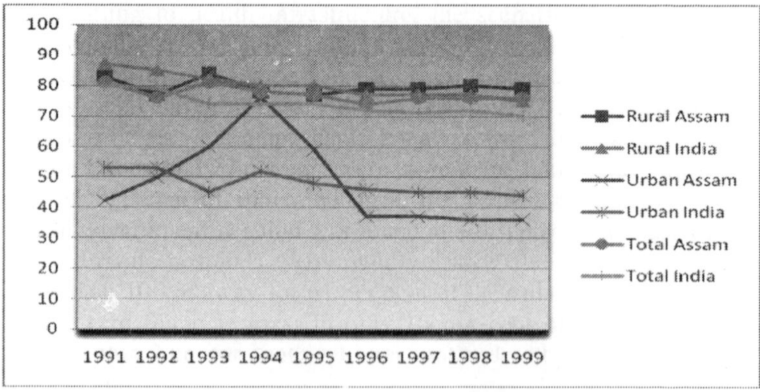

Crude Birth Rate (CBR)

While there is evidence to confirm that the Crude Birth Rate (CBR) has declined significantly in Assam, over the last few decades, the CBR in Assam continues to be higher than the national average.

The Sample Registration System (SRS) data shows that the CBR for Assam decreased in the period 1991-99 from 30.9 (per 1000 population) to 27.0, while in the country as a whole, the CBR declined from 29.5 to 26.1 (per 1000 population) in the same period. In Assam, the CBR is much higher in rural areas as compared to in urban areas. This is true of the country as a whole as well.

Figure 6: Rural-Urban Gap in IMR for Assam

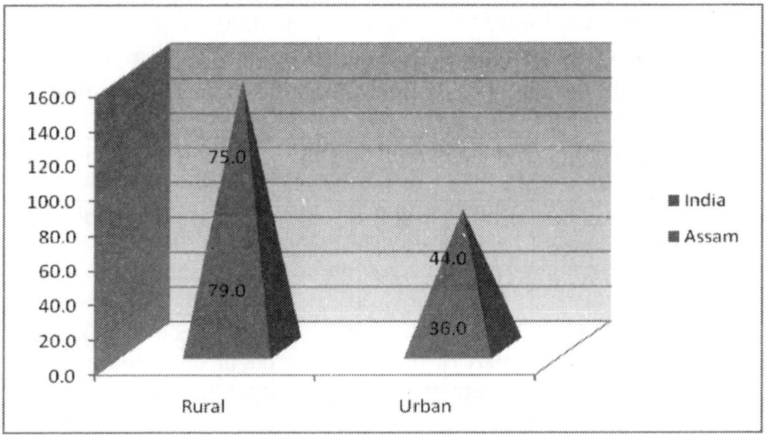

Figure 7: Trend in CBR for Assam and India

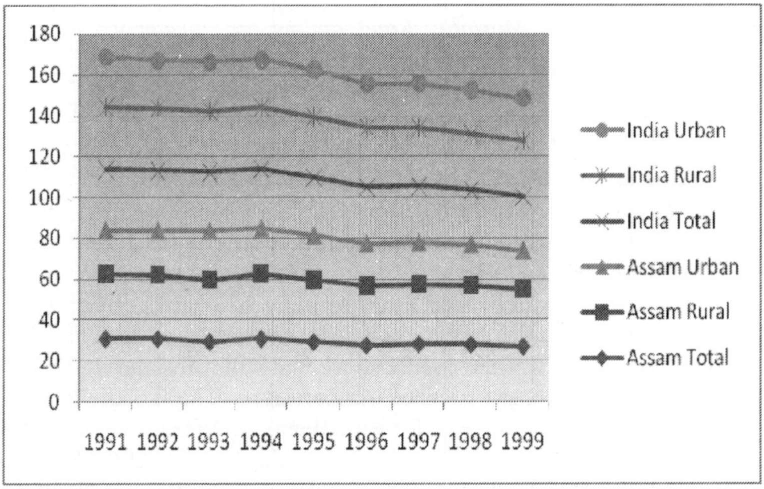

Total Fertility Rate (TFR)

The Total Fertility Rate (TFR) refers to the number of children that would be born per woman if she were to live to the end of her childbearing years and bear children at each age in accordance with the prevailing age specific fertility rates. The total fertility rate (TFR) estimated from SRS data was 3.3 children per woman in 1995-97, a substantial decline from 1980-81, when it was as high as 4.1 children. The TFR for all India was 3.4 in the 1995-97 periods. Estimates made by NFHS-2, put the TFR at 2.3 children per woman. The decline over the 5-year period since NFHS-1, is 35 percent, which is much higher than the decline as per SRS estimates. The NFHS-2 has probably under-estimated the TFR in Assam. In fact the report suggests as much, because it feels the decline of 35 percent is not matched by a corresponding increase in the use of contraceptives, which remained steady at 43 percent. The absence of an upward trend in contraceptive use is inconsistent with a sharp decline in fertility. A part of the bias may occur on account of age misreporting, a problem not atypical of retrospective surveys such as the NFHS. As is to be expected, there is a substantial rural-urban gap in fertility rates as well. The TFR for urban women was 2.1(lower than the all India figure of 2.5 for urban women), while the rural TFR was 3.5 (marginally lower than all India rate of 3.7).

Fertility and Infant Mortality Rates among tea garden workers of Assam

Data on Tea Garden workers in Assam highlights the fact of increasing divergence between population groups, even as indicators at the macro level begin to converge to higher levels. The Crude Birth Rate among tea garden workers is 35.19 compared to 30.9 for Assam (1991) and 29.5 for India (1991). The infant mortality rate is 154.45 (per 1,000 live births) compared to 81 (per 1,000) for Assam and 80 (per 1,000) for India. As many as 70.72 percent of the couples interviewed have experienced three or more live births. More than one-third of the couples reported one or more deaths of their infants, more than one tenth of the couples have had stillbirths and 7 percent of the women have experienced miscarriages. The Total Fertility Rate is 3.63 compared to 3.53 for Assam and 3.39 for India, in 1991. More than 90 percent of the wives and two thirds of the husbands are still illiterate. The mean age of marriage of females is 16.8 years compared to 19 years in India and 21.4 years for Assam.

Crude Death Rate (CDR)

The Crude Death Rate (CDR) is another indicator of the health status of a population. The death rate in Assam declined substantially in the early nineties. In the mid 1990s the decline came to a virtual standstill and the rate even showed a marginal increase. The State has witnessed a decreasing trend in the Crude Death Rate during the 1990s, in rural as well as urban areas. From 11.5 deaths per 1000 in 1991, the CDR came down to 9.7 deaths per 1,000 in 1999. In the same period, the decline in the national CDR was from 9.8 deaths per 1000 to 8.7 deaths per 1000. The SRS data shows that after a fairly rapid fall in the early 1990s, there was no change in the death rate in Assam for three years (1995-97) when the CDR remained constant at 9.6 (per 1000 population). Thereafter it increased to 10.0 deaths per 1,000 in 1998 and then declined to 9.7 deaths per 1,000 in 1999. The reasons for this are not very clear. As in the case of the CBR, the CDR in rural Assam is substantially higher than that in urban Assam, and the same is true for rural and urban India. In case of rural Assam, there was a distinct increase in the death rate after 1994, and it continued to rise for five years, till 1999, when it started declining again but was still higher than the rate recorded in 1994. This is cause for concern. In most countries, male death rates are higher than female death rates, at nearly all ages. South Asia has been an exception and has had higher death rates for females over a large part of the life span. In this respect, the Crude Death Rates in Assam show mixed trends. According to the SRS mortality estimates for 1997, females have higher mortality than males, except at age 60 and over, when males have slightly higher mortality than females. This is indicative of gender inequity. A comparison of age specific deaths over NFHS-1 and NFHS-2 showed that the death rates declined substantially in the youngest age group (under 5 years) and increased substantially at ages 60 and above. In the other age groups, there was not much change.

Health Care Infrastructure in Assam

It is argued in the development literature that infrastructure is one of the driving forces for growth and development. The link between infrastructure and economic growth is, notwithstanding, complex because infrastructure extends both direct and indirect benefits and also a series of positive externalities. It improves communication, transportation and other utility services that may directly create wage employment of various categories. Now, in order to have an idea on the importance of infrastructure on the economies, the present study uses the policy variables like the expenditure of the states on education, medical, health and family welfare as Ratio to Aggregate Disbursements[8] of the states (higher spending on these heads by the states would presumably raise the quality of HDI).

Figure 8: Trend in CDR for Assam and India

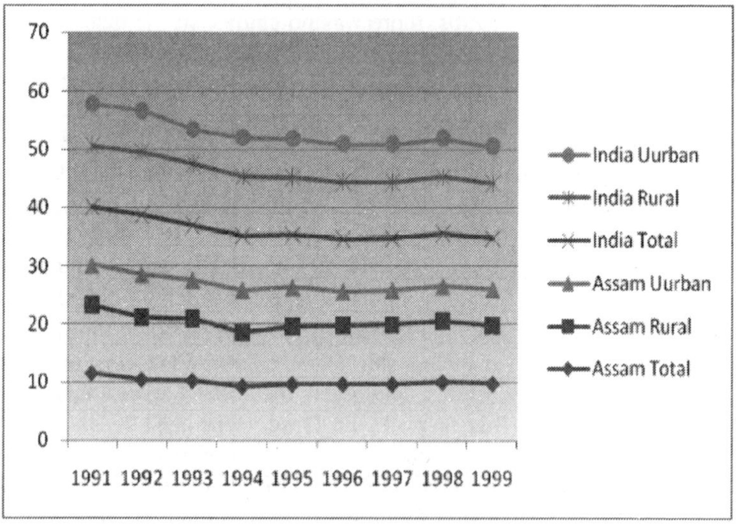

A disturbing scenario of the states that all the states have reduced their expenditure on education from 2000 to 2006 (Table 5) However, the annualized growth rate of this expenditure on education is positive for a few states, precisely three and namely West Bengal, Haryana and Uttar Pradesh[9]. Surprisingly, the initial poor states in terms of HDI have a greater reduction in this expenditure. As is evidenced from the Table 5, states like Bihar, Assam, Orissa and Madhya Pradesh have a greater reduction in the educational expenditure (the annualized growth rate is negative, an indication of the ambivalent attitude towards the most important

[8] Since the data on Education and Health Expenditure of the States as a Ratio to Aggregate Disbursements is not available before 2000, the analysis is limited to the period after 2000 till 2006

[9] Even the growth rates are very minimal for these states

merit good having possibly greatest positive externalities in the economy). Some of the southern states like Karnataka, Kerala, Andhra Pradesh and Tamil Nadu could afford to do this owing to the more efficient role of the private sectors in this regard, but others ought to honour the importance of education in promoting growth and inequality in the states. So far as the expenditure of the states on the health and family welfare is concerned, the situation is not that significantly different though the scenario is better in comparison to the expenditure on education (Table 4.2). The annualized growth rate of this expenditure on health and family welfare is positive for three states, namely Assam, Haryana and Uttar Pradesh[10]. In this case also, the poor states in terms of HDI have a greater reduction in expenditure. However, the Government of Assam is committed to the expansion and development of basic health care. Health facilities are being repaired or constructed and the State has an extensive network of facilities. District and Sub divisional level hospitals are being strengthened and 200-bed hospitals are being constructed in Tezpur, Nagaon, Lakhimpur, Nalbari, Goalpara, Mangaldoi, Karimganj, Barpeta and Haflong.

Table 5: HDI, Education and Health Expenditure and their Growth Rates of the States as a Ratio to Aggregate Disbursements from 2000 to 2006

States	HDI	States	Edu 2000[11]	States	Health 2000[12]	States
BI	0.37	PU	13.20	HY	3.30	PU
AS	0.39	AP	13.30	GU	3.40	AP
UP	0.39	GU	13.60	MH	3.90	MD
MD	0.39	HY	14.60	UP	4.00	OR
OR	0.40	OR	15.90	OR	4.20	GU
AP	0.42	MD	16.30	PU	4.50	KT
RJ	0.42	UP	16.80	AP	4.70	TM
WB	0.47	WB	17.10	AS	4.70	HY
KT	0.48	KT	17.70	TM	4.90	UP
GU	0.48	TM	18.00	KT	5.10	WB
HY	0.51	RJ	18.80	MD	5.10	MH

[10] And the growth rates are relatively higher for these states.

[11] Education Expenditure of the States as a Ratio to Aggregate Disbursements in 2000.

[12] Health Expenditure of the States as a Ratio to Aggregate Disbursements in 2000.

MH	0.52	KR	20.00	RJ	5.20	RJ
TM	0.53	MH	22.30	KR	5.30	KR
PU	0.54	BI	23.70	WB	5.60	BI
KR	0.64	AS	25.50	BI	5.90	AS

contd...

Edu 2006[13]	States	Health 2006[14]	States	GrEd[15] 2000--2006	States	GrHe[16] 2000--2006
11.40	GU	3.20	MH	-4.53	KT	-5.39
11.70	AP	3.40	KT	-4.48	AP	-4.99
12.20	MH	3.40	TM	-4.34	MD	-3.45
12.60	HY	3.50	BI	-4.13	WB	-2.72
12.80	KT	3.50	AS	-3.69	BI	-2.52
13.20	OR	3.70	OR	-3.58	PU	-2.38
13.20	PU	3.70	MD	-3.30	TM	-2.16
14.30	MD	3.90	KR	-1.90	RJ	-1.56
15.20	TM	4.00	PU	-1.83	MH	-1.26
15.70	BI	4.40	RJ	-1.49	OR	-1.15
16.30	RJ	4.50	AP	-1.12	KR	-0.74
16.50	WB	4.50	GU	-0.59	GU	-0.22
17.60	AS	4.90	WB	0.08	HY	2.31
17.70	KR	4.90	HY	0.85	AS	2.86
19.20	UP	6.40	UP	1.32	UP	11.33

Source: State Statistics, RBI, 2006.

The Department of Health and Family Welfare is responsible for the health services, family planning programmes, medical education and training. The Directorate of Health Services has the administrative control of the health services, except for the various teaching institutions, Universities and similar bodies. The only exceptions are the ANM training schools and in-service training centres, which are under the Directorate of Family Welfare. There are 23 district training centres, which have been established under the World Bank funded IPP-IX. The Medical Colleges and the Regional Dental College also produce specialists with postgraduate degrees.

[13] Education Expenditure of the States as a Ratio to Aggregate Disbursements in 2006.
[14] Health Expenditure of the States as a Ratio to Aggregate Disbursements in 2006.
[15] Annualized Growth Rate of Education Expenditure of the States as a Ratio to Aggregate Disbursements from 2000 to 2006.
[16] Annualized Growth Rate of Health Expenditure of the States as a Ratio to Aggregate Disbursements from 2000 to 2006.

Training facilities for laboratory technicians, radiographers and ophthalmic technicians are provided in the Medical Colleges. The major training institutions like the Medical Colleges, apart from training and creating workers for health services, provide specialist care for patients. In addition to the teaching institutions, there is a wide network of institutes, both in the public and private sector, which provide health care services in the State.

Table 6: Health Care Infrastructure in Assam

Distance from Village	PHC	Sub-Centre	PHC/Sub-Centre	Any Hospital	Dispe-nsary	Clin-ic
Within village	10.8	24.4	24.7	4.7	18	31.3
<5 Km.	42.7	42.7	51.7	33.6	37.1	53.9
5-9 Km.	25.5	12.1	8.9	31.6	26.5	6.9
10+ Km.	20.1	14.3	13.8	30.2	18.4	7.5
Don't Know/Missing	0.9	6.6	0.9			
Median Distance	4.4	2.8	2.5	5.8	4.2	2.2

Source: Assam Human Development Report, 2003.

The average availability of facilities in Assam is comparable to the national average as is evident from the table 6. A study of all the available information does suggest that Assam has sufficient facilities, even in rural areas. In some hill districts, the number of sub centres is actually more than the norms set by the Government. There is however an inadequacy of Community Health Centres (CHCs). Some additional Community and Primary Health Centres are under construction, and more are planned. There are imbalances though, between rural and urban areas, and the efficacy of infrastructure in rural, especially remote areas is much less than desired. Private health care institutions are increasing in urban areas. Towns and cities are, however, already beneficiaries of better infrastructure and services from the Governmental system. These imbalances need to be corrected by an effort to improve the availability and quality of services in rural areas.

Accessibility is an important element in utilization. According to NFHS-1, 86 percent of villages did have a health facility within a 5 km. radius. However while the provisioning and accesses are relatively good, the utilization rate is low. The bed occupancy in CHCs was only 51 percent, and the average length of stay was 1.9 days. This indicates underutilisation and inefficient use of scarce resources. Indoor patients prefer to go to District hospitals or Medical College hospitals. At the district level the bed occupancy was as high as 92.5 percent, and the average length of stay was 5.88 days. People do not necessarily visit the facilities, even if they are available. While this may be due to a variety of reasons - credibility loss, poor care and attention, amount of time taken, absence of medicines and sometimes absence of doctors - it has important policy implications. It suggests that it may not be sufficient merely to provide hospital infrastructure: what is required is to make people use the facilities. This will entail considerable work in the community through NGOs, in an attempt to change prevailing attitudes to doctors and medical facilities provided by the Government. While the access to health facilities has improved considerably, especially in recent years, there are remote, riverine and hill areas that continue to have problems of accessibility. For riverine *chars*, the State Government has initiated a scheme of boat clinics. Similarly, mobile clinics have been started in hill areas.

Sanitation and Water Supply

Sanitation and water supply are two important components of well-being and good health. Poor sanitation and water supply leads to ill health and disease.

Sanitation

Sanitation connotes a comprehensive package of measures relating to sanitary disposal of human excreta, liquid and solid waste disposal, food and home sanitation, personal and environmental hygiene, safe water storage and handling practices. Improved health is the principal economic and social benefit of investment in sanitation schemes. Use of sanitary toilets has potential health benefits not only for the households that use them but also for their neighbours. According to the 1991 Census Report, combined (rural and urban) access to toilet facilities in Assam was 37.43 percent, higher than the all India access of 23.70 percent. In rural

Assam, 30.53 percent of households have toilet facilities. The figure for rural Assam is substantially higher than the all India figure of 9.48 percent. In urban Assam, 86.06 percent households had access to a toilet facility. The urban access is also higher than the all India access, of 63.85 percent. There are wide variations across the districts. The districts with the highest percentage of population with access to toilet facilities were Karimganj, (73.17 percent), Cachar (63.27 percent) and Hailakandi (60.97 percent). In Kokrajhar, Dhemaji, Darrang and Nalbari less than 20 percent of the population had access to a toilet facility. Only about 30 percent of the population in Jorhat and Sibsagar had access to toilets.

Rural Sanitation

Rural sanitation programmes in Assam have been undertaken under NREP (beginning in 1986) and have subsequently been taken under the *Indira Awas Yojana*. A Centrally sponsored Rural Sanitation Program (CRSP) for people belonging to Scheduled Castes and Scheduled Tribes, and those below the poverty line was launched in October 1986. This was later included under the 20-point Program. Sanitation programs have also been undertaken under the Minimum Needs Program (MNP) but the coverage is low. One reason for the low coverage of sanitation programs is lack of user commitment to sanitation, compared to that for water. Information, education and communication (IEC) activities have received comparatively less attention from the Government than the construction of toilet facilities.

Urban Sanitation

Urban sanitation consists of the disposal of domestic sewage, solid waste disposal and drainage. In Assam, there is no sanitary sewage disposal (sewerage scheme) facility under any urban local body, including Guwahati city. Sanitary disposal of human excreta is a basic service. Low cost technologies, which are cheaper to construct and require less water to function, are being promoted in Assam. The operation and maintenance (O and M) of these systems can be carried out largely by the users, with the government being responsible in the urban areas for the infrastructure to evacuate the waste beyond the household premises. A low cost sanitation program was started in 58 towns in Assam in 1980-81, but the success has been limited. Loans were given for constructing sanitary toilets but the recovery has been slow. In 1990-91, another low cost sanitation program was initiated, once again with partial success. The inadequate performance of sanitary schemes is partly due to the fact that the user community is often not consulted before a decision is made regarding the kind of system being introduced. Neither are proper feasibility studies undertaken. User preferences need to be taken into account and sufficient provision made for operation and maintenance expenses, if sanitation schemes are to work.

Water Supply

Water is a critical resource. Managing available water efficiently is a challenge. With its high rainfall and river systems, Assam has adequate availability of water. However, access to safe drinking water continues to be low, with less than 50 percent of the population being covered. The quality of water is an important issue. Sewage waste has been identified as a major pollutant in Assam.

Coverage and spread

Access to safe drinking water in Assam is substantially less than the national average. The population in Assam with access to safe drinking water is 45.86 percent, compared to the all India figure of 62.30 percent. Households with access to safe drinking water stand at 43.28 percent in rural areas and 64.07 percent in urban areas. At the all India level 55.54 percent of people in rural areas have access to safe drinking water, while in urban areas, 81.38 percent of people have access to safe water. The main source of safe water supply in Assam is ground water, which accounts for 88 percent of the supply. Only 12 percent of the water comes from surface sources. The water supply is either piped through distribution networks or there are spot sources like hand pumps and ring wells. Drinking water in the small towns in the Brahmaputra Valley comes largely from ground water. The common source of water in the towns of the Barak Valley is river water (surface source) because of unfavourable hydro-geological conditions. During the dry months of April, May and June, there is insufficient drinking water in both rural and urban areas. Data for access to safe drinking water supply shows that the highest coverage (73.66 percent) is in Tinsukia district, followed by Dibrugarh, Nagaon and Morigaon districts. There is significant inter district variation and a noticeable rural-urban gap. People in Kokrajhar district have the lowest access to safe drinking water. Less than 10 percent of the total households are covered, and even in urban areas the coverage is as low at 13.58 percent. Karimganj, Hailakandi, Cachar and Bongaigaon also have low access rates of around 20 percent. Urban access in three out of these four districts is however more than 75 percent, illustrating once again the rural–urban gap.

Rural Water Supply

According to the 1991 Census there are 24,624 revenue villages in Assam, with 70,669 habitations or hamlets, spread over the 23 districts. A status survey conducted in 1993-94, at the instance of the Rajiv Gandhi National Drinking Water Mission (RGNDWM), Government of India, showed that less than half the rural population had access to regular water supply. A population of 87.63 lakhs in 32,547 habitations has access to water supply, at the approved norm of 401pcd (liters per capita, per day). Another 24,462 habitations with a population of 83.27 lakhs have partial access. The Public Health and Engineering Department (PHED) is largely responsible for the implementation of water supply programs. Community Development blocks also takes up small water supply facilities such as those from spot sources. Rural water supply is funded under the Minimum Need Program (MNP). The efforts of the State Government are supplemented by the Central Government through the Accelerated Rural Water Supply Program (ARWSP) and additional plans for the hill districts.

Urban Water Supply

In the State, 64.04 percent of urban households have access to safe water drinking water. However the supply is inadequate and per capita water availability is below the required level in most towns, except in the six towns where the Municipal Services are under Oil and Railway managements. The Assam Urban Water Supply and Sewerage Board (AUWS and SB), established in 1989, is vested with the responsibility of providing water supply to the towns of Assam, except in Guwahati city. (In Guwahati, it supplies water to a part of the city). It has taken up 27 water supply projects for 25 towns. In addition to these, water supply projects in 14 other towns, which were implemented by the PHED, are still being maintained and operated by PHED.

IV: Concluding Remarks and Policy Suggestions

The above analysis shows that there is room for improvement in the health status in Assam. The rate of change of indicators such as CBR, IMR and CDR is lower than the national average. The rise in the CDR in the 1996-99 periods requires serious examination and an attempt to understand the reasons behind this disturbing trend. There is a need to improve the quality of data, the periodicity of its collection and the extent of its coverage. The collection of data, especially disaggregated data, is important; its analysis is even more consequential. Essential to enhancing the efficacy and efficiency of health care systems and services is objective and continuing analysis. More attention needs to be paid to this aspect, to lay the basis for objective and timely changes in policies, in schemes, focus and territorial coverage. Linked to this is the need to prioritize. Resource and infrastructure constraints make it even more imperative to do so, to target those areas and diseases that impact more significantly on the overall health status of the State and its people. Meriting priority attention are the imbalances. The rural-urban gap is significant, and in some cases it is widening. Given the fact of relatively low urbanization, it is clear that the overall health profile and status can only be improved with vastly more attention to the rural sector. In this context, access and utilization are extremely important. Within this framework, the emphasis needs to be on those districts which are most inadequately served, and within districts, on those blocks that have less than adequate access to health services, qualitatively and quantitatively. There are also population groups that have health indicators substantially lower than the State average, for example tea garden workers, tribal women and women belonging to the minority community. Targeted programs that address the particular impediments that these groups face are required, if their health is to be improved. These could be designed and implemented with the participation of the community, to have a good chance of success. The third gap, which in fact encompasses both the earlier gaps, is the gender gap, apparent in life expectancy and maternal mortality rates. Rural women, especially those living in remote and inaccessible areas are among the most disadvantaged groups and have some of the lowest health indicators. The non-utilization of hospital facilities is another important issue. Even where adequate physical infrastructure exists, medical services may be unavailable (no doctors, for example) or deficient (poor quality).

The State Government could have a closer look at the implementation of various measures such as supply of consumables, construction of rural infrastructure and manpower availability in the different health institutions. It is also necessary to assess whether the structural changes brought in the government system have been useful in achieving the broad outputs intended. For example, the construction of various health units in the rural areas should have resulted in reduction of infant mortality, crude death rates and higher number of institutional deliveries, but this has not happened. The reasons for this need to be examined and effective strategies devised for the future. The private sector is expanding rapidly and in the absence of any controls/ regulations the health care that is provided is often substandard. The Government has enacted the Health Establishment Act to control the unplanned proliferation of private hospitals in the State but the rules under the Act are yet to be framed. In fact, all over India, the enforcement of laws relating to control of health care in private hospitals has been poor and Assam is no exception. Laws relating to enforcement of standards in manufacture of drugs and pharmaceuticals have also not been effectively implemented. These areas require attention as well. Undoubtedly resources are important, and the State needs to find the resources that would enable the expansion of the health care system, and allow for its efficient functioning. There are indications that the State would continue to be under fiscal stress, especially in the short term. One possible alternative is to find innovative yet sensitive ways to raise resources from within the sector, through a carefully structured, if necessary cross-subsidized, system of charges for services. Given the fact that private health care systems are expanding, and these provide services at fees certainly higher than in the public domain, it is likely that an increase in revenue generation from health services, at least from people, who can afford to pay, is possible.

The provisioning in sanitation and water supply is less than optimum and there is a substantial rural-urban gap. More resources are needed and mobilization and motivation of the community is required. While the Government does have the primary responsibility in providing services like sanitation and safe drinking water, past experience has shown that the maintenance of these services is inadequate and in some cases schemes are not working at all. The involvement of the user communities both at the program stage and in its implementation is vital to the success of future programs. Water should be managed as a socio-economic good rather than treating it as a free commodity. The key to the success of water supply projects is to ensure sustainability, complemented by a partnership approach. The Government could consider adopting a demand driven approach on the basis of desire and capacity to pay of the user communities. An integrated approach for water supply and sanitation is essential to maximize benefits of improved health of the community. Water must be used in an optimal way, in order to realize potential health and socio-economic benefits.

References

Government of Assam (2003): Assam Human Development Report 2003, Planning and Development Department.

Government of India (2001): National Human Development Report 2001, Planning Commission, New Delhi.

Haq, Mahbub ul (2003): The Birth of the Human Development Index, In Sakiko Fukuda-Parr and A.K. Shiva Kumar (Eds.) Readings in Human Development, Oxford University Press, New York, pp.127-137, First published in Mahbub ul Haq, Reflections on Human Development, 1995, Chapter 4, Oxford University Press.

Reserve Bank of India (2006): State Finance, RBI, Mumbai.

Sen, Amartya (1999): Development as Freedom, Oxford University Press, Oxford.

Sen, Amartya (2003a): Development as Capability Expansion, In Sakiko Fukuda-Parr and A.K. Shiva Kumar (eds.) Readings in Human Development, Oxford University Press, New York. First published in Journal of Development Planning, 1989, No.19, pp.41-58.

Sen, Amartya (2003b): Human Capital and Human Capability, In Sakiko Fukuda-Parr and A.K. Shiva Kumar (Eds.) Readings in Human Development, Oxford University Press, New York. First published in World Development, 1997, 25(12): 1959-1961.

12

Trends and Patterns of Health Expenditure in Andhra Pradesh

T. Subba Lakshmi[1]

I. Motivations

Development of human resources is always been a prime objective of both developing and developed nations. It has been mention in the economic survey of India that the "human development is the ultimate goal of our development and is also crucial for the long run success of economic reforms. Sound, long term development of social services reforms such as education, health is a crucial for sustaining economic growth. According to the human capital theory expenditure on schooling, health, training, migration etc constitute investment in human beings, which enhance the capabilities of the people. Among all other measures [2]health plays superior role in the process of human resources development. Health care expenditure is a very necessary social expenditure for any country. Like any other social expenditure, health expenditure requires a significant contribution from the government.

The ability of the health system of a country to meet the emerging challenges and cater effectively and adequately to the health needs of the population hinges crucially on the financing mechanisms of public health services. Since, public financing of health care has to be met out of scarce public resources, the financing pattern of government needs to be reviewed and analyzed to facilitate better understanding and prioritize allocation optimally. In this connection, the objective of the paper is to study the trend and pattern of health expenditure in Andhra Pradesh, India. We are motivated to conduct this study because of the following reasons. Firstly, the issue of financing health care has assumed greater

[1] M. Phil Scholar,Department of Economics, Pondicherry University, Puducherry

significance in the developing world mainly due to the changing role of the state in providing health care (Guruswamy, et al, 2008). Secondly, the analysis of health care expenditures in general has been a topic of research and discussion in recent times globally. Health is being state subject in India and therefore, analysis of health expenditures by states assumes greater significance (Bhat and Nishant, 2004).

Third, little attention has been given to how individual state performs over time and the role of state government policy in determining state level performance by the researchers, government, policy makers and development planners (Ahluwalia, 2000). Analyzing national expenditures is meaningless, unless the state scenario is simultaneously analyzed. The studies of this nature provide essential information for health policy planning.

The paper has five sections. The motivations behind the study along with the objectives are presented above in section I. section II reviews important relevant literature relating the study. The database and methodologies are explained in section III. The results are analyzed in section IV. The conclusion and policy suggestions are presented in the last section.

II. Review of Literature

Reddy (1992) made an attempt to quantify the total resources devoted to health care in India in the year 1991. He attempts to find out that whether spending pattern across states is on the right lines and in which categories of expenditure influence health status more positively. For that purpose simple correlation matrix and percentages are employed in this study. The author revealed that the expenditure on medical and public health, family welfare, nutrition, water supply and sanitation, social security and welfare are help to improve health of the people directly.

By keeping Infant Mortality Rate (IMR) as a health indicator, he tests the influence of these variables on it. Health expenditure and health indicators are looked in terms of per capita expenditures and IMR. The degree of relationship is lowest in case of water supply and sanitation. He conclude that it is obvious that per capita expenditures hence to be increased to improve health status. But increase in per capita expenditure in India is not on resources and economic backwardness. So he finally concludes that government had to choose program schemes that reallocate the existing resources in a proper manner.

Bansal (1999) examined the status of health financing in India. He analyzed health expenditure of central and state governments, variations in per capita income and the relationship between health status and health financing. To find out whether per capita expenditure on health care truly affects the health status of a population, a health development index was constructed. The results revealed that health expenditure shows an increasing trend in all states and there is a wide interstate variation in allocation of per capita resources to health care. He finally revealed that increasing of health expenditure is mainly due to salary and non- salary components and not because of higher share of health expenditure in state domestic product.

Bhat and Jain (2004) examined the relationship between public health care expenditure and gross domestic product in 14 Indian states from 1990 to 2002. Besides an attempt was made to estimate the income elasticity of health expenditure and find out the target ratio of health expenditure on gross domestic product in these states. The central sponsored schemes like family welfare programs and water and sanitation programs are not included in this study. To estimate the relationship between income and health care expenditure they have taken real gross domestic product (GSDP) for income and real per capita state public health expenditure (PHCE) respectively. Adaptive expectation model was used to estimate the targeted ratio of health expenditure. They showed that at state level, government have target of allocation only 0.43 per cent of state gross domestic product to health and medical care even the income elasticity is 0.68.

Rout (2007) seeks to examine the pattern of public financing of health care in 14 major non- special category states of India during 1990-91 to 2005-06. It is observed that out of 14 states, 13 states have reduced the share of budgetary allocations to health sector during the post crisis period. The poor states particularly Bihar, Uttar Pradesh which have a significantly lower human development index in comparison to Kerala and Gujarat have reduced the health expenditure more. The average share is 5.68 per cent during the study period against 3.08 per cent for Haryana which is the lower in the country. The high income states like Punjab, Haryana and Gujarat allocate relatively lower share of state expenditure towards the health sector in comparison to poor states like Bihar, Orissa and Uttar Pradesh.

The regional inequality measured in terms of coefficient of variation among different states is widening over the years. During the process of reforms the gap between the poor and rich states is rising indicating the poor states are not in a position to allocate more and more resources towards health sector. There exists a negative correlation between ratio of health care expenditure to Gross State Domestic Product (GSDP) and GSDP for 14 major states of the country during the period of analysis. So increasing GSDP does not contribute to the rise in health care expenditure in case of Indian states. He suggested that it is not the allocation alone rather the service delivery mechanism may be improved to translate the outlays to health outcomes. The long route of accountability that exists in the service delivery chain may be broken. In order to improve the quality of delivery of services, the states may put efforts to transfer power to the Panchayati Raj Institutions (PRIs). The states are required to design policies to increase efficiencies of public expenditure and maximize the benefits of every rupee spent for public purpose. This needs well integrated policies and political commitment.

Guruswamy et.al, (2008) examined the levels, trends and patterns of public expenditure on health during 1995 to 2006 in India, both at national and state levels. They found that public expenditure on health as a proportion of GDP has remained stagnant over the years and revenue expenditure accounting for the larger share. Among the states, the relatively poor ones were found to be spending more on health, both per capita and as a proportion of GSDP, compared to the richer states. It was seen that expenditure on health by the state had not grown adequately along the path of overall economic prosperity and the private out-of pocket expenditure seemed to be on the rise. And the author suggested it is imperative that government should increase the finances allotted to health sector by giving priority to alternative health financing options (community based financing of health care, employed based insurance schemes and private health insurance as risk pooling mechanisms) from the perspective of equity as well as to ensure risk free, unbiased access to health care for all.

Mishra et. al. (2003) examines the reasons of the poor health scenario in India and the challenges in the provision of health care in India. The study makes several recommendations relating to the control of communicable disease, the rising threat of non-communicable diseases, reduction of infant and maternal mortality, the emerging thereat of the proliferation of HIV/AIDS infection, financing of health care systems (both public and private), drug policy and regulations, health research, and Indian systems of medicine. Keeping in view the huge inequalities in the present system, the larger proportion of the population still leaving in abject poverty and the states, special responsibility to protect the vulnerable population, an overarching concern about the health care of the poor underpins the entire report.

Mahendra and Mooij (2002) examined trends in the social sector expenditure in the central and state budgets for 1990-1991 to 2000-2001 and looked at several aspects including overall levels of allocation, expenditure on health and education and interstate disparities. The study has included social services as well rural development expenditure in the analysis. It is found that taking centre and states expenditure together the share of social sector expenditure as a proportion of gross domestic product has not increased during the reform period, except in 1999-2000 and it was lower in 1980s and 1990s. As a proportion of total public expenditure, the share of social sector has increased since the mid 1990s and it was higher in the second half of the 1990s than it was in the late 1980s. The expenditure on health and education has declined in 1990s for states. The study suggested that there is an obvious need to step up social sector expenditure and improve fund utilization.

Sharriff et al (2002) made an attempt to analyze trends in public expenditures on social sector and poverty alleviation programs from 1990-91. A considerable proportion of these expenditures is undertaken by the states but the central share seems to be increasing over time. It is found that expenditure on social sector schemes is increasing in real terms but mainly through increased expenditure of the central government. The state governments seem to be easing out of their constitutional commitment to sustain programs in the social sectors. There are large inter sectoral reallocations of funds in the poverty alleviation sectors.

III. Database and Methodology

The study is purely based on secondary data, conducted in Andhra Pradesh in 2009.The sample observations are 21 years. The reference period of the study is 1985-2006. The required information obtained from Handbook of Statistics on State Government Finances, State Finance: A Study of Budget, Various issues, Reserve Bank of India. Handbook of Statistics on Indian Economy is also verified.

In order to examine the trend and pattern of health expenditure (in absolute terms) of Andhra Pradesh, geometric mean, ratios and percentage methods are employed. The average annual growth rate (per cent) is calculated for revenue and capital heads of health expenditure. The average annual growth rate is also calculated for total health expenditure to know the overall percentage change in total health expenditure over the study period. Besides, health expenditure as a percentage of total social service expenditure and total government expenditure and as a percentage of gross state domestic products is also calculated.

IV. Findings

The state government generally owns the health system in India. Expenditure on health care by the state government can be broadly categorized into revenue and capital heads of account. Revenue expenditure mostly comprises recurrent expenditure on salaries, supply of equipment and drugs, public health programs, medical education and training and general operating expenses. Capital expenditure involves non-recurrent expenditure on physical assets and infrastructure, and on-time capital investment in disease control and public health programs.

Table 1 shows the trend and pattern of health expenditure of Andhra Pradesh under economic classification from the period 1985-86 to 2005-06.In absolute terms, the total health expenditure in Andhra Pradesh shows an increasing trend. It was increased from Rs.12, 865 in 1985-86 to Rs.47, 705 in 1995-96. Further, it has increased to Rs.1, 28,336 lakhs in 2005. Thus, in Andhra Pradesh, the total health expenditure has increased to 9.975 lakhs higher in 2005-06. Compared to 1995-96 the total health expenditure has increased by Rs.80631 higher in 2005-06 i.e., it has increased from Rs.47705 lakhs in 2000-01 to Rs.1, 28,336 lakhs in 2005-06. This increase in the expenditure indicates the commitment and determination of government effort to improve the health of masses, to provide medical facilities in backward areas of state and to create a healthy and morbidity free population.

Overall, as a percentage of social services expenditure has come down by 2 per cent and as a percentage of total government revenue expenditure has come down by 1 per cent and the average annual growth (per cent) of revenue expenditure has come down by around 12 per cent over the period of the study in Andhra Pradesh.

Though revenue expenditure shows an increasing trend in absolute terms, it has remained stagnant as a percentage of both expenditure on social services and government total revenue expenditure.

A number of reasons could be possible for such divergent trends in revenue expenditure of Andhra Pradesh. Due to fiscal prudence in recent years, there has been some effort in health financing policy to reduce excess expenditure on health involving salaries for health manpower and other non-essential recurring expenses.

Table 3 shows trends in capital expenditure on medical and public health of Andhra Pradesh. It also shows capital expenditure as a percentage of expenditure on social services and government total revenue expenditure.

Table 3: Trends in Capital Expenditure on Medical and Public Health in Andhra Pradesh

Year	Capital Expenditure (in lakhs)	Average annual Growth of Capital Expenditure (per cent)	As a Percentage of Social Services Expenditure	As a Percentage of Total Capital Expenditure
1985-86	241		5.644	0.380
1990-91	299	4.41	7.250	0.278
1995-96	119	-16.82	2.622	0.032
2000-01	4794	109.42	16.896	0.949
2005-06	549	-35.17	3.521	0.003

Source: Handbook of Statistics on State Government Finances, State Finances: The Study of Budgets, RBI, Various Issues

Capital expenditure on medical and public health has also been irregular in both in absolute and in terms of percentage change over the period of study. Similarly as a percentage of expenditure on social services it has shown massive fluctuations and as a percentage of total capital expenditure has stagnant around 0.1 over the period of the study.

Figure 2: Trends in Capital Expenditure on Medical and Public Health in Andhra Pradesh

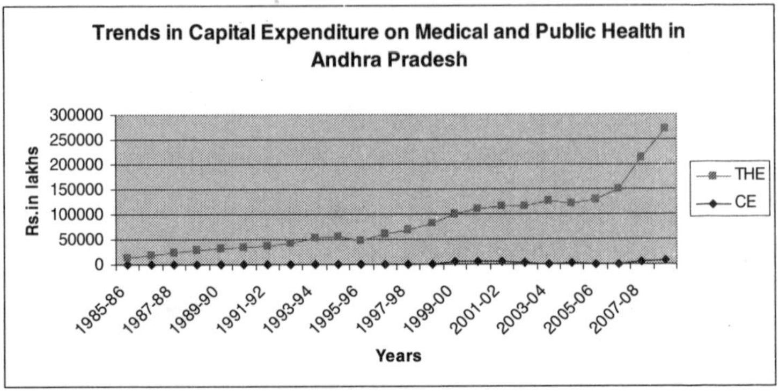

The average annual growth (per cent) of capital expenditure has negative in 1995-96 and it has come up dramatically to 109.42 per cent in 2000-01. As capital expenditure on medical and public health largely includes infrastructural investments, such a pattern of investment may be due to the fact that it has accounted higher percentage during the study period.

Overall, the trends in health expenditure under both revenue and capital heads do not reveal any clear pattern. Moreover, revenue expenditure (i.e. payment of salary) accounted for higher growth (per cent), but capital expenditure (basic physical infrastructure) was not to the extent of revenue expenditure in total health expenditure in Andhra Pradesh. This indicates that new investment in public health sector is almost ceased from 1990-91 to 2000-01. As a result of this the supply of health care in rural and remote areas of the state are far from satisfactory leading to a large scale rural-urban dichotomy. The resources allocated by the government of Andhra Pradesh favour only the urban health facilities.

From the Table 4 it is clear that total health expenditure has increasing trend in absolute terms. It has increased by Rs.115531 in 2005-06 compared to 1985-86 but it has accounted for around 1.11

times over the period of study. Total health expenditure as a percentage of total social service expenditure has stagnant at 10 per cent. Similarly as a percentage of total government expenditure has come down from 5.01 in 1990-91 to 3.33 in 1995-96 and it has increased slightly to 3.77 in 2000-01 and it has declined drastically to 0.641 in 2005-06. Health expenditure as a percentage of GSDP has increased from 0.90 in 1985-86 to 1.04 in 1990-91 and it has come down to 0.82 in 1995-96. Further it has increased to 1.37 in 2000-01 and slightly decreased to 1.22 in 2005-06.

Table 4: Trends in Total Health Expenditure

Year	Total Health Expenditure (THE) (in lakhs)	Average annual Growth of THE (per cent)	As a percentage of Total Social Service Expenditure	As a percentage of Total Government Expenditure	As a percentage of GSDP
1985-86	12,865	-	10.747	3.769	0.909
1990-91	32,979	20.72	15.281	5.011	1.042
1995-96	47705	7.66	10.113	3.335	0.823
2000-01	106126	17.34	12.759	3.774	1.376
2005-06	128336	3.87	10.422	0.641	1.220

Source: Handbook of Statistics on State Government Finances, State Finances: The Study of Budgets, RBI, Various Issues.

Overall, as a percentage of total social service expenditure as well as of total government expenditure has come down by around 3 percent and 1 percent respectively. As percentage of GSDP it has stagnant at 1 percent. The reason for this is that health is virtually absent from public debates and democratic politics in India.

Overall, the annual average growth (per cent) of total health expenditure has come down to around 14 per cent during the period of study. It shows that the state is running out of lack of resources towards financing health sector.

Figure 3: Health Expenditure and GSDP in Andhra Pradesh

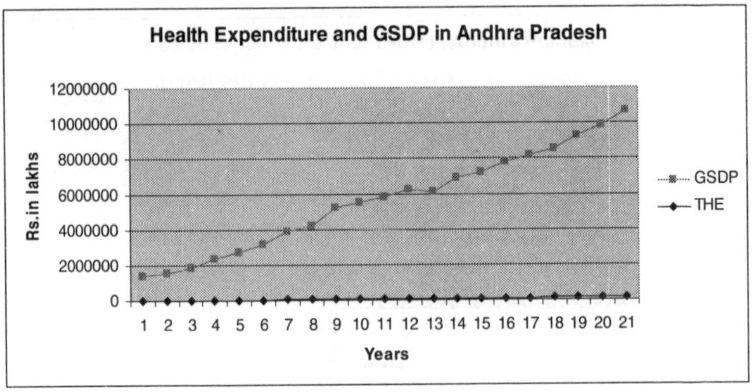

V. Conclusion and Policy Implications

From the above analysis it has to conclude that the health expenditure in absolute terms has increased remarkably during the study period in Andhra Pradesh. However, health expenditure in relative terms showed a mixed trend. The share of total health expenditure as a percentage of total government expenditure and social service expenditure in Andhra Pradesh showed a decreasing trend and stagnant over the study period. The share of revenue expenditure on total expenditure is high in Andhra Pradesh whereas the capital expenditure is too low. Even after implementing economic reforms the revenue expenditure in health sector is still high in Andhra Pradesh and the capital expenditure is on an around the same position. As a result of this supply of health care in rural and remote areas of the state are far away from satisfactory leading to a large scale rural-urban dichotomy. The resources allocated by the government of Andhra Pradesh favour only the urban health facilities. The percentage spending of economic growth on health is around one percent in Andhra Pradesh.

To improve the health status of the people extreme poverty and hunger may be eradicated which is the first goal of the Millennium Development Goals (MDGs). The health planners and administrators may be involved in the planning process of the government to reduce poverty and adopt policies for more equitable distribution of income. They can also recommend to have a specific health tax (an earmarked or so-called hypothecated tax) devoted to health care.

Again spending more on health services does not buy the better health. It needs an efficient management, use of resources and strong political will.

We are aware of the fact that even though health expenditure increases with the income of the state, the resources towards health sector depends to some extent on the socioeconomic and political situations prevailing in the state and local level. Therefore, government should take initiatives to find out additional sources of finance which are broad based, sustainable and suitable to the socioeconomic situations of the rural population. The principle of equality for opportunity for access to services on the basis of need and equal risk, irrespective of ability to pay should be followed.

References

Ahluwalia, M.S. (2000): Economic Performance of States in Post Reforms Period, *Economic and Political Weekly*, 35(19): 1637-48.

Bansal, R.D. (1999): Health Financing in India: Priorities, Issues, Interstate Variations and Challenges, *Health and Population Perspectives and Issues*, 22(3-4): 123-132.

Bhat, R., and Bhat, N. (2004): *Analysis of Public Expenditure on Health Using State Level Data*, Indian Institute of Management, Ahmedabad.

Gupta, Sanjeev (2001): *Public Spending on health care and the Poor*, IMF Working Paper-WP/01/127, IMF, Washington D.C., www.imf.org/external/pubs/ft/wp/2001/wp1127.pdf, accessed on 5 th July 2009.

Guruswamy, M., Sumit, M., and Papiya, M (2008): Public Financing of Health Services in India: An Analysis of Central and State Government Expenditure, *Journal of Health Management*, 10(1): 49-85.

Mahendra Dev, S and Jos Mooij (2002): Social Sector Expenditures in the 1990s, Analysis of Central and State Budgets, *Economic and Political Weekly*, 37(9): 853-866.

Mishra, Rajiv, Rachel Chatterjee and Sujatha Rao (2003): *India Health Report*, Oxford University Press, New Delhi.

Reddy, K. N. (1992): *Health Expenditure in India*, Working Paper No. 14, NIPFP, New Delhi.

Rout, S. K. (2008): Fiscal Reforms and Health Care Spending: An Inter-state Analysis, In A. K. Thakur and A. M. D. Salam

(Eds), *Economics of Education and Health in India*, Deep and Deep Publications, New Delhi.

Sheriff, A, Prabir Ghosh and S.K Mondal (2002): State Adjusted Public Expenditure on Social Sector and Poverty Alleviation Programmes, *Economic and Political Weekly*, 37(8): 767-787.

13

Infrastructure and Human Development in India

Narayan Chandra Nayak[1]

I. Introduction

In course of time, there has been a paradigm shift in the approach towards economic development from growth to human development. Human development approach encompasses three broad dimensions namely income, health and education while putting a thrust on enlarging people's choices and raising their standards of living (HDR, 2009). Human development goes beyond the realm of mere income growth to human capabilities and freedom, empowerment and social inclusion. Considered as an alternative development paradigm, human development is stated to have emerged out of the continued failure of gross domestic product (GDP) growth in ensuring improved quality of life ((Morris and McAlpin 1982; Mazumdar, 1990). To be precise, human development deals with the intrinsic values and not the instrumental values (Spence and Smith, 2009).

In developing countries, even today, half of the population lack access to basic sanitation. About a billion of population is denied access to safe drinking water. As many as 34 million people live with HIV/AIDS. About 30000 children under the age of five die everyday from preventable diseases. About a billion of people of the developing countries are illiterate and as many as 325 million children of school going age are out of schools (Murugan and Swaminathan, 2002). All these reaffirm the need for treating human development as an urgent and critical area of alternative development paradigm.

In the pursuit of achieving high human development, provision of infrastructure, both in quantity and quality, *inter alia* is said to

[1] Associate Professor, Department of Humanities and Social Sciences (HSS), Indian Institute of Technology (IIT), Kharagpur, West Bengal, India

play a pivotal role. It may be ascertained that infrastructure has the potential to not only determine the overall productivity and development of a country's economy but it can also help improve the quality of life of its citizens (Mody, 1997). It is suggested that infrastructure supports the processes of growth on which much of poverty reduction depends and also helps the poor access basic services which can improve their lives and income opportunities. To be specific, infrastructure can create a virtuous cycle through the provision of services leading to growth and then poverty reduction and again provision of services and so on (GOM, 2007). There are several studies that establish positive impact of infrastructure on economic growth and productivity (Straub, 2008; Aschauer, 2000; Macdonald, 2008; Devarajan, Swaroop and Zou, 1993). There are, however, attempts and evidences of infrastructure facilities improving the quality of life (Baldwin and Dixon, 2008; Aschauer, 1998), health and educational attainments (Agénor and Moreno-Dodson, 2006), and regional development (Nijkamp, 1986), thereby contributing to human development.

Infrastructure is defined as "physical framework of facilities through which goods and services are provided to the public" (Khader, 1998, p 13). It is an intermediate input of production (Pillai, 2008). As Hirschman (1958) puts it, it includes those services without which primary, secondary and tertiary activities cannot function. It is a supporting structure that facilitates production, distribution and consumption of goods and services in the economy. Economists have introduced this term into the literature of development economics to use it interchangeably with 'Social Overhead Capital' (Youngson, 1967), which results in facilities and services, and is usually provided free or at subsidized charges to the direct users. The World Development Report (WDR) 1994, which treats infrastructure for development as its main theme, defines infrastructure as an 'umbrella term' encompassing activities that share technical features such as economies of scale and spillover effects from users to non-users (World Bank, 1994, p 2).

The infrastructure required in accelerating the pace of economic development constitutes both economic and social elements. The economic infrastructure is that which directly facilitates the production process. Transport, communication, energy, irrigation, banking etc. are the services comprising of economic infrastructure. The social infrastructure, on the other hand, has an indirect impact on the production process by developing an efficient and productive human resource. It includes education, health, housing, water supply, sewage disposal, sanitation etc. All these help in the attainment of higher growth and also improvement in the quality of life of the people as well. To argue in favour of the latter, it can be stated that better transport and communications provide improved access to health services. Electrification improves the quality of life including health services. Road connectivity to school may increase school attendance. There are evidences of separate toilets for boys and girls improving girls' enrolment (World Bank, 1997). Especially, social infrastructure has a much prominent role to play as compared to its counterpart.

Given the above backdrop, the present paper attempts to analyse the scenario of infrastructure in India and its constituent states. Besides, it makes an account of the level of human development the country and its various states have achieved and draw implications thereon. Accordingly, the remainder of the paper is organized as follows. In section II, a comparative picture of infrastructure and human development across major states of India is presented. Section III draws implications of the findings and concludes the study.

II. Infrastructure and Human Development in India

This section makes an account of the infrastructure scenario in India and in its 15 major constituent states. Analyzing the scenario for the entire country, it may be said that India's progress in infrastructure front is far from satisfactory. According to a study undertaken by Kumar and De (2008), India's rank was recorded to be 54th amongst 104 East-Asian countries in infrastructure index. The aspects of infrastructure covered under their study in the formulation of the index were transport, information and communication technology (ICT), energy and banking. Situation with regard to social infrastructure like education and health is no better. While over the years, significant improvement has been registered in the creation of such infrastructure, availability at a reasonable distance continues to remain a far cry.

Regarding availability of educational facilities, it can be said that since schools up to middle level are exclusively meant for young children only, their benefits can be properly availed of provided schools are located within the villages. Ironically, according to the 58th round of the NSS (Table 1), about one-third of the villages were still devoid of the pre-primary schools within villages and about 28 per cent of villages did not have primary schools within. Only 29 per cent of villages had middle school facilities within and meager 12 per cent had secondary schools within. Added to this, only another 15 per cent of villages had availability of schools within a distance of 2 km. Table 2 provides the pace of change in the availability of educational facilities that the country has witnessed over the period 1991-2002 (between 47th round of the NSS and 58th round). As far as pre-primary schooling is concerned, there has been a phenomenal rise in the availability in these years. Despite that, the attainment of the goalpost remains a challenge. As compared to this, at the subsequent level, the increase in schooling facilities (about 6 per cent at primary and middle level) has been far from satisfactory.

Coming to health infrastructure, the scenario remains by and large equally grim (Table 1). As per the 58th round of the NSS, about 34 per cent of villages had to travel more than 5 km to reach the nearest sub-centre/dispensary during the survey period. Also 54 per cent of villages were more than 5 km away from the nearest Primary Health Centre and 27 per cent were more than 10 km away from that. For 55 per cent of Indian villages, the nearest community health centre/government hospital was found at a distance of at least 10 km away. Private hospitals were awfully scarce, the nearest one being more than 10 km away for 61 per cent of the villages. The medicine shops were found to exist in only 10 per cent of India's villages, while within 2 km for another 13 per cent and within 5 km of another 25 per cent.

With regard to rural road infrastructure, its demand in the country can be better understood by the demand for vehicles. During the period 1990–97, rural roads grew by around 15 per cent, whereas the estimated growth in demand for scooters was 56 per cent, and that of bicycles was 28.5 per cent. However, contrary to the expectations, availability of road infrastructure is, in general, poor for smaller villages with less population (Table 3). As per the Tenth Plan document, there were around 100,000 unconnected habitations with population of more than 500. The average distance from a village to an all-weather road was estimated to be 2 km. On an average, 52 per cent of the people living away from the main village do not have access to all-weather roads (Bery et al. 2004).

As compared to the scenario at the national level, the situation at the state level is far more distressing. This is primarily so because the states are found to experience wide differences in their achievements with regard to infrastructure facilities. While some states have fared remarkably well, there are others which have lagged far behind.

Table 1: Distribution of Villages (per 1000) by their Distance from the Nearest Education and Health-related Facilities

Facility	Within village	Outside the village but at a distance of				
Educational		<2 km	2 km to <5 km	5 km to <10 km	10 km or more	Not recorded
Pre-primary School	665	143	47	14	115	17
Primary	723	162	62	15	25	14
Middle School	289	216	351	78	53	13
Secondary School	119	145	385	200	138	13
Health						
ICDSC (*anganwadi*)	548	113	140	59	125	15
sub-centre/ dispensary	163	160	318	189	156	15
Primary health centre	65	101	278	268	273	14
community/ government hospital	18	37	155	222	553	15
Private hospital	19	38	133	181	614	14
Private clinic/doctor	201	126	246	200	214	13
Medicine shop	103	132	271	217	264	13

Source: Report on Village Facilities, NSS 58th Round, Report No 487, July-December 2002.

Table 2: Comparison of Availability of Educational Facilities between 47th and 58th rounds of NSS

Period	Number of Indian villages (per 1000) having			
	Preprimary school	primary school	Middle school	Secondary school
July-Dec 1991	388	**670**	**242**	**105**
July-Dec 2002	676	**733**	**293**	**121**

Source: Report on Village Facilities, NSS 58th Round, Report No. 487, July-December 2002.

Table 3: Village Connectivity by Size of Village

Population	Connectivity in 1995 (per cent)
<1000	37.5
1000-1500	75.9
>1500	91.7

Source: Bery et al. (2004) as cited in Mahajan, Sahai, and Pasrija (2007).

The present study, in order to compare status of infrastructure across states relies on the data provided by the Centre for Monitoring Indian Economy (CMIE) up to the year 2000 (Profiles of Districts, CMIE, 2000). CMIE has identified eleven important variables under economic and social infrastructure viz. (i) percentage of villages electrified, (ii) railway route length per 100 sq km area, (iii) surfaced road length per 100 sq km area, (iv) unsurfaced road length per 100 sq km area, (v) gross irrigated area as percentage of gross cropped area, (vi) bank branches per lakh population, (vii) post offices per lakh population, (viii) telephone lines per 100 persons, (ix) primary, middle and higher schools per lakh population, (x) primary health centres per lakh population and (xi) hospital beds per lakh population. It clubs the above infrastructural facilities into seven broad categories namely transport, communication, energy, irrigation, banking, educational facilities and health, and assigns weights as 26, 6, 24, 20, 12, 6 and 6 respectively. Accordingly, it computes infrastructure index for each state and union territory.

It is interesting to note from the records of the CMIE that the status of infrastructure facilities varies across states quite significantly (Table 4). For the sake of comparison, only 15 major states have been chosen. Amongst them, Punjab ranks the top followed by Kerala and Tamil Nadu. At the other end, Madhya Pradesh remains at the bottom followed by Rajasthan, Bihar and Orissa.

Table 4: Infrastructure Index across Major States of India

State	Infrastructure Index (Share in per cent)	Rank
Andhra Pradesh	104.01	10
Assam	104.39	9
Bihar	91.31	13
Gujarat	105.33	8
Haryana	133.22	4
Karnataka	106.12	7
Kerala	162.42	2
Maharashtra	106.77	6
Madhya Pradesh	86.66	15
Orissa	101.45	12
Punjab	171.92	1
Rajasthan	87.27	14
Tamil Nadu	145.62	3
Uttar Pradesh	112.04	5
West Bengal	102.09	11

Source: Profile of Districts, Centre for Monitoring Indian Economy, October, 2000.

Going further to analyze state-wise scenario of certain crucial infrastructure services, the situation appears to be decidedly mixed. In respect of roads, telephone connections, villages electrified and bank branches, Kerala, Punjab, Haryana and Tamil Nadu are found to have been consistently doing well. In respect of rail, however, West Bengal tops the list. In primary schooling facilities, Orissa, Assam and Madhya Pradesh are found to have got the maximum attention, thanks to all the efforts in recent years to improve the literacy rates in these states. Madhya Pradesh, Orissa, Rajasthan and

Assam occupy lower ranks in telephone connectivity, banking and electricity (Table 5).

Table 5: Status of Select Individual Infrastructure across Major States of India

State	Road Length in Kilometers (per 100 sq km)		Rail Route Length in Kilometers (per 100 sq km)		Telephone Connections (per 100 persons)	
	2000	Rank	2000	Rank	2000	Rank
Andhra	58.27	10	1.84	10	1.99	8
Assam	87.22	6	3.1	4	0.86	14
Bihar	50.81	11	3.02	6	0.49	15
Gujarat	46.37	12	2.72	8	3.21	5
Haryana	63.71	9	3.42	3	2.63	7
Karnataka	75.09	8	1.59	13	2.79	6
Kerala	374.95	1	2.70	9	4.18	2
Maharashtra	117.61	5	1.80	11	4.10	3
Madhya	45.13	13	1.33	15	1.18	11
Orissa	168.71	2	1.41	14	0.91	13
Punjab	127.78	4	4.25	2	4.59	1
Rajasthan	37.89	14	1.72	12	1.72	9
Tamil Nadu	158.78	3	3.07	5	3.43	4
Uttar Pradesh	86.77	7	3.02	7	1.01	12
West Bengal	19.63	15	4.25	1	1.56	10
INDIA	75.01		1.91		2.15	

contd..

Villages Electrified (per cent)		Bank Branches (per lakh population)		Primary Schools (per lakh population)	
2000	Rank	2000	Rank	2000	Rank
99.92	5	6.51	8	64.49	7
79.97	11	5.14	14	126.69	1
70.85	14	4.96	15	55.88	9
99.44	6	7.68	5	31.14	13

96.72	8	7.48	6	30.41	14
98.51	7	9.13	3	84.21	4
100.00	1	10.15	2	21.62	15
100.00	2	6.76	7	46.33	12
94.37	9	5.68	11	106.38	3
69.86	15	6.11	10	119.17	2
100.00	3	10.69	1	55.52	10
88.56	10	6.25	9	67.52	5
100.00	4	7.79	4	50.59	11
77.20	13	5.24	13	58.06	8
77.21	12	5.44	12	65.59	6
85.95		6.65		69.94	

Source: Profile of Districts, Centre for Monitoring Indian Economy, October, 2000.

Table 6: Number of Villages having Electricity Connection per 1000, and their Distribution by Purpose of Availability

States	Number of villages having electricity per 1000 villages		
	Connections	Street lights only	Household use only
Andhra Pradesh	780	15	15
Assam	554	10	787
Bihar	518	14	382
Gujarat	1000	-	137
Haryana	1000	-	70
Karnataka	1000	45	5
Kerala	1000	15	9
Madhya Pradesh	942	21	160
Maharashtra	871	23	21
Orissa	507	25	616
Punjab	944	-	63
Rajasthan	887	1	151
Tamil Nadu	924	67	
Uttar Pradesh	834	13	159

West Bengal	737	47	391
All India	776	23	236

contd...

Distribution (per 1000) of villages having electricity by purpose of availability of electricity		
Agricultural purpose only	Industrial use only	Two or more of the purposes
-	11	959
-	6	196
50	4	261
2	7	854
-	-	930
-	12	938
7	27	942
19	8	792
-	14	942
-	14	345
-	96	840
182	26	639
1	61	871
52	18	758
16	12	534
29	16	679

Note: In Bihar, the remaining value is non-recorded.
Source: Report on Village Facilities, NSS 58th Round, Report No. 487, July-December 2002.

A further probe into certain crucial aspects of infrastructure reveals the following. With regard to electricity, it is found that till 2002, about one-fourth of the villages of the country were still devoid of electricity (Table 6). Comparing across states, while states like Kerala, Gujarat, Haryana and Karnataka were found to have provided electricity to all their respective villages, the situation in Orissa, Bihar and Assam was found to be very distressing where about 50 per cent of villages were not electrified till 2002. As the NSS suggests, amongst villages with electricity, 23.6 per cent reported that electricity was available for household purposes only, 2.3 per cent for street lights only, 2.9 per cent for agricultural purposes only, and 1.6 per cent for industrial purposes only. Around 68 per cent of the villages which had the facility of electricity reported that it was available for more than one purpose.

In 2002, some source of irrigation was available to about 76 per cent of Indian villages where agriculture was practiced. However, comparing across states, the situation appears to be highly disturbing in two states namely Orissa (28.1 per cent) and Assam (20.1 per cent) (Table 7). As far as sources of drinking water is concerned, in India, during 2002, tube-wells or hand pumps were the major sources of drinking water for 55.1 per cent of villages followed by tap water for 18.5 per cent of villages, wells for 17.6 per cent and tanks or ponds for about 10 per cent. Among the major States, Tamil Nadu had by far the highest proportion of villages using tap water for drinking (70.6 per cent) followed by Haryana (52.5 per cent), Karnataka (47.9 per cent), Andhra Pradesh (46.8 per cent) and Maharashtra (44.9 per cent). As compared to this, in Orissa, Assam, Uttar Pradesh, Madhya Pradesh and West Bengal, tap as water source varied from a low of mere 2.3 per cent in Orissa to little over 6 per cent in West Bengal. Wells were the major source in 85 per cent of Kerala's villages and 40 per cent of Assam's. In all major States other than those mentioned above, and also in Assam, tube-wells and hand-pumps were the most prevalent sources of drinking water. For about 25 per cent of Orissa's villages, spring water continued to remain a major source of drinking water.

All the above analyses suffice the fact that not only is there deficiency of infrastructure at the country level but also the distribution of the same is largely uneven. The states like Orissa, Bihar, Assam and Rajasthan are the ones which show dismal performance in almost all matters barring exceptions. On the other hand, Kerala, Punjab, Haryana and Tamil Nadu are found to be the better performing states. It is interesting to note that as infrastructure facilities are believed to have linkages with human development, states considered under the present study, by and large, present results in conformity with the above (Tables 8 and 9).

For instance, Kerala followed by Punjab, Tamil Nadu and Haryana are found to have topped the list in terms of human development and those are the states which are at the upper end of infrastructure index. Bihar followed by Assam, Uttar Pradesh, Madhya Pradesh, Orissa, Andhra Pradesh, Rajasthan and West Bengal are the ones that have fared miserably in human development front. Interestingly, those are the states that are found to have recorded very low infrastructure index. It may be mentioned here that Uttar Pradesh is the only exception, which despite having occupied 5th rank in infrastructure index, has failed miserably in human development. In the middle are Gujarat, Karnataka and Maharashtra in respect of both human development and infrastructure facilities.

Table 7: Number of Villages having Irrigation Facilities per Thousand, and Number of Villages with Major Sources of Drinking Water according to Major States

States	Number of villages having irrigation facility per 1000 villages	Number of villages per 1000 with major sources of drinking water			
		Tap	Tube Well / Hand pump	Well	Tank/Pond
Andhra Pradesh	796	468	314	78	3
Assam	201	60	458	398	48
Bihar	895	-	647	202	1
Gujarat	891	354	524	110	11
Haryana	979	525	354	113	8
Karnataka	829	479	451	70	---
Kerala	840	112	10	855	-
Madhya Pradesh	925	39	595	348	-
Maharashtra	804	449	266	179	-
Orissa	281	23	502	220	1
Punjab	976	202	786	12	-
Rajasthan	893	186	518	147	87
Tamil Nadu	879	706	107	99	52
Uttar Pradesh	987	4	943	53	-
West Bengal	845	61	727	207	-
All India	762	185	551	176	10

Source: Report on Village Facilities, NSS 58th Round, Report No. 487, July-December 2002.

Although the present study does not attempt to carry out an empirical analysis to prove the linkage between infrastructure and human development in the context of India, a closer look at the cluster of the states may make one convinced that there is a probable linkage between infrastructure and human development (Table 9).

Table 8: Human Development Index for Major States of India

States	1981	1991	2001
Andhra Pradesh	0.298(9)	0.377(9)	0.416(10)
Assam	0.272(10)	0.348(10)	0.386(14)
Bihar	0.237(15)	0.308(15)	0.367(15)
Gujarat	0.360(4)	0.431(6)	0.479(6)
Haryana	0.360(5)	0.443(5)	0.509(5)
Karnataka	0.346(6)	0.412(7)	0.478(7)
Kerala	0.500(1)	0.591(1)	0.638(1)
Madhya Pradesh	0.245(14)	0.328(13)	0.394(12)
Maharashtra	0.363(3)	0.452(4)	0.523(4)
Orissa	0.267(11)	0.345(12)	0.404(11)
Punjab	0.411(2)	0.475(2)	0.537(2)
Rajasthan	0.256(12)	0.347(11)	0.424(9)
Tamil Nadu	0.343(7)	0.466(3)	0.531(3)
Uttar Pradesh	0.255(13)	0.314(14)	0.388(13)
West Bengal	0.305(8)	0.404(8)	0.472(8)
All India	0.302	0.381	0.472
Mean	0.321	0.403	0.463
SD	0.070	0.074	0.073
CV	21.80	18.37	15.75

Note: Figures in Parentheses are HDI ranks in descending order.
Source: Government of India (2002), National Human Development Report 2001, Planning Commission, Oxford University Press, P 25

III. Implications and Conclusion

There is no denying the fact that over the years, there have been phenomenal improvements in the provisioning of all types of infrastructure in the country including the facilities like water, irrigation, educational and health services. Despite that, the country continues to experience deficiencies in several aspects, both in quantity and quality. What is more appalling is the persistence of inequalities in the creation of infrastructure facilities across regions as well as across types. While some states have achieved the level comparable to that in many advanced countries of the world, there are states which continue to face dismal scenarios. These inequalities are said to have bearing on continued differences in human development front across the states.

Table 9: Cluster of States according to Human Development and Infrastructure Index

Cluster	States	Level of Infrastructure	Level of Human Development
I	Kerala, Punjab, Tamil Nadu, Haryana	High	High
II	Gujarat, Karnataka, Maharashtra,	Medium	Medium
III	Madhya Pradesh, Rajasthan, Bihar, Orissa, West Bengal, Andhra Pradesh, Assam, Uttar Pradesh*	Low	Low

*Uttar Pradesh is an exception which has recorded very low human development despite having achieved an infrastructure index higher than those falling under cluster III.

Coupled with this, infrastructure sector is stated to be faced with several other challenges, some implicit and others explicit. It experiences a trade-off between effective delivery and increased availability. It is blamed for its unresponsiveness to public demands leading to poor quality and unreliable service deliveries. Poor maintenance is another area of concern that may require immediate intervention. Coupled with these, financial inefficiencies and continued fiscal drains are regular features (World Bank, 1994). Although the incidence of above challenges is felt in all the developing countries of the world, it has its special significance in India given its persistent poverty, inequality, and poor human development. In the given situation, the following discussions merit attention.

It may be established that infrastructure can contribute towards promoting pro-poor growth, reducing poverty and providing critical services to the poor (GOM, 2007). However, the possibility of a dilemma between growth and human development may arise on two distinct standpoints. First, growth may not imply human development. Past experiences with growth are a testimony to this (Morris and McAlpin, 1982; Mazumdar, 1990). Thus, any infrastructure development directed towards promoting growth of GDP may fail to ensure high human development. Second, there is a problem of social choice with respect to the selection of infrastructure facilities, areas and agencies. In this context, the first and foremost issue is the problem of social choice between public policy and private investment (GOM, 2007). While pro-growth strategies are likely to promote major infrastructure projects leading to large scale displacement, greater investment and private sector participation, pro-poor strategies, on the contrary, would require greater public action and selection of small infrastructure projects. Pro-growth strategies may compromise with regional balance, exclude people from access, affordability and utility of services (GOM, 2007), adopt the principle of allocative efficiency rather than enhancement of economic welfare and may, in turn, only be profit-friendly. The state of India's infrastructure facilities across its states may partly be attributed to this dilemma of social choice.

In this context, the concerns raised and the solutions proposed by the World Development Report 1994 (World Bank, 1994) may be proved to be useful. First and foremost is the selection of the infrastructure facilities for the attainment of high human development. Having known that major infrastructure is difficult, if not impossible, to create, is socially and politically undesirable and has possibly limited impact on human development and poverty eradication, there is a need to create 'small scale infrastructure' specifically designed for the rural poor. They could be rural community feeder roads, rural health centres, rural information and communication technology, community water supply and sanitation, rural schools, etc. These critical infrastructure facilities are required to be located where the poor live, must take care of their needs first, are technologically accessible, break the barriers to physical, economic and financial limitations, have proper geographic spread and adopt acceptable pricing policy for the users (GOM, 2007). It may be ascertained here that although all these facilities are available and/or are being created in certain areas in one form or the other in certain quantities, what is needed is revamping the same in both quantity and quality. Small scale infrastructure specially oriented towards rural development is said to be complementary to large ones and not competitive.

In the absence of incentives to the private sector, it is amply clear that such infrastructure facilities can only be made possible through public provisioning. Thus, the role of the government remains crucial in this respect. In the wake of rising fiscal burden on the government, it is perhaps prudent on the part of the government to leave the major infrastructure projects to private sector participation so that there remains room for reallocation of funds towards creation of alterative infrastructure facilities for the poor. Ironically, contrary to this argument, public sector continues to play a predominant role in the provision of major infrastructure facilities thereby hindering its action towards pro-poor infrastructure. The continued government support may be favoured on the ground that market failure warrants government interventions. However, more probable reason for government's predominance could be the recognition of its political and economic importance (UN, 1995).

Currently, most of the schemes of the government, especially directed towards rural areas, have an implicit agenda of rural asset and infrastructure creation. Schemes directed at creation of rural infrastructure include the Million Wells Scheme for surface water bodies, Indira Awas Yojana for housing, Jawahar Gram Samridhi Yojana for school buildings, Pradna Mantri Gram Sadak Yojana for rural roads, and Swarna Jayanti Swarozgar Yojana to support micro-enterprises. Bharat Nirman Yojana is another such important program meant for rural development. The primary objective of the Bharat Nirman Yojana is to build rural infrastructure and provide a platform to guarantee rural employment, health, and education through Mahatma Gandhi National Rural Employment Guarantee Scheme (MGNREGS), National Rural Health Mission, and Sarva Shiksha Abhiyan respectively.

Amongst all, MGNREGS is considered to be a flagship program of the central government which in addition to providing 100 days of assured employment to each household which demand jobs, has a greater goal of creating durable community assets for sustainable rural livelihood. In course of its operation, several types of rural infrastructure are expected to be created. They could be construction of small roads, school buildings, and pond digging, to mention a few. This scheme is said to be distinct form the rest the schemes in more then one way. Certain key features which make the scheme unique are time bound guarantee, universal targeting to remove bureaucratic discretion, right to information, people's participation in decision making, work site facilities, women empowerment and so on. All these are expected to bring about greater transparency and accountability and in turn, improved service delivery in rural areas (GOI, 2008).

However, the MGNREGS is not free from criticisms. It is argued that the scheme's adherence to 'unskilled manual work' may compromise with the durability of the rural assets created under the scheme. Some economists believe that the scheme suffers from incentive incompatibility (Rastogi, 2007). The studies so far have attempted to draw attention to several other issues like the unevenness in its implementation, low employment creation (CAG, 2007; Biswas, 2007), lack of transparency (Dreze, 2007), inadequacy of manpower, administrative delays, poor quality works (Ambasta, 2008), and underutilization of funds (www.nrega.nic.in). Similarly, Bharat Nirman Yojana also suffers from inherent criticisms of lacking tangible plans for PPP. It is a contractor-client relationship and not a partnership for development. The mission suffers from three risks, namely, non-sustainability, short-term opportunity for a few contractors, and possibility of getting stuck in a low-development trap (Rastogi, 2007).

An important aspect of several rural development schemes is the fund sharing between the centre and the states. It is, however, observed that regardless of the schemes, the state governments are slow in contributing their shares into the schemes. This could be partly attributed to the poor fund position of certain states. Besides, underutilization of funds remains the greatest challenge to almost all the schemes under implementation.

In the wake of fiscal crisis that the government has been facing, it may also be prudent to propose public-private partnership (PPP) in the creation of all types of infrastructure, be it small or large, and economic or social. In recent years, an increasing need for PPP has been felt both by the centre and the states. Under the scheme, Rural Infrastructure Development Fund of the government of India, PPP model has been applied to certain specific schemes. State governments have also been requested to provide feedback on the scope for operationalizing projects under PPP model (Mahajan, Sahai and Pasrija, 2007). However, a lot needs to be done to achieve desired objectives in this front.

There are also suggestions to move from government monopoly to a competitive system of market dominance for the creation of all types of infrastructure. Efficient delivery mechanism demands competition, commercial management and more importantly participation of the users along with other stakeholders (World Bank, 1994). PPP model, if applied in bigger ways, is expected to attain these objectives more meaningfully.

To conclude, it may thus be said that India's effort towards attaining high human development rests inter alia on the availability of infrastructure particularly in rural areas. While undertaking steps to achieve so, it is imperative to ensure adequacy in addition to quality in all the states. Especially the states like Orissa, Bihar, Rajasthan, Madhya Pradesh and Uttar Pradesh need special attention in the allocation of quality infrastructure. It is, in this respect, pertinent on the part of the government to leave major infrastructure projects to the private sector so that is can play a significant role in the creation of rural small scale infrastructure. In addition, the feasibility of PPP model in rural infrastructure may be attempted to overcome the fiscal drains.

References

Agénor, P. R., and Moreno-Dodson, B. (2006): Public Infrastructure and Growth: New Channels and Policy Implications, *The World Bank Policy Research Working Paper* 4064.

Ambasta, P., Shankar, V. P., Shah, M (2008): Two years of NREGA: The road ahead, *Economic and Political Weekly*, 43(8): 41-50.

Aschauer, D.A. (1998): Public Capital and Economic Growth: Issues of Quantity, Finance and Efficiency, Economic Development and Cultural Change, 48(2): 391-406.

Aschauer, D. A. (2000): Do states optimise? Public capital and economic growth, *The Annals of Regional Science*, 34(3): 343-363.

Baldwin J. R., and Dixon, J. (2008): Infrastructure Capital: What Is It? Where Is It? How Much of It Is There? *Research Paper Series 16*, Economic Analysis Division, Statistics Canada.

Biswas, S (2007): India Job Scheme "Disappointing, BBC News, November 10.

Comptroller and Auditor General of India (2007): *Review of NREGA* (draft report submitted to the Ministry of Rural Development).

Devarajan, S., Swaroop, V. and Zou, H. (1993): What do Governments buy? The Composition of Public Spending and Economic Performance, *Public Economic Working Paper Series 1082*, Country Economics department, World Bank, Washington DC.

Dreze, J (2007): NREGA: Dismantling the Contractor Raj, *The Hindu*, November 20.

Government of India (2008): The National Rural Employment Guarantee Act 2005 (NREGA), Operational Guidelines, Third Edition, Ministry of Rural Development, Department of Rural Development, Government of India, New Delhi.

Government of India (2008): The National Rural Employment Guarantee Act 2005 (NREGA), Operational Guidelines, Third Edition, Ministry of Rural Development, Department of Rural Development, Government of India, New Delhi.

Government of Madhya Pradesh (2007): Madhya Pradesh Human Development Report.

Hirschman, A.O. (1958: *The Strategy of Economic Development,* Yale University Press, New Haven, Connecticut.

Khader, S.A (1998): Productivity in infrastructure, *Yojana*, 42(1): 13-18.

Kumar, N and De, P (2008): East Asian Infrastructure Development in a Comparative Global Perspective: An Analysis of RIS Infrastructure Index, Research and Development System for Developing Countries, *Discussion paper No 135*.

Macdonald, R. (2008): An Examination of Public Capital's Role in Production, *Research Paper Series 50*, Economic Analysis Division, Statistics Canada.

Mahajan, V., P. Sahai and S. Pasrija (2007): Financing of Rural Infrastructure, In India Infrastructure Report 2007, Oxford University Press, New Delhi.

Mazumdar, D (1990): Poverty in Asia: An Overview, A paper presented at Policy Dialogue and Pacific Development Centre, Hanvi.

Mehrotra, S (2008): NREGA two years on: Where do we go from here? *Economic and Political Weekly*, 43(31): 27-35.

Mody, Ashoka (1997): *Infrastructure Strategies in East Asia- The Untold Story,* The World Bank, Washington, D.C.

Morris, D M and M.B. McAlpin (1982): *Measuring the condition of India's poor: The Physical Quality of Life Index*, Promia and Co., New Delhi.

Murugan, K., Swaminathan, S (2002): Using ICT in ODL for curbing neo-elitism and building human infrastructure, Conference paper presented in Commonwealth of Learning (2002) Pan-Commonwealth forum on open learning: Open learning: transforming education for development, 29 July - 2 August 2002, Durban, South Africa.

Nijkamp, P. (1986): Infrastructure and Regional development: A multidimensional policy analysis. *Empirical Economics*, 11(1), 1-21.

Pillai, N., Vijayamohanan (2008): *Infrastructure, Growth and Human development in Kerala*, MPRA Paper No. 7017, Online at http://mpra.ub.uni-muenchen.de/7017.

Rastogi, A. (2007): The Infrastructure Sector in India in 2006, In India Infrastructure Report 2007, Oxford University Press, New Delhi.

Satish, P. (2006): Rural Infrastructure and Growth: An Overview, Keynote paper on Subject III "Rural Infrastructure and Growth" presented during the 66th Annual Conference of the Indian Society of Agricultural Economics, to be held at ICAR Research Complex for the NEH Region, Umiam (Barapani), Meghalaya on November 8-10, 2006.

Spence, R. and Smith, M. (2009): Information and Communication Technologies, Human Development, Growth and Poverty Reduction: A Background Paper, DRAFT April 28, 2009, Second Harvard Forum - *A Dialogue on ICTs, Human Development, Growth and Poverty Reduction*, September 2009.

Straub, S. (2008): Infrastructure and Growth in Developing Countries: Recent Advances and Research Challenges, *The World Bank Policy Research Working Paper 4460.*

UNDP (2009): Human Development Report 2009, Oxford University Press, Oxford.

United Nations (1995): The Role of Public Administration in Developing Infrastructure and Protecting the Environment, Report of the Secretary-General, Twelfth Meeting of Experts on The United Nations Programme in Public Administration and Finance New York, 31 July-11 August.

World Bank (1994): World Development Report: Infrastructure for development, Washington DC and New York, The World Bank and Oxford University Press.

World Bank (1997): Development in Practice: Primary Education in India, Washington DC and Allied Publishing, New Delhi.

Youngson, A.J. (1967): *Overhead Capital: A Study in Development Economics,* Edinburgh University Press, Edinburg.

14

Exclusion of Social Infrastructure Menace to Human Development in India

L. Ganesan[1]

I. Introduction

Human Development (henceforth HD) refers to the expansion of people's choices by enhancing their capabilities and functioning (Rout and Panda, 2009). According to UNDP, "HD is a development paradigm that is about much more than the rise or fall of national income. It is about creating an environment in which people can develop their full potential and lead productive, creative lives in accord with their needs and interests. People are the real wealth of nations. Development is thus about expanding the choices people have to lead lives that they value. And it is thus about much more than economic growth, which is only a means – if a very important one – of enlarging people's choices". HD is assumed to have two sides. One is the formation of human capabilities – such as improved health, knowledge, and skill. The other is: how the people make use of their acquired capabilities – for employment, productive activities, political affairs or leisure? A society needs to build up human capabilities as well as to ensure equitable access to human opportunities. Considerable human frustration results if the scales of HD do not finely balance the two sides (Haq, 1995). The HD paradigm is based on the following fairly broad agreements: (i) development must put people at the center of its concern; (ii) the purpose of development is to enlarge all human choices, not just income; (iii) the HD paradigm is concerned with both building of human capabilities (through investment in people) and with using those human capabilities fully (through an enabling framework for growth and employment); (iv) HD has four essential pillars: equality, sustainability, productivity, and empowerment. It regards economic

[1] Assistant Professor, Post Graduate and Research Centre, Department of Economics, S. T. Hindu College, Nagercoil, Tamil Nadu, India

growth as essential but emphasizes the need to pay attention to its quality and distribution, analyses at length its link with human lives and questions its long-term sustainability; and (v) the HD paradigm defines the ends of HD and analyses sensible options for achieving them (Haq, 1995).

India, the largest home to people in the world after China, has a very low level of human development. The recent human development index estimated for 2009 by UNDP puts India in the 134th position among 182 countries with HDI score of 0.612. Compared to the highest HDI score of 0.971, this is much lower. The HDI value has declined from 0.611 in 2005 to 0.602 in 2006 and then increased to 0.612 in 2007. This low value of HDI has to be seen against the country's elevation to a higher growth path in the recent times. Between 1992 and 2002, the gross domestic product (GDP) of India grew at a rate of 6 per cent, much above the growth rate of 5.2 percent registered during 1982-1992. Such a faster growth was observed in the per capita GDP too. Since 2005, the Indian economy is experiencing a high rate of growth of above eight per cent per annum, and it is anticipated to grow at a higher rate in the near future. The impressive economic growth, and the economic reform policies being vigorously followed, also leads many to fear that the high growth might be exclusionary in nature and that it may be characterized by low HDI Rank with low HDI index, jobless growth, ruthless growth, voiceless growth, rootless growth and futureless growth, which UNDP. 1996 warned against. India is recognized as an economy with a 'stunning' but 'jobless growth' (UNDP-ILO-2007) and a booming economy with 'growing gaps' where the spectacular success made have not been shared by all equally (World Bank – 2006). The Planning mechanism has also failed to be sufficiently inclusive and far too many people still lack access to basic social infrastructural services such as health, education, clean drinking water and sanitation facilities without which they cannot be empowered to claim their share in the benefits of growth. As the World Bank (2006) has described, inclusive growth is growth with emphasis not only on the distribution of economic gains but also on the security, protection against vulnerability, empowerment and sense of full participation that people may enjoy in social life. That can be achieved only through focus on human development. Inclusive growth presupposes inclusion of both economic growth and human development by giving top priority to social infrastructure which consists of health and education made accessible to all. The role of these two factors in ensuring inclusive growth is very critical. It is akin to the development strategies such as 'growth with justice', 'growth with equity', 'growth with distribution', 'growth with a human face' and 'pro-poor growth'. The strategies of inclusiveness and broad based participation in the development process call for new emphasis on social infrastructure.

Development of social infrastructure comprising education, health and medical care, nutrition, housing and water supply is instrumental in contributing to substantial improvements in human resources development. This, in turn, initiates and accelerates economic development. Physical quality of life and human well being are pivotal on the enhanced availability of these social services. These services are the key to overall increased productivity. Investment in human development programs enable the poor to help themselves and give a fair chance of getting those rewards on the social front Government had adopted a three – prolonged approach during the successive Five Year Plan periods – augmenting increased resources on social sector, implementing anti-poverty programs in an effective way and accelerating economic growth.

But the social sectors have been the first target for retrenchment in public expenditure is the largely successful bid so far to achieve fiscal balance since liberalization. The state, as a matter of deliberate policy started scaling down, if not retreating from, its constitutional responsibility for providing public goods in such crucial areas as education, health etc. The responsibility has increasingly been transferred to private operators. As a result, there has been a sharp deterioration in the conditions of the poorest and marginalized, particularly socially and economically backward communities. At the time of independence, India had very poor social infrastructure. The planning process during the last six decades has made efforts to strengthen it at various levels. Both large survey-based studies as well as case based studies have repeatedly shown that education and health services in India are characterized by inadequate and inferior infrastructure, poor public service delivery, lack of quality choices for consumers and lack of access especially for the poor mainly because privately provided services are relatively expensive.

With this backdrop, the paper makes an attempt to examine the achievements, shortcomings and failure of human development in India. For this purpose it analyses the levels of human development in India vis-a-via the neighbouring countries with different level of development. In order to determine the factors of human development, this paper has focused on the performance of social infrastructure such as health and education for both All India level and for selected major states.

The major objective of this paper is to study the trend of human development of India over the period of past three decades and to compare its achievements with selected countries.

The second objective is to identify the social infrastructure components which are believed to be the cause for poor performance of HDI. This paper has relied on the various issues of UNDP HDI Reports, India Development Report, Various Issues of RBI Report and Economic Survey for data. It is an exploratory study rather than a descriptive study.

This paper is organized into five sections. The first section briefly gives the introduction of this study. The second section deals with the comparative analysis of various components of human development in India and some selected countries over a period of past three decades.

The third section is focused on identifying the key factors that determine the performance of social infrastructure which is the cause for development of human beings. The fourth section analyses the exclusion of social infrastructure, particularly health and education in India in terms of public expenditure. The last fifth section gives the summary and concludes with a few suggestions for policy making.

II. Comparative Analysis of Various Components of Human Development in India

Human development is defined as the process of enlarging people's choices in terms of knowledge, health and longevity, and levels of income. These choices can be translated to acquire knowledge, to lead a long and healthy life and to have access to resources needed for a decent standard of living.

Table 1 presents Human Development Index for 2007 for India and few selected countries as reported in HDR – 2009. Countries have been grouped under four categories (i) the first category is the group of countries in the HDI range above 0.900. They are classified as Very High Human Development group (HDG), (ii) countries in the HDI range between 0.800 and 0.899 are classified as High Human Development group, (iii) countries in the HDI range from 0.500 to 0.799 are classified as Medium Human Development group, and (iv) countries in the HDI range of less than 0.500 points are classified in the low human development group (Table 3). The data has been collected from 182 countries according to HDI Report of 2009.

Among them 38 countries were in Very High HDG, 48 countries were in High HDG, 75 countries were in Medium HDG, whereas 24 countries were in Low HDG. India's rank was 134 out of 182 countries in 2009. It was a little slip backward from its previous position at 128 in 2005. It was estimated that the long term average annual growth rate of HDI was at 1.33 per cent between the period 1980 and 2007 (see Table 1).

From Table 1, it is evident that the there has been consistent improvement in HDI score of India over the years have increased from 0.427 to 0.612 between 1980 and 2007.

In spite of the progress, the level of human development achieved by India is much lower than that of some of the selected countries (both developed and developing countries) barring Pakistan. Moreover, India has to go a long way to catch up with some of the Asian countries.

A close perusal of the data for the nearly three decades (1980-2009) reveals that all countries are making efforts in varying degree to improve their human development indices. Iran, China, South Korea, Egypt and India, and to a certain extent Pakistan and Bangladesh can be considered as among the very high performers during 1980-2009. If the trend is maintained several medium HDI countries will join the high HDI range.

This is a welcome development. India has improved its HDI from 0.427 in 1980 to 0. 612 in 2007. But it still has a long way to go before India could enter the high HDI group of countries. If she wishes to touch even the top of medium development group, India has to jump over more than 50 countries. Such is the pathetic position held by India in HDI Ranking.

Table 1: Trends in Human Development in India and Selected Countries from 1980 to 2009

HDI Rank	1980	1985	1990	1995	2000	2005
Norway	0.900	0.912	0.924	0.948	0.961	0.968
Canada	0.890	0.913	0.933	0.938	0.948	0.963
Japan	0.887	0.902	0.918	0.931	0.943	0.956
US	0.894	0.909	0.923	0.939	0.949	0.955
Korea	0.722	0.760	0.802	0.837	0.869	0.927
Mexico	0.756	0.768	0.782	0.794	0.825	0.844
Saudi Arabia	..	..	0.744	0.765	..	0.837
Malaysia	0.66	0.689	0.737	0.767	0.797	0.821
Russian Federation	..	..	0.821	0.777	..	0.804
Brazil	0.685	0.694	0.710	0.734	0.790	0.805
Iran (Islamic Republic of)	0.561	0.620	0.672	0.712	0.738	0.773
China	0.533	0.556	0.608	0.657	0.719	0.756
Sri Lanka	0.649	0.670	0.683	0.696	0.729	0.752
Philippines	0.652	0.651	0.697	0.713	0.726	0.744
Indonesia	0.522	0.562	0.624	0.658	0.673	0.723
Viet Nam	..	0.561	0.599	0.647	0.690	0.715
Egypt	0.493	0.552	0.580	0.631	0.665	0.696
India	**0.427**	**0.453**	**0.489**	**0.511**	**0.556**	**0.596**
Pakistan	0.402	0.423	0.449	0.469	..	0.555
Bangladesh	0.328	0.351	0.389	0.415	0.493	0.527
Nigeria	..	..	0.438	0.450	0.466	0.499
Malawi	..	0.379	0.390	0.453	0.478	0.476
Liberia	0.365	0.370	0.325	0.280	0.419	0.427
Central African Republic	0.335	0.344	0.362	0.347	0.378	0.364
Afghanistan	..	..	..	..	..	0.347
Niger	..	..	..	..	0.258	0.330

contd...

2006	2007	Rank 2006	Change in Rank 2006-2007	Average annual growth rates (per cent)		
				Long term 1980-2007	Medium term 1990-2007	Short term 2000-2007
0.970	0.971	1	0	0.28	0.29	0.16
0.965	0.966	4	0	0.31	0.21	0.27
0.958	0.960	10	0	0.29	0.26	0.25
0.955	0.956	12	-1	0.25	0.21	0.11
0.933	0.937	26	0	0.97	0.92	1.08
0.849	0.854	54	1	0.45	0.52	0.50
0.840	0.843	58	-1	..	0.74	..
0.825	0.829	66	0	0.81	0.69	0.56
0.811	0.817	73	2	..	-0.03	..
0.808	0.813	75	0	0.63	0.79	0.41
0.777	0.782	87	-1	1.23	0.89	0.83
0.763	0.772	99	7	1.37	1.40	1.00
0.755	0.759	102	0	0.58	0.62	0.57
0.747	0.751	105	0	0.53	0.44	0.49
0.729	0.734	111	0	1.26	0.95	1.25
0.720	0.725	115	-1	1.16[a]	1.13	0.71
0.700	0.703	122	-1	0.30	1.13	0.81
0.604	**0.612**	**134**	**0**	**1.33**	**1.32**	**1.36**
0.568	0.572	142	1	1.30	1.42	..
0.535	0.543	148	2	1.86	1.96	1.39
0.506	0.511	157	-1	..	0.91	1.31
0.484	0.493	161	1	1.20[a]	1.38	0.44
0.434	0.442	169	0	0.71	1.81	0.77
0.367	0.369	178	-1	0.36	0.12	-0.33
0.350	0.352	181	0	..	..	..
0.335	0.340	182	0	..	..	3.92

Notes: The human development index values in this table were calculated using a consistent methodology and data series. They are not strictly comparable with those published in earlier Human Development Reports. **a** Average annual growth rate between 1985 and 2007.

Sources:
Column 1-8: Calculated based on data on life expectancy from (2009e); data on adult literacy rates from UNESCO Institute for Statistics (2003) and (2009a); data on combined gross enrolment ratios from UNESCO Institute for Statistics (1999) and (2009b); and data on GDP per capita (2007 PPP US$) from World Bank (2009d). **Column 9**: Calculated based on revised HDI values for 2006 in column 7. **Column 10**: Calculated based on revised HDI ranks fro 2006 and new HDI ranks for 2007. **Column 11**: Calculated based on the HDI values for 1980 and 2007. **Column 12**: Calculated based on the HDI values for 1990 and 2007. **Column 13**: Calculated based on the HDI values for 2000 and 2007.

Component wise Analysis of HDI of India and Selected Countries – 2009

Components wise analysis of Table 2 indicates that though India is shining in the performance of its economic variables and is emerging as one among the giant economies in the global level, its position of HDI components shows deteriorating trend. Finally it has slipped into 134th position in 2007 from its previous position of 128 in 2005 in HDI rank The following Table 2 indicates a shock trend when we compared the India's positions of all the components of HDI with other countries.

As per Table 4, the key variables of HDI of India during nearly one decade from 2000 to 2009 indicates that the absolute value of the HDI for India has improved from 0.556 in 2000 to 0.596 in 2005 and further 0.612 in 2007. Despite this, out of 182 countries of the world as against 177 countries of the world in 2000, the relative ranking of India has fallen from 124th position in 2000 to 134th position in 2007. In terms of Gender Development Index (GDI), India ranks 114th position out of 182 countries ranked on the basis of their GDI value. A zero count for HDI rank minus GDI rank for India is indication of almost similar status of gender development and human development. While India's HDI rank reflected low relative achievement in the level of human development till 2005, it has turned worse to 134th position in the recent report. A negative count of –6 for GDP per capita (PPP US$) rank minus HDI rank is indicative that the country has done better in terms of per capita income than in terms of human development. The Gini index of inequality is at 36.8 percent, old age dependency ratio is also increasing to 7.7. The unhealthy life expectancy (the difference between life expectancy and healthy life expectancy) has increased to

10 percent. Out of total allocation aid to the social infrastructure by he government and civil society, the key components of health and education have got more than 50 percent as its share. The situation reinforces the need for greater focus on this area on our development planning. It is this concern that is getting reflected in the 11th plan which seeks to reduce not only differences in allocation of funds to the social sector with other sectors has estimated at 46.6 percent in 2007 which reflect the 11th plan. This situation cause for reinforces the need for greater focus on this area on our development planning which seek to reduce.

Table 2: Component-wise Analysis of HDI of India and Selected Countries – 2009

HDI Rank	HDI Value	Life expectations at birth (years)	Adult literacy rate (per cent)	CGER in education
	2007	2007	1999-	2007
Norway	0.971	80.5		98.6
Canada	0.966	80.6		99.3
Japan	0.960	82.7		86.6
United States	0.956	79.1		92.4
Korea (Republic of)	0.937	79.2		98.5
Mexico	0.854	76.0	92.8	80.2
Saudi Arabia	0.843	72.7	85.0	78.5
Malaysia	0.829	74.1	91.9	71.5
Russian Federation	0.817	66.2	99.5	81.9
Brazil	0.813	72.2	90.0	87.2
Iran (Islamic Republic of)	0.782	71.2	82.3	73.2
China	0.772	72.9	93.3	68.7
Sri Lanka	0.759	74.0	90.8	68.7
Philippines	0.751	71.6	93.4	79.6
Indonesia	0.734	70.5	92.0	68.2
Viet Nam	0.725	74.3	90.3	62.3
Egypt	0.703	69.9	66.4	76.4

India	**0.612**	**63.4**	**66.0**	**61.0**
Pakistan	0.575	66.2	54.2	39.3
Bangladesh	0.543	65.7	53.5	52.1
Nigeria	0.511	47.7	72.0	53.0
Malawi	0.493	52.4	71.8	61.9
Liberia	0.442	57.9	55.5	57.6
Central African Republic	0.369	46.7	48.6	28.6
Afghanistan	0.352	43.6	28.0	50.1
Niger	0.340	50.8	28.7	27.2

contd...

GDP per capita	Life expectation index	Education index	GDP index	GDP per capita rank minus HDI rank
2007	**2007**	**2007**	**2007**	**2007**
53,433	0.925	0.989	1.000	4
35,812	0.927	0.991	0.982	14
33,632	0.961	0.949	0.971	16
45,592	0.902	0.968	1.000	-4
24,801	0.904	0.988	0.920	9
14,104	0.850	0.886	0.826	5
22,935	0.794	0.828	0.907	-19
13,518	0.819	0.851	0.819	-5
14,690	0.686	0.933	0.833	-16
9,567	0.787	0.891	0.761	4
10,955	0.769	0.793	0.784	-17
5,383	0.799	0.851	0.665	10
4,243	0.816	0.834	0.626	14
3,406	0.777	0.888	0.589	19
3,712	0.758	0.840	0.603	10
2,600	0.821	0.810	0.544	13
5,349	0.749	0.697	0.664	-20
2,753	**0.639**	**0.643**	**0.553**	**-6**
2,496	0.687	0.492	0.537	-9
1,241	0.678	0.530	0.420	9
1,969	0.378	0.657	0.497	-17
761	0.456	0.685	0.339	12
362	0.548	0.562	0.215	10

713	0.361	0.419	0.328	-5
1,054	0.310	0.354	0.393	-17
627	0.431	0.282	0.307	-6

Source: HDR 2009.

Table 3: Summary of HDI – 2009 at Global Level

HDI Rank	2007	2007	1999-2007
Very high human development	0.955	80.1	..
Very high HD: OECD	..	80.1	..
Very high HD: non-OECD	..	79.7	..
High human development	0.833	72.4	94.1
Medium human development	0.686	66.9	80.0
Low human development	0.423	51.0	47.7
World	0.753	67.5	83.9

contd...

2007	2007	2007	2007	2007	2007
92.5	37,272	0.918	..	0.988	..
92.9	37,122	0.919	..	0.988	..
..	41,887	0.912	..	1.000	..
82.4	12,569	0.790	0.902	0.807	..
63.3	3,963	0.698	0.744	0.614	..
47.6	862	0.434	0.477	0.359	..
67.5	9,972	0.708	0.768	..	..

Source: HDR 2009.

III. Factors Determining the Performance of Social Infrastructure

The basic purpose of planning in India is to widen people's choices and to improve the well-being of the people. In this context, human development is the key issue Planning should ensure improvement in human development so that people could lead a long and healthy life, could acquire knowledge so as to have better vertical mobility in life and last, but not the least, could achieve a decent standard of living.

It would be, therefore appropriate to examine the factors responsible for the progress of human development in India.

Demographic Factors

A major impediment to progress in human development is the very fast growth of population in India. India's population increased from 620.7 million in 1975 to 1,027 million in 2001 giving a growth rate of 2.0 percent per annum during the period (1975-2001), which is fairly high.

Table 4: Trends of HDI Components for India During 2000 to 2009

Kay Factors	2000	2005	2007 (as per 2009 Report)
HDI Rank	124	128	134
HDI Index value	0.556	0.596	0.612
GDP per capita minus HDI rank	-16	-11	-6
GDI Rank	105	113	114
HDI rank minus GDI Rank	0	0	0
Life Expectancy	64	63.7	63.4
Combine GER	63	63.8	61.0
Physical/ one lakh people	-	60	62
Infant with low birth weight (per cent)	-	45	46
Human Poverty Index	-	-	28.0
Human Poverty Rank	-	-	88th rank out of 182
People living below poverty line	-	-	28.6 per cent
Aid allocate to social sectors	-	-	46.6 per cent
Healthy life expectancy at birth (years)	-	-	57
Unhealthy life expectancy as a per cent or to the life expectancy	-	-	10 per cent
Population not using improved water	-	-	11 per cent
Probability of not surviving to age of 40 years	-	-	15.5 per cent
Old age dependent ratio	-	-	7.7 per cent
Inequality index	-	-	36.8 per cent
Public expenditure on health as per cent of total govt. expenditure	-	-	3.4 per cent
Public Expenditure on education as per cent of total government expenditure	-	-	10.7 per cent

Source: HDI Report, 2009.

It is expected that the growth rate of population during 2000-2015 will come down to 1.3 percent. This would provide a welcome relief and will help to push forward the process of human development. Urbanisation is considered to be a factor which promotes human development. The share of urban population, which was 21.3 percent in 1975, has reached 27.8 per cent in 2001, and by 2015, is expected to reach 32.2 per cent. In absolute terms, urban population was 285 million in 2001 and would reach 407 million in 2015. Another healthy feature of demographic transition is the impact of proportion of children or population under age 15. Their proportion stood at 33.7 per cent in 2001, but is likely to decline to 27.7 per cent by 2015.

Health Indicators

Life expectancy at birth has shown a continuous improvement from 50.7 years during 1970-75 to 62.9 years in 2000-05. However, the probability at birth not surviving to age 40 is 15.3 per cent in 2000-05. India has to improve health facilities as well as nutrition levels so that it can reduce the probability rate at birth not surviving to age of 40 years. Several countries in the medium human development category have much better survival rates. In this context, it would be relevant to take note that 47 per cent of the children under five were underweight in 2009. In absolute terms, 178 million children under five were underweight. Population not using improved water sources was 14 per cent in 2004. Compared with the conditions in the past, this itself was a very healthy development, but in absolute terms 158 million persons were unable to make use of improved water sources and thus became victims of all kinds of water-borne diseases. Similarly, improved sanitation facilities were not available to 33 per cent of the population in 2004. In absolute terms, 375 million persons were living under insanitary conditions. It was really distressing that 49 per cent of the Indian population did not have access to essential drugs in 2008. This implied that 527 million persons were without effective medical cover. This reduced the survival rate in India.

The proportion of under-nourished people in India in 2004 was 20 per cent. This implied that 220 million people were under-nourished. This under-nourishment was primarily due to the existence of poverty. There is a need to strengthen poverty eradication strategies to reduce under-nourishment. There are some positive features too. The survival rate has considerably improved in India. In 1970, infant mortality rate per 1,000 live births was 127; it has been brought down to 60 in 2008. Similarly, under-five infant mortality rate has been reduced from 202 per 1,000 live births to 93 in 2008. These are healthy developments. Likewise, maternal morality rate per 1,00,000 live births have been brought down to 540 during 1985-2008. Control of diseases and improvement in hospital facilities has contributed to improvements in survival rate.

There has been some improvement in the quality of health care over the years (Table 5), but wide inter-state, male-female and rural-urban disparities in outcomes and impacts continue to persist. While population stabilization is in the 'Concurrent List', health is a State subject. The reproductive and child health services reach community and household levels through the primary health care infrastructure. Inadequacies in the existing health infrastructure have led to gaps in coverage and outreach services in rural areas. India's position on health parameters, compared even to some of its neighbours, continues to be unsatisfactory. While India has improved with respect to some important health indicators over the years, it compared very poor with countries like China and Sri Lanka (Table 6).

Though there has been a steady increase in health care infrastructure available over the plan period as per the Bulletin on Rural Health Statistics in India – 2006 – Special Revised Edition, as in March 2006, there is a shortage of 20,903 Sub-Centres (SCs), 4,803 Primary Health Centres (PHCs) and 2,653 Community Health Centres (CHCs) as per 2001 population norm (Table 7). Further, almost 50 percent of the existing health infrastructure is in rented buildings. Poor upkeep and maintenance and high absenteeism of manpower in rural areas have also eroded the creditability of the health delivery system in the public sector. National Rural Health Mission (NRHM) seeks to strengthen the public health delivery system at all levels. In addition to strengthening the health delivery system under NRHM, several other programs in the area of health are being implemented in the country.

Drinking water supply is one of the six components of Bharat Nirman, which has been conceived as a plan to be implemented in four years from 2005-06 to 2008-09 for building rural infrastructure. During the Bharat Nirman period, 55,067 uncovered habitations and about 3.31 lakh slipped–back habitations means these habitations were covered with health infrastructure earlier, but were neglected later. were to be covered and 2.17 lakh quality – affected habitations were to be addressed. Tackling arsenic and fluoride contamination has been given priority. Under Bharat Nirman, in the first two years, impressive achievements have been made. In 2006-07, against the target of cover 73,120 habitations, 1,07,350 habitations have been covered. As on 1.4.2007, there are 29,534 uncovered habitations, 1,74,782 slipped-back habitations and 1,59,348 quality affected habitations. These habitations are proposed to be covered/addressed during remaining terms of the Bharat Nirman period.

Table 5: India – Selected Health Indicators

Sl. No.	Parameter	1981	1991	Current level (2009)
1	Crude Birth Rate (CBR) (Per 1000 Population)	33.9	29.5	23.5
2	Crude Death Rate (CDR) (Per 1000 Population)	12.5	9.8	7.5
3	Total Fertility Rate (TFR) (Per women)	4.5	3.6	2.9
4	Maternal Mortality Rate (MMR) (Per 100,000 live births)	NA	NA	301
5	Infant Mortality Rate (IMR) (Per 1000 live births)	110	80	57
6	Child (0-4 years) Mortality Rate (Per 1000 children)	41.2	26.5	17.3
7	Life Expectancy	(1981-85)	(1989-93)	(2001-05)
	Male	55.4	59.0	62.3
	Female	55.7	59.7	63.9

NA : Not Applicable.
Source: Office of Registrar General India.

The sanitation coverage in 1981 was only 1 percent of the rural population which increased to 11 percent in 1991. By the year 2001, the access to toilets improved to 21.9 percent of the rural population. However, in the last few years, with the launch of demand-based

'Total Sanitation Campaign (TSC)', there has been tremendous improvement in rural sanitation coverage in the country, which has reached 50 percent. In the success of TSC, Panchayati Raj Institutions (PRIs) have played a key role in further acceleration of sanitations coverage. However, in a few States, there is a need to improve the implementation so that goal of total sanitation by the year 2012 is could be achieved.

Table 6: Some Health Parameters: India and its Neighbours

Country	Life expectancy at birth (years)	Under –five mortality rate (per 1000 live births)		Infant Morality Rate (per 1000 live births)		Maternal morality Rate (per 1,00,000 live births)
	2000-05	**1990**	**2005**	**1990**	**2005**	**2005**
China	72	49	27	38	23	45
India	62.9	123	74	80	56	450
Nepal	61.3	145	74	100	56	830
Pakistan	63.6	128	99	96	79	320
Sri Lanka	70.8	23	14	19	12	58
Bangladesh	62.0	144	73	96	54	570
South Asia	62.9	126	80	84	60	NA

NA: Not available.

Source: UNDP, Human Development Report 2007-08.

Table 7: Trends in Health Care Infrastructure

	1991	2005/2006
SC/PHC/CHC[a] (March 2006)	57353	171567
Dispensaries and Hospitals (all)[b] (1.4.2006)	23555	32156
Nursing Personnel (2005)[b]	143887	1481270
Doctors (Modern System) (2005)[b]	268700	660801

Sources: [a]RHS: Rural Health Statistics in India – 2006 – Special Revised Edition. [b] National Health Profile, 2006.

SCs – Sub Centres, PHCs – Primary Health Centres, CHCs – Community Health Centres.

Gender – Factors

Life expectancy at birth of females in 2005 was 65.3 yeas, but for males, it was 62.3 years. Compared with countries in the medium human development category, Indian achievement, though good, is still much lower in relation to Mexico, Venezuela, Russian Federation, Thailand, Philippines, Sri Lanka, Iran, Vietnam, to name a few among them.

Economic Indicators

GDP per capita of India was $3,452 in 2005 (PPP US$). The average annual growth rate of GDP during 1980-90 was 5.8 percent; it declined to 4.2 per cent during 1990-2005. However, the measures of inequality of consumption revealed that the share of the poorest 10 per cent in total consumption in 2004-05 was just 3.6 per cent and that of the richest 10 per cent was 31.3 per cent. Thus, the ratio of consumption between the richest 10 per cent to the poorest 10 per cent was 8.7. Similarly, the share of poorest 20 percent was only 8.1 per cent in total consumption, but the share of richest 20 per cent was 45.3 per cent. Thus, the ratio of consumption of the richest 20 per cent to the poorest 20 per cent was 5.6. Compared with countries in the medium human development category, India shows moderate inequality. A very large number of countries in this group show much higher inequality of income or consumption. However, there is a need to improve the condition of the poorest 10 or 20 per cent of the population so that India is able to reduce inequality still further. Data on amount of public expenditure on education reveals that it was 3.7 per cent of GDP in 1990 and that it has slightly improved to 3.8 per cent in 2002-05. But public expenditure on health was distressingly low at 0.9 per cent of GDP in 2004.

Data reveal that traditional fuel consumption in total energy use declined from 47.5 per cent 1990 to 29.4 per cent in 2004. This was natural and is in accordance with the process of development. However, per capita electricity consumption sharply improved from 173 KWH in 1990 to 618 KWH in 2004. But our record about the proportion of underweight children around 47 per cent is very dismal. Equally distressing is the data that 51 per cent of the population did not have access to life saving drugs. Gender related development indicators revealed the gap between male and female in adult literacy and gross enrolment ratio. Earned income gap was too wide and indicated the existence of a strong gender bias.

Public expenditure on health has been pitiably low at 1.3 percent of GDP in 2007. In nutshell, it may be stated that human development index of India has improved from 0.406 in 1975 to 0.612 in 2009, but India still has miles to go before she can enter the group of countries in the high human development category. For this the process of development has to be accelerated.

IV. Exclusion of Social Infrastructure in Terms of Public Expenditure

Patterns in Social Sector Expenditure

Throughout the history of independent India, the Indian government has claimed that it *is* working towards attainment of social development and the eradication of poverty. On the eve of independence, Jawaharlal Nehru, addressing the Constituent Assembly, declared that independence meant the redemption of a pledge. But he also stated that this achievement 'is but a step, an opening of opportunity, to the great triumphs and achievements that await us ... the ending of poverty and ignorance and disease and inequality of opportunity'.

Combined Expenditure by the Centre and States

The proportion of combined expenditure of the centre and the states provides the best picture of India's commitment towards the social sector. There are different ways of examining the trends in budget expenditure. One way is to look at social sector expenditure as a proportion of GDP, or GSDP in the case of the states. A second way is to calculate social sector expenditure as a percentage of the aggregate budget expenditure. The third option is to look at the real per capita expenditure (at constant prices) for the social sector. Table 8 utilizes all these three methods for the period 1987-88 to 2000-02. India spends around to 6 to 7.5 per cent of its GDP on the social sector. In 1990-91, the share in GDP was 6.78 per cent. Only in 1998-99, a higher level was reached. Throughout the 1990s social sector expenditure, in terms of percentage of GDP, was lower than the value before the onset of the reforms in 1989-90, which was 7.17 per cent. This percentage was, however, reached in 2000-01.

Increasing trend of expenditure on social services by the government (Centre and State combined) in recent years reflects the high priority accorded to these sectors (see Table 9). Expenditure on social sectors as a proportion of total expenditure, after decreasing from 20.4 percent in 2002-03 to 19.5 percent in 2003-04, increased steadily thereafter to 22.3 percent in 2006-07 and 22.5 percent in 2007-08. Expenditure on education as a proportion of total expenditure has increased from 9.8 percent of 2004-05 to 10.4 percent in 2006-07. Share of health in total expenditure has also increased from 4.4 percent in 2004-05 to 4.9 percent in 2006-07.

Table 8: Social Sector Expenditure by Centre and State Governments

Years	Social sector expenditure (revenue and capital)		
	As per cent of GDP	As per cent of agg. pub. exp. (rev. + capital)	Per capita exp. (in Rs.) in 1993-4 prices
1987-88	7.26	25.29	564
1988-89	6.95	25.22	585
1989-90	7.17	25.19	635
1990-91	6.78	24.85	623
1991-92	6.58	24.28	599
1992-93	6.38	24.06	594
1993-94	6.46	24.58	622
1994-95	6.39	25.01	632
1995-96	6.40	25.95	674
1996-97	6.30	26.46	716
1997-98	6.41	26.18	763
1998-99	7.01	27.36	882
1999-2000	7.14	26.75	951
2000-01	7.45	26.56	988
2001-02	7.18	25.31	986

Source: Computed from the data available in Indian Public Finance Statistics, Ministry of Finance, GOI, 1995, 2002.

Intra-sectoral Allocations to Education, Health and Rural Development

Table 10 provides data pertaining to intra-sectoral allocations for education, health and family welfare, and rural development for the post-reform period. It shows that the 1990s witnessed significant shifts within these sectors.

Table 9: Trends of Social Sector Expenditure by General Government (Centre and State Governments combined)

(Rs. Crore)

Items	2002-03	2003-04	2004-05	2005-06	2006-07	2007-08
Total expenditure	6,95,203	7,86,212	8,59,545	9,59,855	11,48,824	13,09,897
Expenditure on social sector	1,41,740	1,53,454	1,72,812	2,03,995	2,56,521	2,94,412
Education	71,298	75,607	84,111	96,365	1,19,199	1,33,284
Health	30,184	33,504	37,535	45,428	56,378	65,158
Others	40,258	44,343	51,166	62,202	80,944	95,970
As percentage of GDP						
Total expenditure	28.32	28.54	27.29	26.81	27.71	27.91
Expenditure on social sector	5.77	5.57	5.49	5.70	6.19	6.27
Education	2.9	2.74	2.67	2.69	2.88	2.84
Health	1.23	1.22	1.19	1.27	1.36	1.39
Others	1.64	1.61	1.62	1.74	1.95	2.04
As percentage of total expenditure						
Expenditure on social sector	20.4	19.5	20.1	21.3	22.3	22.5
Education	10.3	9.6	9.8	10	10.4	10.2
Health	4.3	4.3	4.4	4.7	4.9	5.0
Others	5.8	5.6	6	6.5	7	7.3
As percentage of social sector expenditure						
Education	50.3	49.3	48.7	47.2	46.5	45.3
Health	21.3	21.8	21.7	22.3	22	22.1
Others	28.4	28.9	29.6	30.5	31.6	32.6

Source: Budget documents of Centre and State Governments / RBI Reports.

In education, there has been a sharp increase in the share of elementary education, particularly since 1995-96. This share increased from about 18 percent in 1992-93 to 40 percent in 1995-96 and to 48 percent in 1997-98. Since 1998-99, however, the share has declined and it was 42 percent in 2002-03. A further disaggregation showed that this shift in favour of elementary education was due to the introduction of nutrition programmes and the District Primary Education Programme (DPEP). The shift towards elementary education led to a decline in the shares of secondary, university and higher, technical, and adult education. The intra- sectoral allocations for health and family welfare show that there was a sharp increase in the share of reproductive and child health from around 5 percent in 1992-93 to 15 percent in the late 1990s. In the case of rural development, the share of rural wage employment programmes declined drastically since the mid-1990s. In 2002-03, however, the share increased again. The share for rural housing and other programmes increased in the 1990s. In the case of the latter, there was a twelve-fold increase between 1999-2000 and 2000-01, as a result of the introduction of the rural roads scheme, known as the Prime Minister's Gram Samrudhi Yojana (PMGSY).

Trends in Expenditure by the States

As mentioned above, the main responsibility for social sector development lies with the states. Earlier studies by Prabhu (1997), UNDP (1997) and Chelliah and Sudarshan (1999) have shown that social sector expenditure, either taken as a proportion of GSDP or as a proportion of aggregate expenditure, started to decline for the majority of the states since the mid-1980s and that this trend continued in the early 1990s. Our data confirm this trend for the entire decade of the 1990s. Trend growth rates per annum of the average level of social sector expenditure for all the states during the pre- and post-reform periods were also declining (see Table 11). The trend growth of real per capita expenditure for the social sector declined from around 9 percent in 1980s to around 5 percent in 1990s. The same declining trend can be seen for the growth rates of social sector expenditure as percentage of total expenditure and as percentage of GDP.

Table 10: Intra-Sectoral Allocation to Education, Health and Rural Development: Central Government Expenditure 1992-93 to 2002-03

(Percentage)

	1992-93	1993-94	1994-95	1995-96	1996-97
Education	100.0	100.0	100.0	100.0	100.0
Elementary	18.6	20.2	20.5	39.6	42.0

Secondary	25.0	25.6	24.1	19.9	19.0
Higher Edn.	28.0	24.9	25.6	19.9	19.5
Adult	6.3	7.8	8.5	4.7	3.1
Technical	18.7	18.3	18.6	14.0	14.5
Others	3.4	3.2	2.7	1.9	1.9
Health and family welfare	100.0	100.0	100.0	100.0	100.0
Public health	16.6	16.6	18.0	17.7	19.7
Medical edn.	13.6	12.4	12.3	12.2	12.3
Rural family welfare	17.2	15.8	13.2	13.7	12.4
Maternal and child health	5.4	6.0	6.3	11.0	11.9
Other services and supplies	21.1	26.2	28.5	23.1	19.5
Others	26.1	23.0	21.7	22.3	24.2
Rural development	100.0	100.0	100.0	100.0	100.0
Water supply and sanitation	13.3	13.6	13.2	14.1	14.7
Special programs	13.8	14.5	12.9	10.7	10.6
Social sector and welfare	-	-	-	6.6	7.0
Rural wage employment program	70.5	68.9	70.8	57.3	44.5
Other rural development program*	1.0	1.0	1.2	4.0	6.4
Housing	0.1	0.2	0.3	5.9	15.2
Others	1.3	1.8	1.6	1.4	1.6

contd...

1997-98	1998-99	1999-2000	2000-01	2001-02	2002-03
100.0	100.0	100.0	100.0	100.0	100.0
48.1	42.9	39.0	37.8	44.3	41.7
15.0	15.5	14.4	14.3	15.3	13.6
20.2	25.1	29.6	31.0	20.5	19.4
1.8	1.3	1.1	1.3	2.2	2.4
13.0	13.6	14.1	13.5	15.4	15.0
1.9	1.6	1.8	2.1	2.3	8.0
100.0	100.0	100.0	100.0	100.0	100.0
18.9	16.4	14.1	14.4	12.6	11.5

13.1	15.2	13.1	13.6	12.5	11.7
13.9	15.3	21.4	15.8	15.5	25.0
13.6	15.3	13.6	15.4	16.6	14.6
17.6	16.5	17.9	19.7	20.7	12.2
22.9	21.3	19.7	21.0	22.5	25.2
100.0	100.0	100.0	100.0	100.0	100.0
16.7	17.7	19.3	16.0	14.0	11.0
10.4	9.6	12.1	9.9	9.8	8.8
5.8	6.8	7.6	6.2	4.9	0.0
46.0	42.8	39.8	23.7	31.1	51.6
5.8	5.3	1.9	23.2	20.3	13.6
13.6	16.2	17.7	12.6	13.4	8.4
1.7	1.6	1.6	8.2	6.7	6.6

Note: (1) All the data in this table refer to revised estimates; (2) Others in health and family welfare refers to central government health schemes, hospitals and dispensaries, urban family welfare. Maternal and child health was replaced by reproductive and child health in 1998-99; (3) Special programs for rural development refer to IRDP, TRYSEM, DPAP, Deserts Area development program etc. Rural wage employment programs are JRY and EAS. *Other rural development programs refer to DWCRA, rural roads, million wells scheme and raining.
Source: Vol. II, Budget Papers, GOI.

There are very few states that have been able to increase their social sector expenditure as percent age of GSDP, in terms of real per capita expenditure. However the per capita expenditure is very low in Uttar Pradesh, Bihar and Orissa but which is relatively high in Goa, Gujarat, Kerala and Tamil Nadu. In Table 12, the states are clustered according to their per capita SDP and divided into three categorizes rich, middle and poor. The rich states did slightly better in education. The middle-income states performed better in health, and the poorer states did best in rural development. The intra-group variation is, however, considerable, which makes it difficult to draw group-wise conclusions. Uttar Pradesh, for instance, has done much worse in education, health, and social services than other poor states. In the case of rural development, all except six states recorded a decline in the index in 1999-2000 as compared to that of 1990-91.

V. Comparison of Indian Expenditure with that of Other Countries

Education expenditure (taken as a percentage of GDP or as a percentage of overall public expenditure) was lower in India than in

Malaysia and Thailand. Health expenditure is also very low in India as compared to other countries listed in Table 14. On the other hand, private expenditure on health is higher in India than many other countries (see Table 13).

Table 11: Trend Growth Rates of Social Sector Expenditure of All States

(per cent per annum)

	Education, sports, art, and culture, etc	Health and family welfare	Water supply and sanitation
	(1)	(2)	(3)
1980-1-199-90	7.65	0.18	7.27
1992-3-2002-9	5.91	4.50	6.13
1980-1-199-90	2.80	-4.34	2.10
1992-3-2002-9	1.59	-0.03	1.78
1980-1-199-90	0.94	-6.07	1.82
1992-3-2002-9	-0.05	-1.38	0.16

contd...

Total others	Social services	Rural devel opme nt	Social sector (services and rural development) states	Social sector centre
(4)	(5)	(6)	(7)	(8)
6.09	6.95	-1.25	9.27	14.12
7.41	6.06	1.21	5.44	6.34
1.31	2.13	-6.01	4.34	8.93
2.53	1.57	-4.15	0.85	1.34
-0.52	0.28	-6.26	2.46	5.41
1.37	0.10	-4.48	-0.48	0.82

Source: India Development Report – 2005, Calculated data.

In order to facilitate cross-countries comparisons and monitoring of social sector expenditure over time, the UNDP has proposed the following four ratios (UNDP 1991):

- **The Public Expenditure Ratio**: The percentage of national income that goes into public expenditure. The recommendation is to keep this ratio around 25 percent.
- **The Social Allocation Ratio**: The percentage of public expenditure earmarked for social services. This ratio, according to the UNDP, should be more than 40 percent.

Table 12: Index of Per Capita Real Expenditure on Social Services and Rural Development (at 1993-94 prices) at State Level

	Education, sport, art and culture			Medial, health and family welfare		
	1990-91	1995-96	1999-2000	1990-91	1995-96	1999-2000
Goa	100	94	149	100	86	116
Gujarat	100	113	157	100	102	159
Haryana	100	107	155	100	103	136
Maharashtra	100	117	177	100	100	118
Punjab	100	97	151	100	85	141
Sub-total	100	111	165	100	98	133
Andhra Pradesh	100	96	148	100	104	159
Karnataka	100	119	165	100	115	173
Kerala	100	106	155	100	109	151
Tamil Nadu	100	99	157	100	106	143
West Bengal	100	80	158	100	76	124
Sub-total	100	98	156	100	99	146
Bihar	100	101	179	100	126	165
Madhya Pradesh	100	111	174	100	108	171
Orissa	100	115	186	100	106	137
Rajasthan	100	111	152	100	119	139
Uttar Pradesh	100	89	116	100	87	85
Sub-total	100	101	150	100	105	126
Total	**100**	**103**	**157**	**100**	**101**	**136**

contd...

Social Services			Rural Development		
1990-91	1995-96	1999-2000	1990-91	1995-96	1999-2000
100	94	139	100	58	96
100	106	173	100	71	88
100	135	146	100	55	71
100	116	152	100	137	51
100	100	131	100	95	75
100	113	153	100	108	65
100	124	158	100	70	101
100	120	166	100	73	78
100	105	152	100	90	321
100	103	144	100	58	79
100	81	155	100	86	88
100	105	154	100	73	107
100	103	169	100	81	290
100	114	176	100	126	108
100	120	203	100	56	116
100	117	149	100	79	67
100	90	110	100	46	88
100	104	148	100	70	121
100	**107**	**153**	**100**	**79**	**104**

Source: Estimates based on data from RBI Bulletins.

- **The Social Priority Ratio**: The percentage of social expenditure devoted to human priority concerns. This ratio has to be more than 50 percent.
- **The Human Expenditure Ratio**: The percentage of national income devoted to human priority concerns. This ratio is the product of the above three ratios and the UNDP recommends that it should be about 5 percent.

Table 15 gives these ratios for India in the late 1980s and the late 1990s. It is clear that there had been some progress in the 1990s, but the ratios are still far from the UNDP norms.

VI. Suggestions

1. There should be adoption of *a* decentralization policy based on the discussion above in this paper, which should

help to improve governance, quality of services, enhance political participation.

2. Involvement of Public Private Partnership, Community Based Organizations (CBOs) and Non-Governmental Organizations (NGOs). They can play an important role in creating an environment for social mobilization and for sustainable human development.

Table 13: Composition of Public Expenditure in India and Developing Countries

Major Heads	India (1992-93)	All South Asian Countries (1985-90)	All East Asian Countries (1985-89)	All Developing Countries (1990)
Total expenditure – GDP ratio	27.9	21.3	22.5	20.8
Gen. Adm. And pub. Order	11.6	17.2	17.3	15.3
Defence	11.7	12.0	10.9	1.0
Economic services	29.8	30.6	30.6	21.1
Education	13.5	9.0	20.5	13.6
Health and family welfare	2.9	4.2	7.0	5.9
Housing and community services	4.6	5.4	2.2	2.7
Other social services	3.9	7.9	3.8	9.1
Total social services	25.3	26.5	33.5	31.3
Other expenditure	21.6	13.7	7.5	21.3
Total expenditure	100.00	100.00	100.00	100.00

Source: Rao (1995) quoted in Mundle and Rao (1997).

3. Improving the access to information is one way of increasing the accountability of panchayats, other local bodies, and the delivery system of social sectors in general. Basic to such access is the Right to Information.
4. The pattern of funding also should have the objective of making states more self-reliant with moderate assistance from centre.
5. Proper monitoring and evaluation against the laid down benchmarks in social sector targets along with the use of

modern technology like e-governance can help to obtain better outcomes.

VII. Conclusion

It is obvious from the above facts that the poor performance of 'Human Development' in India is due to inadequacies of social infrastructure in general and in health and education in particular. Though the government has strengthened its efforts for social sector development in recent years, the expenditure of the governments (both central and state) on social infrastructure sector is still too low and it should be stepped up.

Table 14: Public Expenditure on Education and Health: International Comparisons

Countries	Education			Health		HDI rank 2003
	As per cent of GNP 1998-2000	As per cent of total govt. exp. 1998-2000	Primary and secondary as per cent of all education	Public exp. As per cent of GDP 2000	Private exp. As per cent of GDP 2000	
India	4.1	12.7	79.9	0.9	4.0	127
Bangladesh	2.5	15.7	89.7	1.5	2.6	139
China	2.1	12.8	69.6	2.0	3.4	104
Egypt	3.7	-	-	1.8	2.3	120
Korea	3.8	17.4	78.5	2.6	3.3	30
Malaysia	6.2	26.7	66.2	1.8	1.6	58
Sri Lanka	3.1	-	84.3	1.4	1.7	99
Thailand	5.4	31.0	63.1	2.1	1.6	74
Sweden	7.8	13.4	67.3	6.2	1.8	3
Canada	5.5	-	62.2	6.5	2.5	8
United States	4.8	12.3	-	5.8	7.3	7
UK	4.5	11.4	79.9	5.9	1.4	13

Source: UNDP, Human Development Report (2003).

Along with higher economic growth and poverty reduction in recent years, there has been an improvement in many important social sector indicators, but the disparities at the state and regional level are still continuing. Expenditure on social infrastructure have to be supplemented to sustain high level of economic growth in achieving better social sector performance and improvement in the quality of life that, in turn, would lead s to high human development

Table 15: Social Sector Ratios in India

	UNDP norm	Late 1980s	1998-99
Public expenditure ratio	25	37*	25
Social allocation ratio	40	20	27
Social priority ratio	50	34	40
Human expenditure ratio	5	2.5	2.8

Note: Social priority ratio was taken as the share of social sector allocation to elementary education, water and sanitation, public health, maternal and child health, and child nutrition.
Source: India's Development Report 2004-05.

References

Chelliah, R.J. and R. Sudarshan (1999): *Income Poverty and Beyond: Human Development in India*, Social Science Press, New Delhi.

Datt, R. and Sundaram, K. P. M. (2009): *Indian Economy*, S. Chand Publication, New Delhi.

GOI (2008): *Economic Survey – 2007-08*, Ministry of Finance, New Delhi

HAQ (2001): India's Children and the Union Budget, HAQ: Centre for Child Rights, New Delhi.

Mundle, S. and Rao, M. G. (1997): Public Expenditure in India: Trends Issues, In S. Mundle (Ed.), *Public Finance: Policy Issues for India*, Oxford University Press, New Delhi.

Parikh, K. S. and Radhakrishnan, R. (2005): *India Development Report – 2004-05*, Oxford University Press, New Delhi.

Prabhu, Seeta (2001): *Economic Reform and Social Sector Development: A Study of Two Indian States*, Sage Publications, New Delhi.

Rout, H. S. and Panda, P. K. (2009): Introduction, in H. S. Rout and P. K. Panda (Eds.), *Human Development – Dimensions and Strategies*, New Century Publication, New Delhi.

Tilak, Jandhyala B.G. (2007): Inclusive Growth and Education: On the Approach to the Eleventh Plan, *Economic and Political Weekly*, 42(38): 3872-77.

UNDP (1997): India: Road to Human Development, New Delhi Office, June 1997.

UNDP (2009): *Human Development Report 2009: Overcoming Barriers – Human Mobility and Development*, Oxford University Press, New York

UNDP – ILO (2007): Asian Experience on Growth, Employment and Poverty: An Overview with Special Reference to the Findings of Some Recent Case Studies', Colombo, UNDP/Geneva: ILO.

World Bank (2006): India: Inclusive Growth and Service Delivery: Building on India's Success – Development Policy Review, Report No. 34580-iN, Washington DC.

15

Education and Human Development

M. Indira[1]

I. Introduction

Development approach of the 1980s presumed a close link between national economic growth and individual welfare. This was questioned by several development researchers and the need for an alternative development model was recognized. The important factors which influenced the paradigm shift were the failure of 'trickle down' power, identification of human costs of SAPs, spread of social ills even under the strong and consistent economic growth and the emergence of people centered democratization process. The capability approach developed by Amartya Sen and others provided the conceptual foundation for an alternative and broader human development approach.

Human Development Paradigm

The contribution of capability approach to development thinking has broadened the concept of development with a human face. Capability approach focuses directly on substantive freedom of the individuals. Sen suggests that well-being be considered in terms of human functionings and capabilities. Functionings relate to what a person may value doing or being. A functioning is an achievement, where as capability is the ability to achieve. Functionings are more directly related to living conditions, but capabilities are notions of freedom, in the positive sense: what real opportunities you have regarding the life you may lead (Sen. 1987).

Under the new paradigm human development is defined as a process of enlarging people's choices and enhancing human capabilities (the range of things people can be and do) and freedoms, enabling them to live a long and healthy life, have access to knowledge and decent standard of living and participate in the life of their community and decisions affecting their lives.

[1] Professor, Department of Economics and Cooperation, University of Mysore, Mysore – 570006, India

Goods and services are not important in themselves, but in what their characteristics enable people to do and to be, that is, the capabilities that a person can generate from these goods and services and the extent to which a person can generate capabilities from these goods and services depends on the conversion factors. The three important conversion factors are Social factors, Environmental factors and Personal factors.

1. Social factors are determined by the society and education and education systems are one of the important social factors.
2. Environmental factors are determined by the environment in which the persons live.
3. The personal factors are determined by ones mental and physical characteristics.

There are several dimensions of human development when development is defined as enlarging people's choice. Some of the issues which are considered most important to human development are social progress, efficiency, equality, participation and freedom, sustainability and human security.

According to Sen's capability approach, education is one of the critical inputs in the conversion of commodities into functionings and well-being of an individual. The following stylized non dynamic representation of the core aspects of capability approach clearly shows the role of the institutions in the conversion of the utilities from the market and non market production into capabilities leading to greater choice.

Under this framework an attempt is made in the present paper to understand the linkages between education and human development, human development measured in terms of better health and employment opportunities in Indian context.

II. Literacy Status

Literacy rates in India have increased over a period of several years due to Government interventions to promote education. However, still 50 per cent of the population is illiterate in some of the states. For example, according to 2001 census, literacy rate in Bihar is 47.53 per cent and in Jharkhand and Arunachal Pradesh it is 54 per cent. There are several states like Andhra Pradesh, Assam, Chhattisgarh, Madhya Pradesh, Meghalaya, Orissa, Rajasthan and Uttar Pradesh where more than 40 per cent of the people are illiterate. Compared to other SAARC countries like Sri Lanka and Maldives literacy rates are lower in India. Age group wise literacy shows that in the older age group of 45-49 years, 38 per cent women and 68 per cent men are literates. There is an improvement in the younger age group. As of 2005-06, 75 per cent girls and 89 per cent boys in the age group of 15-19 years are literates (see Table 1).

A stylized non -Dynamic representation of the core aspects of the capability

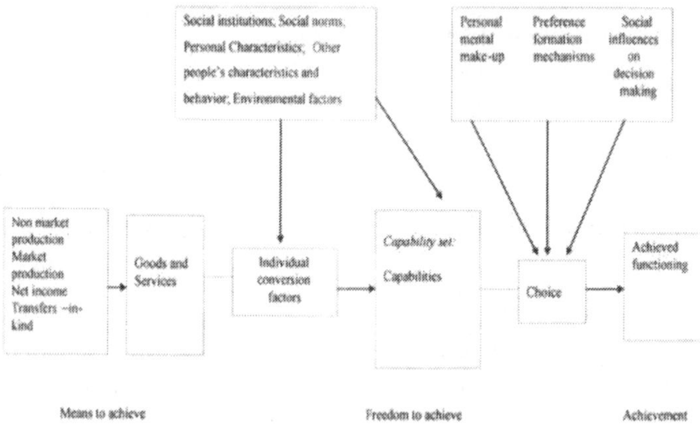

Source: Ingrid Robeyns (2001)

Table 1: Percentage of Literacy According to Age-group

Age Group (Years)	Men	Women
15 – 19	89	74
20 – 24	84	64
24 – 29	81	55
30 – 34	76	48
35 – 39	70	43
40 – 44	69	40
45 – 49	68	38

Source: NFHS – 3.

Interstate Differences in Educational Attainment

Though literacy is an important factor in improving the awareness, the level of literacy and the number of years that an individual spent on education plays an important role in the conversion of this service into capabilities and improved choices. The findings of the NFHS-3 shows that 41.50 per cent of women and 21.9 per cent men in the country have no education at all and 18.10 per cent women and 20.90 per cent men have spent less than 5 years in school. Only 7.60 per cent women and 13.20 per cent men in India have completed 12 or more years in education. Among the states, Bihar has the highest percentage of population without education. Sixty percent of women and 35 per cent of men in Bihar are reported to have no education and 2.70 per cent women and 10.20 per cent men have completed 12 or more years of education.

The other states with more uneducated women are Jharkhand (53.30 per cent), Rajasthan (56.20 per cent) and UP (49.60 per cent). On the other hand there are states like Kerala and Mizoram with only 10 per cent of uneducated women and around 5 per cent uneducated men. But even in Kerala, with 90 per cent of educated women, only 16.5 per cent have completed 12 years of education. Same is the case with men in Kerala. While 16.70 per cent have completed 12 years or more, 24 per cent have completed 8-9 years of education. Delhi has the highest percentage of men and women who have completed more than 12 years. At the all India level, 20.90 per cent of men and 18.10 per cent of women are reported to have completed less than 5 years of education (see Table 2).

III. Employment

Employment status of men and women shows that fewer women are participating in employment compared to men and even among those employed, only 64 per cent are earning cash payment, where as 91.5 percent of the men who are employed earned cash. Even among men, in the states like Chhattisgarh, though 99.4 per cent were employed during the past one year, 87.4 per cent earned cash. Same is the case with Orissa, Nagaland and Karnataka.

Among the southern states Karnataka has the least percentage of men and women who are employed during the past twelve months preceding the NFHS-3 survey. Only 78.7 per cent of the men received cash earnings. But one important observation is that though only 47 per cent of women are employed, 72 per cent of them received cash payment. In the case of Kerala also 29 per cent women are employed and 91 per cent of this received cash payment (see Table 3).

Table 2: State-wise Education Status

States	No Education		Completed < 5 Years		Completed 12 or more years	
	Men	Women	Men	Women	Men	Women
INDIA	21.9	41.5	20.9	18.1	13.2	7.6
A. P.	27.0	45.1	18.7	14.9	12.6	5.6
Arunachal Pradesh	28.9	44.5	25.1	23.1	10.0	5.8
Assam	16.7	29.5	28.4	26.1	10.6	6.6
Bihar	35.3	60.3	21.1	15.4	10.2	2.7
Chhattisgarh	22.4	46.6	26.8	20.7	10.6	4.6
Delhi*	10.8	22.5	12.4	12.2	31.5	27.7
Goa	10.8	21.5	15.9	14.5	21.2	19.0
Gujarat	16.1	34.2	20.9	18.6	12.3	8.6
Haryana	19.0	40.2	15.9	13.5	14.3	8.7
H. P.	11.6	26.7	13.5	12.7	19.2	13.1
J and K	22.0	42.3	15.5	14.4	13.9	9.6
Jharkhand	28.2	53.3	21.7	19.0	11.1	4.7
Karnataka	21.6	37.4	17.8	15.3	15.3	9.0
Kerala	4.9	10.0	18.4	19.0	16.7	16.5
M. P.	26.5	48.00	20.6	19.5	11.8	3.6
Maharashtra	12.1	21.4	20.6	19.3	17.4	10.5
Manipur	12.8	29.8	19.5	17.5	21.6	13.7
Meghalaya	31.6	33.7	25.3	24.5	10.0	8.5
Mizoram	6.8	10.5	26.4	29.3	12.5	8.9
Nagaland	25.0	31.3	22.9	23.0	9.8	6.4
Orissa	22.4	42.2	25.0	20.2	9.6	4.8
Punjab	20.8	33.00	16.1	12.5	13.2	12.7
Rajasthan	25.2	56.2	21.7	17.1	10.8	4.5
Sikkim	21.5	34.6	25.7	22.9	12.7	8.0
Tamil Nadu	14.6	30.6	16.0	14.5	15.6	11.6
Tripura	15.5	24.3	27.9	26.9	9.1	4.9
U.P.	25.6	49.6	21.6	17.8	12.1	6.4
Uttaranchal	14.2	34.9	18.1	14.9	18.2	13.2
West Bengal	22.1	36.00	26.8	25.9	12.3	6.2

Source: NFHS – 3

Table 3: State-wise Employment Status or Men and Women

	Currently Employed		Earning Cash	
States	Men	Women	Men	Women
India	98.8	42.8	91.5	64.2
Delhi	99.5	20.8	99.5	94.7
Haryana	98.3	27.8	96.7	51.9
H. P	97.4	31.1	87.1	33.4
J and K.	99.6	36.1	84.5	35.5
Punjab	99.0	23.2	98.9	78.9
Rajasthan	98.5	56.3	95.9	48.0
Uttaranchal	98.8	45.5	82.3	33.5
Chhattisgarh	99.4	71.4	67.4	44.5
Madhya Pradesh	99.2	56.3	89.2	59.3
Uttar Pradesh	98.4	33.8	94.6	44.6
Bihar	96.3	35.2	88.0	49.8
Jharkhand	99.3	57.7	87.3	47.4
Orissa	98.8	36.1	78.4	72.4
West Bengal	99.3	32.1	94.8	83.2
Arunachal Pradesh	97.1	76.1	75.0	37.0
Assam	97.8	27.0	92.3	85.3
Manipur	98.6	65.3	74.6	76.0
Meghalaya	98.5	42.5	85.9	48.8
Mizoram	98.2	45.2	75.8	61.7
Nagaland	97.8	48.3	69.6	41.5
Sikkim	98.8	32.2	90.0	69.3
Tripura	99.2	29.7	94.1	74.3
Goa	97.7	33.1	95.3	82.6
Gujarat	99.5	51.9	80.9	60.7
Maharashtra	99.3	49.6	97.4	69.6
Andhra Pradesh	99.0	53.3	99.1	83.6
Karnataka	99.6	47.0	78.7	72.0
Kerala	98.9	29.1	97.8	91.3
Tamil Nadu	99.4	48.4	98.6	89.9

Source: NFHS – 3

IV. Economic Status

Income and wealth are important in the life of human beings to provide access to goods and services, which improve the capabilities of individuals. Distribution of wealth indicates how the economic value created in the development process is distributed. According to NFHS-3, 47 per cent of the urban population and 7.40 per cent of rural population are in the highest wealth quintile during 2005-06. On the other hand, 3 per cent of the population in Urban and 27.70 per cent in rural areas are in the lowest quintile. Among the states, Delhi has the highest share of population (69.60 per cent) in the highest quintile. Among the Southern States, Kerala has the highest percent of population (44.8 per cent) in the highest quintile and in Karnataka and Tamil Nadu around 20 percent are in this category. Among the other states, Punjab, Mizoram, Sikkim, Goa, Gujarat and Maharashtra have more than 30 per cent of the population in the highest quintile. Highest percentage of population in Jharkhand (49.6 per cent) is in the lowest quintile and it is followed by Chattisgarh, Madhya Pradesh and Orissa where more than 30 per cent are in this category (see Table 4).

V. Early Childhood Mortality

Neonatal mortality, infant mortality and under five mortality reflect on the health status of the country. Research has shown positive relationship between IMR and number of births. IMR has an impact on the quality of life and the well being of the families. According to the 2001 census, Madhya Pradesh, Orissa, Uttar Pradesh, Rajasthan, Assam and Chhattisgarh have reported IMR of above 70. Kerala has the reported the least number of IMR (10) followed by Manipur (14), Mizoram (14) A and N (15) and Goa (17). Among Southern states AP has reported highest IMR. Latest NFHS-3 has reported an average IMR of 57 in India. IMR has decreased in several states in 2005-06. But the states with high IMR remain to be high, though there is some reduction. In the case of UP, IMR has reduced from 80 to 72 and in Rajasthan it reduced from 78 to 65. Under five mortality is as high as 74 in India and Central India has reported highest under five mortality. MP, UP, Chhattisgarh, Orissa and Jharkhand have reported under five mortality above 90. Among the Southern states AP reported the highest under five mortality of 63 and Kerala has the reported the least (16) (see Table 5).

Table 4: Percentage of Population in the Lowest and Highest Quintile

	Earnings	
State	Lowest Quintile	Highest Quintile
India	20.0	20.0
Delhi*	0.2	69.6
Haryana	4.1	31.0
Himachal Pradesh	1.2	35.1
Jammu & Kashmir	2.8	25.6
Punjab	1.4	48.1
Rajasthan	24.2	19.1
Uttaranchal	6.0	32.8
Chhattisgarh	39.6	10.2
Madhya Pradesh	36.9	13.1
Uttar Pradesh	25.3	13.6
Bihar	28.2	9.4
Jharkhand	49.6	11.9
Orissa	39.5	9.9
West Bengal	25.2	13.9
Arunachal Pradesh	21.1	16.4
Assam	19.8	11.8
Manipur	2.4	16.7
Meghalaya	11.3	16.4
Mizoram	2.5	38.8
Nagaland	7.8	15.0
Sikkim	1.9	32.8
Tripura	11.0	7.6
Goa	2.2	55.3
Gujarat	7.2	31.9
Maharashtra	10.9	32.5
Andhra Pradesh	10.8	17.7
Karnataka	10.8	19.8
Kerala	1.0	44.8
Tamil Nadu	10.6	99.5

Source: NFHS - 3

Table 5: Infant Mortality and under Five Mortality in Different States of India

	Mortality	
	Infant Mortality	Under 5 Mortality
India	57.0	74.3
Delhi*	39.8	46.7
Haryana	41.7	52.3
Himachal Pradesh	36.1	41.5
Jammu & Kashmir	44.7	51.2
Punjab	41.7	52.0
Rajasthan	65.3	85.4
Uttaranchal	41.9	56.8
Chhattisgarh	70.8	90.3
Madhya Pradesh	69.5	94.2
Uttar Pradesh	72.7	96.4
Bihar	61.7	84.8
Jharkhand	68.7	93.0
Orissa	64.7	90.6
West Bengal	48.0	59.6
Arunachal Pradesh	60.7	87.7
Assam	66.1	85.0
Manipur	29.7	41.9
Meghalaya	44.6	70.5
Mizoram	34.1	52.9
Nagaland	38.3	64.7
Sikkim	33.7	40.1
Tripura	51.5	59.2
Goa	15.3	20.3
Gujarat	49.7	60.9
Maharashtra	37.5	46.7
Andhra Pradesh	53.5	63.2
Karnataka	43.2	54.7
Kerala	15.3	16.3
Tamil Nadu	30.4	35.5

Source: NFHS - 3

VI. Maternal Care

Access to maternal care plays an important role in the health status of women and infants. Maternal care in the form of antenatal care, access to health care facility for delivery and post natal checkup are some of the indicators reflecting the maternal care. The NFHS – 3 showed the very poor status of health care for pregnant women. Only 15 percent of the women received recommended antenatal care, 46 per cent of the deliveries are assisted by health personnel and 41 percent had post natal checkup in India. The status of anti natal care is very poor in several states of India. Only 7 per cent of women in MP, 4.1 per cent in UP, 8.6 per cent in Rajasthan, 6.5 per cent in Arunachal Pradesh and 1.9 per cent in Nagaland received all recommended antenatal care. Southern states have shown good antenatal care. While Kerala ranks highest with 63.6 percent of women have taken antenatal care, Tamil Nadu (34 per cent), AP (28.2 per cent), Karnataka (29.6 per cent) are above country average which is 15 per cent. It has been estimated that only 46.6 per cent of the deliveries are assisted by health care personnel in India. In states like Uttaranchal, UP, MP, Bihar, Jharkhand, Nagaland, the percentage of women who delivered with assistance of health personnel is only around 30 per cent. In this indicator also Southern states are performing well with Kerala reporting 99 per cent deliveries under medical supervision. Among the Southern states Karnataka has the least percentage (69.7 per cent) deliveries with health assistance. Post natal checkup is very important for women to regain normal health status and only 37 per cent of women in India are estimated to have post natal check up within two days after the delivery and the status is very poor in central India, Bihar, Jharkhand, Assam and Nagaland (see Table 6).

VII. Impact of Education on Human Development

The relationship between education and human development is analysed by understanding whether the states with high percentage of uneducated people are also the states with lower human development. Human development is measured in terms of engagement in income earning employment, equal distribution of wealth, lower infant mortality rate, professional assisted births and being able to live in a pucca house. The date shows that in Andhra Pradesh with nearly 50 percent of uneducated population still has 91 percent of people, both men and women, earning cash income and has only 10 percent of the population living in lowest quintile and 56 percent are able to live in pucca houses. Nearly one fourth of the births are attended by trained professional and IMR 53. On the other hand we have extreme cases of Bihar where 65 percent of the population are uneducated and only 69 percent are employed for wages and only 20 percent of the population are in pucca houses. But in the case of Mizoram, only 12.5 percent are uneducated, but only 10 percent are living in pucca houses and 69 percent have wage employment.

Table 6: Maternal Care in Different States of India

	Antenatal care	Assisted by health personnel	Post natal Checkup
India	15.0	46.6	37.3
Delhi*	29.0	64.1	58.4
Haryana	14.7	48.9	55.9
H. P.	17.4	47.8	43.2
J and K	17.5	56.5	48.4
Punjab	19.6	68.2	62.0
Rajasthan	8.6	41.0	28.9
Uttaranchal	16.1	38.5	32.4
Chhattisgarh	11.3	41.6	28.4
M. P.	7.2	32.7	28.5
U. P.	4.1	27.2	13.3
Bihar	5.8	29.3	15.9
Jharkhand	7.5	27.8	17.0
Orissa	18.4	44.0	33.3
West Bengal	12.3	47.6	40.7
Arunachal Pradesh	6.5	30.2	22.7
Assam	9.6	31.0	13.9
Manipur	10.5	59.0	46.4
Meghalaya	8.1	31.1	28.8
Mizoram	8.7	65.4	50.6
Nagaland	1.9	24.7	10.6
Sikkim	27.2	53.7	44.9
Tripura	10.6	48.8	30.3

Goa	55.7	94.0	75.5
Gujarat	25.6	63.0	56.5
Maharashtra	21.6	68.7	58.7
Andhra Pradesh	28.2	24.9	64.1
Karnataka	29.6	69.7	58.5
Kerala	63.6	99.4	84.9
Tamil Nadu	34.0	90.6	87.2

Source: NFHS - 3

Table 7: Human Development Indicators in Different States of India

States	Per cent uneducated	Per cent receiving cash for empt.	Percent population in lowest Quintile	IMR	Per cent of profess-ionally assisted birth	Per cent of population leaving in pucca house
A.P	49.55	91.35	10.8	53.5	24.9	56.3
Arunachal Pradesh	51.15	56	21.1	60.7	30.2	20.8
Assam	31.45	88.8	19.8	66.1	31	19.8
Bihar	65.45	68.9	28.2	61.7	29.3	20.4
Chhattisgarh	45.7	55.95	39.6	70.8	41.6	21.7
Delhi*	22.05	97.1	0.2	39.8	64.1	94.9
Goa	21.55	88.95	2.2	15.3	94	73.6
Gujarat	33.2	70.8	7.2	49.7	63	67.3
Haryana	39.1	74.3	4.1	41.7	48.9	61.1
H.P.	24.95	60.25	1.2	36.1	47.8	52.7
J and K	43.15	60	2.8	44.7	56.5	50.3
Jharkhand	54.85	67.35	49.6	68.7	27.8	28.3
Karnataka	40.3	75.35	10.8	43.2	69.7	55.1
Kerala	9.9	94.55	1	15.3	99.4	85.1
Madhya Pradesh	50.5	74.25	36.9	69.5	32.7	26.2
Maharashtra	22.8	83.5	10.9	37.5	68.7	59
Manipur	27.7	75.3	2.4	29.7	59	10.7
Meghalaya	48.45	67.35	11.3	44.6	31.1	15.1
Mizoram	12.05	68.75	2.5	34.1	65.4	22.9
Nagaland	40.65	55.55	7.8	38.3	24.7	20.7
Orissa	43.5	75.4	39.5	64.7	44	31.9
Punjab	37.3	88.9	1.4	41.7	68.2	68.9
Rajasthan	53.3	71.95	24.2	65.3	41	50.1
Sikkim	38.8	79.65	1.9	33.7	53.7	51
Tamil Nadu	29.9	94.25	10.6	30.4	90.6	69.9

Tripura	27.65	84.2	11	51.5	48.8	12.1
Uttar Pradesh	50.4	69.6	25.3	72.7	27.2	28.8
Uttaranchal	31.65	57.9	6	41.9	38.5	49.8
West Bengal	40.1	89	25.2	48	47.6	39.5
STD	13.23	12.74	13.88	15.88	20.94	23.22332
AM	37.48	75.35	14.32	47.27	50.67	43.58621
CV	35.28	16.91	96.94	33.59	41.33	53.28135
r		-0.41	0.658	0.751	-0.73	-0.43252

Source: NFHS - 3

The variation among states in all the selected variables is not uniform. Least variation is observed in the wage employment. Maximum variation is observed in the distribution of wealth which is represented by the percent of people in the lowest quintile. The high variation shows that in some states the distribution of wealth is more skewed against poor. More variation could be observed in the availability of pucca housing. This is due to high values in the case of Delhi, Punjab, Kerala and Tamil Nadu and lowest in Manipur, Meghalaya, Tripura, Arunachal Pradesh and Bihar. Correlation coefficient was calculated to understand the relationship between education and the other variables. All the correlation coefficients have shown expected signs. The negative correlation between the education and the wage employment shows that the states with least number of uneducated are the states with more employed for cash. Since this is a combined work participation and wage employment, it also shows the participation and contribution of women to the livelihoods. Significant positive correlation is observed between education and health indices, negative in the case of IMR and positive in the case of assisted births. Similarly the positive correlation between the education and wealth distribution shows that the states with higher population with no education have greater number of people in the lowest quintile.

VIII. Conclusions

Under the new human development paradigm, the objective of development is to improve the capabilities of people which provide choices to lead the kind of life that they want to lead. Individual well being is given more importance under the human development paradigm. Education plays an important role in giving the opportunity to live with adequate means in a disease free environment. Though there is a considerable improvement in the education status of the people in India, still more than forty percent of the people are not educated. There is a considerable variation across the states in India. The influence of education on the human development indicators which are necessary to lead a minimum standard of living has been analyzed in the present paper. The analysis has clearly shown the strong correlation between education and other human development indicators. The strong policy implication is educating people and it is the biggest challenge India is facing. Government of India has introduced Sarva Shiksha Abhiyan as a flagship programme to universalize elementary education and it is showing positive results. When more and younger generation boys and girls attend to schools and get educated in all the states, the result can be seen in the human development of India in the next decade.

References

Ingrid, Robeyns (2001): Sen's Capability Approach and Feminist Concerns, Paper presented at Conference on Sen's Capability Approach, St. Edmund College, Cambridge.

National Family Health Survey – 3 at www.nfhsindia.org/factsheet.html

Sen, Amartya (1987): The standard of Living, Cambridge University Press, Cambridge.

16

Education, Food Security and Human Development in Orissa

Bidyadhar Majhi[1]

I. Introduction

Access to knowledge through education and access to food and nutritional security are the two important parameters of sound human development of a country, besides other factors. In most of the Human Development Indices education and income to access food grains are used as indicators to show the state of human development of an area. Unfortunately, these two are the most intractable challenge in the human development of a country like India and are result in catastrophic amounts of human suffering. In the World over more than 800 million people are facing the problem of food insecurity and illiteracy. At the policy making levels, efforts are being made to reduce the extent of illiteracy and food insecurity for a sound human development index rating of a country and to minimize these human miseries. For ensuring food security of the vulnerable sections of the society policy initiative includes: rural development-concrete measures to raise productivity and accelerate livelihood promotion strategies through agriculture development. Government interventions including rural infrastructure development (roads, water and irrigation, power, *etc.*), skills training, market support services (farm-based, agro-processing and non-farm), natural resource management and environmental conservation, regulatory framework for food safety and quality, improved access to enhanced social services (education, health, *etc.*). Addressing immediate food needs aimed at ensuring immediate access to food by the most vulnerable groups. It includes ensuring adequate provision of social security and social protection, targeted nutrition programs for the extremely poor, labour intensive public works policies, school meals, targeted conditional cash transfers and subsidies, etc. Programs

[1] Assistant Professor, Indian Institute of Foreign Trade (IIFT), Qutab Institutional Area, New Delhi

cannot be expected by themselves to reduce poverty, food insecurity and vulnerability on a sustainable basis, but rather ensure that people's welfare does not further deteriorate. Similarly, for reducing the extent of illiteracy many policy measures are being undertaken. These measures include increase in the public expenditure on education, incentives to raise enrolment ratio, private participation in higher education, *etc.* Though the policy makers and the researchers are emphasizing the central role of education in promoting human development from many angles, one indirect aspect of education in promoting human development is seems to be missing that is, the role of education in promoting human development via food security in rural areas.

This paper examines the triangular relationship between education (particularly basic education), food security and human development. Education not only directly promotes human deployment but also indirectly promotes human development through securing food grains to the poor people. Education works like a weapon for the poor people to fight against food insecurity. So the basic objective of this paper is to establish the linkages between education, food security and human development. For the purpose, I have taken the state of Orissa for the case analysis. The reason is being Orissa is one of the poorest states in the country with substantially low human development index. Even, the performance of Orissa in the sphere of education is comparable to that of national level, but variation of these parameters within the state is substantial. Some of the districts (coastal region) are performed exceptionally well in education parameters whereas others performance is well below the mark. In this paper I have tried to link various education parameters of different districts of Orissa with human development parameters, their level of development and with food security.

Besides the introductory section, this paper will organize as follows: (ii) socio-economic profile of Orissa, (iii) methodology and data source, (iv) education and human development, (v) the overview of education in Orissa, (vi) the state of food security in Orissa, (vii) education in promoting food security and human development- an analysis of Orissa (viii) conclusions and suggestions.

II. Socio-Economic Profile of Orissa

In order to have a proper understanding of the state of human development in term of education and food security in Orissa, we first provide the socio-economic background of the state in terms of these parameters and the important changes therein. Orissa is one of the poorest states in the country with a total population of 36.8 million; it accounts for 3.6 per cent of the population of India and inhabits 4.2 per cent of the total rural population. It depends largely on an undiversified agricultural economy. The poverty headcount ratio is 47 per cent. Poverty is an overwhelmingly rural phenomenon, more than 87 per cent of the total population of the state are living in rural areas with a large majority of them dependent on agriculture for livelihood and is clearly linked to low land productivity and the lowest agricultural wages in the country. While the state, including some of the poorest districts, is virtually self sufficient in food grains, there is a significant portion of chronic food insecurity associated with particular areas (districts) and population groups. Inequalities are greater between the relatively better off coastal areas and the more remote and inaccessible southern region. Regional differences are closely linked to differences among social groups, with poverty among castes and especially indigenous tribal people being strikingly higher than for other groups. The pervasive and chronic food insecurity of poor communities in Orissa is captured by anthropometric measures as over half of the children between 1 and 5 are stunted. 46 percent of the children under age three are undernourished. The infant mortality rate for Orissa is higher than any other state in India, while child malnutrition in Orissa is significantly higher than the national level. Five million people in the state suffer from calorie undernourishment, while protein consumption in the state was as low as 48 gm against 57 gm at the national level. Overall literacy rate in the state is 63.61 per cent as per census report 2001 as against 49.09 per cent in 1991. Gender disparity is also substantial in the state; 75.95 per cent males are literate whereas female literacy rate is 50.97 per cent in 2001. Inter-district variation in literacy rate is also substantial. Coastal districts performance is much better than other parts of the state. Gross enrolment ratio of the state though not much discouraging but the regional disparities within the state is found to be present. As far as human development is concerned 15 of the 30 district have over 80 per cent households with low standard of living. A total of 18 district having a high of over 50 per cent households as Below Poverty Line (BPL) card holders. As many as eight districts have over 60 per cent households as BPL card holders. On average 18 per cent of the population have access to piped drinking water, in rural areas it is merely 2 per cent. In total, 53 per cent of the households have television while those in rural areas; it is only 36 per cent.

III. Methodology and Data Source

The methodological framework of this paper is basically consists of desk research including: review of existing data on education, food security and various indicators of human development with attention to significant information gap, identification of main vulnerable livelihoods in terms of education and different parameters of human development and linking these information to prove basic education is a key factor for food security and human development, besides other factors. The source of data includes; District- level Household and Facility Survey (DLHS) 2007-08, Orissa Human Development Report, NSSO data, Economic Survey of Orissa, FAOSTAT, India Census 2001 and working papers and research papers of different individuals and institutions.

IV. Education and Human Development

For sound human development of a country education has a direct as well as an indirect instrumental role to play. It directly promotes human development because being educated allows people to have a better quality of life. Also it indirectly brings social changes and help in economic production. Therefore, priority being assigned to education by the policy makers and researchers in human development as well as overall development of a country. From the economist like Theodore W. Schultz (1961), Gary S. Becker (1962), Robert J. Barro (1991) to Amartya Sen and Martha Nussbaum (2003) have all emphasized the role of education in promoting human welfare in different perspective. The central point is that education enhances critical thinking and responsibility which are essential elements for improving the individual and collective well being. As per Martha Nussbaum study there are four categories of life skill that are influenced/enhanced by quality education: learning to know, learning to be, learning to live together and learning to do. The theoretical arguments of researchers matches the indicators used to operationalize the human development concept. The Human Development Index (HDI) as developed by Pakistani economist Mahbub ul Haq and others have also taken education (knowledge measured by adult literacy and mean years of schooling) an important parameter besides, longevity (measured by life expectancy) and standard of living (measured by per capita income adjusted with the purchasing power parity). It is important to outline that education is included as an indicator of human development for its intrinsic value. According to an idea; education is development itself and therefore, higher this component in the human development index implies higher is the level of development of the country. Furthermore, the role played by education is also partially embodied in the other two factors; education can affect the length of the life (especially education received by mothers can influence life expectancy of the children) and it affects the income that a person earns (human capital side of the human capability). It is also treated as a key factor for reducing the extent of poverty, infant mortality and in improving other demographic parameters of life. Besides, education can also contribute in fighting with food insecurity which is one of the most important aspects of promoting human development in rural areas. In the subsequent section, this paper analyses how education (particularly, the basic education) contributes for ensuring food grains to the poor people of Orissa and is a stimulating factor for overall human development of the state.

V. An Overview of Education in Orissa

Even though, the government of Orissa is deeply involved in the promotion of education at all levels (be it primary, secondary or higher education) in the state, still it is some years away from bringing all children up to the age of 14 years into the ambit of education, like many other states in India. But, the satisfying fact is that the performance of the state in the sphere of education is not bad as compared to the national average figures in many respects. Its rank is 24th out of 35 states and union territories in India as per 2001 census. Literacy rate of Orissa is 63.6 per cent whereas it is 65.4 per cent at national level in 2001. Compared to 1991 figure, there is an improvement of 15 per cent. Gross enrolment ratio in primary education for 6-11 years age group (ratio of the number of children enrolled in primary education, regardless of age, to the total population of that age group; it can exceed 100 per cent since enrolled students can include under age as well as over age children) in the state in 1999-2000 is 108.8 per cent whereas at all India level it is nearly 95 per cent (2002). At upper primary level for 11-14 age group this figure is 55.3 per cent in Orissa and at all India level it little higher *i.e.* 61 per cent (2002). So far as school attendance rate is concerned it was 72.1 per cent in 1998-99. The percentage of school dropouts is 26.89 per cent which is a cause of concern. Disparities with respect gender, district and different social group in the state is found to be substantial. The gender disparity ratio (ratio of males to females minus one) is 0.4901 in 2001. 50.97 per cent females are literate in the state in comparison to 75.95 per cent males in 2001. Again, rural urban disparities is also substantial, it is 0.3393 in 2001. Gender parity index (ratio of number of girls to number of boys in schools) in education is 0.66 in 1999-2000. Gross enrolment ratio for girls in primary education is 91.5 per cent in 1999-2000, compared to 125.7 per cent for boys. At upper primary level, it is 43.8 per cent for girls against 55.3 per cent for boys. The astonishing fact about education in Orissa is that there exist huge inter district/region gap with respect to different parameters. Compared to the districts of coastal belt and some of the districts of western part, performance of other districts is miserably low. With respect to the literacy rate in 2001, it is 80.19 per cent in Khurda, 79.61 per cent in Jagatsinghpur, 78.4 per cent in Puri, 77.33 per cent in Kendrapara, 76.13 per cent in Cuttack, whereas it is 31.26 per cent in Malkanagiri, 34.26 per cent in Nabarangpur, 35.61 per cent in Rayagada, 36.20 per cent in Koraput, 41.73 per cent in Gajapati, 42.29 per cent in Nuapara and 46.20 per cent in Kalahandi. Marked inter-districts gender disparities are also found. It is 1.2599, 1.2531, 1.1272, 0.9478, 0.9366, and 0.9337 for the districts Nuapada, Nabarangpur, Kalahandi, Rayagada, Malkanagiri and Kandhamal respectively. Whereas it very low for the districts like; Khurda-0.2437, Jagatsingpur-0.2719, Cuttack-2911, Kendrapara-0.3021, etc. In respect to enrolment ratio, the inter-district variation is also very large. It is 50.72 per cent in Nabarangpur, 63.90 per cent in Koraput, 66.79 per cent in Malkanagiri, 69.10 per cent in Rayagada and 73.93 per cent in Gajapati whereas this ratio for coastal districts is much higher. Similarly education deprivation index (it is the sum total of percentage of out-of-school children plus adult literacy rate) is higher than the state average (74.05 per cent) in many of the badly performed districts in the state like; Koraput, Kalahandi, Ganjam and Balangiri. It is 114.33 in Koraput, 97.96 in Kalahandi, 87.47 in Ganjam, 82.12 in Balangiri. Inter-district variation with respect to educational infrastructure in the state is also substantial. These educational disparities is one of the reasons, I assume, for which majority people of these districts fails to ensure food grains for their livelihood, despite so many government schemes (both central and state governments) is in operation in the state.

VI. The State of Food Security in Orissa

Food security refers to the availability of sufficient food grains at a reasonable price so that each and every individual can access food grains as per his/her requirements. According to United States Agency for International Development (USAID), a country attains food security when all the people at all times have both physical and economic access to sufficient food to meet their dietary needs for a productive and healthy life. As per this definition, food security has three dimensions viz., availability of sufficient food grains, access to the available food grains and utilization of the available food grains by the concerned household. Availability implies there must be sufficient food supplies in the country. Access to food grains means the ability of the people to acquire sufficient quantity of food grains. Utilization of food grains refers to actual consumption according to biological capacity (or requirement) of the individuals and households. Of these three aspects of food security problem, adequate food availability is a fundamental parameter or a basic issue. In Orissa, food security problem in terms of all its three aspects has been persisting historically. Even though Orissa is virtually self-sufficient in food grains, there is a significant prevalence of food insecurity in the state and around 9 per cent of the population is classified as extremely food insecure (consuming less than 1,800 kcal per day). The situation varies significantly within the state: 15 per cent of the population in the southern region is extremely food insecure compared to 3 per cent of the population living in the coastal areas. Besides poor basic education, other reasons of this food insecurity includes limited physical as well human asset base, slow economic growth, limited or no access to welfare provisions and public services, lack of land reforms and difficulties in accessing credit institutions. As per the study of FAO (2007), in the coastal belt 43 per cent of labouring rural households had an average daily energy intake of less than 1800 kcal, and there were 57 per cent in the Northern Region and 69 per cent in the Eastern Ghats. Rural agricultural households are the vulnerable group category with the most extreme food insecurity followed by marginal farming households and labouring rural households (52 and

58 per cent). Nutritional status of children and women, is one important indicator of social well being is in miserable state in Orissa. According to International Institute of Population Sciences (IIPS), 48 per cent women in Orissa suffer from nutritional deficiency. It is 54.60 per cent for illiterate woman, 55.5 per cent for scheduled tribe woman and 55.2 per cent for the women who are with a low standard of living. In the age group of 15-49 married women in the state, 63 per cent found to have some degree of anemia. 20.7 per cent of children below 3 years of age are severely underweight and another 54.4 per cent are moderately underweight (on the basis of weight of age). On the basis of height for age measure, 17.6 per cent of children suffer from chronic under nutrition of severe type and another 44 per cent of the moderate type. As many as five million people in the state suffer from calorie undernourishment, while protein consumption in the state was as low as 48 gm against the national average of 57 gm. If we analyse production side, the productivity of major crops is pretty low in comparison to those in better producing states as well as national average. The total food grains production in the state in 2006-07 is about 8.30 million tones. Looking at the food security outcome index, five districts (Nuapada, Rayagada, Gajapati, Malkanagiri and Kandhamala) are extremely food insecure and thirteen districts (Balangir, Nabarangapur, Jajpur, Sambalpur, Sonepur, Sundergarh, Keonjhar, Bhadrak, Bargarh, Boudh, Kalahandi, Ganjam and Koraput) are severely food insecure districts. Interestingly, most of these districts are performed badly in respect of education parameters.

VII. Education in Promoting Food Security and Human Development - An Analysis of Orissa

Having analyzed the present state of education and food security in Orissa, this section focuses on to link these parameters/determinants to draw the desired conclusion that basic education is a stimulating factor for food security and human development. As stated above, there are three broad indicators that influence food insecurity in one way or other viz., production factor (influencing availability), access to food by the households and individual and, ability to absorb foodgrains. Availability of food grains depends on agricultural production and productivity which is a necessary but not sufficient condition of food security, access to food grains including, physical and economic access, certainly depends on income of the households, efficiency of public distribution system, infrastructure, transportation, etc. Absorption/utilization is concerned with actual consumption according to the biological capacity of the individual and households. Though food insecurity problem in terms of all these three aspects persist in Orissa, one of the most important aspect responsible for food insecurity is lack of access to public information regarding health, nutrition and hygiene. Acquiring knowledge about how to avoid and face illness is essential since people with disease requires more calorie to be food secure. The public information can be acquired through basic education. Further, if parents are educated, they will definitely give priority to the nutritional requirement of their children (children with less educated parents score poorly on nutritional status indices- Mukudi, 2003). Thus, education is fundamental to promote agency, which expresses the capacity of rural poor to escape from poverty and hunger with their own power. An educated person is always concern about certain valuable objectives of life like, access to food for the household, health and nutrition. Educated people are more likely to find a job, as he/she has capacity to use the recourses rationally which he/she has. Female's education has much more influence on family food security than the male because females are more concerned to the well being of their children (female literacy… is found to have an unambiguous and statistically significant reducing impact on under five mortality- A.K. Sen, 1999). Another aspect of education in promoting food security is through social relations. In Orissa, 20 villages in Balangir district formed a community grain bank to fight food insecurity and are being successful in achieving its goal. The process was initiated by some of the literate people in the village and is actively participating in the functioning of the community grain bank. Education also makes people ambitious and self confident which in turn gives a psychological contribution to food security. An educated person can contribute more towards agricultural productivity through scientific cultivation and can earn income through commercial crops and from non farm activities. Awareness on various government schemes has also is an important bearing on food security. An educated person can take these benefits easily.

Linking the educational parameters of Orissa with the food security parameters reveals an interesting trend. The districts with potentially poor with educational parameters are more food insecure and districts with better of in education are comparatively food secure. In educationally advanced districts less percentage of population are living below poverty line, on the contrary in educationally backward districts more percentage of the population are living below poverty line. Districts like, Kandhamal, Nuapada, Rayagada, Gajapati, Malkanagiri, Balangir, Koraput are poor in education parameters and also perform badly in food security outcome index. Similarly, district like, jagatsinghpur, Cuttack, Puri, Khurda, Balasore, Nayagarh, Jharsuguda performed well in education parameters as well as in food security index. Table 1 links different educational and food security parameters of some of the districts of Orissa.

Four parameters each of education and human development for 14 districts of the state is given in the Table 1. It is clear that first seven districts perform well in respect to educational as well as human development indicators whereas rest seven districts performed badly in respect of all these parameters. Districts with higher literacy rate, gross enrollment ratio and education index are ranked well in human development index and vice-versa. Income index of educationally better of districts are comparatively higher than the districts which are performed badly. For example, districts like, Khurda, Jharsuguda, Cuttack, Kendrapada have higher literacy rate, gross enrollment ratio thus, their HDI ranks are 1, 2, 3, and 10 respectively whereas districts like Malkanagiri, Koraput, Gajapati have lower literacy rate, gross enrollment ratio thus, their HDI ranks are 30, 27 and 28 respectively. This shows a trend in Orissa that education has a significant bearing on human development in the state. In relating the education indicators of some of the districts with food security indicators (District Level Household and Facility Survey-3, 2007-08); a similar trend is also observed. The set of eight districts namely, Malkanagiri, Kandhamala, Kalahandi, Boudh, Rayagada, Koraput, Nuapada, Nabarangapur presents a very dismal HDI in respect to all the yardsticks. In these districts more than 60 per cent of the population is BPL card holder hence living below the poverty line. In Kandhamal, 65 percent people are BPL card holder. Interestingly, in these districts education parameters are well below the better performed districts. Therefore, education is one of the key factors in determining the economic and social parameters of life.

Table 1: Education and Food Security Indicators in Orissa

Sl. No	Name of the District	Literacy rate (2001) in Percentage	Overall Literacy Rate Index	Gross Enrollment Ratio (Primary)	Education Index	DDP Per Capita (1998-99)	Income Index	HDI Value	HDI Rank
I	II	III	IV	V	VI	VII	VIII	IX	X
1	Khurda	80.19	0.802	93.03	0.845	7353	0.639	0.736	1
2	Puri	78.4	0.784	90.02	0.823	4933	0.527	0.657	7
3	Jagatsingh Pur	79.61	0.796	90.97	0.833	5340	0.549	0.557	19
4	Kendrapada	77.33	0.773	89.95	0.815	3964	0.466	0.626	10
5	Cuttack	76.13	0.761	91.64	0.813	6116	0.587	0.695	3
6	Jharsuguda	7147	0.715	89.00	0.773	11210	0.757	0.722	2
7	Bhadrak	74.64	0.746	89.81	0.803	3916	0.463	0.645	8
8	Malkanagiri	31.61	0.313	84.73	0.491	4436	0.497	0.370	30
9	Koraput	36.2	0.362	88.12	0.535	5148	0.539	0.431	27
10	Kalahandi	46.2	0.462	83.03	0.585	4043	0.471	0.606	11
11	Kandhamal	52.95	0.530	87.68	0.645	4737	0.516	0.389	29
12	Gajapati	41.73	0.417	84.82	0.561	5498	0.558	0.431	28
13	Nuapada	42.29	0.423	90.13	0.582	4018	0.470	0.581	14
14	Rayagada	35.61	0.356	88.21	0.443	5300	0.547	0.589	25

contd...

Source: Orissa Human Development Report, 2004-05.

VIII. Conclusions and Suggestions

In conclusion, it can be argued that education is very much relevant in strengthening food security to the poor people thus, promotes human development significantly. As discussed, basic education contributes directly as well as indirectly for the well being of the people. It not only raises the people's capacity to earn more but also provides life-skills to the people. Data pertaining to different districts of Orissa in our case analysis provides the evidence that higher the literacy rate or school attendance rate implies comfortable income and human development parameters, thus, less is the problem of food insecurity. Therefore, priority of government policy should also aim to reduce the extent of illiteracy and to increase the gross enrolment ratio. The governments and donors aiming to tackle the problem of food insecurity should focus their attention in investing on basic education which in turn will help in solving the problem of food insecurity, besides other measures. Such a policy should be adopted with a specific emphasis on rural areas because of the dramatic incidence of illiteracy, food insecurity, and poor state of human development index.

References

Anand, S. and Sen, A. K. (1999): *Human Development Index: Methodology and Measurement*, United Nations Development Program, http://hdr.undp.org/publications/papers.cfm.

Burchi, Francesco (2006): Education, Human Development, and Food Security in Rural Areas: Assessing Causalities, Paper for the International Conference of the Human Development and Capability Approach, Groningen.

De, Haan A. and Dubey A (2003): Poverty in Orissa: Divergent Trends, paper presented at "Monitoring of Poverty in Orissa, 26-27 Feb."

Deaton, A. and Dreze, J. (2002): Poverty and Inequality in India, a re-examination, *Economic and Political Weekly*, 37(36): 3729-48.

ESA Working Paper No 07-28 (2007): Understanding the Dynamics of Food Insecurity and Vulnerability in Orissa, India. FAOSTAT (http://faostat.fao.org/)

Government of India (2001): National Human Development Report, Planning Commission.

Government of India (1996): National Sample Survey (NSS) 50th and

55th Round, 1993-1994 and 1999-2000.

Government of Orissa and UNDP (2004): Orissa Human Development Report.

Majhi. Bidyadhar (2009): Food Security in India vis-avis the Policy of Waiving Farm Loans, Southern Economist, 47-18.

Patra, Sanjeev Kumar (2009): Orissa Poor in Human Development Index, Express Buzz.

Padhi, Arbind K (2009): Agriculture and Food Security in Orissa, www.odisha.in.

Rout, Sarita Sundari (2009): Food Insecurity in Rural Orissa, Orissa News.

Tilak, Jandhyala B.G (2002): Education and Poverty, *Journal of Human Development.* 3(2): 191-207.

Tripathy D. and Misra J.K. (2004): Seasonality and Food Security: A Programme for Food Security for All, DJ Research and Consultancy for Planning and Coordination Department, Orissa.

Ul-Haq, Mahbub (2003): The Birth of the Human Development Index, In Sakikon Fukuda-Parr and A.K. Shiva Kumar (Eds.), *Readings in Human Development.* New York: Oxford University Press, pp. 103-113 Article originally published in 1995, *Reflections on Human Development*, Chapter 4, Oxford University Press.

UNDP (1990): *Human Development Report: Concepts and Measurement of Human Development*, Oxford University Press, New York.

17

Technology and its Impact on Human Development

K. Joseph Raj[1]

Introduction

People are the real wealth of nations. Development expands the choices of people they value to leave. Fundamental to enlarging these choices is building human capabilities, the range of things that people can do or be in life. The most basic capabilities for human development *are those that enable them* to lead long and healthy lives, to be knowledgeable, to have access to knowledge, to have access to the resources needed for a decent standard of living and to be able to participate in the life of the community.

Philosophers, economists and political leaders have long emphasized human wellbeing as the purpose, the end of development. Aristotle said that Wealth is evidently not the good we are seeking, for it is merely useful for the sake of something else. Human development shares a common vision with human rights. The goal is human freedom. People must exercise their choices and participate in decision making that affects their lives. Human development and human rights are mutually reinforcing, helping to secure the well being and dignity of all people building self respect and the respect of others.

The Past and Present Human Development

Of the 4.6 billion people in developing countries, more than 850 million are illiterate, a billion lack access to improved water sources, and 2.4 billion lack access to basic sanitation. Nearly 325 million boys and girls are out of schools. And 11 million children under the age of five die each year from preventable causes. Around 1.2 billion

[1] Assistant Professor of Economics, Department of Economics, S.T. Hindu College, Nagercoil, Tamil Nadu

people live on less than $ 1 a day and 2.8 billion on less than $ 2 a day (HDI Report 2001). Since 1990 adult literacy rates have risen from 75 percent to 82 percent, reducing the number of illiterate people in the world by 100 million. Women still account for about two thirds of adults' illiteracy. The bad news is that 115 million children are still out of schools (HD Report 2006) .

A child born today is expected to live eight years longer than that of one born 30 years ago. The share of rural facilities with access to safe water has increased fivefold. The average income in developing countries has almost doubled in real terms between 1975 and 1998 from $ 1300 to $ 2500.

All types of development are backed by technology. Technology has been at the heart of human progress since earliest time. The technological improvement has been followed by the first human species named Homo babilies to modern human. All types of technologies have been used for human development. The digital, genetic and molecular breakthroughs are pushing forward the frontiers of how people can use technology to eradicate poverty and lead the decent living. Many technologies are tools of human development that enable people to increase their incomes, live longer, be healthier, enjoy better standards of living, participate more in their communities and lead more creative lives. It enables people to lift themselves out of poverty.

Technological innovation affects human development in two ways. First, it can directly enhance human capabilities. Many products, drought tolerant plant varieties for farmers in uncertain climates, vaccines, for infectious diseases, clean energy sources for cooking Internet access for information and communications has directly improved people's health, nutrition, knowledge and living standards and has increased people's ability to participate more actively in the social, economic and political life of a community.

Second, technological innovation is a means to human development because of its impact on economic growth through the productivity gains it generate. It raises the crop yields of farmers, the output of factory workers and the efficiency of service providers and small business. It also creates new activities and industries such as the information and communication technology sector – contributing to economic growth and employment creation.

Figure 1

LINKS BETWEEN TECHNOLOGY AND HUMAN DEVELOPMENT

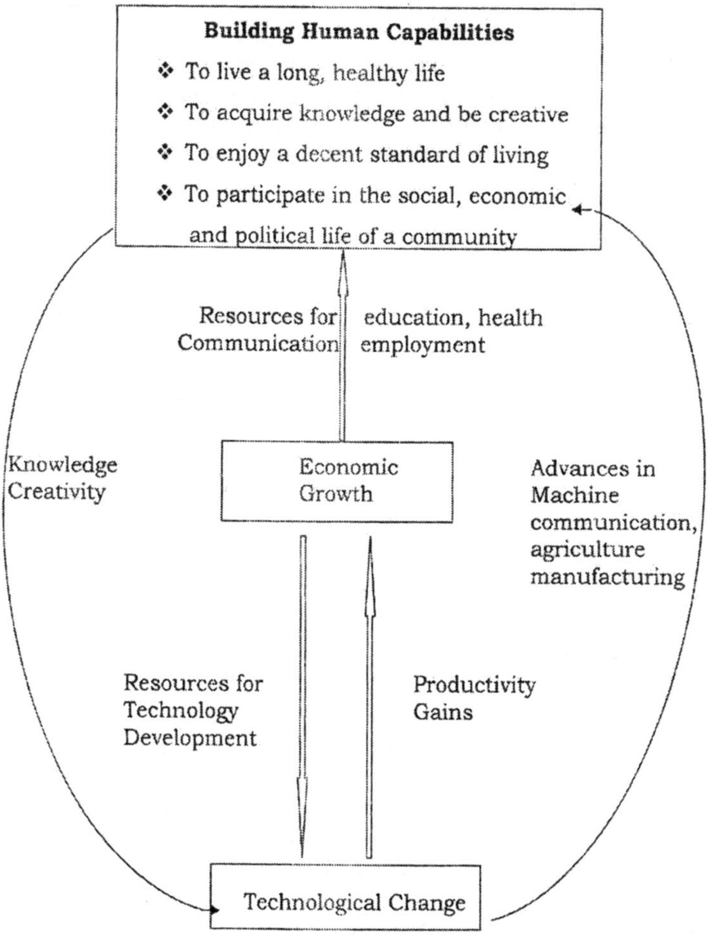

Human development and technological advance can be mutually reinforcing, creating a virtuous cycle. Technological innovations in agriculture, medicine, energy, manufacturing and communications were important to break the barriers on progress.

Survival and Health

Medical breakthroughs, such as immunization and antibiotics have resulted in faster gain in Latin America and East Asia than in Europe. Human health and survival began to improve dramatically in developing countries. The 1980s saw the impact of two new breakthroughs – oral rehydration therapy and vaccines, which were better adapted to conditions in developing countries.

Life expectancy at birth has continued to increase globally over the years. Trends in life expectancy of people show that people are living longer. They have a right to a long life in good health.

Table 1: Expectation of Life at Birth in India

Year	Life expectancy (in Years)
1951	32.06
1961	43.29
1971	45.55
1981	50.45
1991	58.60
1999	62.90
2003	63.30
2004	63.60
2005	63.70

Source: 1. Human Development Reports, 2002, 2005, 2007/08.
2. Economic Survey, Govt. of India, 2008-09.

Table 1 reveals that the life expectancy at birth increased from 32.06 years in 1951 5o 63.70 years in 2005. This increased trend is because of improvement in health conditions contributed by the technology. No doubt, that life saving medicines has been invented and technological upgradation implemented to produce them in mass scale *so that they could* reach the hands of needy people.

Food Grain Production and Nutrition

Technological progress has played a similar role in accelerating food production. Starting in 1960s a green revolution of plant breeding, fertilizer use, better seeds and water control transformed land and labour productivity around the world. Their dynamic effects increased food production and reduced food prices eliminating much of under-nutrition and chronic famine in Asia, promoting human development.

Food Grains Production in India

Green revolution is backed by technological development. The shortage of food grains production is solved by technological innovations.

Table 2: Foodgrains Production

Year	Production (in tons)
1960-61	82.0
1970-71	104.4
1980-81	129.6
1990-91	176.4
2000-01	196.8
2008-09	229.9

Source: Economic Survey, 2008-09.

Table 2 indicates that the food grains production increased from 82 million tons in 1960-61 to 229.9 million tons in 2008-09. This much of growth in production is because of high yielding variety of seeds, mechanized farming, use of pesticides and chemical fertilizers. The per capita net availability per day increased from 394.9 grams in 1951 to 442.8 grams in 2007.

Participation

The printing press, telephone, radio and television have opened up communications, reducing isolation, enabling people to be better informed and to participate in decision making that affect their lives positively. Tied to these technologies is the free media, a pillar of all functioning of democracies.

Employment and Economic Growth

The acquisition and adoption of manufacturing technology brought rapid gains in employment and income to all sections of the people. The industrial revolution was triggered by technological change. *E*conomists argue that technological progress plays a vital role in sustained long term economic growth.

Table 3: Employment and Economic Growth

Year	Employment (in Lac)	Economic Growth
1991	267.33	5.0
1994	273.75	5.9
1996	275.25	6.5
1997	279.41	7.3
1998	282.45	8.1
1999	281.06	4.5
2000	281.13	6.7
2001	279.80	6.4
2002	277.89	4.0
2003	270.00	6.0
2004	264.43	4.0
2005	264.58	8.5
2006	269.93	7.5

Source: Economic Survey, 2008-09.

Table 3 shows that employment both in organized and unorganized sector increased from 267.33 lakhs in 1991 to 282.45 lakhs in 1997 and went up *to* 269.93 lakhs in 2006. The economic growth of the country has attained a significant level. This economic growth is caused by technological improvement and liberalized policy of the government. This growth and employment have reduced the poverty of the country.

Technology, Education and Human Development in India

Education is an engine vital for human development. Technology and education are inter-related. Education promotes technological diffusion and creation. Technological development is higher in countries where education is given much importance.

Table 4: Education and HDI in India

Year	Education in Index	HDI
1999	0.56	0.571
2003	0.61	0.602
2004	0.61	0.611
2005	0.62	0.619

Source: Human Development Report, 2005, 2006, 2007/08.

Table 4 indicates that education index increased from 0.56 in 1999 to 0.62 in 2005. Similarly human development index increased from 0.571 in1999 to 0.619 in 2005. There is a direct relationship between education and human development. Besides, education helps to improve technology.

Information, Communication, Technology and Human Development

Information and communications technology involves innovations in microelectronics, computing, telecommunication and microprocessors and semi conductors. Fibre optics linking computing devices are allowing them to communicate with each other. Individuals, households and institutions are linked in processing of information. These promote the human development.

Benefits to Human Development

These new technologies dramatically increase access to information and communication, breaking barriers to political participation and giving greater transparency, generating income to a notable number of people in the country.

Health problems are compounded by lack of information, and new solutions are emerging. Nurses can use a digital camera to record patients' symptoms. The pictures are sent electronically to a nearby town to be diagnosed by a local doctor. It enables them to process that information efficiently, cooperate with medical institutions worldwide and provide information on emerging outbreaks of diseases. Biotechnology has also been applied to seemingly intractable health issues, such as determining which genes are responsible for creating or enabling disease processes, how these genes control these processes and what might be done to stop them. These technologies are then used to modify crops and food plants.

New technology, new drugs and treatments based on genomics and related technologies offer potential break-through for tackling major health challenges. Genomics can speed up plant breeding, new crop varieties and disease resistance. It could develop technologies with less environmental stress and produce foods with more nutritional value.

Internet

This new facility connects the people throughout the world. It breaks barriers to knowledge. Access to information is pivotal to acquire knowledge and build human capabilities. It is breaking barriers to participation and breaking barriers to economic opportunities.

Technology achievement Index of India

There are parameters which are used to calculate the technological achievements. The parameters are technology creation, diffusion of recent innovations, diffusion of old innovations and human skills.

Table 5: Technology Achievement Index of India

Country	Technology achievement Index value (1999)	HDI
Leaders		
Finland	0.744	0.925
US	0.733	0.934
Sweden	0.703	0.936
Japan	0.698	0.928
Potential Leaders		
Spain	0.481	0.908
Malaysia	0.396	0.774
Dynamic adapters		
China	0.299	0.718
Sri Lanka	0.203	0.735
India	0.201	0.571
Marginalized		
Pakistan	0.167	0.498
Nepal	0.081	0.480

Source: Human Development Report, 2002.

Table 5 shows that there are five categories on the basis of value scored. The USA, Finland, and Japan have obtained a value more than 0.5. They are categorized as leaders. Those with a index value ~~is~~ up to 0.35 are categorized as the potential leaders; those with a index value up to 0.2 are categorized as dynamic adapters – those with a index value up to 0.266 are categorized as the marginalized and the rest of the countries are termed as 'others' category. India and China fall under the category of dynamic adapters.

Table 6 shows that the number of telephones mainlined, cellular subscribers and internet users are increasing. The developed countries like the US, Finland, Sweden and Japan spent more on research and development; and the number of persons involved in research there are also comparatively higher. Similarly their Human Development index is also higher than that in other countries. The people involved in research and development in Asian countries is comparatively lower than that in developed countries.

Human Development Trends in India

Human development is contributed by many factors. Among them technology achievements, technology diffusion and creation are less in developing countries. India is a country, which gives more importance for the development of information technology, computer literacy programs and research and development.

Table 7 indicates that the human development index increased from 0.419 in 1975 to 0.619 in 2005. These figures lead us to infer that there is an increasing trend of human development in India.

Conclusion

Technology helps in all walks of life. Owing to the improvement in technology, death rate and infant mortality rate in our country has decreased year by year. Not only that life expectancy has increased, but food production has also increased; consequently per head availability of food grains has also increased. As a result poverty reduction is achieved successfully. Technological development is paving way to improve human development. Educational level of the country is improving. Besides technology diffusion and creation are improving to a larger extent both in developed and developing countries of the world. India is gradually moving towards the path of improving education and this leads to improvements in technology. On the whole, improvements in education and technology have advanced the people's life and this is getting reflected in human development.

Table 6: Technology Diffusion and Creation in India and other Countries

Country	Telephone mainlines (per 1000 people)		Cellular subscribers\ (per 1000 people)		Inter users (per 1000 people)	
	1990	2005	1990	2005	1990	2005
Finland	535	404	52	997	4	534
US	545	606	21	680	8	630
Sweden	683	717	54	935	6	764
Japan	441	460	7	742	-	668
Spain	325	422	1	952	-	348
Malaysia	89	172	5	8771	0	435
China	6	269	-	302	0	85
Sri Lanka	7	63	-	171	0	14
India	6	45	0	82	0	55
Pakistan	8	34	-	82	0	67
Nepal	3	17	0	9	0	4

contd...

Patents grants to residents (per million people)	Receipts of royalties license fees US $ per person	R and D Expectation of GDP	Researchers in R *D per million people	HDI
2000-05	2000-05	2000-05	1990-2005	2005
214	230.9	3.5	7832	0.925
244	191.5	2.7	4605	0.591
166	367.7	3.7	5416	0.956
857	138.0	3.1	5287	0.953
53	12.9	1.1	2195	0.949

-	0.0	0.3	97	0.811
16	0.1	1.4	708	0.777
3	-	0.1	128	0.743
1	-	0.8	119	0.619
0	0.1	0.2	75	0.551
-	-	0.7	59	0.534

Source: Human Development Report, UNDP, 2006, 2007/08

Table 7: Human Development Trends in India

Year	HDI
1975	0.419
1980	0.450
1985	0.487
1990	0.521
1995	0.551
2000	0.578
2005	0.619

Source: Human Development Report 2007/08.

References

UNDP, (2002): Human Development Report, New York.
UNDP, (2005): Human Development Report, New York.
UNDP, (2006): Human Development Report, New York.
UNDP, (2007/8): Human Development Report, New York.
Government of India (2008): Economic Survey, New Delhi.

18

Human Development and Environmental Quality: Issues of Harmony and Conflict

Nirmal Chandra Sahu[1]

I. Introduction

Human development (HD) recognizes the limitation of economic growth that high rates of material prosperity do not automatically translate into high levels of human well-being. Human capability and deprivation are the two important defining elements behind the measurement of HD, which combines three essential components of life, namely longevity, knowledge and decent living standards. The efforts of UNDP since 1990 have helped to standardize a methodology to combine the attainments of an economy in respect of these components and express the same through the HD Index (HDI), which has gained currency as a strategic policy tool. The strength and appeal of HDI lie in the fact that it brings the twin objectives of economic progress and social development together. However, it does not fully address the issues of compatibility and conflict between environment and development, which is the substantive subject addressed in this paper.

II. HD Theory and Heterodox Economics

HD theory is the most pronounced output of heterodox economics, which is an umbrella term used to cover various separate unorthodox approaches, schools, or traditions outside of the mainstream. These include institutional, post-Keynesian, socialist, marxian, feminist, austrian, ecological, social economics and so on. Beyond the rubric of non-neoclassical economics, it promotes pluralism in economics and permit distinct paradigms to develop. HD theory merges ideas from ecological economics, sustainable development, welfare economics, and other social sciences. Like ecological economics it focuses on measuring well-being and detecting uneconomic growth that comes at the expense of the health

[1] Professor, Post Graduate Department of Economics, Berhampur University, Orissa

of the human economy. However, it goes further in seeking not only to measure but to optimize well-being by some explicit modelling of how social capital and institutional capital can be deployed to optimize the overall value of human capital in an economy. The role of individual capital is a major focus of the theory. The most notable proponent of HD theory is Amartya Sen, who asked, in Development as Freedom, "What is the relationship between our wealth and our ability to live as we would like?" This question cannot be answered strictly from an energy, feminist, family, environment, health peace, social justice, or ecological well being point of view, although all of these may be factors in our happiness, and if tolerances of any of these are violated seriously, it would seem impossible to be happy at all. Thus the HD theory is a major synthesis, which is not confined within the bounds of conventional economics or political science, nor even the political economy that relates the two.

The concept of human well-being based on the capability approach formulated by Sen was the basis of the first HD Report published by UNDP in 1990. The HD paradigm focused its attention on how development could enlarge people's choices by expanding freedoms and capabilities. It implied expansion of the real freedom that individuals enjoy and attention must be shifted away from the means that allow liberties to expand such as economic growth, increased personal income, technological progress or social modernization towards the ends which are the liberties themselves. In the first report Mahbub ul Haq had the explicit purpose to shift the focus of development economics from national income accounting to people centered policies. To produce the HDRs, Haq brought together a group of well known development economists including Paul Streeten, Frances Stewart, Gustav Ranis, Keith Griffin, Sudhir Anand and Meghnad Desai. But it was Sen's work on capabilities and functionings that provided the underlying conceptual framework.

However, HDI is a summary indicator. It does not fully represent the comprehensive notion of Sen's HD. Therefore, attempts have been made to supplement the HDI with more specialized indices to capture certain other aspects of social well-being, namely the gender-sensitive dimension of socioeconomic deprivation. Yet another dimension relates to environmental quality, which is now widely considered as a welfare determinant. While the 1994 HD Report covered environmental security as an important component of human security, no effort has been made to integrate environmental issues with HD. The recent reports have recognized that climate change is the defining HD issue of our generation as it threatens to erode human freedoms and limit choice.

III. The Economy-environment Interface

The economy-environment nexus is portrayed in Figure 1. The left hand side represents a simple circular flow model of an economy. The right hand side shows the natural environment in terms of the three economic functions – Resource supply, Amenity value and Sink service (Common, 1988 and Hanley et al., 1997). A fourth function of the environment is shown as the boundary of the Figure. This role relates to the life-support services provided by the environment. Such services include maintenance of an atmospheric composition suitable to life, maintenance of temperature and climate, recycling of water and nutrients, maintenance of biodiversity and ecological stability, and so on. The economy-environment system is characterised by a number of interrelated features, which include the following:

- ✓ Material balance principle: Since matter, can neither be created nor destroyed, any economy must eventually have the same amount of materials disposed of in the form of waste (output) as it initially used in the form of raw materials (inputs) in production and consumption.
- ✓ The entropy law: Because of the Second Law of Thermodynamics, the economic process always requires low entropy matter and continuously makes it to move towards high entropy (disordered) matter. This implies that there are definite limits to the economic process.
- ✓ Uncertainty and irreversibility: There is extensive uncertainty about the workings of the economic-ecologic systems. The environmental impacts mostly come in our lives as surprises and novel experiences. Moreover, a major implication of the entropy law is that the environmental impacts of the economy are irreversible.
- ✓ Scale effect and synergies: As the volume of economic activity increases, the scale of the impact on the environment tends to rise with multiplicative effect. The natural environment is characterized by the existence of thresholds and discontinuities, which result in large scale damages once the thresholds are exceeded.

Figure 1: Economy–Environment Interactions

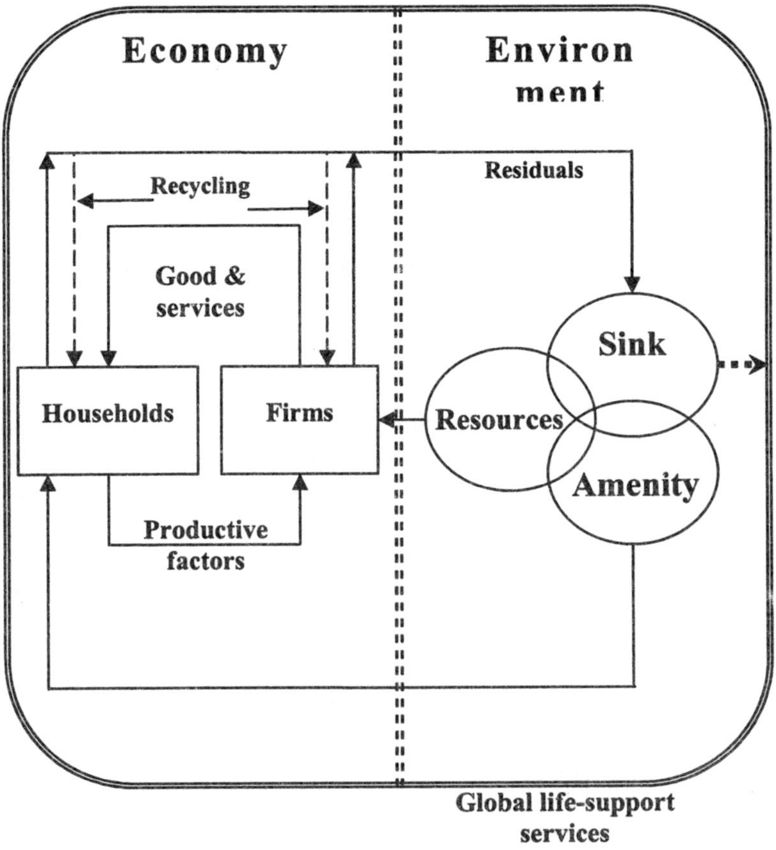

✓ Cost shifting and distance phenomenon: Cost shifting refers to the process of pushing (or shifting) a part of the adverse consequences (or cost) of one's behavior on to the others to bear. This has been recognised in economics as the problem of externalities or external costs. Economic activities lead to social costs that are not (fully) translated into private costs, or internalised into the private decision making mechanism.

- ✓ Institutional failures: There are at least three categories of failures - transaction failure, empowerment failure and governance failure - within the institutional arrangements of an economy, which cause injury to environment. The transaction failures, among other things, include market system failures covering inefficient markets and absence of markets (as in the case of many indirect benefits of biodiversity), and preference failures, due to inadequate knowledge and information. Empowerment failures take place when there is inadequate or inappropriate social mobilisation for environmental conservation compared with what would be optimal. These problems arise from the inadequacies in the relationships between different kinds of economic agents, such as individuals, state and non-governmental organisations in so far as they deal with economically relevant transactions and decisions, and their repercussions on the biodiversity. The government failure includes at least four sub-categories: (a) correction failure: lack of policies to address biodiversity depletion; (b) co-ordination failure: deficiencies in arriving at inter-state mechanisms or agreements to deal with environmental problems; (c) failures in the intervention itself, such as inappropriate target setting or lack of instruments; and finally (d) administrative failure: inefficiencies in enforcement and implementation, lack of internal co-ordination, etc.
- ✓ Public good properties: Environmental quality is a public good. Many environmental resources, often referred as the commons, common property resources or common pool resources (CPRs) and open access resources (OARs), suffer from the problem of 'free ride'.
- ✓ Tragedy of the commons and social trap: The combination of ineffectual property right and inadequate legal protection against overuse together with free or cheap use of the CPRs by the people inevitably lead to abuse and quality degradation. Professor Garrett Hardin has captured the

essence of this phenomenon in the evocative phrase of the Tragedy of the Commons in 1968. Being caught in a 'social trap', the individuals take a decision, which is collectively harmful. What is optimal from an individual short-run perspective is not optimal from a social long-run perspective.

Over the last few decades, a great deal of attention has been given to the role of natural resources and the environment in promoting the fundamental aspects of human well-being and the quality of life. Attention has gradually shifted from a vision of environment as a limit to economic growth (Meadows et al., 1972) to its active role in reducing poverty, achieving higher living standards (WCED, 1987) and increasing human development levels. The first few HD reports have not explicitly considered the role of the natural environment in enhancing people's choices but in more recent editions, the environment and more broadly sustainable development have been progressively introduced (UNDP, 1996). In the year 2000, the definition of the Millennium Development Goals by the United Nations definitively recognized the full integration of human development and the environment as mutually reinforcing development goals. From a theoretical perspective, an integrated Sustainable Human Development paradigm has been defined as development that promotes the capabilities of people in the present without compromising the capabilities of future generations (Sen, 2000). In this context, two different approaches seem to be most appealing for appreciating the integrated paradigm: the effects of natural resources endowment on development as analysed through the Resource Curse Hypothesis (RCH) and the effects of economic growth and development on environmental quality as formalized in the Environmental Kuznets Curve (EKC) hypothesis.

IV. Resource Curse Hypothesis (RCH)

The Resource Curse Hypothesis maintains that countries with high natural resources endowments have experienced lower economic growth rates than countries with scarce stocks of natural resources. The resource curse is paradoxical because production of natural resources has been the initial source of nearly all development, providing an almost immediate source of foreign exchange, attracting foreign capital and skills and increasing the availability of both raw materials for processing and a market for manufactured inputs. Nonetheless, over the last fifty years, countries rich in natural (commercial) resources (e.g., Russia, Nigeria and Venezuela) experienced economic growth that was somewhat lower than the countries with scarce resources (Auty, 2001). Sachs and Warner (1995) provided a first formulation of an empirical RCH, claiming that the resource curse is a historically common pattern and the abundance of natural resources is one of the most evident causes of low economic performances. Countries that base their economies on natural resources tend to be examples of development failures. In contrast, countries such as Japan, Hong Kong, Korea and Ireland experienced high economic growth rates although they had relatively lower endowments of natural resources.

One of the first explanations for the observed slow growth rate despite the resource endowments in some countries has been attributed to the substantial terms of trade volatility in primary commodity exports (Mikesell, 1997). Empirical investigations have not been able to find a strong relationship between terms of trade volatility and per capita growth (Sachs and Warner, 1999; Sala-i-Martin and Subramanian, 2003), and have turned to other transmission channels in order to explain such a curse. The main body of literature suggests five different explanations (Auty, 2001; Ross, 1999) such as the Dutch disease effect, misallocation of revenues from resource exploitation, rent seeking behavior, quality of institutions, and role of human capital.

First, the Dutch disease hypothesis, coined in 1977 by the Economists to describe the decline of the manufacturing sector in the Netherlands after the discovery of a large natural gas field, suggests that a resource boom will divert a country's resources away from activities that are more conducive to long-term growth. The theory is that an increase in revenues from natural resources will de-industrialize a nation's economy by raising the exchange rate, which makes the manufacturing sector less competitive. Secondly, misallocation of revenues from exploitation of natural resources implies negative values of Genuine Savings (GS), which means that income growth has been obtained through the dissipation of natural capital without appropriate investments to replace the exhaustible resources. From a sustainability point of view, such growth progress will not last long, as overexploitation will negatively affect the long-term economic growth (Atkinson and Hamilton, 2003). The third explanation of the RCH is linked to the presence of rent seeking behavior, based on the assumption that resource rents are easily appropriable and this, in turn, leads to distortion in public policies and pressure from lobbies and oligopolistic companies to seek public favors (Torvik, 2002). Concentration of rents in the hands of a few private owners directs revenue away from human resources, infrastructures, traditional agriculture, small enterprise towards consumption and rent dissipation. A fourth explanation looks deeply at the relationships between the quality of institutions and the capacity to effectively and optimally manage the resources (Mehlum et al., 2005 and Bulte et al., 2005). Destruction of institutions and obstacles to the formation of solid institutions associated with resource abundance leads to poorer economic performance. Finally, a fifth explanation classifies recent contributions that have stressed the importance of characteristics linked to the absence of adequate investments in enhancing human resources. Gylfason (2001) has emphasized that resource abundance may have the effect of "crowding out" the accumulation of human capital, reducing the incentives for investments in education or knowledge sectors. Atkinson and Hamilton (2003) have pointed out that public investment in human capital accumulation makes a great contribution to economic growth in resource abundant countries, whereas countries with higher government consumption have generally experienced a significant resource curse.

V. Environmental Kuznets Curve (EKC) Hypothesis

Under static assumptions about technology, tastes and environmental investments, economic growth will inevitably hurt the environment. However, if the assumptions are relaxed, for which there is evidence in the real world, alternative relationships are possible. The relation between per capita income growth and environmental degradation can take the form of an inverted-U. With this form of relationship, pollution per capita rises until per capita income reaches the turning point, and thereafter actually it declines (Perman et al., 1999). This implies that economic growth can improve the environment, after a certain stage. It has been hypothesized that such relationship holds for many forms of environmental degradation. This relationship, now widely described as the EKC, was first observed in the studies of Selden and Song (1992). The term is derived from the famous Kuznets Curve, which was named after Simon Kuznets, the 1971 Nobel Laureate, who in

1955 hypothesized an inverted-U shaped relationship between a measure of inequality in the income distribution and the level of income. The EKC has been observed as an empirical regularity in several studies for some index of environmental degradation (Sahu, 2005). The EKC behaviour, of course, has a bearing not only with the per capita income as an index of economic growth, but also with the state of environmental property rights, policy mechanisms and resource subsidies (Pachauri 1997). The World Bank (1992) has identified four factors, which together play a very important role in determining the environmental impact per unit of economic activity. These are:

- Structure: the goods and services produced in the conomy;
- Efficiency: inputs used per unit of output in the economy;
- Substitution: the ability to substitute away from resources that are becoming scarce; and
- Clean technologies and management practices: the ability to reduce environmental damage per unit of input or output.

The extent to which these factors impact upon environmental quality depends upon the incentive structures facing agents, and policy settings. As incomes rise, demand for environmental quality will rise along with resources available for investment on environmental promotion. Thus, economic growth yields factors and practices conducive to the EKC relationship. The reasoning behind the validity of the hypothesis has been explained through a certain process of economic evolution. At low levels of development both the extent and intensity of environmental degradation is limited to the impacts of subsistence economic activity on the resource base and to limited amounts of biodegradable wastes. As economic development accelerates with the different types of resource extraction processes, the intensification of agriculture, and the take-off of industrialisation, the rates of resource depletion begin to exceed the rates of resource regeneration. The wastes and pollution generated in the economy increase in quantity and toxicity. However, at higher levels of development, structural changes set in taking the economy towards information-intensive industries and services, coupled with increased environmental awareness, enforcement of environmental regulations, efficient technology and higher environmental investments. All these result in a leveling off and gradual decline of environmental degradation. Because of the evidence for the relationship, it has been argued that at the end the best, and probably the only, way to attain a decent environment in most countries is to become rich.

Two main arguments have been proposed to explain the EKC. On the demand side, there is the role of public opinion in requiring policy actions to reduce environmental degradation where environment is no more a luxury good, as it is in poor economies and on the supply side, the role of structural changes in the economic system where economic growth is followed by technological innovation and change in the productive structure (from basic industries to high-tech services) producing a reduction in polluting emissions (Barbier, 2003). The specific nature of the abatement technologies with increasing returns to scale could constitute a further explanation of the EKC where high fixed initial investment costs for pollution abating techniques reduce the capacity of poor countries to implement pollution control policies (Andreoni and Levinson, 2001).

If EKC hypothesis is consistently and widely valid, then economic growth is not a problem for the environment, but a solution to the environmental problems. The counter arguments to such observations are many. Ekins (1993) criticised the hypothesis as purely conjectural, as its evidence is not found in reality over a long period. A team of influential scholars comprising four economists and seven ecologists led by the Nobel laureate economist Professor Kenneth J. Arrow has made a consensus statement that "economic growth is not a panacea for environmental quality" (Arrow et al., 1996). Stern et al. (1996) have spotted several major problems in the literature on the EKC, relating to its partial validity, turning points at high levels of income, assumptions on people's preferences, data problems and a need for systematic ecological reforms.

VI. Need for Synthesis

In order to relate the EKC and RCH with human development, modified approached have been developed. The inverted U-shaped relation between GDP per capita and pollutant emissions (EKC) is re-formulated by using a modified EKC (MEKC), replacing the GDP per capita with a modified Human Development Index (HDIM) that does not include the income factor and replacing the pollution emissions with the negative value of Genuine Saving per capita (-GS) as a measure of non-sustainability. The absence of the GDP index in the HDIM eliminates multi-collinearity between the GS and the HDI. The value added of such analysis is the presence of depletion and degradation value of natural resources contained in the GS index compared with the simple pollutant emissions considered in a classical EKC model (Costantini and Monni, 2005). In addition, using a HD measure and not a simple economic growth (EG) level allows broader considerations to be made on the sustainability of the development path or if future generations could enjoy the same well-being level (and not only income). In line with classic EKC, the inclusion of other control variables such as trade flows and manufactures as the share of value added even allows researchers to analyze the effects of economic globalization on sustainable development. Estimates of MEKC that account for human development and sustainability give results that are quite similar to traditional EKC. Such analysis also put emphasis on the role of institutions as an engine for economic growth and sustainable development (Bulte et al. 2005). Attempts have also been made to develop and estimate integrated models that account for a RCH - including the role on institutions - and a MEKC.

In such studies, the role of HD dimensions is quite clear and unanimous. A higher initial level of HD corresponds to positive effects on institutional quality and indirectly on EG. With regard to sustainability, increasing HD is first associated with increasing exploitation of natural resources until a threshold level where such relation becomes positive and an increase in HD positively affects sustainability. An increase in EG and in HD is associated with growing resource consumption in the first stages of development. The industrialization process first requires great efforts from primary industries and then development of heavy (polluting) industries. If the EG and HD processes are followed by sufficient human capital accumulation with better institutions and qualified human resources, the industrialization process will move towards a further development stage characterized by the major role of services while reducing pollution and using less natural resources. A virtuous circle of this kind could be reinforced by public investments for health and education and more widely for social capability. The role of skilled labor force in conjunction with higher income level are necessary for an environmentally-friendly consumption path and production techniques (Costantini and Monni, 2006). Natural resource endowment could be a source of low economic growth rates if the institutions in a country do not have the ability to manage the resources in the right way. Therefore, investment policies geared towards human capital formation (education and high skilled labor forces) are to be considered the most effective actions for reaching a higher development level. At the same time, during the first stages of the development process, a large consumption of natural resources without appropriate investment policies to replace depleted resources - as explained by the Hartwick rule, or the investment of the Hotelling rent coming from the exploitation of natural resources - could produce a development path that is not sustainable in the long run (Hanley et al., 1997).

VII. Concluding View

Since environmental and natural resource accounting has been standardized over the years, it should be possible to develop a measure of environmentally sustainable HD by adding the elements and indices on environmental security and access to resources in the HDI. Different causal linkages analyzed in economic growth, human development and environment offer some general principles with regard to the sustainability of a human development process. It is possible to reduce (and invert) an unsustainable growth path at some medium level of development and reverse the process of environmental degradation. Human capital accumulation represents an effective channel of reaching and maintaining higher consumption path in the future. The positive role of health and education attainments is much bigger than the negative effects linked to natural resources endowments. The resource curse would not occur if appropriate investments are made in human capital accumulation for promoting the quality of institutions. Better institutions represent one of the most efficient conditional variables for achieving better sustainable HD and environmental quality. Thus in order to win over the resource curse and turn it into a blessing, it is necessary to concentrate on human capital accumulation and consequently on the quality of institutions. Achieving a higher standard of living and maintaining natural capital could be complementary to each other mutually reinforcing an upward spiral of HD, which should be the first objective of international development policies, as an increase in human well-being is necessary to provide a sustainability path. So the developing countries should promote environmental protection and the industrialized countries should help this process through coordinated know-how and technological transfer so as to avoid great degradation and depletion of natural resources through out the world.

References

Andreoni, J. and Levinson, A. (2001): The simple analytics of the environmental Kuznets curve, *Journal of Public Economics*, 80(2): 269-286.

Arrow, K., B. Bolin, R. Costanza, P. Dasgupta, C. Folke, C. S. Holling, B-O. Jansson, S. Levin, K-G. Maler, C. Perrings, D. Pimentel (1996): Economic growth, carrying capacity, and the environment, *Environment and Development Economics*, 1(1): 104 - 110.

Atkinson, G. and K. Hamilton (2003): Savings, Growth and the Resource Curse Hypothesis, *World Development*, 31(11): 1797-1807.

Auty, R. M. (2001): The political economy of resource-driven growth, *European Economic Review*, 45(4-6): 839-846.

Barbier, E. B. (2003): The role of natural resources in economic development, *Australian Economic Paper*, 42(2): 253-272.

Bulte, E.H., R. Damania, R. T. Deacon (2005), Resource Intensity, Institutions, and Development, *World Development*, 33(7): 1029-1044.

Common, M. (1988): *Environmental and Resource Economics: An Introduction*, Longman Group UK Limited, London, 319 pp.

Costantini, V. and S. Monni (2005): Sustainable Human Development for European Countries, *Journal of Human Development*, 6(3): 329-351.

Costantini, V. and S. Monni (2006): Environment, Human Development and Economic Growth, *Working Paper No. 62*, Department of Economics, Roma Tre University, Rome, Italy.

Ekins, P. (1993): Limits to growth and sustainable development: grappling with ecological realities, *Ecological Economics*, 8(3): 269 - 288.

Gylfason, T. (2001): Natural resources, education, and economic development, *European Economic Review*, 45(4-6): 847-859.

Hanley, N., J. Shogren, and B. White (1997): *Environmental Economics in Theory and Practice*, Macmillan Press.

Meadows, D. H., D. L. Meadows, J. Randers and W. Behrens (1972): *The Limits to Growth*, Universe Books, New York.

Mehlum, H., K. Moene, and R. Torvik (2005): Cursed by resources or institutions? Department of Economics Working Paper No. 10, Norwegian University of Science and Technology, Norway.

Mikesell, R. F. (1997): Explaining the resource curse with special reference to mineral-exporting countries, Resources Policy, 23(4): 191-199.

Pachauri, R. K. (1997): Development and environment, *Yojona*, 41(8): 7-9 & 134.

Perman, R., Y. Ma, J. McGilvray, and M. S. Common (1999): *Natural Resources and Environmental Economics*, 2nd Edition, Longmans.

Ross, M. L. (1999): The political economy of the resource curse, *World Politics*, 51(2): 297-322.

Sachs J. D. and A. M. Warner (1995): Natural resource abundance and economic growth, *NBER Working Paper No. 5398*, Cambridge, MA.

Sachs J. D. and A. M. Warner (1999): The big push, natural resource booms and growth, *Journal of Development Economics*, 59(1): 43-76.

Sahu, N. C. (2005): The Environmental Kuznets Curve: A critique', in N. C. Sahu and A. K. Choudhury (Ed.), *Dimensions of Environmental and Ecological Economics*, University Press (India) Limited, (Distributed by Orient Longman Pvt. Ltd.), Hyderabad, pp. 469 – 480.

Sala-i-Martin, X. and A. Subramanian (2003): Addressing the Natural Resource Curse: An Illustration from Nigeria, *IMF Working Paper No. 139*, International Monetary Fund, Washington DC.

Sen, A. K. (2000): The ends and means of sustainability, Keynote Address at the International Conference on Transition to Sustainability, Tokyo, May 2000.

Selden, T. M. and D. Song (1994): Environmental quality and development: Is there a Kuznets Curve for air pollution? Journal of Environmental Economics and Environmental Management, 27(2): 147-162.

Stern, D. I., M. S. Common and E. B. Barbier (1996): Economic growth and environmental degradation: The Environmental Kuznets Curve and sustainable development, *World Development*, 24(7): 1151-1160.

Torvik, R. (2002), Natural resources, rent seeking and welfare, *Journal of Development Economics*, 67(2): 455-470.

World Commission on Environment and Development (WCED) (1987): *Our Common Future*, Oxford University Press, Oxford.

World Bank (1992): *World Development Report: Development and the Environment*, Oxford University Press, New York.

19

Impact of Environmental Degradation on Human Development

Barun Kumar Thakur[1]

I. Introduction

One of the goals of MDG was to ensure Environmental Sustainability. For ensuring environmental sustainability (Goal 7 of MDG), the mechanism calls for integrating the principles of sustainable development into country policies and programs and reverse the loss of environmental resources (Target 9). The overarching goal were to ensure sustainable delivery of ecosystem services to human societies and manage the wastes and byproducts of production and consumption process that threaten human and ecosystem health. It can be defined[2] "as meeting human needs without undermining the capacity of the environment to provide for those needs and support life over the long term".

The concept of environmental degradation is as old as 'human civilization', but environmental concerns were neglected for long time. The first international concern held in Stockholm (5 to 16 June) in 1972 on United Nations Conference on the Human Environment (UNCHD) which prepares "Action plan for human development". Later in the World Commission on Environment and Development (WCED) report in 1987 advocated idea of 'sustainable development' and defines it as "development that meets the needs of the present without compromising the ability of future generations to meet their own needs". Later on the Rio declaration on Environment and development which held at Rio de Janeiro from 3 to 14 June 1992 gives further improvement on the concepts. Therefore, the environmental concerns that had been neglected from a long time became global and important issues in development strategies across the globe. Environmental problems which causes environmental

[1] Research Associate, Madras School of Economics, Chennai-600025

[2] Taken from Environment and human well-being: a practical strategy (page no. 44).

degradation are multidisciplinary in nature and the scale of problem varies based on the level of the problem. Some problems are global while some are local in the nature. Problems like Climate change, depletion of ozone layer, loss of bio-diversity and extinction of endangered species are global problems in nature and it requires international co-operation for their solution. Problems such as land degradation, water pollution, vehicular and air pollution are local in their nature and requiring policies at national / Regional level. Environmental degradation is mostly occurred due to the excess extraction of natural resources which is basically so called means for development. Environmental degradation is the deterioration in environmental quality from ambient concentrations of pollutants and other activities and processes such as improper land use and natural disasters (OECD).

This paper tries to list out the problem, both global and local which generates the problem of environmental degradation and how finally it will affect on human development. But it will specially concern about the local problems in Indian context. First section is introduction; second section give details about causes of environmental degradation, third section is on how environmental degradation and human development linked with each other; fourth section talks about India's major environmental problems; fifth section tells about what are the legal and policy mechanism in theoretical as well as other aspects in India's concern. Fifth section also deals mainly with all the theoretical and policy mechanism for India and on environmental pollution prevention and control in Indian contexts, followed by suggestion and conclusion.

II. Causes for Environmental Degradation

Environmental degradation is said to occur when uncontrolled extraction of natural resource takes place rapidly. The rapidly growing trend of industrialization, population and economic development and uncontrolled growth in urbanization is prime concern for environmental degradation. Environmental degradation can be naturally occur or causes by human beings or both. When habitats are destroyed, biodiversity is lost, or natural resources are depleted, the environment is hurt and causes environmental degradation.

Environmental degradation can be local, regional and global. Social, economic and institutional factors are also effecting the environmental degradation. Population, poverty and urbanization are social factor. Protection, conservation and development of environment in India are the sole responsibility of ministry of environment and forest (MOEF) and come under institutional factors. Environment (Protection) Act, 1986 is the key legislation governing environment management. Other important legislations in the area include the Forest (Conservation) Act, 1980 and the Wildlife (Protection) Act, 1972. A detail has been discussed in the legal and policy mechanisms section.

Local as well as global environmental problems hurt poor people most. Local environmental concerns like water pollution and contamination, air pollution, waste disposal, deforestation and soil degradation have direct impact on human-being. Waste and water related diseases are increasing and they affect the livelihood and survival of the poor people most. Water pollution and contamination, air pollution, domestic solid waste, industrial hazardous waste, soil degradation and desertification, deforestation and loss of biodiversity are some local environmental concerns which mostly causes for environmental degradation.

Water pollution and contamination affect the people globally, but by far the greatest impact on human well-being is in developing countries, especially in the poorest. In developing and least developed countries 29 and 43 per cent are people without access to safe water and 58 and 68 per cent respectively are people without access to basic sanitation. Air pollution from industrial emissions, vehicle exhaust and the burning of fuels at home kills more than 2.7 million people every year. According to WHO report deaths from indoor pollution and outdoor pollution in India is more than 1000. Deaths from indoor pollution in rural is higher than urban in India. Domestic solid waste in both absolute and per capita terms is in increasing. In developing countries 25-50 per cent of the waste generated remains uncollected. Industrial hazardous waste like toxic effluents from mines, chemical producers, pulp and paper plants, and leather-tanning factories are playing an increasing role in environmental degradation. The Bhopal disaster in India is the example for that which killed more than 8000 lives and more than 50,000 people in different ways due to swept of lethal gases from the Union Carbide factory.

Soil degradation and desertification problems are increasing in Asia and Africa and mostly effect to poor. According to MA report, nearly one third of the global population – mostly poor depends directly on what they can grow, gather or catch. Deforestation is prominent and important factors of environmental degradation. One third forests have disappeared and two-thirds of what is left is changed. India increased its forests area by more than 6 million of hectares in 1980's. Loss of biodiversity refers to diversify the species of life in different forms. Erosion of biodiversity has more ecological consequences. Due to erosion, shrimp farming is in trouble and results in increasing mangrove area loss. In Table 1 relationship between mangrove loss and shrimp production has been shown.

Table 1: Relationship between Mangrove Loss and Shrimp Production

Country	Mangrove area loss by 1989 (000 of hectares)	Shrimp production in 1995 (000 of tons)
Thailand	200	280
Ecuador	120	90
Viet Nam	67	37
India	35	96
Bangladesh	9	34

Source: Shiva 1997a

III. Environmental Degradation and Human Development

Miller stated on the consideration of the law of the Conservation as "matter cannot be created or destroyed; it can only be changed from one form to another. Every waste material we believe we have managed is still with us in one form or another; there is no away"[3]. In Ramcharitmanas[4] also described that chhiti, jal, pawak, gagan and sameer are the five fundamental elements from which our body is meant. In ancient Indian civilization and literature e.g. Vedas, Upanishads Smiritis and dharmas preach a worshipful attitude towards earth, sky, air, water, plants, trees, and animals and enshrine a respect for nature and environmental harmony and conservation. It

---

[3] Miller, T.G (1992), living in the environment, 7th edn (Belmont, CA: Wadsworth publishing Company).

[4] Ramcharitmanas is most popular epic for Hindu religion which is written by Goswami Tulsidas. Tulsidas mentioned that human body is made from five element (earth, water, fire, cloud and air), but modern scientist acclaimed that these are not a single element.

regards sun, air, fire, river, earth and forests as god and goddesses[5]. Many animals, birds, trees and plants are associated with the names of gods and goddesses. This really shows the respect given to the civilization so that the human being respect the natural resources and don't degrade it.

Under the auspices of the United Nations, the Millennium Ecosystem Assessment was conducted to assess the consequences of ecosystem change for human development and also to establish the action needed to enhance the conservation and sustainable use of ecosystems and their contribution to the human well-being on the scientific basis. Millennium Ecosystem Assessment (MA) finds four main findings. These are as[6]

(a) Over the past 50 years, humans have changed ecosystems more rapidly and extensively than in any comparable period of time in human history, largely to meet rapidly growing demands for food, fresh water, timber, fiber and fuel. This has resulted in a substantial and largely irreversible loss in the diversity of life on earth.
(b) The changes that have been made to ecosystems have contributed to substantial net gains in human well-being and economic development, but these gains have been achieved at growing costs in the form of the degradation of many ecosystem services, increased risks of non-linear changes, and the exacerbation of poverty for some groups of people. These problems, unless addressed, will substantially diminish the benefits that future generations obtain from ecosystems.
(c) The degradation of ecosystem services could grow significantly worse during the first half of this century and is a barrier to achieving the Millennium development goals.
(d) The challenge of reversing the degradation of ecosystems while meeting increasing demands for their services can be partially met under some scenarios that the Millennium Assessment considered, but these involve significant changes in policies, institutions, and practices that are not currently under way.

---

[5] Taken from Sankar, U (2009)

[6] These four measures were taken from the Millennium Ecosystem Assessment (2005), Ecosystems and human well-being: synthesis, island press, Washington D.C.

From the above four findings it is evidently clear that how important role of human well-being with resource depletion or degradation. In Table 2 ecosystem services and constituent of well-being has been shown. In the figure it has been depicted the strength of linkages between the components of ecosystem services and components of human well-being that are commonly encountered, and includes indications of the extent to which it is possible for socioeconomic factors to mediate the linkages. The Millennium Ecosystem Assessment (2003) recognized five dimension of human well-being: basic material for a good life, freedom and choice and action, health, good social relations, and security. Ecosystem services are the benefits people obtain from ecosystems. These include provisioning, regulating and cultural services. Which directly affect people, and supporting services needed to maintain the other services. Changes in these services affect human well-being through impacts on security, the necessary material for a good life, health, and social and cultural relations. These constituents off well-being are in turn influenced by and have an influences on the freedom and choice available to people. From Table 2 details of linkages between ecosystem and constituent of well-being can be seen.

IV. India's Major Environmental Problems

India is the 2nd largest country in the world population and seventh largest in the area wise. India has about 17 per cent of the global population but only 2.54 per cent of the global area and 1.8 per cent of the forest area. India is one of the 12 countries which are mega biodiversity in the world. As a norm of 33 per cent of forest land coverage out of which India's forest coverage of land area is 20.6 per cent. About 41 per cent of forest cover has been degraded, 70 per cent of forests have no natural regeneration and 55 per cent are prone to fire. Forest cover of India is 67.71 million ha, which is 20.60 per cent of its geographical area. Of this, 5.46 million ha (1.66 per cent) is very dense forest, 33.26 million ha (10.12 per cent) is moderately dense and the rest 28.99 million ha is open including 0.44 million ha of mangroves. The policy target is to have 33 per cent forest and tree cover ultimately which will require additional coverage of 16 million ha.

Table 2: Ecosystem services and the human well-beings linkages

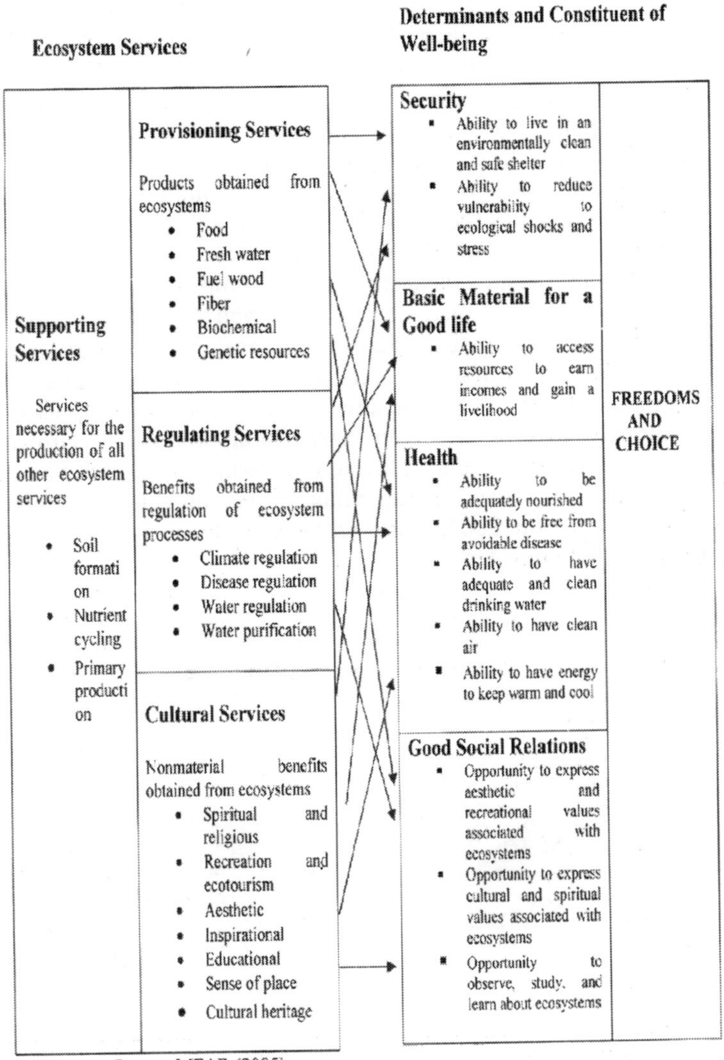

Source: MEAR (2005)

Agriculture

Rapid Industrialization, green revolution and intensive farming[7] and discharge of untreated effluents in water bodies has resulted in soil erosion, salinity / alkalinity of soil, micro nutrition deficiency, water logging and other problems. Land area which is under cultivation is degrading day by day. An estimate about that 60 per cent area under cultivation is degrading. Due to access use of pesticides and fertilizers and dependence of only one crops leads to loss of topsoil which is estimated of 5400 million tones annually. Therefore it concerns the decline of productivity, food security and sustainable cropping pattern. After green revolution, introduction of high yield variety and genetically modified crops has also generated controversy regarding there sustainability and suitability to Indian ecosystem. In certain part of Punjab, Haryana, Andhra Pradesh and Western Uttar Pradesh due to excess extraction of water resources underground water level is declining and it has both directly as well as indirectly adverse effect on Agricultural production. Growing population need more food. Therefore, growing food requires more efficient use of water for Agriculture. According to Millennium development report 2009, water usage in different sectors can be seen from the Figure 1.

Figure 1

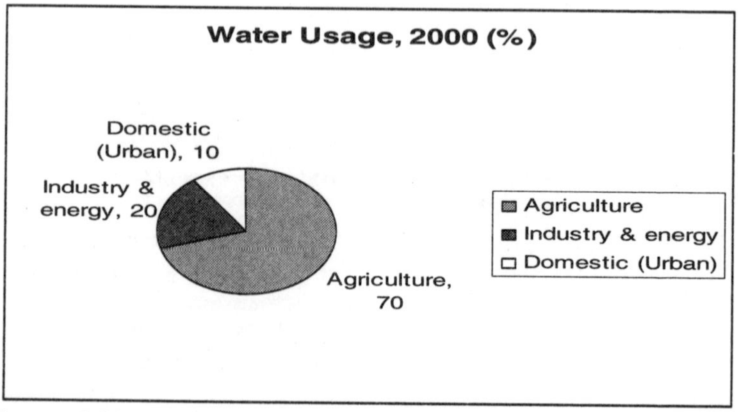

Source: Millennium development report, 2009

[7] Intensive farming is mainly used after green revolution and basically used high yielding varieties, fertilizer and pesticide uses in more manners.

Water

Water is one of the most components for human being to survive. It is becomingly a scarce resource day by day. Water disputes among different user groups, within the different states of the same country and also in globally are increasing. Water-borne diseases are on monotonous path of increasing day by day. 10 per cent of the people have no access to drinking water and access to safe drinking water is still more. Chemical contaminations are increasing. Industrial water pollution leads of excessive nitrate leached into groundwater and it's also affect the water borne disease. In the last two decades, it has been observed that there is a decline in water quality in almost all the sources. The water problem has been seen in the metro cities in the last 2 decades and its increasing. Increasing importance of water usage can be seen from Figure 1.

Air and Vehicular pollution

In the last 30 years, there has been tremendously increased in the air pollution mostly in the larger segment in urban and industrial centre. The rapid industrialization and exceeding extraction of natural resources are primarily responsible for that. Initially air pollutants were sulphur dioxide, black smoke and lead, which were mainly resulted from the use of combustions of fossil fuels. In recent year's nitrogen monoxide, nitrogen dioxide and ozone have also appeared in air pollution. In India, Central pollution control board (CPCB) monitors air quality of 95 cities and towns with respect to 3 main pollutants: SO2, NOx and RSPm. In the case of large and medium scale polluting units very few have pollution control devices. In the case of unorganized sector and small units problem is more serious. Due to increase in pollution level, respiratory and other related diseases are phenomenally increasing over the last 15 years. Vehicular pollution also causes air pollution and it is increasing due to increasing number of vehicles. The drastic increase in number of vehicles has also resulted in a significant increase in the emission load of various pollutants. The quantum of vehicular pollutants emitted is highest in Delhi followed by Mumbai, Bangalore, Calcutta and Ahmadabad. The daily pollution load generated due to automobiles in 12 metropolitan cities is shown in Table 10.1. Carbon monoxide (CO) and hydrocarbons (HC) account for 64 per cent and 23 per cent, respectively, of the total emission load due to vehicles in all these cities considered together (CPCB 2005).

Solid Waste

With the increasing trend in consumerism and progress in human civilization the waste generated will became more complex by nature. With the generation of more and more non-biodegradable solid waste not only air gets more polluted but also the earth became more polluted. The increased growth of population and urbanization is also solely responsible for the increasing trend in solid waste. According to World Bank estimates, in the early nineties the economic value of depletion and degradation was around 4.5 per cent of GDP where growth rate was nearly around 5 per cent.

The problems in solid wastes are as[8] a) Households and other wastes in cities and towns: sorting[9] and safe disposal, b) Disposal of fly ash in thermal power stations, c) Handling of bio-medical wastes in hospitals and d) Safe disposal of hazardous wastes in chemical and other polluting industry.

V. Legal and Policy Mechanism

(a) Theoretical Mechanism

A different approach has been given on this view. Mainly Pigou (1920), Coase (1960), Hotelling (1931), Hardin (1968) and Baumol and Oates (1988) has been argued on that. Pigou view was that environmental problem arises due to the absence of regulations, decision makers(both producers and consumers) is likely treating environmental good as "free good". To behave in a socially responsible manner, Pigou suggests a unit tax on the polluting firm's output equal to the marginal social damage[10]. Later this idea became basis for the "polluter pays principle".

In Cosean framework, environmental problem arises because of the transaction cost and property rights. He further argued that environmental problem arises because (a) property rights either do not exists or when do they exists they are either not defined or ill defined or poorly implemented, and (b) higher transaction costs between polluters and pollutees. He suggested for reaching binding agreements between polluters and pollutees.

---

[8] This has been taken from Sankar (2009) on S. Ambirajan eighth memorial lecture on 'the state of environment and environmental policy in India' on March 18, 2009.

[9] In solid waste management generally when we are talking about sorting it refers to all polluting mechanisms like biodegradable, non-biodegradable and hazardous elements.

[10] Marginal social damage is generally the difference between the marginal social cost and marginal private cost.

Hotelling considers the problem of optimum rate of exhaustible resources. He argued that the price of an exhaustible resource must grow at a rate equal to the rate of interest. Hardin argued with the problem of over exploitation of grazing lands with open access. He used the terms "tragedy of commons" and argued that tragedy of commons arises because each man is forced to increase his herd without knowing the limit of it. But he further argues that tragedy of commons reappears in problems of pollution in a completely reverse way. He recommends coercive laws or tax devices that make it cheaper for the polluter to treat his pollutants than to discharge them untreated.

Baumol and Oates argued that Pigouvian tax requires information about marginal social damage corresponding to the socially optimum level of output. As there is set of asymmetric information, they suggest a second-best solution.

At the global level three policies has been recommended: a) WCED (1987): Policy on Sustainable development; b) UNCED (1992): Rio Declaration and its principles; and c) UNCED (1992): Agenda 21: Objective of Environmental Policy---where talks about mainly on sustainable development and environmental degradation.

(b) Policy Mechanism for India

India has made and amended constitutional provisions, legislations and policy statements and also judicial activism on environmental protection. Despite all these regulation India's state of environment continues to deteriorate. To protect and improve the environment, India made certain constitutional as well as judicial amendment. The 42nd constitutional amendment act which was amended on 1976, talked about the directive principle of state policy under article 48A and fundamental duties under 51A (g). 51A (g) talks about to protect and improve the natural environmental including forests, lakes, rivers, wildlife and to have compassion for living creatures. Indian constitution also amends the 73rd and 74th constitutional amendments, 1992. Schedules 11 and 12 which contain environmental activities can be undertaken by panchayats and municipality respectively. The doctrine of public trust states that state is trustee of all natural resources.

Principles

- The polluter pays principle
- The precautionary principle

- Sustainable Development and Inter-generational Equity.

Legislations: Some of the legislation which is dealing with the industrial pollution

- The Water (Prevention and Control of Pollution) Act, 1974.
- The Water Cess Act, 1977.
- The Air (Prevention and Control of Pollution) Act, 1981.
- The Environment (Protection) Act, 1986.

Policy statements

- The National Forest Policy, 1988.
- The Policy Statement for Abatement of Pollution, 1992.
- The National Conservation Strategy and Policy Statement on Environment and Development, 1992., and
- The National Environment Policy, 2006.

Some important legislations and law dealing with forest, wildlife, biodiversity and dealing with liability:

- The Public Liability Insurance Act, 1991.
- The National Environmental Tribunal Act, 1995 and the National Environmental Appellate Authority Act, 1997.
- The Indian Forest Act, 1927.
- The Wild Life Protection Act, 1972 and the Wild Life Protection Amendment Act, 2002.
- The Forest Conservation Act, 1980.
- The Biodiversity Act, 2002.

In 2007, the government of India made amendment on the Scheduled Tribes and Other Traditional Forest Dwellers (Recognition of Forest Rights) Act. But after so many legislations and policy mechanisms Indian environment is continued to deteriorate.

(c) Environmental Pollution prevention and control in Indian context

The national environmental policies (NEP) are solely for recognizing the problem and also find the solutions. There is an argent need for not talking in rhetoric way and implement that kind of policy which prevent the pollution. In another dimension we can say that there is a need of such kind of policies which encourage preventing the pollution. It is very interesting that India's per capita emission of CO2 is only 1.2 metric tons which is far less than the world average emission of 4.2 metric tons. USA is the highest which account for 20 metric ton per capita. India is exempted from emission reduction requirements under Kyoto protocol. However, national action plan on climate change (NAPCC) identifies measures that promote our development objectives while also yielding co-benefits for addressing climate change effectively also. In 2009, India renounces its national ambient air quality standards according to environmental protection act 1986. After invention by the Supreme Court[11], the EPCA is pursuing to implement plan of action of white paper priority measures for air pollution control. Issues which were achieved were as:

- Fuel quality
- Premixed oil dispensers
- Measures to prevent adulteration of fuels
- Improvement in vehicular technology; and
- Emission warranty

VI. Conclusions and Suggestions

In the last 50 years due to excess extraction of natural resources environmental degradation has been in its peak. It is known fact that environmental issues, especially the unequal impacts of environmental degradation and its impacts of damages mostly occurs on poor people needs an urgent attention. The adverse impacts occurred from dirty water, indoor and outdoor air pollution; deforestation causes natural disasters which claim million of death every year. India has amended certain norms related to environmental related problems. But, in policy perspective it won't give priority to environmental considerations. India is achieving high GDP growth, almost in the range of 8-9 per cent in the last few years. After such a healthy growth rate there must be a two way linkages between poverty and environment quality, it should be essential that government give equal weightage to both growth and improvement in the environmental quality to the future scenario. Not a single government gave important priority to the environmental degradation. Government has to take it seriously because of the high growth rate there must be an irreversible damages and decline in the natural resource capital. It has been seen that in the Indian cases, the

[11] On its order dated November 16, 1998 Supreme Court recommended to implement the P.K.Kaul committee which was based on "white paper on pollution with an action plan".

rights of people in the forests areas and in the other ecosystems are not well defined and not implemented. Healthy environment became a scarce resource now these days and in the coming era it will be going more scarce if we degrade our environment in the same manner in which we degraded it in the last 50 years. It is well known fact that every individual behaviour (be it consumers or producers) affect the environment quality. It is the responsibility of the every individual be it ethically or morally to become environmentally conscious by internalizing environmental costs into the decision making. The changes would be to structural shifts in natural resource use, in both the consumption and production patterns of societies as well as individual beings. Otherwise, days will not much far that we will also be in the list of the endangered species.

References

Baumol, W. J., and W. E. Oates (1988): *Theory of Environmental Policy*, Cambridge University Press.

Coase, R. (1960): The Problem of Social Cost, *Journal of Law and Economics*, 3(1): 1-44.

Government of India (1992): Policy Statement for Abatement of Pollution 1992, Ministry of Environment and Forests, New Delhi.

---------- (2006): National Forest Report 2006, Ministry of Environment and Forests, New Delhi.

---------- (2006): National Environmental Policy 2006, Ministry of Environment and Forests, New Delhi.

---------- (2007): India's Forest 2007, Ministry of Environment and Forests, New Delhi.

---------- (2008): Annual Reports 2008-09, Ministry of Environment and Forests, New Delhi.

---------- (2009): State of Environment Report India 2009, Ministry of Environment and Forests, New Delhi.

Hardin, G. (1968): The Tragedy of Commons, *Science*, 162(3859): 1243-1248.

Hotelling, H (1931): The Economics of Exhaustible Resources, *Journal of Political Economy*, 39(2): 137-75.

Jahan, S. (1998): Unequal Human impacts on environmental damage, In *Human Development Report 1998*, Oxford University Press, New York.

Millennium Ecosystem Assessment (2005): *Ecosystems and Human Well-being: Synthesis*, Island Press, Washington D.C.

Miller, T.G (1992): Living in the environment, 7th edition, Wadsworth publishing Company, Belmont, CA.

Pigou, A. C. (1920): The Economics of Welfare, Macmillan and Company Limited.

Sankar, U. (2001): Environmental Economics, Oxford University Press, New Delhi.

——(2007): Trade and Environment: A study of India's Leather Exports 2007, Oxford University Press, New Delhi.

——(2009): The State of Environment and Environmental Policy in India presented on Dr. S. Ambirajan Eighth Memorial Lecture on 18th March, 2009.

Shiva, Vandana (1997a): Biodiversity, Consumption Patterns and Globalization, Background paper for Human Development Report 1998. UNDP, New York.

United Nations (2009): The Millennium Development Goals Report 2009, New York.

UN Millennium Project: task force on environmental sustainability (2005): Environment and human well-being: a practical strategy, EARTHSCAN London.

United Nations Conference on Environment and Development (1992): Agenda 21, Rio de Janeiro.

United Nations Conference on the Human Environment: Action plan for the human environment (1972): Stockholm 5-16 June, Sweden.

World Commission on Environment and Development (1987): Our Common Future, Oxford University Press.

20

Sustainable Development and Human Development as a Two Way Relationship: A Case for Clean Cooking Fuels for Indian Rural Households

Robin Singhal[1]

I. Introduction

In the economic literature, 'development' is defined as 'growth plus change', and 'growth' is referred to as 'sustained increase in the level of output of an economy'. It is expected that a higher level of economic growth will trickle-down to the masses in terms of better health facilities, higher life expectancy, improved standard of living and the like. In order to assess the efficacy of this process, several human development indicators have been developed over time such as human development index (HDI), physical quality of life index (PQLI) etc.

However, it is increasingly being recognized that the effects of strategies for achieving development in terms of material well-being of the individuals, has brought human civilization to a point where it is threatening its own existence. The implicit assumption of these growth strategies has been that there are in fact no limits to growth, and if any, can be resolved by technological progress. The role of nature is recognized mainly as a source of raw material and as a sink for assimilating all wastes generated from different economic activities, which has led to its gross undervaluation. The environmental problems such as global warming, ozone depletion and loss of biodiversity are some of the fallouts of such growth oriented development strategies.

In this regard, the two broad but vital concepts conceived by the 20th century as guiding principles for economic planning in the 21st century are 'Sustainable Development' and 'Human Development'.

---

[1] Research Scholar, Centre for Economic Studies and Planning (CESP), Jawaharlal Nehru University (JNU), New Delhi

On the one hand, 'sustainable development' defined as 'meeting the needs of the present generation without compromising the ability of the future generations in meeting their own needs' highlights the unsustainable production and consumption patterns in the industrialized countries while on the other hand 'human development' defined as 'the process of enlarging people's choices' brings in to focus the lack of basic amenities of life to people in the developing world.

II. Sustainable Development and Human Development

A two-way relationship

Sustainable development, as defined by the Brundtland Commission in its report titled "Our Common Future", offers a broad framework for designing development strategies. Instead of advocating a common solution, the report emphasises that every nation should devise its own development path which are sustainable in the long run. Such development paths are expected to differ across countries, since they will ultimately be influenced by nations' resource endowments, geographical locations, size of population, cultures and traditions. As Langhelle (1999) puts it "Our Common Future is more coherent and potentially more radical than either adherents or critics seem to be aware of". Thus, sustainable development should be viewed 'as a process of development' based on fundamental and guiding principles (Figure 1).

On the one hand, the strategies for sustainable development should have economic, environmental and social sustainability as its fundamental principles while on the other hand, concepts such as carrying capacity, inter-generational and intra-generational equity and justice, gender equality, biodiversity conservation, preserving social and cultural diversities, should be the guiding principles of any such development strategy.[2] According to Goodland (1995) even though there exists an overlap between economic, environmental and social sustainability, efforts should be made to define components separately under each head. This can help in designing strategies

---

[2] 'Carrying capacity' is defined as the 'number of individuals of a given species that can be sustained indefinitely in a given space'. 'Inter-generational equity' refers to the 'use of earth's resources between generations in a manner that the present generation does not consume it to its exhaustion' whereas 'intra-generational equity' refers to 'the fairness in the utilisation of resources among human members of present generations, both domestically and globally'.

which can effectively guide us to environment friendly and socially equitable models of development. When 'sustainable development' is analysed in its broadest sense as discussed above, enlarging human choices is found to be central to the idea of sustainable development.

Figure 1: Fundamental and Guiding Principles for Sustainable Development

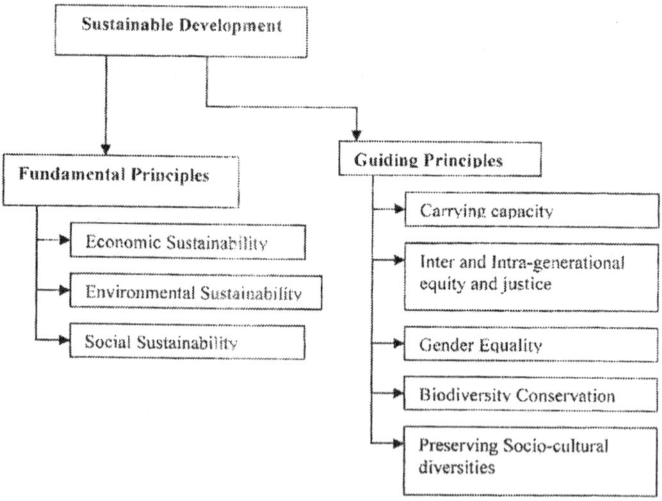

The first World Human Development Report (WHDR) published by United Nations Development Programme (UNDP) in 1990, defined 'human development' as a 'process of enlarging people's choices'. This report highlighted the importance of factors other than income, such as health, education for ensuring that every individual "live a long and healthy life, to be educated and to have access to resources needed for a decent standard of living". Besides, human development was measured through Human Development Index (HDI). The three indicators used in the construction of this index were life expectancy at birth, education and GDP per capita (purchasing power parity in terms of US $). The key aspect of human development is that it emphasises upon the advancement of individuals' well being as the measure of nations' development, which makes it an essential 'end' in itself. However, it must be understood that human development is not just an 'end' in itself but can be an effective 'means' to achieve sustainable development as well.

Note that 'choices' are dynamic in nature. They undergo a change as economy develops. The change in choice patterns can be in any direction, it can either lead to sustainability or unsustainability. Thus, the sustainable development of a nation ultimately depends upon the choices made by its people. For an economy as a whole, besides expanding people's choice base, it is equally important to ensure that the choices which people make are sustainable in the long run. Thus, human development as a 'concept' needs to be oriented towards making choices that are sustainable in the long run. This may involve a short-term trade-off but will have long-term sustainability implications.

Hence, there exists a fundamental relationship between sustainable development and human development. This relationship is effectively two-way in nature (Figure 2). Expanding human choices explores only one side of the relationship between sustainable development and human development whereas ensuring that the choices made by the society are sustainable in the long run, makes this relationship two-way in nature.

Figure 2: 'Two-way relationship' between 'Sustainable Development' and 'Human Development'

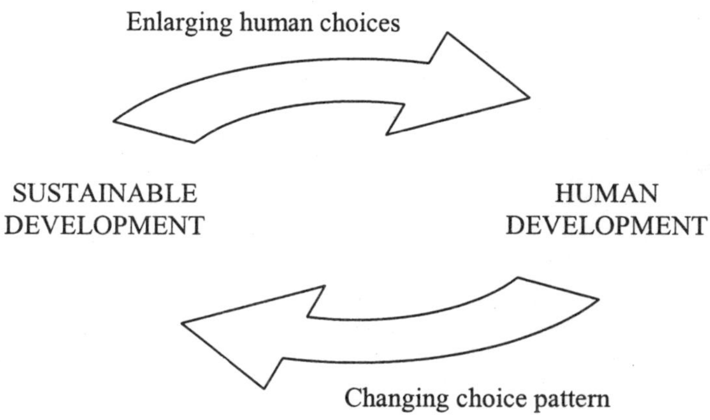

Energy services, human development and sustainable development

On the one hand, the development of the energy sector having a dominant share of renewable energy sources, employing environmentally sound technologies, limiting the negative environmental externalities and ensuring safe and clean energy supply at affordable prices is a major challenge faced by both - the developed and the developing world - whereas on the other hand, a large majority of population in developing countries still depends upon non-commercial energy sources for meeting their day-to-day needs such as cooking, lighting, water and space heating.

As a result, the role of energy in bringing 'human development' in the developing countries is being increasingly emphasised. According to Reddy (2001), direct measures can play a far more effective role in eliminating poverty in comparison to the economic policies based on 'trickle down approach'. These direct measures can even result in a significant improvement of a country's HDI. He has emphasised the relationship between energy and HDI as being one such potential measure.

There is a growing literature which establishes a relationship between a country's level of per capita energy consumption (PCEC) and its human development index (HDI). Martinez and Ebenhack (2008) have studied the relationship between United Nations HDI and PCEC for 120 nations.[3] They found that for 90 countries (excluding the rest 30 nations who are major energy exporters) a 'saturation curve'[4] fits well to the observed relationship of HDI and PCEC (Figure 3).

On the basis of the distribution of countries along the curve, they are classified into three different categories a) 'Energy poor nations' situated in the steep rising region of the curve, b) 'Transitioning nations' situated near the point of inflexion of the curve and c) 'Saturated nations' situated near the horizontal segment of the curve, characterised by high per capita energy consumption with a high level of human development (above 0.9). Countries with HDI less

[3] The relationship between human development index and per capita energy consumption has been studied by other researchers – Carlous Suez, undated cited in Reddy, 2001; Pasternak, 2000; Goldemberg, 2001; Smil, 2003 and Dias, Mattos and Balestieri, 2006 (cited in Martinez and Ebenhack, 2008).

[4] According to Martinez and Ebenhack (2008), this saturation phenomenon has been used earlier to explain natural processes such as 'molecular absorption, ideal operation of a continuous flow stirred tank reactor with dead volume and oxyhemoglobin dissociation'.

than 0.7 are classified as energy poor nations and in case of developing countries which have a high dependence on biomass (i.e. above 60 per cent) in meeting their energy needs, HDI is found to be less than 0.6 for every such nation. Thus, it is argued that since energy poor nations are situated in the steep rising portion of the curve, increased energy access to people in these countries can bring significant improvement in their level of human development.

Figure 3: Relationship of HDI and PCEC

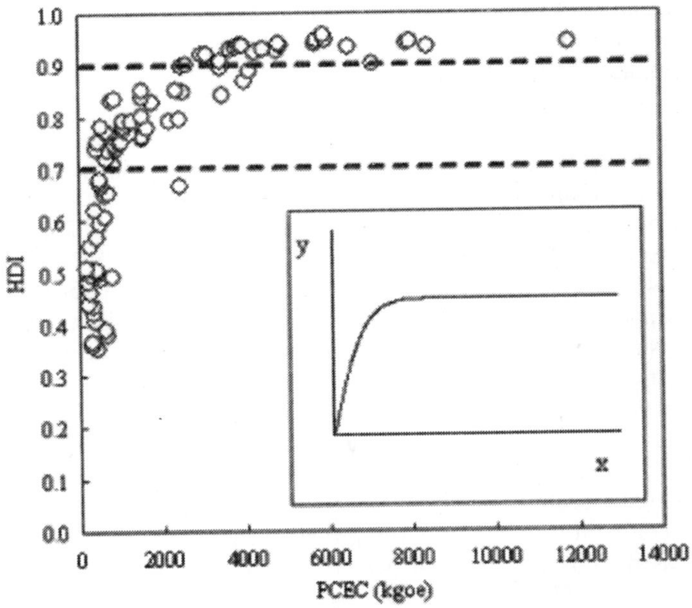

Source: Adapted from Martinez and Ebenhack (2008)

On the basis of a similar relationship for Organization for Economic Cooperation and Development (OECD), Dias, Mattos and Balestieri (2006) argue that there is a significant scope of reduction in per capita energy consumption without adversely affecting their level of well being. The study estimates an energy saving potential of 29.3 per cent of the total energy consumption in OECD countries.

Thus, human development can be an effective 'means' to achieve sustainable development. The relationship between energy services, human development and sustainable development is one such example.

III. An Indian scenario

In India, the 11th Five Year Plan lays special emphasis on achieving a 'faster, more broad-based and inclusive growth'. In order to achieve a higher rate of economic growth and to ensure that the growth is 'inclusive' in nature, the development of a sustainable energy sector is an important challenge (GOI, 2006a). While the Indian energy sector is heavily dependent on the fossil fuels, the residential sector (particularly in rural areas) depends largely upon non-commercial energy sources in meeting their energy needs such as cooking, water heating (GOI, 2006b).

The case of petroleum products

In India, crude oil consumption has been growing rapidly. In 1970-71, the total quantity of crude oil consumed was estimated to be 18,505 thousand tonnes (tt) which increased to a level of 26,755 tt in 1980-81, 53,720 tt in 1990-91, 1,06,523 tt in 2000-01 and 1,44,846 tt in 2006-07. Thus, between 1970-71 and 2006-07, the consumption of crude oil increased by eight times. Indian economy has been heavily dependent upon imports in meeting the growing domestic demand for crude oil (Graph 1). In 1970-71, domestic production of crude oil accounted for only 37 per cent of the total quantity of crude oil supplied to the economy. In 1970's, the imports were as high as 60 per cent. In 1980's, the import dependence though registered a decline. However, since 1995-96 the share of imports in total crude oil supplied has been growing. The share of imports has increased from a level of 44 per cent in 1995-96 to 70 per cent in 2000-01, and 77 per cent in 2006-07.[5]

At the same time, the consumption of petroleum products which was estimated to be 19,135 thousand tonnes (tt) in 1970-71, increased to a level of 32,261 tt in 1980-81, 57,745 tt in 1990-91, 1,06,974 tt in 2000-01 and 1,30,474 tt in 2006-07. Between 1970-71

[5] This heavy dependence on the imported crude oil has resulted to a sharp increase in the crude oil import bill. The total value of imported crude oil was estimated to be Rs 107 crores (cr.) in 1971, which increased to a level of Rs 3,349 cr. in 1981, Rs 6,118 cr. in 1991, Rs 30,695 cr. in 2000 and Rs 1,21,000 in 2004-05 (Subramanian *et al,* 2005).

and 2006-07 the total consumption of petroleum products registered a seven fold increase (Graph 2).

Graph 1 - Percentage share of domestic production and net imports in total quantity of crude oil supplied, 1970-71 to 2006-07

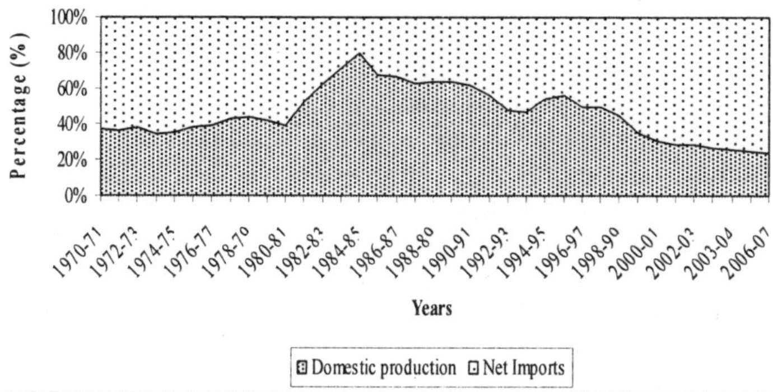

Graph 2 - Total consumption of petroleum products in India, in '000 Tonnes

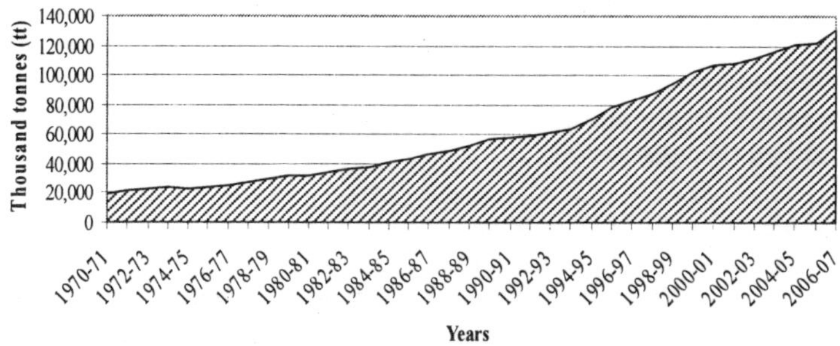

If we analyse the share of different sectors of the economy in the total petroleum products supplied to the Indian economy in 2005, we find that the share of transport sector is the highest at 33 per cent, followed by the residential sector (20 per cent), industry (18 per cent). The other energy consuming sectors such as agriculture and commercial and public services account for a very small share. If we analyse the share of different fuels in meeting a sector's total energy needs, in case of transport and residential sector, we again find a dominant share for petroleum products. In case of transport, the dependence on oil has increased from a level of 46 per cent in 1971 to 89 per cent in 1990 and 96 per cent in 2005. In case of residential sector, the share of petroleum products in the final commercial energy is estimated to be 65 per cent in 1971, 80 per cent in 1990 and 63 per cent in 2005 (Sengupta, 2007).

The petroleum products such as Motor gasoline (or petrol), High Speed Diesel (HSD) Oil and Aviation Turbine Fuel (ATF) are consumed by the transport sector whereas the consumption of products such as Kerosene oil and Liquefied Petroleum Gas (LPG) comes mainly from the residential sector. The share of these petroleum products have been increasing steadily. As percentage of the total petroleum products, the share of the five petroleum products (i.e. Petrol, HSD, ATF, Kerosene and LPG) taken together, is estimated to be 49 per cent in 1970-71, 55 per cent in 1980-81, 64 per cent in 1990 and 59 per cent in 2005-06 (Graph 3). The Indian transport sector is expanding at a fast pace and its growing demand for petroleum based fuels is one of the key areas of concern. The Indian government is promoting the development of biofuels such as ethanol and biodiesel, which can be used as a substitute or as a blend with petrol and HSD respectively. For producing ethanol, the use of sugarcane molasses – a byproduct of the process of producing sugar from sugarcane juice is being encouraged, and the use of non-edible oilseeds such as jatropha curcas is being promoted for producing biodiesel (Singhal, 2009).

Residential sector and cooking energy needs

There exists a sharp contrast between the nature of fuels consumed in the urban and rural households in meeting the essential energy needs for cooking, water heating, lighting etc. Pachauri and Jiang (2008) analysed residential energy consumption taking into consideration the aggregate level of energy consumed, changes in the per capita energy use over time and changes in percentage of users across different fuels, for both urban and rural households in India as well as China. In case of India, though the share of biomass in total energy consumed by Indian households has declined from above 90 per cent in 1980-81 to slightly above 80 per cent in 2004-05, the absolute quantity of biomass consumed has been steadily increasing over the same period. The study also finds the stark differences in the pattern of per capita energy consumption between Indian rural and urban households. In case of rural households, the per capita energy consumption is found to be rising steadily and is much higher than their urban counterparts. An important reason highlighted for this trend is the continued dependence of rural households on inefficient biomass sources for meeting their energy needs such as for cooking, heating.

Graph 3 - Fuel-wise share in total petroleum products consumed in India, 1970-71 to 2006-07

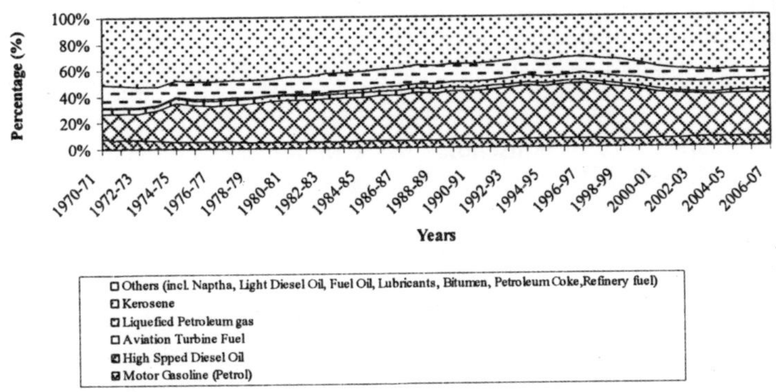

Vishwanathan and Kumar (2005) have studied the pattern of energy consumption for rural and urban households across 16 major states (covering 90 per cent of India's total population) for the period 1983-2000. The pattern of consumption of cooking fuels has been studied for the population ranked according to the monthly per capita expenditure (MPCE), for both the rural and urban households across states. At an all India level, the study finds a low penetration of clean fuels among the rural households. In case of urban households, the share of expenditure on clean fuels have increased from 39 per cent in 1983 to 70 per cent in 1999-2000 whereas in case of rural households, the share of cooking fuel expenditure on clean fuels is estimated to be only 22.5 per cent in 1999-2000. In case of rural households, the share of expenditure on dirty fuels have remained more or less stagnant – 78.6 per cent (in 1983), 79 per cent (in 1993-94) and 76.5 per cent (in 1999-2000). Further, the study reports large inter state variations across rural and urban households as per their expenditure on clean fuels. In 1999-2000, the expenditure shares on clean fuels for rural households across all states studied is found to lie in the range of 12 per cent (in Rajasthan) to 36 per cent (in Maharashtra) whereas in case of urban households the expenditure shares are found to be in the range of 41 per cent (in Kerala) to 88 per cent (in Maharashtra). The study finds increasing trends in expenditure on clean fuels in urban households across all states whereas the 'stagnant or decreasing' share of expenditure on clean fuels in case of rural households is a major cause of concern.[6]

Table 1 below shows the dependence of rural and urban households on dirty and clean cooking fuels for the period 1999-2000 and 2004-05. In rural India, 93 per cent of the households were dependent on dirty fuels (firewood, chips, dung cakes, coal and coke etc) in 1999-2000 and even in 2004-05 close to 90 per cent of the households were still using these fuels for cooking. Though the percentage share of households using dung cakes and coal/coke has declined marginally, share of households using firewood and chips has remained stagnant. As a result, the percentage of rural households using clean fuel such as LPG has increased marginally from 5.4 per cent in 1999-2000 to 8.6 per cent in 2004-05. On the other hand, a large percentage of urban households have been consuming clean cooking fuels. The percentage of urban households using kerosene has declined from 22 per cent in 1999-2000 to 10 per cent in 2004-05. In 2004-05, more than 57 per cent of urban households were using LPG for cooking.

Across all states, we find that a large percentage of rural households are using dirty fuels in comparison to urban households. In states such as Assam, Bihar, Chhattisgarh, Jharkhand, Karnataka, Madhya Pradesh, Orissa, Rajasthan, Uttar Pradesh and West Bengal, more than 90 per cent of rural households are dependent on dirty

[6] In case of three north Indian states namely Himachal Pradesh, Uttar Pradesh and Rajasthan, more than 90 per cent of households use biofuels for meeting their cooking needs. In case of Himachal Pradesh, where the use of clean fuels is relatively higher in comparison to other states, the study reports that 66 per cent of the households use clean fuels as complementary to traditional biofuels (Parikh, Biwas and Karmakar, 2003).

fuels. Even in states such as Bihar, Chhattisgarh, Jharkhand, Kerala, Madhya Pradesh, and Orissa, more than 30 per cent of urban households are found to be still dependent on dirty fuels.

Table 1: Fuel-wise Distribution of Indian Rural and Urban Households using Dirty and Clean Cooking Fuels, 1999-2000 and 2004-05

S. No.		Rural		Urban	
		1999-2000	2004-05	1999-2000	2004-05
1	**Dirty fuels**				
	Firewood and chips	75.5	75	22.3	21.7
	Dung cakes	10.6	9.1	-	-
	Other incl. coal, coke	7.4	6	11.1	6.4
	Sub-total	93.5	90.1	33.4	28.1
2	**Clean fuels**				
	Kerosene	-	-	21.7	10.2
	LPG	5.4	8.6	44.2	57.4
	Sub-total	5.4	8.6	65.9	67.6
3	**No cooking arrangements**	1.1	1.3	0.7	4.3
	Total	100	100	100	100

Source: Author's compilation based on NSSO 55th and 61st rounds.

Note that these solid (or dirty) fuels may be available to rural households either free of cost or at low private cost, but true social cost of using these fuels is very high. Indoor air pollution (IAR) is considered to be a major disadvantage of using such fuels. Young girls and women have to spend a lot of time in collecting and using these dirty fuels, who in turn get exposed to hazardous pollutants such as particulate matter, carbon monoxide, nitrogen dioxide, formaldehyde, polycyclic organic pollutants, and carcinogens like benson-a-pyrene.

According to Batliwala (1983) besides income, factors such as land ownership, geographic factors and agricultural productivity levels plays an important role in determining the availability of fuels such as firewood, crop residues to the rural women. Further, she argues that the use of low efficiency traditional cooking devices influences not only the quantity of fuel required and cooking duration but can even result to a change in the dietary patterns which can adversely affect the nutrition status of a rural household particularly women.

Several studies have been conducted which report the adverse health impacts for women, young girls and even the elderly people, due to the exposure to harmful emissions from these fuels. The exposure to these emissions is found to be the major reason for diseases such as bronchitis, asthma, chest infection, eye infection and even tuberculosis. (for details see Parikh, Biswas and Karmakar, 2003; Balakrishnan et al, 2004; Planning Commission, 2006; 11th Five Year Plan, GOI and Duflo, Greenstone and Hanna, 2008).[7]

Table 2: Objectives for Providing Clean Cooking Fuels

1. Enlarging human choices	
The objective should be to ensure that every household should have 'access to clean energy for meeting cooking energy needs'.	
2. Sustainability	
a. Economic sustainability	The choice of the fuel should be such that 'it is available at reasonable prices on a sustained basis'.
b. Environmental sustainability	The fuel chosen should be such that its 'production and consumption is environment friendly'.
c. Social sustainability	The objective should be to ensure that 'maximum number of households has access to clean cooking fuels across states'.

[7] In case of India, the national burden of disease on account of the use of the solid fuels by households is estimated to be 3.5 per cent (WHO 2002 cited in Duflo *et al* 2008).

In view of the above discussed pattern of energy consumption of Indian households for meeting their cooking energy needs, there should be special emphasis on ensuring clean cooking fuels. In this context, Table 2 summarises the broad set of objectives which needs to be achieved as per the framework of sustainable development and human development (discussed in section 2 of this paper).

As Goldemberg et al (2004) highlights that LPG despite of being a petroleum based product, would still remain to be the most preferred cooking fuel worldwide. In this context, the recent scheme announced by the government of India under the head 'Rajiv Gandhi Gramin LPG Vitrak' which aims to increase the penetration of Liquefied Petroleum Gas (LPG) for cooking in the rural areas is a major policy step in the right direction. In the first phase, the scheme will be implemented in states where the LPG coverage is found to be less than 50 per cent.

The immediate focus of this scheme is to put in place an efficient distribution channel for LPG particularly in rural areas or the low potential areas (GOI, 2009). However, this initiative can address only the issue of 'availability' whereas the other sets of issues such as 'accessibility' and 'affordability' require immediate attention as well. For example, the pricing of the LPG cylinder is one such important issue. As Mcdade (2004) points out that 'the most difficult consumer transition' is to bring a shift from the traditional cooking patterns using traditional stoves and fuels to modern energy fuels and devices.

In case of India, the HDI value has increased from 0.427 in 1980 to 0.489 in 1990, 0.511 in 2000, 0.596 in 2005 and 0.612 in 2007. However, in 2007, on the basis of the HDI India ranked 134th among the 182 nations, and is classified in the category of 'medium human development' (UNDP, 2009). Thus, increasing per capita energy consumption and ensuring a higher level of penetration of modern energy services is imperative even from human development point of view.

V. Conclusion

In this paper, the 'two-way' relationship between sustainable development and human development has been emphasised. It is argued that human development is not just an 'end' in itself but can be an effective 'means' to achieve sustainable development.

In Indian context, on the one hand we find that consumption of petroleum products is growing rapidly while on the other hand, the penetration of clean cooking fuels (such as LPG) is very low in rural areas. The transport sector and the residential sector are found to be consuming the significant proportion of the total petroleum products consumed in the economy.

In 2005-06, the share of petroleum products consumed by these two sector accounts for approximately 60 per cent of the total petroleum products consumed in India. The use of LPG as a cooking fuel is found to be concentrated largely in urban areas whereas rural households are still using dirty fuels (such as firewood, chips, and dung cakes) as their primary cooking fuels.

In order to achieve sustainable development, while it is important to find alternative sources for meeting the energy demands of the growing transport sector, it is equally important to ensure that rural households have access to clean cooking fuels.

References

Balakrishnan, Kalpana, Sankar Sambandan, Padmavathi Ramaswamy, Sumi Mehta and Kirk R Smith (2004): Exposure assessment for respirable particulates associated with household fuel use in rural districts of Andhra Pradesh, *Journal of Exposure Science and Environmental Epidemiology*, 14(S1): S14 – S25.

Batliwala, Srilatha (1983): Women and Cooking Energy, *Economic and Political Weekly*, 18(52 – 53): 2227-2230.

Dias, A Rubens, Cristiano R. Mattos and Jose A. P. Balestieri (2006): The limits of human development and the use of energy and the natural resources, *Energy Policy*, 34(9): 1026 – 1031.

Duflo, Esther, Michael Greenstone and Rema Hanna (2008): Cooking Stoves, Indoor Air Pollution and Respiratory Health in Rural Orissa, *Economic and Political Weekly*, 43(32): 71 – 76.

Goldemberg, Jose, Thomas B. Johansson, Amulya K. N. Reddy, and Robert H. Williams (2004): A global clean cooking fuel initiative, *Energy for Sustainable Development*, 8(3): 5 – 12.

Goodland, Robert (1995): The Concept of Environmental Sustainability, *Annual Review of Ecology and Systematics*, 26(1): 1 – 24.

Government of India (2009): Rajiv Gandhi Gramin LPG Vitrak (RGGLV), Ministry of Petroleum and Natural Gas.

Langhelle, Oluf (1999): Sustainable Development: Exploring the Ethics of "Our Common Future, *International Political Science Review*, 20(2): 129 – 249.

Martinez, Daniel M., and Ben W. Ebenhack (2008): Understanding the role of energy consumption in human development through the use of saturation phenomena, *Energy Policy*, 36(4): 1430 – 1435.

McDade, Susan (2004): Fuelling development: the role of LPG in poverty reduction and growth, *Energy for Sustainable Development*, 8(3): 74 – 81.

Pachauri, Shonali and Leiwen Jiang (2008): The Household Energy Transition in India and China, Interim Report (IR-09-09), International Institute for Applied Systems Analysis, Luxembourg, Austria.

Parikh, Jyoti, Haimanti Biswas and Shyam Karmakar (2003): Cooking with Biofuels Risk Factors Affecting Health Impact on Rural Women, *Economic and Political Weekly*, 38(26): 2681 – 2692.

Planning Commission (2006a): *Towards Faster and More Inclusive Growth – An Approach to the 11th Five Year Plan*, Government of India.

Planning Commission (2006b): *Integrated Energy Policy - Report of the Expert Committee*, Government of India.

Reddy, A. K. N. (2001): *Overview of Available Energy Technologies for Rural Development*, Paper presented at the Second Meeting of the Global Forum on Sustainable Energy at the international institute for Systems Analysis, Laxenburg, Austria.

Singhal, Robin (2009): *Development of Biofuels and Agricultural Land Use in India*, M.Phil Dissertation submitted to Jawaharlal Nehru University, New Delhi.

Sengupta, Ramprasad (2007): *High Economic Growth, Equity, and Sustainable Energy Development of India*, Research Institute for Economics and Business Administration, Kobe University, Japan, Discussion Paper Series no. 213.

Subramanian, K. A., S. K. Singhal, Mukesh Saxena and Sudhir Singhal (2005): Utilization of liquid biofuels in automotive diesel engines: An Indian Perspective, *Biomass and Bioenergy*, 29(1): 65 – 72.

United Nation Development Program (2009): World Human Development Report, New York.

Viswanathan, Brinda and K. S. Kavi Kumar (2005): Cooking fuel use patterns in India: 1983 – 2000, *Energy Policy*, 33(8): 1021 – 1036.

21

Challenges in Human Development: A Case Study of West Bengal

Mitrajit Chatterjee[1]

I. Introduction

Development is essentially a multi-dimensional concept and has varied facets like economic, social, cultural, political, institutional, psychological, ecological and ethical. It is often deemed as a process that attempts to improve the economic conditions of the people or to increase human welfare or to improve quality of life. Human development implies the attainment of the human community of an area to a satisfactory standard of living with quality life and environment. The human community of all parts of a country should enjoy the guarantee of equal share on the basic resources they need to live and should avail common opportunities to improve their living conditions. Irrespective of caste, creed, religious faith and political ideology, all of them need equal right to make choices about their lives.

II. Objectives

The objectives of the present study are

a. to give an overview of the nature of human development in the state as a whole;
b. to look into the degree of differences in the HDI and GDI among the districts of the state;
c. to throw light upon the challenges in human development in the state; and
d. to propose some measures to combat the challenges and improve the condition of human development in the state.

III. Data and Methodology

The data and information sources for the paper are the Human Development Reports on World, India and West Bengal published at

[1] Assistant Professor, Department of Geography, Dr. Gour Mohan Roy College (The University of Burdwan), Monteswar, Burdwan West Bengal, India

different times by government and non-government agencies, the Census of India reports as well as from various websites. Empirical observations have also been incorporated in the paper.

A Glimpse of the Study Area

The state of West Bengal is located in eastern India. The state comprises of 19 administrative districts *viz.* Darjiling, Jalpaiguri, Kochbehar, Uttar Dinajpur, Dakshin Dinajpur, Malda, Murshidabad, Birbhum, Bankura, Barddhaman, Nadia, Hugli, Puruliya, Purva Medinipur, Paschim Medinipur, Haora, North 24-Parganas, South 24-Parganas and Kolkata. The area extends from 85° 50' E to 89° 50' E Longitude and from 21° 38' N to 27° 10' N Latitude. West Bengal covers an area of 8872 km² with a total population of 80176197 persons, thus accounting for a population density of 904 persons per km² (Census 2001). The state is bordered by Nepal, Bhutan and the state of Sikkim on the North, Goalpara district of Assam and Bangladesh on the East, Bay of Bengal on the South, Orissa state on the South-west and Jharkhand and Bihar states on the west.

West Bengal is the fourth most populous state of the Indian federation. About 72 per cent of the people live in rural areas. The percentages of scheduled caste and scheduled tribe populations are 28.6 and 5.8 respectively in the rural areas and 19.9 and 1.5 respectively in the urban areas. Among the minorities, Muslims are the dominant section, accounting for 33.3 per cent of the urban and 11.8 per cent of the rural population. SC, ST and Minority groups together account for more than half the population of the state, and are also the poorest groups in rural West Bengal (WBHDR, 2004), thus, experiencing less development. The geographical concentration of these social groups well displays an uneven distribution. The dominance of the Scheduled Caste population is significantly higher than the state average in Koch Behar, Jalpaiguri, Uttar and Dakshin Dinajpur, Bankura, Birbhum and South 24 Parganas Districts; concentration of Scheduled Tribe population is significantly high in Darjiling, Jalpaiguri, Dakshin Dinajpur, Puruliya and Bankura districts, and Muslim population is much higher than the state average in Malda, Murshidabad and Birbhum districts (Census, 2001). The development indices measured in the districts of West Bengal show striking low values for the districts just mentioned with nominal exceptions.

Analysis of HDI and GDI of the State

Human development in West Bengal presents a mixed picture, and this picture is further complicated by the variations across districts in the state. Table 1 presents the Human Development Index for the different districts, as well as for the state as a whole. The table refers to undivided Dinajpur and Medinipur, because of the nature of the data available for consumption, poverty and life expectancy. There are very substantial differences across districts, such that the HDI ranges from a high of 0.78 for Kolkata, to a low of 0.44 for Malda i.e. a difference of 0.34 which is enough to be considered as 'critical gap' (WBHDR, 2004).

Table 1: District-wise Human Development Indices and Ranks

Districts	Health index	Income Index	Education Index	HDI value	HDI rank
Darjeeling	0.73	0.49	0.72	0.65	4
Jalpaiguri	0.61	0.38	0.6	0.53	10
Koch Bihar	0.5	0.41	0.65	0.52	11
Uttar and Dakshin Dinajpur	0.62	0.39	0.53	0.51	13
Malda	0.49	0.36	0.48	0.44	17
Murshidabad	0.57	0.29	0.52	0.46	15
Birbhum	0.53	0.27	0.61	0.47	14
Barddhaman	0.74	0.47	0.71	0.64	5
Nadia	0.65	0.41	0.66	0.57	9
North 24 Parganas	0.72	0.49	0.76	0.66	3
Hugli	0.77	0.46	0.67	0.63	6
Bankura	0.67	0.26	0.62	0.52	11
Puruliya	0.61	0.18	0.55	0.45	16
Medinipur	0.68	0.45	0.74	0.62	7
Haora	0.77	0.53	0.75	0.68	2
Kolkata	0.82	0.73	0.8	0.78	1
South 24 Parganas	0.71	0.4	0.68	0.60	8
West Bengal	0.7	0.43	0.69	0.61	-

Source: West Bengal Human Development Report (2004).

Gender discrimination has been an important feature of economic and social processes in West Bengal, and while it has declined in some respects in the recent past, it remains significant.

But it is more evident in economic variables and in literacy than in the longevity data, which indicate improving health position of women relative to men. This comes out very clearly in the calculations of the Gender Development Index which are presented in Table 2.

Table 2: District-wise Gender Development Indices and Ranks

Districts	Health index	Income Index	Education Index	GDI value	GDI rank
Darjeeling	0.731	0.356	0.714	0.600	2
Jalpaiguri	0.614	0.281	0.581	0.492	11
Koch Bihar	0.497	0.287	0.628	0.471	13
Uttar and Dakshin Dinajpur	0.616	0.291	0.527	0.478	12
Malda	0.491	0.291	0.465	0.416	17
Murshidabad	0.566	0.176	0.527	0.423	16
Birbhum	0.533	0.178	0.595	0.435	14
Barddhaman	0.740	0.270	0.669	0.560	7
Nadia	0.649	0.215	0.653	0.506	9
North 24 Parganas	0.721	0.219	0.752	0.564	6
Hugli	0.764	0.259	0.720	0.581	3
Bankura	0.662	0.215	0.605	0.494	10
Puruliya	0.606	0.161	0.506	0.424	15
Medinipur	0.683	0.323	0.728	0.578	4
Haora	0.773	0.194	0.742	0.570	5
Kolkata	0.824	0.320	0.783	0.642	1
South 24 Parganas	0.705	0.192	0.666	0.521	8
West Bengal	0.697	0.270	0.681	0.549	-

Source: West Bengal Human Development Report (2004).

It is worth noting that the rankings of the GDI broadly follow the same pattern as the HDI rankings, in that districts with low HDI also tend to have low GDI. However, some districts such as Haora, North 24 Parganas, Bardhaman and Koch Behar tend to have worse ranking in terms of GDI than HDI, suggesting especially acute gender discrimination. The very low "Income index" component of the GDI essentially reflects the low workforce participation of women in West Bengal, which in turn suggests a combination of greater restrictions on women's economic agency as well as social lack of recognition of women's unpaid work. Both of these suggest a major undercurrent of gender discrimination in society.

IV. Challenges to Human Development in the State

There are a lot of challenges that West Bengal has to face in the path of human development. The chief among them are enumerated below.

1. **Natural Control:** Variation in the ***physical environment*** of the state is the most fundamental challenge. West Bengal may broadly be divided into three regions on the basis of topographic and landform characteristics: *the Himalayan mountainous region of the north, the plateau region of the west* and *the extensive plains.* Each region has a different set of challenges which widely varied in nature.
2. **Population Density:** Greater ***population pressure*** inevitably puts more pressure on basic infrastructure as well as on the provision of health and education services. The extremely high population density (nearly 3 times the national average) obviously affects per capita resource allocation, so whatever West Bengal has achieved has been in spite of this critical negative factor of having the highest population density in the entire nation.
3. **Locational Factor:** West Bengal happens to be situated in a relatively ***poor and economically stagnant region*** of India, as well as near relatively backward countries, such that there have been very few economic growth stimuli coming from the surrounding region.
4. **Macroeconomic Conditions:** West Bengal, like all the states in the country, has been crucially affected by ***macroeconomic conditions*** that prevail in the country as a whole, and the economic policies of the central government continue to have the dominant effects on the basic conditions of life and work of the people. Since the early 1990s, there has been concentration of fiscal powers and reduced flow of resources to state governments from the Centre, which have dramatically affected both the fiscal position and the ability to engage in productive expenditure, of the state government. Therefore, despite the fact that formally speaking the responsibility for several of the factors that affect

human development (such as health and education) rests with the state government, in reality the power to alter these conditions significantly is relatively limited.

5. **Political Factor:** West Bengal is the only state in India to have been ruled continuously for more than a quarter of a century (32 years) by a Left Front government. The state has been particularly affected because the ruling Left Front government in the state has continuously had to deal with a central government led by an ***oppositional political formation***. This has obviously affected its ability to attract or extract any concessions from the Centre.
6. **Landlessness:** A disturbing feature of the very recent past has been the rapid increase in ***landlessness*** among rural households. By the end of the decade, nearly half of the rural households in West Bengal were landless. There have been recent reports of increasing land alienation by pattadars, and of eviction of bargadars.
7. **Financial Devolution:** West Bengal was the first state in the country to make a serious effort at devolving funds from the state government level to lower tiers of administration. However, actual financial devolution has been relatively constrained, especially from the mid 1990s onwards, when the state government's own severe ***fiscal problems*** reduced both the ability to make available untied funds and even the amount of planning and other departmental funds which could be utilised by the panchayats. In general, more backward districts have tended to receive larger per capita allocations from the state government. Some major anomalies remain in terms of financial devolution and the control, and even the financial information, provided to the panchayats.
8. **Poverty amidst agricultural labourers:** Though the most remarkable acceleration of growth in West Bengal occurred in agriculture, ***agricultural labourers remain the poorest section*** of the population, and have also experienced the lowest decline in poverty rates. Even in 1999-2000, nearly half of such households were absolutely poor. The group of cultivating households showed a broadly stable extent of poverty, at around one-fifth of such households.
9. **Employment Trends:** In West Bengal, much as in the broad all-India trends, ***employment growth lagged well behind output growth***. Rural employment has suffered more than urban employment. In the rural areas, population growth has been more

than double the rate of growth in the number of main workers, while the number of marginal workers has increased at a rapid rate. In urban areas, the employment picture looks slightly better: while marginal work is clearly the most dynamic with a very high annual rate of growth, main workers grew faster than total population growth.

Within the overall stagnation of aggregate employment in the West Bengal countryside in the recent past, one very significant shift has been the diversification into non-agricultural activities. Much of the employment diversification away from agriculture in rural West Bengal represents positive and dynamic processes and tendencies. However, there are doubts about the sustainability and continued viability of several of these activities, either from an ecological or an economic perspective. Thus, it is not known whether small-scale local manufacturing industry will be able to compete effectively over time with the products of large-scale companies or branded multinational products benefiting from superior marketing and distribution techniques. Also, the expansion of alternative activities such as prawn farming and fisheries has ecological implications which cannot be dismissed and which raise question about the future effects.

Rates of urban employment generation have slowed down in the most recent period. While rates of employment growth for men have not declined, the decline has been sharp for women. In Kolkata, unlike the state as a whole, the proportion of male main workers to male population has increased over the 1990s. The reversal of employment generation for urban women in the latter part of the 1990s is a very serious issue which requires specific policy focus in order to redress. This is especially the case given that labour force participation rates for women in West Bengal were already very low. Also, there is a substantial gender gap in wages, which stems primarily from the fact that most female employment in the urban areas is in low income occupations.

10. **Nutrition:** The data on ***nutrition*** overall indicate that the average level of nutrition in the state, and especially among women, is low by several criteria. The overall ***anaemia status of children in West Bengal is very poor*** as it ranks as low as nineteenth among 25 states. The proportion of children with anaemia (78 per cent) is higher compared to the Indian average of 74 per cent. In the rural areas, 82 per cent of children are estimated

to have anaemia, compared to 64 per cent in urban West Bengal and 60 per cent in Kolkata. Severe anaemia is also higher in rural West Bengal, at 5.3 per cent compared to 4.6 per cent in the urban areas and 0.7 per cent in Kolkata. The ***nutritional status of women in West Bengal is significantly worse*** than the national average. Compared with the national average of 52 per cent, 63 per cent of ever-married women in West Bengal were characterised as having iron-deficiency anaemia in 1998-99. The most deprived nutritional group consists of children between 1-3 years of age.

Food security is obviously one of the prime factors for nutritional well being, and therefore an important determinant of the overall health condition. Food security in turn is affected by aggregate production within the state, the ability to access outside production, and the distributional features within the state that determine the access to food of households in different geographical areas as well as households of different income and occupation groups. In this context, the recent deterioration of the public food distribution system, and its declining ability to reach households across the state and provide the desired range of foodstuff, is a source of concern.

The prevalence of malnutrition is possibly a major cause for certain health problems in the state. The data on ***morbidity*** among the general population indicate very ***high incidence of asthma and jaundice***. These are diseases which are affected by the extent of atmospheric pollution and the availability of safe water and sanitation. There are some diseases for which West Bengal appears to have much higher incidence than any other state. For example, 40 per cent of the reported cases of measles in India in 2001 were from West Bengal. This is even though the rate of measles immunisation in West Bengal is higher than the all-India average. The state also has a higher than expected incidence of some diseases that can be prevented by timely vaccination, such as neonatal tetanus (21 per cent of all reported cases in India) and diphtheria (17 per cent of all reported cases).

11. **Health:** The ***public health system in West Bengal bears an exceptionally large burden***, because in addition to the high demographic pressure in the state, the bulk of curative services are in public hands, such that 76 per cent of the health institutes in West Bengal are run by the government, compared to less than 40 per cent elsewhere in India and as little as 25 per cent in states like

Kerala and Tamil Nadu. The panchayat system has a lot of potential in terms of mobilization and ensuring effective vaccination and personal and community cleanliness which contributes to the control of disease. However, to a significant extent this potential has not really been utilised in West Bengal so far. The state has a ***very low rank in terms of coverage of vaccines such as DPT, OPV and measles***.

Furthermore, there is evidently a very high dropout rate with respect to successive immunisation for DPT and OPV, which has obvious effects on the efficacy of the vaccination. The problem of maintaining continuity in services is evident even in antenatal care. The data indicate a good beginning in terms of coverage, but subsequently gradual fallout among women who receive ANC. The reason could be lack of motivation or gaps in service delivery itself.

12. **Literacy:** As per Census 2001, 27 per cent of households in rural areas and 12 per cent of all households in urban areas did not have any literate adult (15 years and above). The proportion of households without any female adult literate was substantially higher, at 51 per cent and 31 per cent in the rural and urban areas of West Bengal respectively. Further, the ***literacy status of Scheduled Castes, Scheduled Tribes and minority community households is significantly worse than for other households, especially in rural West Bengal. Even among the literate population, around 17 per cent is only literate at "below primary" level***. The relatively most deprived occupation group appears to be that of agricultural labour households, of whom more than half of all such population, and nearly two-thirds of the females, are non-literate. ***Gender gaps remain substantial***, and women of rural labour households (both in agriculture and non-agriculture) are the worst off among the rural population in terms of illiteracy. Gender gaps in literacy are slightly less marked in urban parts of the state. Here, casual labour households are the worst off, and nearly half the women in such households are illiterate.

Income categories are also relevant in determining access to education. People from the bottom 20 per cent of households according to income are more than twice as likely to be illiterate as those from households in the top 20 per cent income category. About 66 per cent of rural females of age 7 years and above are non-literate in the lowest quintile as compared to 30 per cent in the richest quintile.

Literacy among persons of age 7 years and above in the ST households is uniformly lower as compared to all other social categories. The problem of illiteracy is particularly acute among rural women from ST households, with 70 per cent of them being non-literate. The low levels of literacy among ST households indicate that the problem also has a spatial or regional dimension, since ST households tend to be concentrated in certain regions/districts/blocks, and poor physical infrastructure in such areas makes communication and the provision of basic public services including education much more difficult. In SC households, more than half of the women are illiterate. The gender gap is approximately equal across caste category, indicating that gender discrimination in not more marked among any particular caste group, but is shared across all castes.

13. **Primary Education:** ***School attendance rates*** for boys were generally slightly lower than the all-India average in both urban and rural areas. However, attendance rates for girls aged 6-10 years in rural West Bengal were generally better than the all-India average, although in urban areas the rate in West Bengal was slightly lower. Never enrolled children tend to be more concentrated among the lower income groups and the Scheduled Tribe and minority populations. The reasons for the relatively low ratio of attendance at schools in rural West Bengal include the sheer physical lack of schools in the vicinity of children. ***Lack of basic infrastructural facilities continues to be a serious concern for the proper growth of primary education in West Bengal.*** There are not enough schools; even those that exist often do not have buildings to speak of, not to mention other facilities and equipment. Despite the rapid increase in the number of schools and school teachers over the 1990s, there are ***very severe gaps in physical availability of schools***. The number of schools with no room is depressingly high, and amounts to nearly one-fifth of all schools. When a school does not have a building, it does not only affect the quality of the learning experience; it can even affect the quantity of instruction, since such schools cannot function, for example, on rainy days. Schools with only one room amounted to nearly another one-fifth. While the average number of teachers per school is 3, this is still below the number of classes, which must

cover at least Class I-IV and sometimes also Class V. This means that at least two classes would be taught together on average. In addition, there are major inadequacies with respect to the physical condition of schools and the absence of necessary fitting and fixtures, toilets and basic equipment and teaching materials such as blackboards. Many rural school buildings are characterised by poor natural light and often no electricity, with inadequate toilet facilities (especially for girl students) and mostly very insufficient furniture, which make them unattractive places to be in for young children. Separate urinals for girls are very rare, while latrine facilities do not exist in most rural schools.

Available dropout rates may be overestimates, mainly because enrolment itself is over estimated at the primary stage and therefore subsequent data for later classes do not capture similar numbers. Therefore the problem of high dropout at primary level may not be as severe as generally imagined. The typical reasons for dropout include lack of interest in education, inability to meet the expenses, distance of the school from the home, and the need to attend to domestic and other household duties, including collection of fodder and water. In urban West Bengal, the most important reason is the inability to meet the expenses associated with schooling.

There are serious and continuing concerns about the quality of primary education, in both urban and rural areas, including poor infrastructure and inadequate equipment in schools; sporadic and irregular attendance of some teachers; lack of accountability of teachers; and inadequate school inspection. There may be a need to restructure the organisation and administration of schools, to make them amenable to greater local community control.

Apart from proper infrastructural facilities, quality education is another important factor to be considered immediately for these otherwise out-of-school children. In many more backward areas where such education is really required, it is difficult to find a woman above 40 years who is able to teach primary children. More importantly, the basic assumptions, that anyone can teach children and that pedagogy is unimportant at elementary school level, must be faulted.

14. **Vulnerability to Natural Disasters:** West Bengal is prone to various kinds of ***natural disasters***. The most significant of these has been ***floods***, which have been the major cause of agony due to

natural disaster. In addition, ***cyclones*** have also wreaked substantial damage periodically. The recent cyclone ***'Aila'*** has caused severe damage in South Bengal especially in the *Sundarbans*. It has been estimated that more than 45 per cent of the villages in the state were susceptible to floods, and more than 40 per cent of the land area of the state has been identified as flood-prone. Among all natural calamities, the devastation caused by cyclones tends to be the most sudden and severe. The western districts of the state, especially Birbhum, Bankura and Purulia, are ***drought-prone*** and tend to receive inadequate rainfall.

Devastation caused by the Cyclone 'Aila' in South Bengal

15. **Water and Arsenic Poisoning:** ***Water*** is an increasingly scarce resource, in West Bengal as in most other parts of India. While most districts have near universal or at least adequate coverage of habitations and population in terms of water supply, there is ***distinct inadequacy*** in some districts, where at least 15 per cent of the population is not covered. The worst affected districts in this regard are South 24 Parganas, Haora and Nadia, while Medinipur, Koch Behar and North 24 Parganas also require attention. One problem with regard to water pollution which has recently assumed critical proportions relates to ***arsenic poisoning*** through tubewell water, which has affected at least 75 blocks spread over 9 districts, accounting for an estimated population of over 13.5 million people.
16. **Air Pollution:** Air pollution is dominantly an urban problem. In the twin cities of Kolkata and Haora quite a large number of

industrial units are located within the residential areas. In general, Haora is more polluted than Kolkata. In addition, about half of the total air pollution load of Kolkata and Haora is contributed by automobile exhausts, especially from diesel driven vehicles. Indoor air pollution is also a problem in rural areas, mainly affecting women and girl children who are responsible for household cooking.

17. **Regional Issues:** Human development in West Bengal has strong regional dimensions. The central importance of Kolkata means that levels of human development tend to be highest in the greater Kolkata region, and deteriorate in concentric circles according to distance from this region.

There are ***three particular sub-regions*** in West Bengal which face particular problems of development and constraints on improving the conditions of well-being, due to historical reasons, or distance and locational considerations, or social composition. Therefore, they tend to be more backward in terms of nfrastructure development and also human development indicators. It is noteworthy that these three regions also have in common higher proportions of SC/ST population relative to the rest of the state.

In **North Bengal**, the Uttar Banga and DGHC blocks span the two major watersheds of the Tista and the Mahananda. The hilly blocks of the DGHC region, the Terai and the Duars share some characteristics, although Koch Behar is more similar to the two Dinajpur districts. In this region, the presence of Siliguri in Darjeeling district creates a more developed centre, but the ***economic and developmental linkages to surrounding areas are still weak***. Within North Bengal, three further sub-regions can be identified with different characteristics: (i) *Malda and Dinajpur* (ii) *Darjeeling, Cooch Behar and Jalpaiguri* and (iii) *the "chicken neck" of North Dinajpur*. These areas are not only geoecologically distinct, but also were until recently separated with little interaction in terms of transport or trade, especially after the Partition of India broke pre-existing links. The region as a whole has a much higher rate of in-migration than other parts of West Bengal. The advantages are that migrants bring in new skills and also tend to be better educated, so they utilise local educational and other resources better. But this also raises questions, for example the problem of the local deprived groups, such as the SCs/STs in the area. In this region a particular role is played by the substantial presence of tea gardens, especially in

Darjeeling and Jalpaiguri districts. While the expansion of such tea estates, including into Uttar Dinajpur district, has been associated with the decline of small-holder subsistence cultivation, there is also ***a recent tendency for closure of some of these plantations, because of worsening international market conditions***. There is a lot of wasted land on plantations, which produce only 41 per cent of the tea used in the local tea factories. These factories deal with tea blends that include both local and imported tea leaves. Conditions of labour on the tea estates are cause for some concern. There have been increases in labour productivity, but a ***simultaneous increase in the casualisation of labour***, especially of women workers. Female work participation is much higher in the tea areas, but this is mostly in the form of casual labour.

Secondly, there is the **Sunderbans** area in the southernmost part of the state, mostly in South 24 Parganas and some blocks of North 24 Parganas, a special region with an ***exceptionally fragile environment of mangrove forests and estuaries***. The crucial problem for future development in the area is of ***creating a balance between the delicate and threatened ecosystem, the needs of the local population, and the demands of resource exploitation and material development***. The human development problems in the area go beyond those determined by the lack of productive employment and the poor physical infrastructure. The population of this area is very heterogeneous, with a rich history of in-migration especially in the post-Independence period, with new migrants (often displaced people from the east) pushing into a relatively harsh natural environment, clearing forests for habitation and cultivation. This process of ***uncontrolled population growth has reduced the per capita cultivable land, and created overcrowding and high rates of disguised unemployment in agriculture, as well as overexpansion of pisciculture and brackish water shrimp farming which have created a range of ecological and socio-economic problems*** in the region. The consequent difficulties in ensuring livelihood have also led to high rates of out-migration, especially among young male workers. The economy of the region suffers from very ***substantial structural underemployment***. A large part of the population is basically dependent upon rain-fed monocropping (recently dominated by *boro* rice) and whatever subsidiary activities are available. About half of the households are those of landless labourers. The limited possibilities of extending cultivation and the features of the area, have led to an increase in dependence upon fishing and the collection of *bagda* prawn seeds. There are ***complicated issues of social cohesion, given the diversity of the population and the contradictions between fringe villagers and relatively new migrants***. Also, because of inaccessibility, the ***panchayat system is less developed*** and integrated into society than in other parts of the state, and therefore the use of local government institutions to further human development goals, while still possible, is more constrained.

Collection of Bagda Prawn seeds in the Sunderbans

Finally, the **Paschimanchal region** in the west of the state spans the all the blocks of Birbhum and Purulia, and some blocks of Bankura, Medinipur and Bardhaman. These blocks are ***relatively isolated, with poor transport infrastructure, and therefore tend to be backward***. The western parts of the state include some of the most backward areas from the point of view if infrastructure and material development, with the lowest levels of per capita income and also relatively poor HDI rankings. The relative inadequacy of transport and communication networks, and the inadequate physical provision of basic public goods and services are compounded by the fact that this region is relatively speaking the ***driest*** in the state; it receives the least amount of annual rainfall and is more ***prone to drought*** than other parts of West Bengal. Nevertheless, the ***problems of the Paschimanchal region appear to be more tractable than those in the other regions, because they stem more directly from poor infrastructure and lack of material development***. Many of the social requirements for improved human development and empowerment of disadvantaged groups are more developed in this region than in some other parts of the state.

V. Latest Challenges

Frequent ***Bandhs and strikes*** in Bengal have struck at the root of the state's development. Bandhs and strikes have become a common weapon to be used by all the political parties and many other secessionist, sectarian and separatists for their narrow gain. Of late, the state is facing violent agitation demanding a separate hill state and the movement is led by *Gorkha Janamukti Morcha*. Apart from this, another violent and armed struggle has begun against the state by the Maoists who with their foreign ideology want to capture power through armed struggle. Another secessionist movement by Kamtapuri Liberation Army demanding a separate state to be named *Greater Coochbehar* has added fuel to the fire. The entire state has become a dreadful dream for the common peace-loving people and at the same time is posing hindrance to human development in the state.

Areas to be focussed on:

There are particular areas that require specific intervention. Some of these are described very briefly here:

1. In the area of land relations, the recent increase in landlessness needs to be analysed in terms of its causes and the viability of peasant cultivation needs to be strengthened.
2. There is a very strong case for giving panchayats and municipal bodies greater administrative and functional control over many of the local social sector delivery institutions, such as in health and education.
3. Urban-rural income disparities need to be addressed; in particular, the growing gap between the metropolitan area of Kolkata and the rest of the state is a cause for concern.
4. In terms of poverty alleviation, the single most affected group is that of rural wage labour households, whose needs need to be specially considered.

5. More than half of the villages in West Bengal lacked connection by roadways in the mid-1990s. This obviously has important implications for the provision of a range of basic services and utilities, as well as health and education infrastructure.
6. Employment generation has got to be a critical focus of future policy. The change in the pattern of job creation towards more casual, marginal, part-time and insecure contracts or self-employment is a major source of concern. Improvements in this area will require diversification away from those sectors which are exhibiting low employment elasticity, or changing the pattern of growth in these sectors.

   Clearly, employment generation has to be a critical focus of future policy in the state. This can be achieved dominantly through diversification away from those sectors which are exhibiting low employment elasticity, or changing the pattern of growth in these sectors. Ideally, employment diversification has to be based on activities using locally available resources. This can involve activities such as agro-processing as well as fishery development and so on. There should also be an attempt to exploit the opportunities created for the increase in rural services, either because of the indirect effects of government spending or because people take up activities such as petty trade for want of alternatives. In the urban areas, simply encouraging the diversification of activities away from employment towards manufacturing and services may not be sufficient to cause employment expansion in the urban areas, given the current pattern of growth in these sectors. What may be needed is a change in the nature of such growth, which would make these activities not only more dynamic, but also more labour-using than they are at present.
7. The low nutritional status of women and young children requires urgent attention. Areas of public intervention that can be usefully pursued in his regard include the provision of sanitary facilities and campaigns to improve food consumption practices to ensure adequate nutrition.
8. The recent deterioration of the public food distribution system, and its declining ability to reach households across

the state and provide the desired range of foodstuff, is a source of concern.

9. Health service delivery needs overall improvement at all levels. In particular, preventive health delivery systems need to be strengthened.

   The broad health indicators, such as the birth rate, death rate, life expectancy at birth, neonatal mortality rate, infant mortality rate, child mortality rate are better in West Bengal as compared to India. The state also has a better morbidity profile of diseases like diarrhoea and malaria. However, the service indicators suggest that there are gaps in its service delivery mechanisms and also in the involvement of the community in the entire process of the health delivery system. There is tremendous potential to improve the health care and delivery service, not only through increased public expenditure, but also by involving panchayats and local communities more generally. The empowerment of women is a crucial instrument towards better health for the society in general.

   The current aim of the state government is to involve panchayats in creating community health consciousness, and also to take over some of the more basic activities of the Primary Health Centres which currently are still run in a centralised way from Kolkata. These measures are designed to increase the involvement of local government and local communities in the public health services, which will therefore become more directly accountable to the people. However, care must be taken in such measures, to ensure that they do not result in a lower track parallel system of health care provision under the supervision of the panchayats, operating with community involvement but with fewer resources. Some further system of ensuring local accountability of the public health system needs to be devised. At the same time, it is also necessary to regulate the activities of private medical practitioners and institutions. All these measures are part of a broader programme based on the philosophy that the people's health is in the people's hands.

10. There is utmost necessity to improve the infrastructure of the schools and at the same time it is necessary to devise

ways of making the formal system more responsive to local needs and to the specific requirements of children from disadvantaged groups, perhaps by increasing community participation in the supervision of such education. There is therefore a strong case for increasing the control of panchayats over the formal school system in the state.

11. Arsenic poisoning is an urgent problem requiring immediate public intervention.
12. In recent years, improved forecasting, better disaster preparedness in highly exposed regions and more systematic response by local authorities have tended to reduce the human and animal deaths caused by cyclones, even if they have not managed to reduce the damage to property and real assets. The western districts of the state, especially Birbhum, Bankura and Purulia, are drought-prone and tend to receive inadequate rainfall. Drought management requires a combination of sustained and improved water harvesting techniques which reduce dependence upon any one rainy season, and much improved transport and communications links between the drought-affected areas and the rest of the state and neighbouring regions, such that greater supply of food and other commodities is provided during and just after the drought. The improvement of transport links is critical in this regard.
13. The specific problems of certain regions (North Bengal, *Sunderbans* and Paschimanchal) highlight several policy areas relevant for improving human development: the role of infrastructure in redressing development imbalances; the importance of institutions, in a range of areas such as banking, marketing, research, education, health, industrial development; the simultaneous significance of both decentralisation and co-ordination in the planning process. The problem of ensuring sustainable development with social cohesion is especially marked in these regions.

VI. Conclusion

The experience of West Bengal highlights ***three significant relationships*** that have crucial implications for human development anywhere.

- The first is the inherent difficulty of an autonomous development trajectory within a constituent province of a country, even with a federal system of government, and the role of broader macroeconomic processes in determining outcomes even within the state.
- The second is the importance of mobilising resources for public intervention, and the possible limitations upon the advance of human development imposed by fiscal constraints.
- The third is the crucial two-way relationship between institutional change and economic processes, as well as the importance of continued mobilisation and involvement of ordinary people in the infrastructure and delivery mechanisms necessary for improving conditions of human development.

Thus, the two crucial planks of a forward looking strategy therefore are: increasing the efforts for resource mobilisation to enable more state government spending in necessary areas; and innovating and strengthening institutions and mechanisms to ensure the better delivery of public services. Such a strategy would help to generate a virtuous cycle of human development and economic growth positively reinforcing each other.

References

Bhattacharya, Kapil (1959): *Bangladesher Nad-Nadi O Parikalpana* (in Bengali), Vidyodaya Library Pvt. Ltd., Kolkata.

Census of India (2001): *Final Population Totals*, West Bengal.

Chatterjee, A. B., Gupta, A., and Mukhopadhyay, P. K. (1970): *West Bengal*, K. L .Mukhopadhyay, Kolkata.

Delhi Human Development Report (2006): Oxford University Press, New Delhi.

Human Development Report (1999): Oxford University Press, New Delhi.

Human Development Report (2004): Oxford University Press, New Delhi.

Hussain, Majid (2005): Human Geography, Third Edition, Rawat Publications, New Delhi, pp. 273-315.

National Council of Applied Economic Research (1999): *India: Human Development Report*, Oxford University Press, New Delhi.

Rao, Shankar C. N. (2006): *Sociology: Principles of Sociology with an Introduction to Social Thought*, S. Chand and Co., New Delhi.

West Bengal Human Development Report (2004): Development and Planning Department, Govt. of West Bengal.

World Bank (1998): *Reducing Poverty in India: Options for More Effective Public Services*, Washington D.C.

22

Travel and Tourism Competitiveness Index and Human Development

Y. Venkata Rao[1] and B. Thrinadha Rao[2]

I. Introduction

In the realm of globalization, the success and prosperity of a nation largely depends on the availability of indigenous industries with competitive capabilities. Many strategy scholars argue that the competitiveness of local business firms is one of the key determinants of a country's competitiveness (Porter, 2004). As, the travel and tourism (T and T) sector, worldwide, is showing significance in the economic development of the Nation s, competitiveness of the sector is an essential element for extensive contribution to a nations employment, national income, and improvement in balance of payments. Given the importance of the T and T sector, four years ago the World Economic Forum (WEF), together with its Industry and Data Partners, embarked on a multi-year research effort aimed at exploring various issues related to the T and T competitiveness of Nation s around the world. Research also indicates that the human development Index is becoming crucial for developing as well as for developed economies for economic, political, and social growth (Kevin Watkins, 2006). Therefore, the human development is an important segment which also takes significant share in building competitiveness of a nation.

II. Human Development (HD) and Competitiveness

Human Development: It is about putting people at the centre of development and realizing their potential, increasing their choices and enjoying the freedom to lead lives they value (Kevin Watkins, 2006). HD also refers to create environment in which people can

[1]Associate Professor, Department of Tourism Studies, Pondicherry University, Puducherry

[2]Research Scholar, Department of Tourism Studies, Pondicherry University, Puducherry

develop their full potential and lead productive, creative lives in accordance with their needs and interests, thus bringing the focus back onto people (Jeni Klugman 2009). People are the real wealth of Nations. Development is thus about expanding the choices people have, to lead lives that they value and improving the human condition so that people will get the chance to lead full lives.

Competitiveness: The World Economic Forum (Jennifer Blanke and Thea Chiesa; 2009) defined the competitiveness as a 'set of institutions, policies, and factors that determine the level of productivity of a country'. Asia Pacific Research and Training Network on Trade (ARTNeT) (2009) defined the competitiveness in three levels. They are:

- *Company level:* the ability to provide products and services more effectively and efficiently than the relevant competitors.
- *Industry level:* the ability of the Nation's firms to achieve sustained success against foreign competitors without protection or subsidies.
- *National level:* the ability of the Nation 's citizens to achieve a high and rising standard of living.

III. Significance of HD and Competitiveness

Health and wealth are the two factors which determine a Nations growth or development. Mostly, both these factors are mutually correlated in all over the world nations. A wealthy country has population with high standard of healthy conditions. HDI indicates living conditions, education levels and purchasing power of people in a country. TTCI depicts health and education, infrastructure development, government policies and regulations in a country are contributed towards the nation's economic development, eradication of poverty by creating high volume of jobs and attracting more foreign direct investment. With the help of these two Indexes i.e. HDI and TTCI one can draw the inferences and feasible solutions for, why some countries are prosperous in economy and some are lagging behind? In the same way, why people in some countries are having high standard living conditions with high life expectancy, where as others are not? It is also responsible for developing co-operation among the organizations and individuals with in the country to increase their competitiveness and human development Index levels against the rest of the world organizations and countries. As the World Economic Forum (Jennifer Blanke and Thea Chiesa;

2009) opinion that the 'economic progress without human / social development is not sustainable, while human development without economic development is not feasible'.

IV. Contribution of Travel and Tourism Industry to Economic Development

Travel and Tourism act as a critical source of economic growth and development of a nation. It is one of the fastest growing economic sectors in the world. In some countries this is the primary sector for their nation's economic growth. According to World Economic Forum reports, the Travel and Tourism Industry generates receipts from US$2.1 billion (1950) to US$622.7 billion (2004). The number of International Arrivals increased from 25 millions (1950) to 924million (2008). The World Travel and Tourism Council (WTTC) estimated that the travel and tourism industry is accounted for 9.9 per cent of world GDP, 10.9 per cent of world exports, and 9.4 percent of world investment in the year 2009. T and T Industry is one of the major sectors which creating high volume of jobs in the world's job market. In the year 2007, it created 234 million jobs and is responsible for 8.2 per cent world's employment.

V. Index Assessment Agencies

United Nations Development Program (UNDP): UNDP is the UN's global development network, an organization advocating for change and connecting countries to knowledge, experience and resources to help people build a better life. It is on the ground in 182 countries, working with them on their own solutions to global and national development challenges. UNDP helps developing countries attract and use aid effectively. It encourages the protection of human rights and the *empowerment of women*. The annual *Human Development Report*, commissioned by UNDP, focuses the global debate on key development issues, providing new measurement tools, innovative analysis and often controversial policy proposals. The global Report's analytical framework and inclusive approach carry over into regional, national and local Human Development Reports, also supported by UNDP.

World Economic Forum (WEF): The World Economic Forum (WEF) is a Geneva-based non-profit foundation best known for its annual meeting in Davos, Switzerland which brings together top business leaders, international political leaders, selected intellectuals and journalists to discuss the most pressing issues facing the world including health and the environment. The World Economic Forum, earlier called as The European Management Forum, was founded in 1971 by Klaus M. Schwab, a business professor in Switzerland. Beyond meetings, the Forum produces a series of research reports and engages its members in sector specific initiatives.

VI. Assessment Criteria for HDI and TTCI

The UNDP has chosen following three dimensions as a criterion for assessing the human development of 182 countries all over the world (Jeni Klugman; 2009). They are:

- *Life expectancy:* Life expectancy is the expected (in the statistical sense) number of years of life remaining at a given age. Life expectancy at birth, as an Index of population health and longevity.
- *Literacy:* Knowledge and education, as measured by the adult literacy rate (with two-thirds weighting) and the combined primary, secondary, and tertiary gross enrollment ratio (with one-third weighting).
- *Standard of living:* Standard of living is generally measured by standards such as real (i.e. inflation adjusted) income per person and poverty rate. Other measures such as access and quality of health care, income growth inequality and educational standards are also used.

The TTCI has been developed within the context of the World Economic Forum's Industry Partnership Program for the Aviation, Travel and Tourism sector. The aim of TTCI is to measure the factors and policies that make it attractive to develop the T and T sector in different countries. It is based on three broad categories of variables that facilitate or drive T and T competitiveness. These categories are summarized into the three Sub-Indexes (Jennifer Blanke and Thea Chiesa, 2009). They are (a) the T and T regulatory framework Sub-Index; (b) the T and T business environment and infrastructure Sub-Index; and (c) the T and T human, cultural, and natural resources Sub-Index. Each of these three Sub-Indexes in turn consists of 14numbers of pillars of T and T competitiveness. They are: 1. Policy rules and regulations; 2. Environmental sustainability; 3. Safety and security, 4. Health and hygiene; 5. Prioritization of Travel and Tourism; 6. Air transport infrastructure; 7. Ground transport infrastructure; 8. Tourism infrastructure; 9. ICT infrastructure; 10. Price of Travel and Tourism; 11. Human resources; 12. Affinity for Travel and Tourism; 13. Natural resources and; 14. Cultural resources.

VII. HDI and TTCI – An Inter-relationship Perspective

The correlation between HDI and TTCI of 132 countries is analyzed by categorizing all the countries into four – 1. Very high human development courtiers (36) and competitiveness rank; 2. High human development courtiers (37) and competitiveness rank; 3. Medium human development courtiers (46) and competitiveness; 4. Low human development courtiers (13) and competitiveness rank. In each category, correlation was measured to find the strength of a relationship between two variables i.e. human development and competitiveness. There are noteworthy finding in all categories of the countries in between the two variables. On the whole, largely, the interpretation indicates that the positive correlation was found, which means the two variables move in the same direction.

Table 1 shows the ranking of very high HDI countries (36) including the year 2009 TTCI. It is evident from the table that the top country in HDI i.e. Norway has secured 19th rank in TTCI. It is interesting to note that a set of countries like Canada, Sweden, Finland, Denmark, New Zealand, Greece and Korea were almost all coinciding their HDI with TTCI. Whereas, notable gap between the two variables was observed in case of Iceland, Ireland, Netherlands, Japan, Luxemburg, Italy, United Kingdom, Germany, Kuwait, Cyprus, Portugal, Czech Republic and Malta. Among these countries, there are around ten ranks differences between the two variables. It also indicates from the table 1 that among the very high human development countries, by and large their competitiveness of T and T is less than the HDI. On the whole, the Table 5 subscribes that the positive correlation between the HDI and TTCI among very highly human developed countries.

Table 2 presents the ranking of high HDI countries (37), besides the year 2009 TTCI. In this category, countries like Bahrain, Slovakia, Lithuania, Latvia, Mexico, Panama, Romania and, Colombia have more or less similar HDI and TTCI. The rest of the countries have the differences of around ten ranks. It is noteworthy to mention form the Table 2 that the Libyan Arab Jamahiriya's competitiveness of T and T (rank 112th) is higher than the HDI (rank 55th) from the rest of the countries in this category.

Table 1: Very High Human Development Countries (36) and Competitiveness Rank

Sl. No.	Country	Competitiveness Rank (T and T)	HD Rank
1	Norway	19	1
2	Australia	9	2
3	Iceland	15	3
4	Canada	5	4
5	Ireland	18	5
6	Netherlands	13	6
7	Sweden	7	7
8	France	4	8
9	Switzerland	1	9
10	Japan	25	10
11	Luxembourg	23	11
12	Finland	14	12
13	United States	8	13
14	Austria	17	14
15	Spain	6	15
16	Denmark	14	16
17	Belgium	22	17
18	Italy	28	18
19	New Zealand	20	20
20	United Kingdom	11	21
21	Germany	3	22
22	Singapore	10	23
23	Hong Kong	12	24
24	Greece	24	25
25	Korea	31	26
26	Israel	36	27
27	Slovenia	35	29
28	Brunei	69	30
29	Kuwait	95	31
30	Cyprus	21	32
31	Qatar	37	33
32	Portugal	17	34
33	UAE	33	35
34	Czech Republic	26	36
35	Barbados	30	37
36	Malta	29	38

Source: Prepared based on given data from Human Development Report, 2009, and the Travel and Tourism Competitiveness Report 2009.

In contrast to the very high human developed countries category, the high developed countries have largely more TTCI and the HDI. However, among all the countries, there are no much differences in the two variables. It is also supported by the Table 5 positive correlation.

Table 3 indicates the ranking of medium HDI countries (46) along with the year 2009 TTCI. Among the medium HDI counties, Thailand, South Africa and India have some similarities in HDI and TTCI. These three countries depict less human development and more T and T competitiveness. In case of Algeria and Bolivia, competitiveness of T and T is less than the human development. Unlike very high and high human developed countries, in the medium human development countries more variation between the two variables was found. In this category, no country's two variables Index was matching. It is supported by the Table 5 of correlation between HDI and TTCI. Table 4 shows the ranking of low HDI countries (13) with corresponding TTCI of the year 2009. Among the low HDI counties, Zambia, Gambia and Senegal have some differences in HDI and TTCI. These three countries depict less human development and more T and T competitiveness. The rest of the countries didn't show much difference in the two variables. It is supported by the Table 5 of correlation between HDI and TTCI.

VIII. Status of India

India is the youngest Nation in the world, with 1/5th of world's population under the age of 24 years being Indian citizens. The academic and the policy makers all over the world are in a pre-conceived notion that, India would be more productive and have a competitive edge over other Nations. But it is quite surprising to note that the health standards of India are relatively poorer than many other Nations. Access to safe drinking water and decent sanitation is still a distant dream to the majority of Indians. The mushrooming urban slums are compounding the health problems. India ranks 62nd in Travel and Tourism Competitiveness Index, the rankings given by World Economic Forum (Jennifer Blanke and Thea Chiesa; 2009), 134th in Human Development Index report-2009, the rankings given by United Nations Development Programme. India ranks 103 in the rankings given by World Economic Forum based on health indicators. We are still below the standard of many Sub Saharan Nations in access of good sanitation. India has the highest number of malarial deaths as compared to Africa in 2008(Thierry Geiger and Sushant Palakurthi Rao; 2009). Indian citizens are not only less healthy but also more malnutritioned, with 21 per cent of our population falling into this category. It is 50per cent more than the average of lower and middle income grouped countries average i.e.14percent and also more than twice of China i.e.9percent (Thierry Geiger and Sushant Palakurthi Rao; 2009). Even to attend to the casualties, we have only 6 physicians for every 10,000 people. It is far below the standards of developed nations. Even the number of physicians available in rural India is still worse. Even India's life expectancy rate is 64.7 years (As per United Nations World Population Prospects 2005-2010) which is below the world average (67.2 years) and the standard of East Asian countries.

India falls short in providing basic education to its citizens. As per World Bank-2009 report India stands in the 100th place in world rankings, where as its counter part China is in 42nd position and Malaysia in 24th position. India scored around 4 points on a scale of 7 on the aspect of providing primary education. The enrolment rate in primary education has almost reached 90 per cent (aged 5-14 years).For this India placed in 89th rank with 3.2 score. India spends 3.2 percent of GDP on education. There is only one teacher for every 40 pupils at school.1/5th primary school pupils in rural areas enrolled in private schools, with better average class performance. With all our young population, it shall be a hard struggle to attain more productivity and increased competitiveness, with our population suffering from diseases and malnutrition, lack of decent living conditions and quality education conditions to the majority. These issues need to be addressed with utmost urgency for a qualitative growth.

IX. Conclusion

This paper has explored the interrelationship between HDI and TTCI of 132 countries under four categories. It was developed based on the two reports - Human Development Index of the United Nations Development Programme and Competitiveness of Travel and Tourism Index of the World Economic Forum. All the counties were categorized into four groups based on the HDI into very high, high, medium and low human development countries. In the line of these four categories, correlation was identified and inferences were drawn. There are some countries with less human development index, but their competitiveness of T and T was very high. Though India is in the lesser side in human development (rank 134th), the competitiveness of T and T (rank 62nd) is better than the other counterparts. Where as, very highly human development countries were showing less competitiveness of T and T. On the whole, largely, the interpretation indicates that the positive correlation was found, which means the two variables move in the same direction.

Table 2: High Human Development Countries (37) and Competitiveness Rank

Sl. No.	Country	Competitiveness Rank (T and T)	HD Rank
1	Bahrain	41	39
2	Estonia	27	40
3	Poland	58	41
4	Slovakia	46	42
5	Hungary	38	43
6	Chile	57	44
7	Croatia	34	45
8	Lithuania	49	46
9	Antigua and Barbuda	44	47
10	Latvia	48	48
11	Argentina	65	49
12	Uruguay	65	50
13	Mexico	51	53
14	Costarica	42	54
15	Libyan Arab Jamahiriya	112	55
16	Oman	68	56
17	Venezuela	104	58
18	Saudi Arabia	71	59
19	Panama	55	60
20	Bulgaria	50	61
21	Romania	64	63
22	Trinidad and Tobago	84	64
23	Montenegro	52	65
24	Malaysia	32	66
25	Serbia	88	67
26	Albania	90	70
27	Russian Federation	59	71
28	Macedonia	80	72
29	Dominica	67	73
30	Brazil	45	75

31	Bosnia	107	76
32	Colombia	72	77
33	Peru	74	78
34	Turkey	56	79
35	Ecuador	96	80
36	Mauritius	57	81
37	Kazakhstan	92	82

Source: Prepared based on given data from Human Development Report **2009,** and the Travel and Tourism Competitiveness Report 2009.

Table 3: Medium High Human Development Countries (46) and Competitiveness Rank

Sl. No.	Country	Competitiveness Rank (T and T)	HD Rank
1	Armenia	91	84
2	Ukraine	77	85
3	Azerbaijan	76	86
4	Thailand	36	87
5	Georgia	73	89
6	Dominican Republic	95	90
7	China	47	92
8	Jordan	54	96
9	Suriname	99	97
10	Tunisia	44	98
11	Jamaica	91	100
12	Paraguay	122	101
13	Sri Lanka	78	102
14	Algeria	115	104
15	Philippines	86	105
16	El Salvador	94	106
17	Indonesia	81	111
18	Honduras	83	112
19	Bolivia	114	113
20	Guyana	102	114
21	Mongolia	105	115
22	Vietnam	89	116
23	Moldova	93	117
24	Kyrgyzstan	106	120

25	Guatemala	70	122
26	Egypt	70	123
27	Nicaragua	103	124
28	Botswana	79	125
29	Tajikistan	109	127
30	Namibia	82	128
31	South Africa	61	129
32	Morocco	75	130
33	India	62	134
34	Cambodia	108	137
35	Pakistan	113	141
36	Nepal	118	144
37	Madagascar	116	145
38	Bangladesh	129	146
39	Kenya	97	147
40	Tanzania	98	151
41	Ghana	110	152
42	Cameroon	125	153
43	Mauritania	127	154
44	Lesotho	132	156
45	Uganda	111	157
46	Nigeria	128	158

Source: Prepared based on given data from Human Development Report **2009,** and the Travel and Tourism Competitiveness Report 2009.

Table 4: Low Human Development Countries (13) and Competitiveness Rank

Sl. No.	Country	Competitiveness Rank (T and T)	HD Rank
1	Malawi	117	160
2	Benin	120	161
3	Timor- Leste	126	162
4	Cote D' lvoire	130	163
5	Zambia	100	164
6	Senegal	101	166
7	Gambia	87	168

8	Ethiopia	123	171
9	Mozambique	124	172
10	Burundi	131	174
11	Chad	133	175
12	Burkina Faso	126	177
13	Mali	119	178

Source: Prepared based on given data from Human Development Report **2009**, and the Travel and Tourism Competitiveness Report 2009.

Table 5: Correlations between Human Development and Competitiveness of Countries

Sl. No	Tools	Very High HD Counties	High HD Countries
1	Correlation	0.527816	0.49821469
2	COVAR (returns covariance)	105.2886	128.993827
3	LINEST	0.843204	0.75899736
4	PEARSON	0.527816	0.46645874

contd...

Medium HD Countries	Low HD Countries	For All Countries
0.5908708	0.27943435	0.842654
313.8752363	22.64497041	1676.601
0.620712021	0.078084	0.611781
0.5908708	0.27943435	0.842654

Source: Prepared based on given data from Human Development Report **2009**, and the Travel and Tourism Competitiveness Report 2009.

References

Ali, A. J. (2006): Rethinking Competition, *Competitiveness Review*, 16(3-4): 171-173.

Blanke, J. and T. Chiesa, (2008): The Travel and Tourism Competitiveness Index: Measuring Key Elements Driving the Sector's Development, In The Travel and Tourism Competitiveness Report 2008: Balancing Economic

Development and Environmental Sustainability, World Economic Forum 3–26, Geneva.

Dwyer, L., P. Forsyth, and P. Rao (1999): Tourism Price Competitiveness and Journey Purpose, *Turizam*, Special Issue on Competitiveness in Hospitality and Tourism 47 (4): 283–99.

IATA (International Air Transport Association) (2007): Aviation Economic Benefits: Measuring the Economic Rate of Return on Investment on the Aviation Industry, IATA Economics Briefing No. 8, IATA, Switzerland, available at http://www.iata.org/whatwedo/economics/issue_briefing_new.htm

Jeni, Klugman (2009): Human Development Report 2009, Overcoming barriers: Human Mobility and Development.

Jennifer, Blanke and Thea Chiesa (2009): *The Travel and Tourism Competitiveness Report 2009*, World Economic Forum.

Kevin, Watkins (2006): Human Development Report 2006, United Nations Development Program.

OECD (Organisation for Economic Co-operation and Development). (2008): *Tourism in OECD Countries 2008: Trends and Policies*, OECD, Paris.

Pearce, B. (2008): What Is Driving Travel Demand? Managing Travel's Climate Impact, In *The Travel and Tourism Competitiveness Report 2008: Balancing Economic Development and Environmental Sustainability*, World Economic Forum. 83–90, Geneva.

Porter, M. E. (2004): Building the Microeconomic Foundations of Prosperity: Findings from the Business Competitiveness Index, In M.E. Porter, K. Schwab, X. Sala-i-Martin and A. Lopez-Claros (Eds.) *The Global Competitiveness Report 2004–2005*, Palgrave Macmillan, World Economic Forum: New York, pp. 19–50.

Sharkey, J. (2008): Travel Industry Shaken by Economic Downturn, *The New York Times*, October 7, available at http://docenti.luiss.it/tourism-lazzerini /files /2008 / 10 / http.wwwnytimescom_2008_10_07_business_07outlook.pdf.

Sullivan, Arthur; Steven M. Sheffrin (2003): *Economics: Principles in action*. Upper Saddle River, New Jersey 07458: Pearson Prentice Hall, pp. 473.

Thierry, Geiger and Sushant Palakurthi Rao (2009): The India Competitiveness Review 2009, World Economic Forum.

UNWTO (United Nations World Tourism Organization) (2008): *Tourism Highlights: 2008 Edition*, available at. www.unwto.org.

------ (2009): International Tourism Challenged by Deteriorating World Economy, Press Release, January 27, UNWTO, Madrid, available at http://www.unwto.org/ media/news/en/press_det. php? id= 3481

World Economic Forum (2008): The Travel and Tourism Competitiveness Report 2008: Balancing Economic Development and Environmental Sustainability. Geneva: World Economic Forum.

WTTC (2004): Competitiveness Monitor, World Travel and Tourism Council, available at: www. wttc.org/frameset3.htm accessed 15 February 2007.

Yeoman, I. (2008): Prospects for World Tourism: Economic Squeeze or Prosperity, hospitalityNet, July 9, available at http://www.hospitalitynet.org /news/ 4036736. search?query= prospects+for+world+tourism+.

23

Gender Discrimination in the Recognition of Work and Earnings in Rural India

Swarna Sadasivam Vepa[1]

Labour force participation and Work Participation of Women

Work participation ratio gives the number of females working per thousand females in the population. Labour force participation on the other hand consists of those who are working and those who are unemployed, but seeking work and willing to work. Labour force excludes person who are not willing to work and not seeking work. As per the development theory, as the country develops and female education improves, the labour force participation of women increases. It also helps relevant human resource availability for development. People shift from low paid jobs in agriculture to high paid jobs in non-agriculture. The shift also helps improvement in labour productivity of those left behind in the primary sector. Shift of population leads shortages in agriculture necessitating mechanization.

Another important feature is that the labour force participation ratios is that they had fallen for all the age groups and for all the categories of workers, (principle, subsidiary, both usual status and current daily status work) had fallen both for male and female population from 1993-94 to 1999-2000 and again increased from 1999-2000 to 2004-05. The point to note here is that labour force participation of men had fallen slightly in rural areas from 561 per thousand in 1993-94 to 555 per thousand in 2004-05. For rural women, the labour force participation had increased marginally from 331 per thousand in 1993-94 to 333 per thousand d in 2004-05 (Table 1).

For rural men labour force participation ratio was slightly lower in 2004-05, compared to 1993-94 probably due to migration and decline in the number of able-bodied men in the labour force. It

[1] Visiting Professor, Madras School of Economics, Chennai, India

could also be due to boys going to school and not participating in the labour force.

Table 1: Labour Force Participation Rate (LFPR) According to Usual, Current Weekly and Current Daily Status during 1993-94, 1999-2000 and 2004-05

Status	Number of persons / person-days in labour force					
	Male			Female		
	1993-94	1999-2000	2004-05	1993-94	1999-2000	2004-05
Rural						
Usual (ps)	549	533	546	237	235	249
Usual (ps+ss)	561	540	555	330	302	333
cws	547	531	545	276	263	287
cds	534	515	531	232	220	237
Urban						
Usual (ps)	538	539	566	132	126	148
Usual (ps+ss)	543	542	570	165	147	178
cws	538	539	566	152	138	168
cds	532	528	561	132	123	150

Source: NSS Report No. 515, Employment and Unemployment Situation in India, 2004-05.

Labour force participation ratios increased for urban men as a whole from 542 to 570 over the decade ending in 2004, both due to the educational achievements, as well as due to rural-urban migration of able-bodied men for manual work. The migration of men has lead to a slight increase in the labour force participation of women in rural areas. The labour force participation of women in the age groups of 25 and above was higher in 2004-05 than in 1993-94, where as it is lower for men in 2004-05 compared to 1993-94 (Table 2). All the same the labour force participation ratios for women appear to be very low at 33.3 per cent for rural India and 17.8 per cent in urban India, compared to that of men at 55.5 per cent in rural areas and 57 per cent in urban areas.

Table 2: Age Specific Labour Force Participation Ratios

Age Group	Rural Males		Rural Females	
	1993-94	2004-05	1993-94	2004-05
5-9	11	3	14	3
10-14	139	70	142	75
15-19	598	529	371	331
20-24	902	891	470	435
25-29	980	982	528	530
30-34	988	988	587	593
35-39	992	991	610	642
40-44	989	985	607	627
45-49	984	982	594	616
50-54	970	963	543	562
55-59	941	931	468	509
above 60	699	645	241	254
All 0+	**561**	**555**	**331**	**333**

Source: NSS Report 515, 2004-05

There are several reasons for the apparent low labour force participation of women reported in rural India, compared to men. It could be due to underestimation or women's work. First, in rural India, women's work participation is not adequately recognized and hence a large number of women who are making substantial contributions to the rural economy are not considered as workers. Most of such un-recognized work is unpaid work in the family enterprises, farming and home based production and value addition. Labour force participation in high paid skilled work outside the house is also low for women due to low levels of educational achievement and their inability to secure high paid jobs. Less than 20 per cent of women achieved primary level of education.

It is obvious that Indian rural women may not have shared the fruits of agricultural development, for various reasons. First, the labour force participation in paid work is low. The migration of men to urban areas may have lead to an increase in the labour force participation of women in the age groups of 30-50 in unpaid/ low-paid farm work. The literacy levels and educational achievements are limited and work opportunities are limited, leading to redundancy and withdrawal of women in the lower age groups from the labour force.

Work participation is normally considered as a positive factor for women, as it is expected to gives them control over income and decision-making in the household. It is expected to be positively correlated with literacy.

However, in the Indian rural context, work participation is high among the illiterate, poverty groups and deprived sections, than the better-off sections of population (Table 3). Work participation is high among the rural women compared to urban women though the literacy rates of urban women are higher than that of rural women. Further work participation in the rural context may not put any money in the hands of women.

They may not have any decision-making capacity either in the economic work or in the household. Hence, some are skeptical about using work participation as a symbol of gender equity. However since their contribution to the National Income is substantial and they contribute substantially to the family income.

Work participation ought to be considered as a positive factor for gender equity. The very dependence of the rest of the family on the women for the livelihood ought to give them some amount of bargaining power. Alternatively, they can use the skills possessed and the time spent on the economic activity outside the house in paid employment.

Hence, work participation would improve the bargaining capacity of women both inside and outside the house.

Women's Paid Work and Unpaid Work

To understand the implications of women's paid and unpaid work, some clarity on various definitions adopted and issues involved may be necessary. First let us look at the definitions and then at the issues. Women's work needs to be looked at in a holistic manner of all the work performed by women, adolescent girls and girl child inside the household and outside. The SNA work and extended SNA work. SNA and Extended SNA work, paid work and unpaid work are substitutable to each other. All the domestic work that women perform has an economic value for the household members.

Table 3: LFPR, WPR, According to Usual Status Principles and Subsidiary Status in India

HH social group	Male		Female		Person	
	LFPR	WPR	LFPR	WPR	LFPR	WPR
Rural						
Scheduled Tribe	568	562	466	464	518	514
Scheduled Caste	554	545	338	333	448	441
;lkl ,;;OBC	545	537	337	330	443	436
Others	568	557	270	262	422	412
All	555	546	333	327	446	439
Urban						
Scheduled Tribe	538	523	254	245	396	384
Scheduled Caste	568	537	210	200	398	377
OBC	573	554	199	185	394	378
Others	571	550	147	134	368	351
All	570	549	178	166	382	365

Source: NSS Report No. 516, 2004-05, Employment and Situation among Social Groups in India.

Definition of work under SNA, Extended SNA and Non SNA

The International Standard for National Accounting, popularly known as UN SNA or simply SNA includes activities connected to primary production, secondary activities related production, including trade business and services. SNA refers to activities falling within the production boundary. Extended SNA are activities falling outside the SNA production boundary but within the general production boundary consisting mainly of household work, which remains unpaid in many Societies. As has been pointed out by some scholars[2], there is no watertight line between the two sets of activities, as the economy develops, the domestic services are hired which increases the national income and the work force.

Women's activities within the household that contribute to the household enterprise have been excluded from the SNA for a long time. More recently women's contribution to Household enterprise has been included in the SNA. At present SNA activities include fetching water, collection of fuel wood, wild foods and so on in

[2]Indira Hirway (2007) ,"Underestimation of Women's Contribution to National Income: Implications to Gender Justice"' Report of the Workshop on Gender Concerns and Food Security , 26th and 27th February,2007, MS Swaminathan Research Foundation, Chennai (Mimeo)

addition to livestock rearing and participation in the family enterprises in the household premises.

Household work such as cooking and cleaning, "care economy" consisting of child bearing, child rearing and care of the sick and the aged on the other hand have been included as Extended SNA and still excluded from the SNA by the United Nations. Community work and voluntary work is also excluded in the SNA but included in extended SNA.

Issues involved in Paid Work vs. Unpaid Work

There are three distinct issues involved. The first one is the underestimation of women's contribution to Gross Domestic Product of the country and the underestimation of female main workers in the economy for the activities that fall within the production boundary of the System of National Accounting.

This is broadly a national issue. It is important to carefully consider the implications. While recognition is the first step in the right direction for awareness creation, the ultimate aim is just not correcting the estimation of the contribution of women's SNA work to GDP and correcting the number of main female workers. The ultimate aim is to bring all women workers under the labour protection laws including equal wages[3] and provide suitable support services to all of them and providing necessary access to resources that enable women to realize their full potential. The lack of recognition of unpaid work is the chief contributor to women's poverty in and around the world.[4]

The second issue is the recognition of the activities performed by women as falling under the general production boundary but the refusal by the governments all over the world to bring them under the International System of National Accounting. They come under the caption of Extended SNA activities. UN recommends a separate satellite accounting. They essentially include household work and voluntary work. They are not valued, as they are not the services offered by the market. Women's household work involving cooking, cleaning, gardening, teaching and caring for the children, the sick and elderly, come under this category. Most of these activities are

[3] Equal wage is denied to many female workers as they are considered as marginal workers contributing less and working fewer hours than their male counterparts, even though they work as long and contribute as much as their male counterparts.

4 FAO Focus "Women and food Security", www.fao.org

interchangeable with the market. Women within the household normally perform these services but they are also available in the market for a price as paid services. It is erroneous to recognize the monetized activities and ignore non-monetized activities in the GDP. This leads to the misinterpretation of the overall GDP, when it gets monetized during booms and demonetized during recession.[5]

The public policy can increase or decrease the burden of unpaid Non SNA work of women in the economy. Sub-standard public services increase the burden of women's Non SNA work. For example, sub-standard teaching in schools, lack of primary and secondary health care facilities, reduction in the social security for old age, etc., increases the unpaid work burden on women at home. An increase in the disease burden including HIV AIDS, on the other hand increases women's time spent on taking care of the sick. Hence, there is a need for looking at the problems of women's unpaid extended SNA work in the Indian context and evolve suitable public policies, as the women bear the brunt of the failure of the public services delivery system.

It is true that voluntary workers do not receive labour protection, all over the world. However, the large number of women from poor communities drawn into voluntary work as a part of participatory development approach in developing countries, need labour protection and compensation for the time spent on these activities that contribute to the GDP. Here again, non-allocation of resources for development shifts the burden to the women. It is a matter of gender insensitive public policy.

The third issue is about a large proportion of unpaid work compared to paid work and women's increasing burden of work in general. When women are spending their time on unpaid work, they are not doing paid work. Because only the latter is paid, earning potential of women decreases dramatically.

Women's work burden is increasing in the recent years due to their roles as homemakers, workers in agricultural and non-agricultural activities out side the house and their role as voluntary community workers. This is the triple burden of work on women.

Policy Implications of Non-recognition of Work

Recognition of women as workers is important in view of the Unorganized Sector Workers' Social Security Bill of 2007

5 UNIFEM (2004) "Valuation of Unpaid work", Gender Fact sheet No.3

introduced in the parliament. Non-recognition of women as workers would exclude all of them from the benefits of social security. The implementation of the bill also needs to be gender sensitive. The Unorganized Sector Workers' Social Security Bill, 2005 seeks to extend benefits for the first time to the unorganized sector. Most of the existing legislation in India, such as the Factories Act, Provident Fund Act, etc; apply only to the formal sector where the employer-employee relationship is clear. The bill specially addresses the needs of the unorganized sector. The implementation details of the bill are not yet ready. The Unorganized Sector Workers' Social Security Bill, 2005 when implemented will establish a 'National Social Security Authority for the Unorganized Sector'.

This Bill redefines the term 'worker' to include all types of workers such as self-employed, casual, contract, home-based, etc., and will identify each worker with a unique Social Security Number. This Bill will establish a Central Supervisory Board along with similar Boards at the State level. The implementation mechanism would be via Worker Facilitation Centers. A network of Facilitating Agencies would manage these centres to reach the village level.

As envisaged in this legislation, a variety of social security benefits including Health Insurance, Maternity Benefit and Pensions would accrue to workers in this sector. Thus, this legislation will provide a minimum amount of benefit and funds to this sector through a participatory structure involving the Government, Civil Society, quasi-Government Organizations with qualified record of accomplishment.

Three important areas need public action. First is to reduce the work burden among women through the introduction of basic drudgery reducing, affordable technologies at home as well as work place. Second is the provision of efficient public services such as sanitation, drainage, water for drinking and cleaning, fuel for cooking and lighting, communications, health care, education and old age security. They would go a long way in reducing the work burden of women. The third aspect is provision of support services and hygienic noon meals for women and children. The crèches are necessary for all workers including own account unpaid workers.

Extent of Women's Unpaid Work in India

Women's unpaid work may be divided into four categories:

1. Unpaid work that falls within the production boundary and

considered as a part of the System of National Accounting.

2. Unpaid Household work including child care, care of the sick and elderly comes under care economy and is included under Extended SNA.
3. Unpaid voluntary work related to self help groups, work related to community in natural resource management or health monitoring and any such work assigned to women, which is also included under Extended SNA.
4. Unpaid personal work related to personal care, learning and personal entertainment etc., which comes under Non SNA.

In India, there is no estimate of the women's contribution to GDP, or the value of women's unpaid work in various categories. Only information available is the time spent by women and men in six states on SNA and Extended SNA and Non SNA activities.[6] In this paper we have only considered the women's unpaid SNA work in the rural areas to have an idea about the inequity in burden of unpaid SNA work and possible underestimation of GDP and the number of female workers.

In the rural work atmosphere, a large amount of work performed by women that contributes to the National income is not considered in the System of National Accounting. Also a large number of women involved in such work are not recognized as workers in the census. To get an idea of the magnitude of such work, Time use surveys have been conducted in six states. They show that Women's total contribution to GDP is apparent not only in crop production but also in the other activities that form part of the System of National Income Accounting, (SNA). In all the six states, women had spent as much time or much more time on non-crop production, SNA activities as on crop production. The first item called, "Primary production" in the Time Use Surveys included only crop production activities. The non-crop SNA activities include livestock, fisheries, forestry, processing storage etc. An average of 10.20 hours per week had been spent by women on crop production activities in the year 2000. This alone has translated into 43 percent of female workers to total workers in crop production in the year 2001 in these states. An additional time of 10.37 hours a week was spent on non-crop agricultural activities by women. Total time spent on agricultural activities was about 20.57 hours per week by women, which would

6 Government of India, Central Statistical Organization, Ministry of Statistics and Programme implementation (2000) "Report of the Time use Surveys, New Delhi.

mean either there are more women workers in agriculture than reported in the census or more main workers spending more time on these activities (Table 4).

Table 4: Weekly Average Time Spent on Crop Production and other SNA Activities

State	Crop Prod.	Non-crop Ag. Activities	All Ag. Activities	Other Activities	All SNA Activities	% of unpaid Work	% of Female Workers
	1	2	3	4	5	6	7
GJ	12.00	9.63	21.62	2.28	23.90	44.67	41.71
HY	3.14	18.04	21.18	2.26	23.49	85.99	45.52
MP	13.60	6.51	20.07	2.55	22.62	52.40	43.77
MGH	13.60	12.32	25.89	3.23	29.12	76.39	45.80
OR	6.61	10.15	16.76	2.27	19.03	69.44	35.70
TN	12.40	5.57	17.92	5.54	23.46	32.45	45.52
Average	10.20	10.37	20.57	3.02	23.60	60.22	43.00

Note: Columns1-6: CSO, "Time Use Survey" April 2000; Column 7: Census of India 2001 (% of Female workers to all farm workers); SNA= System of National Accounting

Time taken to travel to the Work place is included in the SNA activities, both for men and women. Women mostly work closer to the house than men. They take up work with in the premises of the house or closer to the house, as they also need to attend to the household work and caring for children and family members etc.

Rural women can more effectively combine their housework and the work that contributes to the household income. Women perform activities such as livestock rearing, poultry and growing of vegetables, etc., closer to the house. Thus time spent by men on travel to work is almost double that of women. As against 2 hours spent by women per week on travel to work, men spend close to 5 hours a week on travel. In effect, women work more than men do, as the travel time is less. Time use surveys also under estimate the time spent by women on SNA activities that add to the national Income.[7] (Appendix 4.1)

Appendix 4.1: Weekly Average Time Spent on Travel to Work on SNA Activities (Rural Hours)

S. No.	State	Primary Production Activities Rural		Secondary Activities Rural		Trade, Business and Services Rural		Average Weekly Time Spent on travel	Average Weekly Time Spent on travel	Total SNA Activities Time spent on work	
		Male	Female	Male	Female	Male	Female	Male	Female	Male	Female
1	Haryana	2.48	2.18	0.69	0.02	0.96	0.07	4.13	2.27	37.98	23.49
2	M.P	5.16	2.79	0.27	0.07	0.43	0.05	5.86	2.91	43.55	22.62
3	Gujarat	4.39	2.34	0.43	0.06	0.85	0.19	5.67	2.59	44.83	23.90
4	Orissa	2.68	0.78	0.35	0.04	0.30	0.03	3.33	0.85	39.54	19.03
5	Tamil Nadu	3.55	1.71	0.47	0.13	0.81	0.14	4.83	1.98	42.02	23.46
6	Meghalaya	4.47	2.71	0.54	0.02	0.47	0.18	5.48	2.91	48.28	29.12
	Combined	3.94	2.00	0.40	0.07	0.63	0.10	4.97	2.17	42.31	22.53
	Sample size	11764	6591	1246	253	1857	378	14867.00	7222.00	17693	15339

contd...

Source: Ministry of Statistical and Programme Implementation, GOI, "Time-use survey".

7 Indira Hirway,(2002) 'How good is NSS data? EPW, 25th May

Women's contribution to national income and their status as workers, not being recognized is also apparent from the recent study of National sample survey where the percentage of women principally engaged in household work but engaged in certain specific activities that contribute to National Income have been studied.

The study showed that 58.4 percent of the rural women of the age 15 years and above, principally engaged in household work were performing activities, which enter into the system of national accounting (Table 5).

Type of Work Available to Women

In the rural areas, paid employment opportunities are lower for women than men. Self-employment is the main category of employment available to both for men and women. When we consider the usually employed persons of both principal as well as subsidiary economic status, we find that 63.7 per cent of women are self-employed in 2004-05 as against 58.1 per cent of men. Only 3.7 per cent of the women in rural areas are in regular employment as against 9.0 per cent of men. Casual labour employment is slightly lower for rural women at 32.6 per cent as against 32.9 per cent for rural men. In urban areas, self-employment and casual labour employment are higher for women where as regular employment is higher for men. Thus, it is obvious for the most of the employment opportunities available to rural women are either unpaid or low paid in self-employment and casual labour (Table 6).

Further, self-employment increased marginally for rural men by about 4 per cent but increased substantially in the past decade by more than 5 per cent for rural women. Casual labour work opportunities in rural as well as urban areas declined for men and women, over the past decade. Self-employment of rural women is not the same as the self-employment of men. While men are recognized as farmers and owners of businesses that they run, women are considered as workers in the enterprises. They often lack the control over the income generated from the family enterprises. Women's management control, and control over assets in the family enterprises is also limited, unless women run the enterprise independently. The point is that the self-employment in family enterprises has increased and thus unpaid work has increased for women.

Table 5: No. of Women of Age 15 years and above Usually Engaged in Household Duties (principal status) and also Participating in Specified Activities per 1000 Women Usually Engaged in Household Duties - All India

	Specified additional activities	Rural			Urban		
	activities	With SS € Work	Without SS € Work	All SS €	With SS € Work	Without SS € Work	All
1	Maintenance of kitchen garden	164	129	135	80	31	33
2	Work in household. Poultry etc.	543	276	319	219	37	44
3	Either item 1 or 2	591	328	370	262	62	70
4	Free collection of fish etc.	179	147	152	46	11	12
5	Free collection of fire wood etc.	534	370	396	164	50	55
7	Any of item 1,2,4 or 5	817	540	584	355	99	110

contd...

Source: NSS Report No.465,"Participation of Indian women in household work and specified activities", 1999-2000
Note: SS = Subsidiary work Status

Declining Casual labour employment Opportunities

The decline in casual labour employment of rural women is very sharp at 6 per cent compared to less than 1 per cent for men. Similar sharp decline occurred for women compared to men even in urban areas, the decline being 2 per cent for men and more than 9 per cent for women. Thus, illiterate women faced larger shrinkage in work opportunities than men did. The reason for overall decline in casual employment could be due to use of machinery in all types of work, agriculture, non-agriculture, construction, road building and so on. Not only the work opportunities had shrunk but also the wages for casual work is lower for women than men.

Table 6: All India - Per thousand Distribution of the Employed Usually employed - principal status+ Subsidiary status

	Self employed		(F-M)	Regular employees		Casual labour		(F-M)
	Male	Female	gap	Male	Female	Male	Female	Gap
Rural								
1993-94	577	586	9	85	27	338	387	49
2004-05	581	637	56	90	37	329	326	-3
Urban								
1993-94	417	448	31	422	292	161	260	99
2004-05	448	477	29	406	356	146	167	21

contd...

Source: NSS Report No. 515, Employment and unemployment situation in India, 2004-05.

Small gain in regular employment

The only positive trend is an improvement in the regular employment of women, showing a reduction in gender gap in regular employment. Regular employment, though insignificant for rural women, increased from 3.7 per cent by 1 per cent over the decade. For urban women the regular employment was 35.6 per cent as against 40 per cent for urban men. Over the past decade the regular employment for women grew faster than that of men reducing the gender gap in regular employment.

Larger number of women in unpaid family enterprises and casual labour widens the gender gap in income earning opportunities and control over resources. In the casual work as well as regular employment, women earn less than what men get. The next two sections would examine these two aspects of women's unpaid work and lower earnings.

Wages Differentials in Employment

Gender discrimination exists in the earning between women and men with equal skills and educational background, leaving alone the differential access to education and skills and training and asset ownership structure. Recent National Sample survey data of 2004-05 highlighted the differential. Even for regular wage and salary earners the differentials are higher for illiterate women. Discrimination continues due to gender bias of the employers, possible movement in and out of labour force, and ineffective government policies (Tables 7 and 8).

Table 7: Average Earnings per day of Regular Employees Aged 15-59 (2004-05)

S. No.	General Education Level	RURAL		URBAN	
		Male	**Female**	**Male**	**Female**
1	Not Literate	72.47	35.74	98.79	48.70
2	Literate and up to primary	98.59	47.75	111.44	64.79
3	Secondary and higher secondary	158.04	100.19	182.58	150.41
4	Diploma / certificate	214.38	200.40	274.87	237.02
5	Graduate and above	270.02	172.70	366.76	269.17
	All	**144.93**	**85.53**	**203.28**	**153.19**

Source: NSS Report 515: Employment and Unemployment Situation.

The earning differentials clearly show that gender discrimination is higher for illiterate women than literate women in regular employment both in rural and urban areas. They get 51 per cent less than men do. Gender gap in earnings is high for various levels of educational achievements. However it is quite interesting to note that for one group of persons who hold a diploma or certificate after finishing higher secondary education, the gender gap in earnings appear to be very narrow. For this small group in rural areas women's earnings are 93 per cent of men's earnings and in urban areas women earn 86 per cent of what men get as shown in the table.

Table 8: Average per day Earnings of Women as a Ratio of Men in Regular Employment (Gender gap in earnings)

S. No.	General Education Level	Rural F/M ratio	Urban F/M ratio
1	Not Literate	0.49	0.49
2	Literate and up to primary	0.48	0.58
3	Secondary and higher secondary	0.63	0.82
4	Diploma / certificate	0.93	0.86
5	Graduate and above	0.64	0.73
	All	**0.59**	**0.75**

Source: NSS report 515 (2004-05).

Rural women employed on regular salaried jobs earn 41 per cent less than men do. This explains why the regular employment of women is growing faster than that of men in rural areas. Urban women employed in regular jobs also earn 25 per cent less than what men earn. This is one of the reasons for sharper increase in regular employment of women compared to men in urban areas. The wage differentials also reflect the higher unemployment rates of women and their willingness to work even for less. Obviously only low paid regular employment is available to women. The distressing fact is that gender gap in earnings does not decline much with Primary education. Only beyond secondary education does the gender gap in earnings decline. Unless we reduce the gap in educational achievement between girls and boys, gender equity in earnings would remain high.

Another interesting observation seems to be that the skill improvement through certificate and Diploma after secondary education suits the market demand that reduces the gender gap in earnings both in rural and urban context. Vocational training for girls after high school probably assumes importance.

The gender gap in earnings is interestingly higher for higher levels of education above under-graduation compared to diploma and certificate holders. Probably this category contains a larger proportion of older age groups than the category of diploma and certificate holders. In general, older women get higher discrimination than the younger women do for several reasons. Maternity and child rearing responsibilities make older women to move in and out of the job market and hence they loose out on experience and continuity.

The gender bias in promotions and hitting a glass ceiling and so on happen even for those who do not go out of the labour market. The gain in earnings due to acquiring a higher degree seems to be considerably less for urban women than for urban men. The earnings for men increase by about Rs. 90/- per day due to higher education while earning go up only by Rs. 32/- per day for women. In this context, an observation made by a recent study of London School of Economics seems to be relevant in essence even in the Indian situation. "*Women continue to choose family over career at some point in their life. When they return to the labour market, our labour market severely punishes those who sacrifice career for family.*" Women's groups often argued that the reproductive roles and child-care responsibilities of women made work participation discontinuous, over a life time, over a week or even during the 24 hours that constitutes a day and hence they need to be compensated for it.

Gender Gap in the Wages of Casual Labour on Non-public Works

The plight of women in casual labour appears to be even worse. Not only do they confront shrinking opportunities and low wages, but they also face discrimination. The wages of female casual labour (other than public work) are particularly low in some states. Madhya Pradesh, Orissa, and Andhra Pradesh and Karnataka seem to pay the lowest wages for women in absolute terms, which is between Rs.23 and Rs.27 in 1999-2000.

In 2004-05 the situation has not changed much. The average female wage in rural Chhattisgarh and Maharashtra are about Rs. 28 and in Orissa it was about Rs. 29 and in the wages are around Rs. 30 in Andhra Pradesh and Madhya Pradesh. It has been reported that Female wages could fall to the lowest levels of Rs.10/- in drought hit areas such as Mahbubnagar of Andhra Pradesh, that records 48 per cent poverty in the lean seasons.[8]

---

8 Govt. of Andhra Pradesh (2004) 'Report on Mahabub Nagar district"

To indicate the wage inequality among the states, female wage was taken as a proportion of male wage. Ideally, it should be one, indicating no wage differentials. In 1999-2000, the ratio was low in three states at 0.51 in Tamil Nadu and 0.56 in Goa and Kerala. In 2005-06, five years later, situation substantially improved in Goa and the wage gap was 0.67. In Tamil Nadu, the gap remained almost the same at 0.52, while in Kerala the situation deteriorated to 0.48. Though the wage levels are not very low in absolute terms in these states, the gender gap is high due to higher wages for men. In the past five to six year the rise in men's wage was higher than the rise in women's wage.

The female wage in absolute monetary terms declined in Jammu and Kashmir and the male wage increased by about 30 percent, widening the gap in 2005-06. In Kerala the female wage increased by Rs.10/- while the male wage increased by Rs.33/-, widening the wage gap. In some of the northeastern States, rise in male wages was high, while female wages had a modest rise. For the country as a whole, gender inequity in daily wages for casual workers increased. The female wage as a ratio of male wage has declined to 63 per cent in 2004-05, compared to 65 per cent in 1999-2000. The gender gap in wages widened for casual labour in ten states out of 30 states for which data are available.

The states in which wages are high, the percentage of female labour is also relatively low. In states such as Punjab where the wages are high and wage differential is relatively low, female agricultural labour constitute only 25 per cent of total agricultural labour. In Andhra Pradesh and Karnataka where the female wages are quite low at Rs.26/- and Rs.27/- in 1999-2000, the percentage of female labour in the total agricultural labour is high at 46 percent and 43 percent respectively. The absolute wages are the lowest for women in Madhya Pradesh and Orissa and they have large percentage of female labour to the total agricultural labour. About 48 percent of agricultural labour in Orissa and about 53 percent of agricultural labour in Madhya Pradesh are women.

Further, the average number of days of employment of casual labour during the year for women had declined sharper than that of men in rural areas as per the National sample survey data. It has declined from 235 days in 1999-2000 to 227 days for men and from

199 to 184 days for women[9] (Appendix 4.2).

Appendix 4.2: Average Daily Wages (Rs. 0.00) for Casual Workers of Age 15-59 Years Engaged in Works other than Public Works (Rural)

S. No.	States	Male Wage	Female Wage	Wage Differentials
1	Andhra Pradesh	50.30	30.88	0.61
2	Arunachal Pradesh	104.38	50.60	0.48
3	Assam	62.59	53.29	0.85
4	Bihar	45.41	37.42	0.82
5	Chhattisgarh	37.60	28.55	0.76
6	Gujarat	52.80	43.17	0.82
7	Haryana	75.26	59.34	0.79
8	Himachal Pradesh	88.88	62.00	0.70
9	Jammu & Kashmir	100.24	53.39	0.53
10	Jharkhand	51.11	37.93	0.74
11	Karnataka	48.33	30.74	0.64
12	Kerala	134.86	65.75	0.49
13	Madhya Pradesh	38.58	30.53	0.79
14	Maharashtra	47.37	28.16	0.59
15	Orissa	42.29	29.65	0.70
16	Punjab	75.14	53.10	0.71
17	Rajasthan	64.33	52.03	0.81
18	Tamil Nadu	70.45	36.53	0.52
19	Uttaranchal	69.66	56.20	0.81
20	Uttar Pradesh	53.37	39.54	0.74
21	West Bengal	49.88	39.99	0.80
	All India	55.03	34.94	0.63

Source: NSS Report No. 515, Part I "Employment and Unemployment Situation in India, 2004-05"

9 National Commission for enterprises in the un-organized sector (2007) op. cited.

24

Factors behind Low Yield of Rice in Assam

Dipali Bosumatari[1] and Phanindra Goyari[2]

I. Introduction

Assam is one of the important agricultural states in India. Assam is one of the economically backward states in the country. Agriculture occupies a vital position in the state's economy engaging about 53 percent of total working force (2001 census). Agriculture contributed about 31.19 percent of the net state domestic product at constant prices in 2003-04 and about 40 percent to state gross domestic product (Economic survey Assam 2003-04). Agriculture in Assam has been basically cereal-based, where around 80 percent of total area is devoted to food grain production. The small and marginal farmers accounting nearly 70 percent of the total cultivators still dominate the agriculture sector.

The soil and climatic conditions of Assam are congenial for paddy cultivation. Among the food crops, rice occupies nearly 64 percent of gross cropped area. In Assam, rice cultivation is unique, as it is grown in all the three seasons in an agricultural year, viz., kharif (winter or sali), rabi (summer or boro) and pre-kharif or autumn (ahu). The yield of summer rice is generally higher than the other two rice varieties. Rice is grown both in irrigated and rainfed ecosystems. Assam occupies a special place in the rainfed rice production system in the eastern India. Due to low irrigation facilities, many farmers till depend heavily on rainwater for cultivation. According to Bhowmick et al. (2005), around 79 percent of total rice area in Assam is rainfed.

The main motivation to carry out the present study comes mainly due to the fact that only very few studies have been done so far on Assam agriculture sector in general and on present topic in particular. Some of the recent studies on Assam agriculture sector

[1] Research Scholar, Department of Economics, University of Hyderabad, Hyderabad
[2] Assistant Professor, Department of Economics, University of Hyderabad, Hyderabad

include Goswami and Chatterjee (2003 and 2006), Borah et al. (2001), Bhowmick et al. (2005) and Goyari (2005). The present study proceeds to examine the trends in area, production and productivity of rice cultivation and factors behind low yield level of rice in Assam.

Another important motivation is due to the special characteristics of Assam as an agricultural state. Assam has various natural resources like fertile land, forest and available water sources. Along with available naturally flowing water ways, Assam also receives heavy rainfall almost every year. But in spite of having several resources and advantages, the rice productivity in kg per ha in Assam has been one of the lowest in the country till now. The problems of agricultural development and increment of the rice productivity have been a topic of discussion for the policy makers and agricultural scientists in India. Several earlier studies, both state level and national level, carried out by various agricultural economists on the productivity of cereal based have constantly pointed out various problems and offered suggestions for bringing up higher productivity. Based on various studies on rice development, efforts have been subsequently made to improve the productivity by providing various kinds of developmental programs and schemes. However, in spite of various policy implementations and steps undertaken, Assam's rice yield has been remaining almost stagnant. Thus, it is necessary to carry out a continuous study on the rice sector in Assam to gain better understanding of various problems associated with rice production and productivity. Since rice is the major food crop in the state and yield per ha can have several implications on the agricultural economy of the state, a study on the factors influencing rice yield assumes importance.

II. Objectives

The specific objectives of present study are:

1. to examine the trends in area, production and productivity of rice in Assam;
2. to estimate the growth rate of area and yield of rice with a view to examine the technological progress in the cultivation of rice; and
3. to examine the factors behind the low level of rice yield in the state.

III. Data sources and Methodology

Data on area, production and productivity of rice, fertilizer usage, irrigation, rainfall, area under HYV, and other related variables were collected from secondary sources like various issues of Statistical Handbook of Assam, Economic Survey of Assam and Fertilizer Statistics, Rice in India- A Hand Book of Statistics 2006 (GOI), Department of Agriculture and Co-operation, Patna various issues of CMIE.

To examine Assam's position in area, production and productivity of rice, the entire study period is divided into two sub-periods, viz., 1980-81 to 1991-92 and 1992-93 to 2003-04. The average and percentage shares were calculated for each sub-period. For the decomposition analysis of output growth, the exponential growth rate has been estimated by the semi-log linear regression model on area, production and productivity of rice. The model is:

$$\ln Y_t = a + b.t + U_t$$

where Y_t = dependent variable, t = time in year, a and b are linear parameters and U_t is error term. The annual compound growth rate (r) has been calculated from the formula $r = e^b - 1$. To test the statistical significant of estimated growth rates, the student's t test has been applied.

The rice yield response function has also been estimated by fitting a log-linear regression model. First we specify the yield function for rice in Assam in the Cobb-Douglas production function form as below:

$$Y_t = AF_t^{\alpha 1} H_t^{\alpha 2} I_t^{\alpha 3} e^{Ut} \qquad (1)$$

Where, the dependent variable is Y_t, the yield of rice in kg per ha at time t. We have included only three explanatory variables, viz., fertilizer consumption (Ft), area under High Yielding Varieties of paddy seeds (Ht) and irrigation (It). The chemical fertilizer consumption (Ht) has been measured in kg per ha. The HYV (Ht) variable is the area under HYV paddy seeds in thousand hectares. The third variable, It, is the total irrigated area under paddy, measured in thousand hectares. The time period for estimation is 24 years, i.e. t =1980-81, 1981-82........ 2003-04. While A and α_i (i=1, 2, 3) are parameters to be estimated, Ut is the disturbance term at time t and e is the base of natural logarithm.

The yield function specified in the model (1) is non-linear in parameters. So, it cannot be estimated directly by applying the ordinary least square (OLS) method. However, the model (1) can be made linear by taking log on both sides as follow:

$$\ln Y_t = \alpha_0 + \alpha_1 \ln F_t + \alpha_2 InH_t + \alpha_3 InI_t + U_t \qquad (2)$$

Where lnA= α_0. The main objective of the present model estimation is to examine the response of rice yield in Assam to each of the above mentioned explanatory variables.

The main focus of the present paper is on Assam state. However, for comparison, data for some states of the country have also been taken into account wherever required. Therefore, as a representative of every region, present study has chosen the following major rice growing states from the rest of India, i.e., Andhra Pradesh and Tamil Nadu from the southern region, Haryana and Punjab from the north western region, Uttar Pradesh from the central region and West Bengal from the eastern region.

The entire analysis is carried out using the secondary data. The analysis is restricted to 24 years period from 1980-81 to 2003-04. The choice of the study period is guided by the data availability for all the study variables at the time of analysis. As stated above, the whole study period has been divided into two sub- periods-(i) pre-reform period (1980-81 to 1991-92) and (ii) post-reform period (1992-93 to 2003-04). This enables us to examine the growth pattern of rice area, production and productivity during the pre and post liberalization period.

IV. Trends in Area, Production and Productivity of Rice

The position of Assam's rice acreage in all India and other major rice growing states are presented in Table 1. It shows that Assam has been cultivating rice in vast area. The percentage share of rice area of Assam in national level slightly increased from 5.7 percent in pre-reform period to 5.8 percent in post-reform period. The share of rice acreage of Assam to all India acreage was higher than some states namely Tamil Nadu, Punjab and Haryana. But rice area in Assam is less, as compared to Andhra Pradesh, Uttar Pradesh, and West Bengal. It is also observed that West Bengal is the leading rice growing states in India followed by Uttar Pradesh in terms of area.

Rice is important not only in terms of area coverage in total cropped area, but also due to the fact that it constitutes the main staple food for almost the entire population of the state of Assam. The absolute quantity of rice production of Assam increased from

2654 thousand tonnes during 1980-91 to 3552 thousand tones during 1992-03. However, in percentage share, total rice production remained almost constant in both the period at about 4 percent. In terms of production, Assam's share was lower than that of Punjab, Uttar Pradesh, Tamil Nadu, Andhra Pradesh and West Bengal. But Assam produced more rice compared to Haryana (Table 1).

Table 1: Acreage, Production and Yield of Rice in Assam and Some States in India

States	Acreage in thousand ha		Output in thousand tonnes		Yield (kg/ha)	
	1980 -1991	1992-2003	1980-1991	1992-2003	1980-1991	1992-2003
West Bengal	5347 (13.1)	5855 (13.5)	8657 (13.9)	13117 (15.9)	1607	2240
Uttar Pradesh	5070 (12.4)	5415 (12.5)	7148 (11.5)	10808 (13.1)	1404	1989
Andhra Pradesh	3770 (9.2)	3690 (8.5)	8244 (13.2)	9874 (12.0)	2179	2674
Assam	2354 (5.7)	2530 (5.8)	2654 (4.3)	3552 (4.3)	1125	1403
Tamil Nadu	2147 (5.2)	2050 (4.7)	5338 (8.6)	6294 (7.6)	2522	3028
Punjab	1659 (4.0)	2377 (5.5)	5209 (8.4)	8135 (9.9)	3119	3419
Haryana	568 (1.4)	917 (2.1)	1465 (2.4)	2393 (2.9)	2568	2623
Others	13960 (34.8)	14279 (33.1)	17579 (28.3)	21341 (25.9)	..	..
All India	40958	43260	62225	82520	1514	1906

contd...

Note: Figures in brackets are percentage shares to all India average in respective periods

Source: Calculated from data of various issues of 'CMIE'.

In terms of total acreage and production, Assam's position is higher than some major rice growing states of India. For example, in terms of production, Assam's total rice production was higher than

Haryana during the study period. But in terms of yield per hectare, Assam has no supremacy over many rice growing states and national average. During the pre-reform period, the rice yield of Assam was 1125 kg/ha, which was below the country's average productivity of 1514 kg/ha. Thus, there was about 389 kg/ha yield gap between national level and Assam. Comparison of state level yield performance shows us that the productivity of rice in Assam was far below than other states, namely, Punjab, Haryana, Tamil Nadu, Andhra Pradesh, West Bengal and Uttar Pradesh during the pre-reform period. In the post-reform period, there was an increase of productivity for all the states of the country. It also showed overall increase of national productivity level. The rice productivity increased to 1403 kg/ha during the post-reform period in Assam. Thus, there was an increase of about 278 kg/ha over the earlier period. Even though there was an increase of rice yield in Assam during period II, Assam was still lagging behind by about 503 kg/ha of the country's productivity.

Thus, the study on rice yield level per hectare for Assam and some other states in the country showed that Assam was lagging behind in term of productivity of rice as compared to national average and states mentioned in Table 1 during the study period.

V. Decomposition of Output Growth Rate

Output growth of any crop can be decomposed into area growth and yield growth. The yield growth of any crop is largely influenced by technological progress. Thus, in a situation where the yield growth rate is much higher than the area growth rate for a crop during a particular period, it can be inferred that technological progress has penetrated in the cultivation of that particular crop. With that idea in mind, growth rates in area, yield and output have been estimated for rice in some states in India.

The estimated results of growth rates on area, yield and production of rice are presented in Table 2. The results show that in Assam, the contribution of yield factor was higher (1.77 percent) than the area factor (0.85 percent) towards the output growth rate during the whole period. Growth rates of all these three components were significant at 5 per cent level of significance. The total growth rate of rice production in Assam was 2.35 percent which was also significant at 5 percent level of significance. At the country level there has been a significant growth rates in area, production and productivity of rice during the period of 1980-81 to 2003-04. The contribution of productivity in accelerating rice production during the study period was three times higher (1.97 percent) as compared to that of area growth (0.45 percent) in India. For the whole period (1980-81 to 2003-04) the estimated result shows that the area growth rate was marginally higher in Assam than national level. On the other hand, the yield growth for India was higher than that of Assam by about 0.2 percentage points during the study period. The estimated result also shows that the yield contribution towards the rice production was higher than the area factor.

Among the study states mentioned in Table 2, rice area growth in Tamil Nadu, Andhra Pradesh and Uttar Pradesh were lower than the growth rate of rice area in Assam during the whole period. But the growth rates of rice area in Punjab, Haryana and West Bengal were more than Assam during the whole period.

The estimated results of growth rates on rice area, production and productivity of Assam for two different time periods are also given in Table 2. This was done with a view to understand the impact of reform period in the growth rates. It is observed that in Assam, the contribution of yield growth factor was higher than the area growth factor towards the growth of output of rice in both the periods. This shows that some level of technological progress has taken place in the cultivation of rice crop in Assam during the study period. However, it must be noted that growth rate in yield was as low as about 2 percent only during both sub periods.

VI. Factors Responsible for Low Productivity of Rice

The yield of rice per unit of land is influenced by several factors. For example, systematic use of fertilizers, HYV seeds, irrigation, pesticide etc. may increase the paddy yield per hectare. Paddy yield also tends to be high in a region having fertile soil and suitable agro-climatic conditions. However, excessive rainfall and consequent heavy floods, droughts, pest attacks etc. tend to make the rice yield low in a region.

Technique of cultivation, modern or traditional, can also determine the level of yield per unit of land. Such studies examining effects of those factors on paddy yield are not rare. Studies like Saha and Mooley (1978), Yoshino and Suppiah (1984), Goyari (2005), Shah et al. (2009) elaborate the bad impact of flood, drought and excess/insufficient rainfall on paddy productivity. Kainth and Mehra

(1985) examine varying effects of droughts, attack of insects and pests, fertilizers, demographic factors, number of markets, tractors intensity, pesticide dealers, climatic conditions, technological and institutional factors on the productivity of paddy. Studies such as Mahajan et al. (1986), Shukla et al. (2003), Haque (1985) and Ramasamy et al. (1986) etc. emphasis the importance of fertilizer consumption, irrigation, HYV seeds et cetera on the yield of rice.

Table 2: Annual Compound Growth Rates of Area, Production and Productivity of Rice

States	Variables	Period I – 1980-81 to 1991-92	Period I – 1991-92 to 2003-04	Overall – 1980-81 to 2003-04
Assam	Area	0.74	0.27*	0.58
	Yield	1.45	1.53	1.77
	Production	2.18	1.80	2.35
Andhra Pradesh	Area	0.80	-1.04*	-0.19*
	Yield	1.88	1.46	1.71
	Production	2.68	0.42	1.52
Haryana	Area	2.60	3.44	3.79
	Yield	0.70	-0.09*	0.21*
	Production	3.28	3.35	3.99
Punjab	Area	5.09	2.15	3.25
	Yield	1.10	0.60*	0.80
	Production	6.13	2.75	4.05
Tamil Nadu	Area	-1.98*	-3.07*	-0.96*
	Yield	5.52	-1.17*	1.74
	Production	3.54	-4.24	0.78
Uttar Pradesh	Area	0.39*	0.56	0.52
	Yield	5.60	1.64	3.15
	Production	5.99	2.20	3.67
West Bengal	Area	1.17	0.12*	0.74
	Yield	5.21	2.07	3.12
	Production	6.38	2.19	3.86
India	Area	0.62	0.18*	0.44
	Yield	3.08	0.84	1.97
	Production	3.70	1.02	2.41

Note: All growth rates are statistically significant at 5 % level except those marked with*
Sources: Estimations from CMIE and Rice in India-A Handbook of Statistics 2006, Patna.

Although several factors in Assam are responsible for the low yield of rice, non-availability of continuous time-series data for all variables restrict us from examining each and every factor. Therefore, we examine only some selected variables responsible for the low yield of rice per unit of land in the state. Some of these factors include modern farm inputs in rice production (fertilizer consumption, area under HYV seeds, irrigation and water management, electricity consumption in agriculture and credit used) and climatic factors (such as rainfall and floods).

(i) Use of fertilizers: Use of chemical fertilizers in appropriate doses plays a crucial role in increasing the productivity of paddy in any region. A fertilizer is an important element in agriculture sector. Being the key input, fertilizer increases the productivity by providing essential nutrients to the plants that soil cannot supply in adequate and appropriate amount. However, inadequate and imbalanced supply of required nutrients reduces the productive capacity of land which results in the low productivity. Sometimes, even very fertile land becomes less fertile due to continuous cultivation on the same land for a long time which leads to further depletion of most deficient nutrients in the soil.

Table 3 shows the consumption of fertilizers in Assam with other states of India. Data in the Table show that the consumption of fertilizers in kg per hectare in Assam has been low during the study period. It was 5.82 kg per ha in period I compared to 50.21 kg per ha at the national level. Although per ha fertilizer consumption in Assam is low, it has been increasing over the period of time. From a low level of 5.82 kg per ha, Assam's fertilizer consumption increased to 25.12 kg per ha during the period II, i.e., during 1992-93 to 2003-04. However, this level was still much lower than that of the national level (81.58 kg per ha) during the same period.

Assam is lower in fertilizer consumption not only compared to all India average, but also when compared to some of the states in India as shown in Table 3. There may be several reasons behind the low level of fertilizer consumption in kg per ha in Assam. The low level of fertilizer consumption may be one of the reasons behind the low level of rice yield per unit of land in Assam. Contrary to this, states like Punjab and Andhra Pradesh had higher fertilizer consumption per ha and at the same time, they experienced much higher paddy yield per ha compared to Assam during our study period.

Table 3: Fertilizer Consumption (N+P+K) in Agriculture (in kg/ha)

Period	Assam	Punjab	A.P.	Tripura	Manipur	India
1980-81 to 1984-85	3.66	130.04	58.96	8.12	17.92	38.58
1984-85 to 1989-90	5.94	153.12	89.74	23.56	33.12	54.44
1980-81 to 1991-92	**5.82**	**145.09**	**82.18**	**18.03**	**29.14**	**50.21**
1990-91 to 1994-95	10.66	161.70	122.32	22.44	46.92	68.26
1994-95 to 1999-00	19.16	167.68	141.74	21.24	71.82	83.16
2000-01 to 2003-04	43.53	179.03	151.94	22.99	103.26	89.81
1992-93 to 2003-04	**25.12**	**169.81**	**140.45**	**21.03**	**76.02**	**81.58**

Sources: Calculations from data of 'Assam Agriculture at a Glance' June 2006, Directory of Indian Agriculture 1997, various issues of CMIE, Statistical Handbook of Assam & Fertilizer Statistics.

(ii) Area under HYV of paddy seeds: Many studies have shown that High Yielding Varieties (HYV) of seeds can give higher yield per ha than traditional varieties of seeds. In some places, HYV paddy seeds can give yield level double the yield level of the traditional paddy seeds. Although rice occupies the largest area share among individual crops in Assam, the use of HYV paddy seeds is still not so popular. Many farmers in Assam are still using traditional paddy seeds.

Data shown in Table 4 are evidences of this fact. During the period I of our study, more than 50 percent of the total rice area was under the traditional paddy seeds. Although the area under HYV seeds increased over the years in Assam, only 51.84 percent of the total rice area was under the HYV paddy seeds during the period II, i.e., 1992-93 to 2003-04. This percentage share is very low compared to the national level (76.02 percent) and states like Punjab (92.18 percent) and Andhra Pradesh (92.39 percent) during the same period. The low share of area under HYV paddy seeds may be one of the reasons behind the low level of total rice yield in Assam.

Table 4: Percentage of Area under HYV Rice in Assam, AP and Punjab

Period	(As % to total area under rice)			
	Assam	AP	Punjab	India
1980-81 to 1984-85	38.47	81.45	88.02	50.30
1984-85 to 1989-90	45.35	87.76	90.15	59.14
1980-81 to 1991-92	**42.78**	**83.44**	**89.91**	**56.41**
1990-91 to 1994-95	46.64	86.43	93.07	67.00
1994-95 to 1999-00	49.85	90.32	90.09	74.85
2000-01 to 2003-04	58.47	95.05	94.60	83.16
1992-93 to 2003-04	**51.84**	**92.39**	**92.18**	**76.02**

Sources: a. various issues of 'Fertilizer Statistics', Statistical Handbook of Assam, 'Economic Survey of Assam and Handbook of Statistics, 2006.
b. Calculations are by the authors

(iii) Irrigation and water management: Along with the other inputs, irrigation is also key input to increase the productivity of agriculture sector. Irrigation is also an ingredient for proper exploitation of modern agricultural technology. Among individual crops, rice cultivation requires huge irrigation water. Rice yield per ha tends to increase under systematic irrigation facilities. Assam, which has subtropical climate and where the rainfall is unevenly distributed and the crop transplantation rate is higher in winter, assured and controlled water supply is more important to carry out the proper production. The modernization of agricultural practices vis-a-vis increase in productivity of crops cannot be conceived in the absence of assured irrigation facilities. The importance of irrigation in a state like Assam, therefore, needs special emphasis. Like other states in India, the program for irrigation development has been launched under two heads, major and medium irrigation and minor irrigation in Assam. At present, three departments i.e. irrigation department, agriculture and panchayats and rural development are associated with the development of irrigation facilities in Assam. The department of irrigation development maintains all major, medium and minor irrigation schemes in the state whereas other two departments are confined with only minor schemes (Economic Survey, Assam, 2004-05).

Irrigation potential created and utilized: One of the important aspects of poor irrigation development in Assam is the low utilization rate of the irrigation potential created in the state. The total irrigation potential created in Assam has been increasing over the years. But the percentage of utilization of irrigation potential created has been declining over the years; it was about 51 percent in period I which came down to about 26 percent in period II. Thus, the irrigation potential utilization has not been able to keep pace with the potential created in the state.

Percentage of irrigated area under rice to total rice area: Table 5 shows the gross irrigated area under rice cultivation as percentage to total rice area in the state. Data show that Assam is lagging behind in terms of irrigation facilities under rice crop compared to states like Andhra Pradesh and Punjab. Rice being the important crop in Assam, the efficient use of irrigation potential created is very important basically in rice cultivation. Out of the total rice area in Assam, only 19.15 percent of rice cultivation area was irrigated during 1990-91 to 2003-04. However, in Punjab 98.58 percent of rice cultivation area was irrigated as against of 19.15 in Assam. In Andhra Pradesh also, out of the total rice area, 95.09 percent of rice area was irrigated in the same period. In Assam only 19.15 percent of the total rice area was brought under irrigation facility and remaining about 80 percent of rice area mainly depends on rainfall.

(iv) Electricity consumption in agriculture: Consumption of electricity in agriculture is another indicator of irrigation development in a state. Electricity is necessary for mechanization in agriculture sector, i.e., for running pump sets, bore wells et cetera Data in Table 6 show a very low share of electricity consumption in Assam agriculture during 1980-81 to 1984-85. The percentage share of electricity consumption in agriculture to total electricity consumption in Assam was very low as compared to states like Punjab and Andhra Pradesh and even compared to the national average.

Table 5: Irrigated Area under Rice in Assam, AP and Punjab

Year	As % to total rice area			
	Assam	AP	Punjab	India
1990-91	33.08	94.86	99.21	45.13
1991-92	32.64	94.31	99.65	46.32
1992-93	21.09	94.46	99.26	48.11
1993-94	21.06	94.98	99.24	48.75
1994-95	21.71	94.70	97.38	49.96
1995-96	21.25	94.80	99.39	50.09
1996-97	21.35	95.60	98.98	51.30
1997-98	21.06	96.37	99.16	50.20
1998-99	21.98	95.94	99.19	52.26
1999-00	20.11	94.70	86.87	51.94
2000-01	8.11	95.23	99.21	53.97
2001-02	8.23	95.73	100.00	54.87
2002-03	8.19	95.29	99.17	52.37
2003-04	8.22	94.28	99.31	52.78
1990-91 to 2003-04	**19.15**	**95.09**	**98.58**	**50.58**

Source: Calculations from data of Irrigation Department Govt. of Assam, Statistical Handbook of Assam and CMIE (various issues).

The consumption electricity in Assam agriculture was only 1.33 percent during the pre-reform period as against 38.16 percent in Punjab and 31.59 percent in Andhra Pradesh. But during the post-reform period, the percentage share of electricity consumption in Assam agriculture to total electricity marginally increased to 2.38 percent. Because of the non-availability of electricity supply, almost all pump sets and bore wells used in irrigation purposes are run by diesel and petrol. This increases the cost of cultivation per unit of land. Ultimately, higher cost of cultivation discourages farmers from adopting mechanization (like pump set or bore well irrigations). This might be one of the reasons behind the low rice yield in the state.

(v) Credit used in agriculture: Credit is considered as one of the most important inputs for conducting all agricultural development programs. Farmers borrow credit from various sources (organized and unorganized) for various purposes. Farmers basically borrow credit of various types (short, medium and long term) to purchase their required inputs such as fertilizers, improved seeds, agricultural equipments, land etc. Thus, availability of credit facility can transform the behavior of using various inputs in agriculture sector. It is very important input to increase the productivity level of any crop. Total credit flow to farmers per ha through primary agricultural credit societies (PACs) and scheduled commercial banks (SCBs) in Assam, Punjab and at national level at 1980-81 constant prices is presented in Table 7. It is observed that the credit use in agriculture sector per ha in Assam was very low and well below the national level and even compared to states like Punjab. The credit use in agriculture sector in Assam was Rs. 343.2 per ha in the year 1988-89. In the same year, Punjab's credit disbursement to agriculture sector was Rs. 989.7 per ha and it was Rs. 592.4 per ha at the national level.

Table 6: Consumption of Electricity in Agriculture Sector

Period	As % to total electricity consumption			
	Assam	Punjab	AP	India
1980-81 to 1984-85	0.92	34.96	20.47	18.42
1984-85 to 1989-90	1.31	38.29	33.18	22.86
1980-81 to 1991-92	**1.33**	**38.16**	**31.59**	**21.75**
1990-91 to 1994-95	2.18	41.44	43.21	28.7
1994-95 to 1999-00	2.35	35.28	42.62	30.25
2000-01 to 2003-04	2.45	27.28	41.40	25.8
1992-93 to 2003-04	**2.38**	**33.52**	**42.52**	**28.52**

Source: Calculations from data of "CMIE" (various issues).

The credit use in per ha amount in Assam agriculture was not only low, but it was also declining over the years. However, the national level average and Punjab showed an increasing trend in per ha credit use in agriculture sector during 1988-89 to 1996-97. It is very probable that due to low level of credit amount, many farmers might not have been able to buy required inputs like fertilizers, improved paddy seeds, necessary implements etc. Under such circumstances, it is very likely that farmers may not be able to take proper production decisions to increase rice productivity per unit of land. Thus, low level of credit use per ha may be one of the reasons behind low level of rice yield during our study period.

Table 7: Credit Advanced to Agriculture Sector in Assam and Punjab (at 1980-81 prices)

Years	Rs.in Crores		Total (Rs/ha)	Rs.in Crores	
	PACS	SCBs		PACS	SCBs
1988-89	3.6	116.1	343.2	230.0	502.1
1989-90	3.9	130.1	374.2	286.7	497.2
1990-91	4.9	111.4	320.5	208.8	539.2
1991-92	3.6	112.7	315.2	249.2	500.4
1992-93	1.1	96.4	266.4	435.7	461.1
1993-94	0.8	90.0	249.3	429.9	460.4
1994-95	3.0	94.8	272.4	424.3	475.3
1995-96	0.3	87.5	240.8	317.2	458.3
1996-97	0.1	86.8	237.9	354.4	471.5

contd...

Total (Rs/ha)	Rs.in Crores		Total (kg/ha)
	PACS	SCBs	
989.7	2641.9	8157.0	592.4
1060.4	2714.7	8195.2	598.2
997.0	1764.7	8250.6	538.7
997.1	2069.7	7834.2	543.4
1187.5	3348.7	7877.4	604.8
1168.0	3301.1	7463.7	576.9
1169.4	2784.1	7406.6	541.6
1000.5	2875.5	7905.4	758.1
1053.1	3085.3	8171.2	788.2

Note: PACs and SCBs denote Primary Agricultural Credit Societies & Scheduled Commercial Banks respectively.

Source: Taken from 'Assam Developmental Report', Planning Commission of India, 2002

(vi) Rainfall and problems of floods: Assam is situated in the sub-tropical monsoon zone, which receives abundant rainfall during the kharif season as a result very high humidity level. The hot and humid condition during kharif season favours the spread of pests and diseases, which results in crop losses. The excessive humid condition during the kharif season contains a higher level of moisture. Therefore, sometimes farmers are forced to sell their output at a very low price. Even though, Assam receives heavy rainfall in the country, the distribution of rainfall in a single year is not uniform.

The average annual rainfall in Assam was much higher than the national average every year during the study period. In the period I (1980-81 to 1991-92) of our study, the average rainfall in Assam was 2331.67 mm against 1185.10 mm at the national level. During the period II, the average rainfall in Assam increased to 2362.83 mm against 1776.89 mm at the national level.

No doubt, rainwater is very useful for farmers in a state like Assam where the agricultural production activities depend on heavily on the nature and extent of rainfall. But the state's agricultural sector suffers from excess rainfall during kharif season and almost no rainwater or low rainwater during rabi reason. Since rainfall is not uniform throughout the agricultural year, many farmers can not cultivate summer paddy even if they want to do due to lack of proper irrigation facilities. Thus, the overall paddy yield tends to be low.

Occurrence of frequent flood due to excess rainwater during kharif seasons in every year is another important problem faced by farmers in Assam. Flood is a major natural disaster regularly causing damage of various crops, population of animals and houses in the state. According to flood control department of Assam, approximately 3 lakh hectares of crops area is subjected by annual flood every year. Out of the 23 districts in Assam, 21 plain districts are subjected to flood. These districts suffer from severe flood situation, which causes enormous damage to crops, livestock, and property and brings miseries to the people. Every year the south west monsoon starting from June to October receives heavy rainfall which results in heavy flood in the state. Flood occurs not only single time but four to five waves of flood occurs in the state. In a normal year, mainly three months from June to august receives flood. But during heavy rainfall, it occurs even from May to September. An analysis of flood damages and their impacts on the agricultural sector in Assam can be found in Goyari (2005). The available data on flood damage in Assam shows that, the intensity of flood has not been decreasing even at the present days. The total damage by flood in Assam has been increasing over the period. The total damage by floods was estimated about Rs 39.8 crore during 1980-81 and it increased to Rs 497.0 crore at current prices during 1998-99 (Table 8).

Table 8: Damages in Crops Area and other Public Utilities caused by Flood in Assam

Period	% of area to state's total area	% of crop area to CGA	Total damages
1980-81 to1984-85	11.80	7.12	35.22
1985-86 to1989-90	17.20	13.74	315.28
1980-81 to 1990-91	**13.75**	**9.54**	**166.10**
1990-91 to 1994-95	9.16	3.00	66.88
1995-96 to 2001-02	8.33	7.44	166.44
1991-92 to 2001-02	**8.90**	**6.04**	**129.54**

Note: 'Total damages' include crops, houses & public utilities in Rs. crores.

Source: Compiled from Goyari (2005).

In the Table 8, the damage of crops area, value of crops damage, human lives lost and total damage of crops, houses and public utilities are given. According to the available data on area affected, about 15.8 percent of total area, 3.8 percent of crops area was damaged and 57 human died in the state due to flood during 1980-81. During 1988 huge number of areas, population, human's lives; cattle and villages were affected by flood in the state. About 48.7 percent, out of the total area was affected by flood in the state and recorded highest damage in these two decades. In the same year, the crop area affected was 31.9 percent of the CGA. This was the first time heart breaking loss occurred, which was miserable to all the people in the state. The situation came back in normal during 1990s. Area affected, human's lives lost, cattle and villages damage caused by flood reduced significantly during 2001-02. This uncertain condition makes farmers to frighten to invest modern costly inputs such as HYVs seeds, chemical fertilizers and other costly farm inputs in production system, results in subsistence level of production rather than commercial purpose. The excessive floods damage the rural economy in Assam.

Excess rainfall and consequent floods in Assam have bad impact on the agricultural sector. As reported by Goyari (2005), among individual crops, rice is the worst hit by frequent floods. First, many farmers do not want to use costly purchased inputs like chemical fertilizers, HYV seeds etc. due to the fear of being washed away by excess rainwater and floods. Second, many HYV paddy plants are of short height. Many farmers in Assam cultivate paddy in low-lying areas. During heavy rainfall and floods, paddy plants are submerged and are damaged if flood water continues to stay for long days. Under such situations, it is very difficult for many farmers in the state to adopt modern techniques of cultivation to increase the production and productivity of rice. Thus, along with other factors, erratic rainfall and frequent floods may be responsible for the low rice yield per ha in Assam during our study period.

VII. Rice Yield Response Function Estimation

We have already discussed that the yield of any crop is influenced by various factors like modern farm inputs (fertilizer, HYV seeds, pesticides, systematic irrigation etc.), basic agricultural infrastructures (marketing, storage and transportation facilities etc.), prices, agro climatic factors, socio-economic condition etc. The yield response function can provide information of the direction and extent of farmer's response to those factors. Most of the earlier supply response studies of crops are based the Nerlovian supply response model. Some of such studies are Krishna (1963), Cummings (1975), Narayana and Parikh (1981) etc. Many studies modified the basic structure of Nerlovian model essentially by including required exogenous variables in their models.

Generally, the rice yield per ha in a region tends to increase with the increase in HYV paddy area, appropriate dose of fertilizer application and available systematic irrigation facilities. So, we can expect the estimated coefficients of those three explanatory variables to be positive in our model estimation.

The double log linear model (2) reported in section 3 has been estimated by the OLS method. The model has been estimated for the yield of total rice, winter rice, summer rice and autumn rice. The estimated results have been shown in Table 9. Interpretations of estimated coefficients of variables have been given below:

Fertilizer: The estimated results show that the impact of fertilizer (kg/ha) on the yield of total rice was positive during the study period in Assam. The influence was statistically significant at 1 percent level for all types of rice yield. Keeping the other factors constant, a one percent increase in the fertilizer consumption (kg/ha) led to an increase in rice yield by about 19 percent during the study period. In case of rice yield function of three seasons also, a positive and significant impact of fertilizer consumption (kg/ha) on the paddy yield was observed from estimation results.

Table 9: Estimated Coefficient of Rice Yield Functions in Assam during 1980-81 to 2003-04

Inputs	Parameters	Total rice	Autumn rice	Summer rice	Winter rice
(1)	(2)	(3)	(4)	(5)	(6)
Constant	α_0	7.496 (13.403)*	8.154 (6.964)*	6.156 (4.891)*	7.173 (12.037)*
Fertilizer	α_1	0.188 (8.068)*	0.215 (4.448)*	0.109 (2.654)*	0.149 (6.130)*
HYV	α_2	0.166 (1.883)**	0.347 (1.875)**	0.063 (1.726)**	0.090 (0.0958)
Irrigation	α_3	0.060 (2.068)**	0.083 (1.415)***	0.074 (3.967)*	0.055 (1.872)**
	R^2	0.91	0.66	0.79	0.86
	d.f.	20	20	20	20
	dw	1.98	1.97	1.96	1.99

contd...

Notes: t-statistic values are given in parentheses, d.f. = degree of freedom, *, ** and *** denote statistical significance at 1% level, 5% level and 10% level respectively.

HYV: In addition to fertilizer use by farmers, the impact of HYVs on the yield of total rice and three seasonal rice crops was positive and significant in explaining the variation of paddy yield in the state during the study period. While the estimated coefficients of HYV variable were found to be significant in case of total rice, autumn rice and summer rice, it was not statistically significant in case of winter rice yield. This shows that the impact of the expansion of area under HYV paddy seeds was not so strong in raising the yield of winter rice. The winter rice in Assam is cultivated during June-July, during which the state receives heavy rainfall and consequently floods occur in most of the years. Since many varieties of HYV paddy plants are of short stems, many farmers may feel reluctant to cultivate HYV paddy varieties in low lying prone areas. This may be one of the reasons behind statistically insignificant impact of HYV area on the winter rice yield in our estimation results.

Irrigation: Like fertilizer and HYV, the impact of irrigation on the rice yield, total rice and seasonal rice, was found to be significantly positive during the study period in Assam. This means, with the expansion of systematic irrigation facilities, rice yield in the state increased. A one percent increase in the irrigated area under total rice led, on average, to an increase of total rice yield by about 6 per cent, other things remaining constant.

Thus, estimated yield function results show that all three explanatory variables (fertilizer, HYV and irrigation) influenced the rice yield in kg per ha in Assam during the study period. This indicates that by increasing the appropriate dose of fertilizer consumption per ha, systematic irrigation facilities and area under good quality HYV paddy seeds, rice yield in the state may be increased further.

VIII. Main Findings and Conclusion

The paper examined the various factors behind low yield of rice per unit of land in Assam during the last two decades. The analysis was based on the state level secondary data. Rice is the most dominant crop among individual crops in Assam in terms of area allocation. But, in terms of yield level per hectare, Assam rice has been very low and well below the national level average as well as some selected states like Punjab and Andhra Pradesh. The contribution of yield growth recorded higher than the area growth component towards the growth of rice output in Assam during the study period. But, this yield growth rate was as low as 2 percent only. Use of low level of modern farm inputs like fertilizer, HYV seeds, low irrigation, low credit, adverse climatic conditions like heavy rainfall and consequent floods, inadequate basic infrastructure facilities like marketing centres and transport connectivity, etc. are some of the important possible reasons behind low level of rice yield per hectare in Assam. The estimated yield function results showed that all three explanatory variables (fertilizer, HYV and irrigation) influenced the rice yield in kg per ha in Assam positively during the study period. This indicates that by increasing the appropriate dose of fertilizer consumption per ha, systematic irrigation facilities and area under good quality HYV paddy seeds, rice yield in the state may be increased further.

Above findings have enormous an importance on the policies for the increase in the rice productivity as well as in the overall agricultural development in Assam. In this perspective, following suggestions can be made. First, government should take proper steps to increase the use of modern farm inputs like fertilizers and HYV paddy seeds. The state is having available water sources. Thus, various policies on surface and ground water based irrigation development should be implemented properly. Since rice requires huge water, priority should be given to expand irrigation facilities in the rice growing districts. Since the state suffers from frequent floods every year, both short term and long term steps should be taken to control flood problems in the state permanently. Second, at least one agricultural marketing centre should be established in each sub-division of the state. This may prevent farmers from getting low price of their produces and exploitation from middlemen. Third, rural road connectivity should be improved in the state. Finally, credit and other financial assistance facilities should be extended even in remote villages for the benefit of all farmers. Existing co-operative societies and formal financial institutions should be strengthened.

References

Borah, B.C., Rajeev Betne and B.C. Bhowmick (2001): Status of Rice Production System in Assam, A paper presented at the National Seminar on Prioritization of the Strategies for Agriculture in North Eastern India, Jorhat, Assam.

Bhowmick, B.C., B.C. Borah, Sushil Pandey and N. Barthakur (2005): Changing Patterns of Rice Production Systems and

Technology in Assam, A policy paper no. 22, National Centre for Agricultural Economics and Policy Research.

Cummings, J.T. (1975): 'The Supply Responsiveness of Indian Farmers in the Post-Independence Period', *Indian Journal of Agricultural Economics,* 30(1): 26-40.

Goswami, Kishor and Bani Chatterjee (2006): Factors Influencing the Yield of Paddy in Assam: An Econometrics Analysis, *ICFAI Journal of Agricultural Economics,* 3 (3): 34-43.

Goswami, Kishor and Bani Chatterjee (2003): Measurement of Growth and Instability in Paddy Production in Assam; A District level Analysis, *ICFAI Journal of Applied Economics,* 2(1): 65-80.

Goyari, P. (2005): Flood Damages and Sustainability of Agriculture in Assam, *Economic and Political Weekly*, 40(26): 2723-2729.

Haque, T. (1985): Factors Accounting for Low Yield of Rice in West Bengal, *Agricultural Situation in India,* 39(13): 775-783.

Kainth, G.S. and P.L. Mehra (1985): *Rice Production Potential and Constraint; A Case Study of Productivity Backward Region*, Inter-India Publications, New Delhi.

Krishna, Raj (1963): Farm Supply Response in India-Pakistan: A case Study of the Punjab Region, *The Economic Journal.* Vol. 73(291): 477-487.

Mahajan, R.K., A.V. Rao and D. Gandhi (1986): Rice Production in India during Nineteen Seventies, *Indian Journal of Agricultural Economics,* Vol. 40(11): 987-996.

Narayan, N.S.S. and K.S. Parikh (1981): *Estimation of Farm Supply Response and Acreage Allocation: A Case Study of Indian Agriculture',* International Institute for Applied Systems Analysis, Luxemburg.

Ramaswamy, C., M. Chandrasekaran and R. Prabhakaran (1986): Sustaining Rapid Growth in Fertilizer Use in Rice Region, *Indian Journal of Agricultural Economics,* 41(4): 503.

Saha, K.R. and D.A. Mooley (1978): Fluctuations of Monsoon Rainfall and Crop Production, In *Climate Change and Food Production,* K. Takahashi and M. M. Yoshino (Eds), University of Tokyo Press, Tokyo, PP 73-80.

Shah, T., A. Kishore and Hemant P (2009): Will the Impact of 2009 Drought be Different from 2002?, *Economic and Political Weekly,* 44(37): 11-14.

Shukla, N.D, S.K. Sharma and Krishna Murari (2003): "Determinants of Inter-State Disparities in Rice Productivity", *Agricultural Situation in India*, 60(9): 565-573.

Yoshino, M. M. and Ramasamy Suppiah (1984): "Rainfall and Paddy Production in Sri Lanka", *Journal of Agricultural Meteorology*, 40(1): 9-20.

Index

Index